*Consumer
Choice
in the
American
Economy*

CONSULTING EDITOR:

Donald Dewey

COLUMBIA UNIVERSITY

Consumer Choice

in the

American Economy

BY

Carolyn Shaw Bell

WELLESLEY COLLEGE

RANDOM HOUSE *New York*

FIRST PRINTING

© *Copyright, 1967, by Random House, Inc.*

All rights reserved under International and Pan-American Copyright Conventions. Published in New York by Random House, Inc. and simultaneously in Toronto, Canada, by Random House of Canada Limited

Library of Congress Catalog Card Number: 66–19846

Manufactured in the United States of America by American Book–Stratford Press, Inc.

Designed by Leon Bolognese

For my father,
CLARENCE E. SHAW

Acknowledgments

I wish to thank the American Association of University Women, whose grant of the Shirley Farr Fellowship enabled me to undertake part of the research for this book. I am also grateful for the suggestions of students and colleagues at earlier stages of the work and for the encouragement and endurance shown by my husband during all its stages.

My special thanks go to Mary Jane Latsis for help that cannot be adequately acknowledged.

Contents

ix

CONTENTS

Tables

TABLES

Chapter 3

TABLES

Figures

Figures

*Consumer
Choice
in the
American
Economy*

Introduction

C*onsumer* choice in the American economy depends upon competition in the market. In simplest terms, families and individuals select their purchases from among all the goods and services that competing sellers offer. The process of consumer choice and the shopping process by which the consumer obtains the goods and services that he has chosen have been examined by psychologists and sociologists, statisticians and engineers, government policy-makers and businessmen. This book applies economic analysis to the study of consumer choice and market competition.

What does an economist have to contribute? Lionel Robbins has defined economics as "the science which studies human behaviour as a relationship between ends and scarce means which have alternative uses."[1] The consumer—whether an individual, a family, or a household—is an economic unit that faces the problem of choice described in this classic statement. The relationship between ends and scarce means is parallel to the goals of the consumer and his limited income. Consumer choice determines how the "scarce means" of purchasing power will be apportioned among the many alternatives of spending and saving. But "human behaviour" is more than just a matter of consumer choice. Consumer decisions must be carried out in the market where the process by which choices are translated into purchases of goods, services, or assets is a form of economic activity.

What tools of economic analysis can be used to investigate consumer choice and the shopping process in the market? Two models exist: the theory of consumer choice dealing with the individual household, and the theory of monopolistic competition dealing with the individual seller. These can be linked since market competition influences consumer choice, and consumer tastes and preferences shape the forms of market competition. There is yet another link that exists between the fields of economics and marketing; the concept of the consumer's shopping process may be used to analyze distribution and selling methods. Economic statistics provide the basic data for the study—figures on income, savings, debt, expenditures, sales, and sellers show how the models of consumer choice and the shopping process apply to the American economy.

Before embarking on an analysis of statistical data or theory, the consumer choice problem needs to be placed in historical perspective. How have the present conditions of consumer choice and market competition developed? The opening chapter of this book provides the background for the analysis of consumers' scarce means and their choices of spending and saving.

4

chapter *1* Consumer
Choice:
An Historical
Sketch

The United States currently enjoys the "highest standard of living" in the world: more food, clothing, bathtubs, automobiles, household appliances, and toothpaste is available per consumer than in any other country; everything is bigger or better or more plentiful than elsewhere. By and large, Americans take their material well-being for granted or, when they do reflect about it, credit it to American progress. For not only are American consumers better off than their contemporaries in other countries, but their possessions and their way of life clearly surpass those of Americans of an earlier generation. In 1900 some 8,000 passenger cars were registered in this country, one car for each 10,000 people; in 1964 1,000 times as many automobiles were sold, and registrations came to one car for every 3 people. In 1900 8 per cent of the homes used electricity, half the children were in school, and life expectancy at birth was less than 50 years; today electrical service exists in all but one per cent of the homes, 96 out of 100 children are in school, with more than half the high school graduates going on to college, and life expectancy at birth exceeds 70 years. The "highest standard of living" in the world reflects the "greatest progress" in the world.

Depending on one's individual point of view, one or another cliché can be drawn on to explain the phenomenon: the enormous change in the American way of life can be attributed to native ingenuity or imported skills, industrious labor or the risk-taking entrepreneur, abundant natural resources or Yankee thrift, free enterprise or antitrust laws, mass production and the assembly line or craftsmanship and the instinct for tinkering. Despite the differing emotions such well-worn phrases arouse, they agree in one significant respect: they all focus on production. Nowhere is there any reference to the audacity of those consumers who used the first telephones, drove the first automobiles, ate the first canned tomatoes, or wore the first "factory-made" clothes. Yet no change in production, no new production function, can succeed without a change in consumption. Families and individuals must come to accept the new alternatives, must spend their incomes in a different way. Tracing the effect of "progress" on consumption and describing how the "highest standard of living" has evolved will build an historical foundation for subsequent analysis. How have the alternatives available, the specific consumer goods and services, changed over the past 60 years? Has there developed a general pattern of consumption choice?

The sources that tell of the changes in consumption have varied widely in their goals and, consequently, in their methods of investigation. Today there are massive studies of consumption choices, such as the Bureau of Labor Statistics 1960–61 *Survey of Consumer Expenditures,* with its two-inch thick schedule of questions, its three-stage sample of 13,000 dwelling units, and its detailed tables of figures. Yet these owe much to 100 years of effort in collecting and analyzing data and to the work of the pioneers Frederic LePlay and Ernst Engel.

Early Investigations

Frederic LePlay, who was born in 1806, was hailed as "the creator of social science" by no less a person than Auguste Comte, partly because he insisted on the use of scientific method in investigating social problems and partly because he refused to restrict his interests to either production or consumption. Trained as a mining engineer, he had begun making observations on differing rates of productivity in widely separate localities. But his first trip through rural Germany convinced him that differences in mining technology were probably less responsible for different levels of output than were differences in the way miners lived. Subsequently he devoted years of constant travel to studying workers, their working conditions, and their ways of life. For 6 months out of every year, from 1829 to 1853, he kept detailed notebooks, according to a standard procedure, of his findings in Scandinavia, Russia, Hungary, Turkey, England, Spain, Italy, and Germany, as well as in his native France. His hypothesis solidified into a conclusion:

Gradually he became aware that technical process played only a minor part and that the essential condition was linked up, most of the time, with a moral factor, a feeling of permanence, stability, a binding attachment for the land as well as collective production and the community to which one belongs.[1]

For data to substantiate his findings, LePlay examined closely the living conditions of workers' families. Relying on the advice of local clergy, landholders, and employers, he selected for each area or occupation a "typical" workingman and then recorded exhaustive data on how he and his family lived. LePlay had to gain the complete confidence of his subjects; often he lived with them in order to be sure of his facts, sharing such varied accommodations as the hovel of a Parisian ragpicker and the cottage of an agricultural laborer in Eastern Europe. For each family he drew up a record, which he called a "budget," of money receipts and expenditures and of income in kind, such as firewood for miners in the Harz Mountain area and produce from the home gardens of agricultural workers. A selection of his case studies, *Les Ouvriers Européens* (1855), stimulated others to adopt his methods and collect similar data. In 1890 the Société Internationale des Études Pratiques d'Économie Sociale had over one hundred family monographs on file; by then, however, LePlay himself had moved on to larger questions of social reform.

As a youth he had pondered the optimistic doctrines of Rousseau and Saint-Simon, and like many nineteenth-century political philosophers, he questioned the changes brought about by the French revolutions: had there been reforms or should something of "l'ancien regime" be restored? His comparative studies convinced him that custom and tradition were as essential to family well-being as income and expenditure, and he found the materialistic emphasis of the economist insufficient:

Economics . . . is literally the science of wealth; it studies how it is produced and distributed. Now, the question today is much less how to develop wealth than it is how to guarantee stability, social peace, in a word that happiness which is man's legitimate right. That is the aim of social science when it is based on fact.[2]

In short, LePlay took human happiness as his subject matter, rather than the more limited area of analysis outlined in the Introduction; when in 1869 he became consultant to Napoleon III, it was on questions of social reform, not economic policy. His contributions to the field, however, include definitions of income in kind, the arrangement of spending and

8

consumption in standard categories of food, housing, education, recreation, etc., and the delineation of consumption from payments for taxes, insurance, or saving. Although large-scale surveys have superseded his emphasis on the case-study approach to a "typical" family, many investigations today are reminiscent of those made by LePlay, particularly Ferdinand Zweig's work in Great Britain and the "small group studies" used in market research.

LePlay's great German contemporary, Ernst Engel (1821–1896), was also trained as a mining engineer and also became head of a government statistical bureau. Accompanying LePlay on some of his travels, Engel became interested in the relationships he discovered among the data, and is famous for his "laws" of consumption, which he evolved after studying many different statistical series. Engel was also concerned with the reliability and validity of basic data; he purged the Prussian statistical office of its tendency to twist figures under political pressure, and he founded a "seminar" to improve the training and skills of younger statisticians. Convinced that published data could be widely used, he wanted to compare, to analyze, and to draw conclusions rather than to present forbidding tables of figures.

Engel's conclusions were two: "that the poorer a family is, the greater is that portion of the total expenditures which must be used for procuring nourishment, and furthermore, that, under similar circumstances, the measurement of the expenditures for nourishment is an accurate and truthful measurement of the material well-being of a people."[3] The work of both Engel and LePlay was widely discussed by statisticians and social workers on both sides of the Atlantic;[4] but Engel's laws were widely misinterpreted. Each of the two Europeans, however, set forth a methodology that was used in early investigations in the United States.

Sporadic attempts to collect data on wages and prices had

been made by the Labor Departments of various states, following the pioneering work of Carroll Wright, who conducted a survey of some 400 wage-earning families in 15 Massachusetts cities and towns in 1875. As the first United States Commissioner of Labor, Wright nurtured what is now the Bureau of Labor Statistics, and based studies of both wages and prices on the hard facts of consumer incomes and expenditures reported by consumers themselves. The earliest attempt at a national survey, resulting in the collection of data from 25,440 workingmen's families living in 33 states, took place in 1901 under Wright's direction. The list of food items that was used for the cost-of-living index of the Bureau of Labor Statistics came from these data; as the index needed revision, the Bureau conducted similar large-scale studies in 1918, 1934–36, 1942, 1950, and 1960–61.

Both the publication presenting Wright's 1875 survey and his 18th Annual Report as Commissioner of Labor, presenting the 1901 data, contained a statement of Engel's laws that gained widespread circulation despite its inaccurate interpretation of what Engel had said. Wright's version was as follows:

First. That the greater the income the smaller the percentage of outlay for subsistence.

Second. That the percentage of outlay for clothing is approximately the same whatever the income.

Third. That the percentage for lodging or rent and for fuel and lighting is invariably the same whatever the income.

Fourth. That as the income increases in amount the percentage of outlay for sundries becomes greater.[5]

Data from all the early surveys, both local and national, were painstakingly analyzed for verifications of these laws. The fourth one, however, posed major problems. "Sundries" often seemed equivalent to "luxuries," as opposed to the "necessities" of food, shelter, and clothing. But if the percentage of income spent on luxuries increased steadily as incomes rose, how could a minimum level of living be defined for determining a "fair" wage? The purely quantitative data of the early surveys provided no answers to this question, but nevertheless other investigators struggled with it. The tables of figures in the 1901 survey were enhanced by the writings of contemporary social workers and economists who followed LePlay's methods. Especially for the earlier years of this century, the descriptions of life among the steelworkers in Homestead, the cottonmill operatives in Fall River, or the immigrant families in a tenement district of New York City enrich the meaning of consumer choice.

Food

Engel's first law, however misinterpreted, focused the attention of early investigators on family spending for food, and more detailed data exist for this category than for any other. Both broad surveys and case studies of families turned up the same figure for food expenditure, 43 per cent of the total. But such calculations tell nothing about the alternatives for consumer choice. The following menus, for workers' families in Southern and Northern mill towns in 1909, provide a base point.[6]

	SOUTH	NORTH
Breakfast	sausage, butter, biscuit, coffee	eggs, bread and butter, coffee
Dinner	pork and peas, greens, corn bread, biscuit, cake	corned beef and cabbage, potatoes, apple pie, tea, bread and butter
Supper	pork, peas, corn bread, milk	ham, bananas, tea, bread and butter
Breakfast	biscuit, butter, syrup, coffee	fish, bread, sugar, coffee
Dinner	pork, peas, corn bread, syrup	boiled beef, tea, bread and butter
Supper	biscuits, pork, milk	ham, eggs, tea, bread and butter

The changes in food consumption since 1900 are often presented as in Figure 1, which emphasizes the great shift away from grains and potatoes, and in favor of dairy products, fruits and vegetables, eggs and meat. Even these figures, which are based on per capita civilian consumption, lack detail. Table 1 contrasts the *kinds* of foodstuffs bought in 1901 with those bought in 1955; many of the items listed for the later year were not available earlier. Even at that time food consumption had already changed substantially. Early in the history of this country, the diet consisted largely of corn or corn products—pork, meal, or whiskey. In the last quarter of the nineteenth century, the developing railway network provided more wheat and beef, although the isolated South continued to rely heavily

Figure 1. Per Capita Civilian Consumption, 1910–1960 (1947–1949 retail prices as weights; 5-year moving average centered)

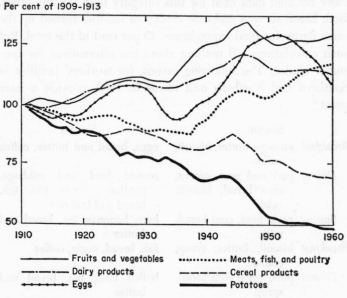

Per cent of 1909-1913

Fruits and vegetables ·············· Meats, fish, and poultry
Dairy products ————— Cereal products
Eggs Potatoes

Source: U.S. Department of Agriculture, Economic Research Service Neg. ERS 93-61(4).

on corn in its various guises, as the family menu shows. Along with the railways, the emergence of giant firms and trusts also altered food staples: the 10¢ per pound differential between raw and refined sugar had dropped to 3¢ by 1876; at the instigation of the millers, hard wheats, which could be more highly refined, replaced the soft varieties, and white flour was produced.

The menus and Table 1 emphasize, however, how few kinds of food were then available. Whether measured in quantity or in money spent, food consumption consisted chiefly of bread and meat. Seasonal production severely limited variety; almost half the meat consumed was preserved with salt. Although cabbage, carrots, onions, and turnips were available in the winter months and fresh string beans, tomatoes, and lettuce in the summer, dried beans and peas made up the bulk of vegetable consumption all year round. Fruits were also seasonal: dried apples and prunes in the winter, fresh berries in the summer. Sweets, pickles, and the "condiments" of preserves and sauces did a little to lessen the fare's monotony.

Even with these limited choices, food consumption differed sharply at different income levels. An early writer on economizing[7] suggests a nourishing diet for 5¢ to 15¢ per person, daily: potatoes, rye meal, corn meal, wheat flour, barley, oats, dried peas and beans, salt cod, halibut nape, "any meat with little bone," oleomargarine, and skimmed milk. A middle-income household with 15¢ to 20¢ a day to spend on food, per person, could choose beef, mutton, and any meat not over 25¢ per pound, wheat bread from the baker's, suet, butter, whole milk, cheese, dried fruits, cabbages and other vegetables "in their season," sugar, fish, and bacon. The rich, with up to $1.00 a day for food per person, could feast on choice cuts of meat, chickens, green vegetables, "garden stuff and vegetables out of season," confections, cakes, tea and coffee. Table 2 lists one week's food expenditures at the turn of the century by two

Table 1

Quantities of Food Purchased by Families During One Week,
1901 and 1955

Food Item	Unit	1901 Quantities (Average family size, 5.3)[a]	1955 Quantities (Average family size, 3.64)[a]
Fresh beef	pounds	6.73	4.35[b]
Salt beef	pounds	.93	.06
Fresh hog products	pounds	2.20	1.73
Salt hog products	pounds	2.13	2.21[c]
Other meat	pounds	1.49	2.32
Poultry	pounds	1.30	2.71
Fish	pounds	1.54	1.49
Eggs	dozen	1.64	2.14
Milk	quarts	6.82	11.82
evaporated, dried, condensed milk	pounds		1.17
ice cream, ice milk	pounds		1.14
Butter	pounds	2.25	.70
margarine	pounds		.69
Cheese	pounds	.31	1.10
Lard	pounds	1.60	.50
shortening, salad and cooking oils, salad dressing	pounds		1.24
Tea	pounds	.20	.09
Coffee	pounds	.90	.84[d]
soft drinks, cocoa, chocolate, syrups	pounds		3.28
Sugar	pounds	5.16	2.91
jellies, jams, candies	pounds		1.13
Molasses	pounds	.08	.04
other syrups, honey	pounds		.51
Flour and meal	pounds	13.09	3.80
prepared flour mixes	pounds		.65
breakfast cereals	pounds		.86
baby cereals, hominy, popcorn, pasta, other cereal	pounds		2.55
Bread	loaves[e]	4.86	4.98
baked goods other than bread	pounds		2.09

Food Item	Unit	1901 Quantities (Average family size, 5.3)[a]	1955 Quantities (Average family size, 3.64)[a]
Rice	pounds	.48	.40
Potatoes	pounds	16.80	6.37
frozen, canned, dehydrated, potato chips and sticks	pounds		.24
Per Cent Total Food Expenditures			
Other vegetables		5.77%	4.92% (9.26 lbs.)
Fruit		5.05%	4.13% (9.95 lbs.)
frozen, canned and dried fruits and vegetables, including juices			5.12% (8.80 lbs.)
Vinegar, pickles, and condiments		1.26%	
Other food		6.24%	3.62%[f]

[a] Since no details exist on family consumption in 1901, no adjustment in family size was made.
[b] Includes frozen meats.
[c] Smoked and cured; includes .19 pounds salt pork.
[d] Includes .04 pounds instant coffee.
[e] Various weights; see pp. 17 and 21.
[f] Includes nuts and peanut butter, canned and dried soups, prepared baby foods, puddings and other mixes, relishes, sauces, and seasonings.
SOURCES: *Eighteenth Annual Report of the Commissioner of Labor,* Washington, D.C., 1903, p. 82; and USDA, *Food Consumption of Households in the United States, 1956,* various tables.

families, one in a "workingman's neighborhood" (Family A) and the other in a "residential suburb" (Family B).

Milk, cream, butter, fresh fruits and vegetables were "luxuries" at this time. But for any income level, such lists make it clear that food expenditures were chiefly for raw materials: home preparation was substantial. Contemporary home economists, in evaluating typical diets, pointed out that nutritive

Table 2

Food Expenditures During One Week, Two-person Families at Different Income Levels, 1904–1905

1904: Family A		1905: Family B	
Item	Total Cost	Item	Total Cost
Round steak	$ .09	6 lbs. rib roast of beef	$1.08
1¼ lbs. steak	.20	1½ lbs. steak	.38
4½ lbs. smoked ham	.60	Deerfoot Farm sausages	.25
Pork chops	.60	3 lamb chops	.18
Bologna	.06		
Meat	.15		
Cooked corned beef	.10		
Sturgeon	.06		
2 lbs. flounder	.10		
2 qts. milk	.10	6 qts. milk	.48
1 can condensed milk	.09	5 bottles cream	.50
½ lb. butter	.13	2 lbs. butter	.52
¼ lb. cheese	.04	¼ lb. cheese	.06
Eggs	.26	20 eggs	.50
Bread and rolls	.25	Lard	.38
3½ lbs. oatmeal	.12	Cream of wheat	.15
Quart potatoes	.10	Potatoes (measure)	.20
Onions	.02	Quart onions	.15
1 head cabbage	.10	Head of lettuce	.05
1 can peas	.10	Tomatoes (3 measures)	.45
		Cauliflower	.15
		Sweet potatoes	.15
		6 ears of corn	.15
Bananas	.15	Concord grapes	.45
Pickles, pie	.06	Crackers, cakes, olives	.30
Staples (sugar, soda, tea, sundries)	.45	Staples (salt, cream of tartar, gelatine)	.26
Total	$3.43	Total	$6.79

SOURCE: Louise Balard More, *Wage-Earners' Budgets* (New York: Henry Holt, 1907), p. 234.

values were lost and both food and fuel wasted by improper home preparation.

The consumer of 1901 spent time and effort in buying

food. Fresh meats came from a butcher shop; almost everything else was sold in bulk and frequently ladled from the barrel or bin in the store directly into the buyer's container. What processing or packaging existed was far from standardized: butter sold by the roll or in 2-pound pails; dried cod by the piece or in 2-pound bricks; a loaf of bread varied from 14 ounces to 2 pounds. Price quotations depended on the particular shop as well as the locality: corn meal sold by the quart, the peck, the bushel, or in 50-pound bags; poultry was sold by the bird rather than on a net weight base; meat cuts differed in different areas; and to compare prices required considerable skill. Income limitations added to the problem:

The poor housewife knows what good bargains are, but the meagerness of her purse often times prevents her from purchasing supplies except in very small quantities. . . . She is buying potatoes . . . a bushel would not be an oversupply and that quantity can be bought for a dollar; but the outlay of a dollar for potatoes may not be possible. Instead of spending a dollar for a bushel she spends eight cents for a quarter of a peck, paying at the rate of $1.28 a bushel, losing nearly thirty-nine per cent by the transaction. . . . She has gone the rounds of the markets and has nearly finished her purchases, but there are still butter, sugar, coffee and salt to be bought and besides some matches are needed. For all these things she has twenty-five cents remaining. Butter is thirty cents a pound; sugar, five cents; coffee, fifteen cents; salt, five cents a large sack or three cents a small sack (the latter being half as large as the former); matches, 3 boxes for five cents or two cents a box. . . . Practice has taught our housewife the art of making skillful divisions. She buys a quarter of a pound of butter for eight cents, a half-pound of sugar for three cents, half a pound of coffee for eight cents, a small sack of salt for three cents, a box of matches for two cents, and has one cent left with which to buy an onion for the soup. She has lost heavily on every one of these articles including the onion, and she knows she has lost.[8]

The shift from farm to factory in the growing economy changed the alternatives available to consumers. The first major change in food was the combination of packaging, processing, and quality control, which accelerated in pace during the first decades of the century. Late in the nineteenth century the first pioneers had began to lobby against widespread food adulteration, and one of the most outspoken, Harvey Wiley, feared that the dangers from unprotected food would increase as food preparation was shifted from the kitchen to the factory.[9] Government regulation had some effect, but the forces of market competition played a major part.

In 1907 the Federal government began the inspection of meat and established the Pure Food and Drug Administration; in 1913 Congress enacted a law that required all packaged foods in interstate commerce to state the quantity of the contents; 1914 saw the beginning of extension work, including education in home economics for the Department of Agriculture's rural clients; in 1917 fruit and vegetable inspection and grading began at terminals. Local laws dealt with sanitation, after investigators had discovered the role of bacteria-laden milk in spreading typhoid, tuberculosis, and other diseases. Doctors and dairymen set up commissions to encourage sanitary milk production, and by 1907 several states had passed legislation adopting the word "certified" from the commissions and setting standards for its use: only milk produced under sanitary conditions, with a minimum bacteria count and a standardized chemical composition, and meeting nutritional standards, could be sold as "certified" milk.

But the discovery that there were profits to be had from brand names and advertising hastened the use of processed and packaged foods. "Processed" foods meant first the canning industry. Apparent annual consumption per person of all canned vegetables was 15 pounds in 1909, 21 pounds in 1921, and 26 pounds ten years later. Two-thirds of the 1909 total consisted of peas, tomatoes, and corn; by 1929 these accounted for only half, after packers successfully canned green beans, sauerkraut, spinach, asparagus, beets, pumpkin, and sweet potatoes. Over the same period, per capita consumption of canned soup (most of it tomato) increased from .3 pounds to 3.9 pounds. Figures for canned fruits are similar: 2.9 pounds per person in 1909— chiefly applesauce, apricots, peaches, and pears; 12.1 pounds per person in 1929, including cherries, cranberries, pineapple, plums, fruit salad or cocktail combinations.[10] Processing also changed other food staples. The growth of the cereal industry —both ready-to-eat varieties, such as cornflakes and shredded wheat, as well as prepared wheat and oats for home cooking— helped introduce trade names to the language. Processed cheese and baked beans provided variety in the diet and some lightening of the housewife's load. Prepared shortening, baking powder, and yeast added new cooking ingredients.

Aside from the specific items, these changes introduced the new dimension of standardization into consumption choice. As food companies packaged and processed foods with brand names, consumers shifted from bulk purchases to mass-produced packages, with considerable assurance that the sack of flour bought this month would be identical to that brought home last month, and used successfully during the weeks since. Sweetened condensed milk was an economical spread for bread and a nourishing addition to tea or coffee in the days when butter could go "off" in a warm spell and milk was apt to be watered. Similarly, packaged cereals, bakers' bread, canned salmon, and pails of Crisco were more reliable, as sources of good nutrition, than homemade foods that used raw materials whose quality varied daily, despite all the consumer's efforts to buy "wisely."

It was to the producer's interest to maintain standardized quality. When consumers bought in bulk, their complaints about rancid butter, moldy flour, or fly-specked meal fell upon unidentifiable ears; no household purchaser could force an improvement of quality by threatening to buy from another supplier. When purchasers bought Cream of Wheat, Kellogg's Cornflakes, Crisco, certified milk, Campbell's soup, Kraft cheese, they depended on the same familiar, accepted foods. Packaging staple groceries offered opportunities for profit if advertising directed consumers' purchases to the branded product, and package labels identified the brand. But these profits could vanish if the quality of the product varied or was in blatant contradiction to the advertising claim. The use of brand names on produce required inspection and grading to control quality; these were supplied by the producers' associations, which reaped the benefits of a brand name, as consumers learned to ask for Sunkist oranges, Diamond walnuts, and Sun Maid raisins. Finally, brand names for coffee and tea were publicized, as major importers shifted to food retailing. By the early twenties "standard brands" were common, and the food price index listed items by weight instead of by the ambiguous peck, dozen, or loaf.

These consumption changes show up dramatically in the food items used by the Bureau of Labor Statistics for its cost-of-living index. From 1890 to 1902, 814 merchants in 33 states submitted monthly prices on the following articles:

> Evaporated apples, dry beans, prunes, Irish potatoes, rice
> Wheat flour, corn meal, wheat bread
> Fresh beef (roasts and stews), fresh beef (steaks), salt beef, chickens, fresh fish, salt fish, mutton and lamb, fresh pork, salt pork (bacon), salt pork (dry or pickled), salt pork (ham), veal
> Butter, cheese, eggs, lard, fresh milk
> Coffee, molasses, sugar, tea, vinegar

The Bureau struggled in vain to work out standard definitions for these items. Meat cuts varied by locality; "sirloin" was known as rump in Fall River, but as porterhouse in Boston, Providence, Manchester, and Philadelphia. Lard prices came chiefly from bulk sales; some pails of 3 to 5 pounds were included. Wheat flour quotations varied regionally: merchants in 30 cities quoted on the basis of a bag equal to an eighth of a barrel (its weight ranged from 23 to 24½ pounds), but in the East many sales were made in bags containing one-sixteenth and one thirty-second of a barrel. The Bureau noted that "in a few of the cities the price of the flour is 'protected'; that is, the flour manufacturer fixes a minimum selling price for the retailer." The term "butter" referred to "creamery extra," with "no dairy butter nor brands designated as special or fancy" to be included. Cheese could be "full cream" or "whole milk," usually from New York or Wisconsin but occasionally of local origin.[11]

Not surprisingly, by 1908 half the original list had been dropped because of rapid changes in quality and the difficulties of comparing items from place to place. But the growth of standardization made quite a different list of foodstuffs possible after World War I. Wartime regulations themselves had helped; the Food Administration adopted standard-weight loaves of bread in December 1917, and from 1918 on, prices were collected for a one-pound baked loaf of bread. Sugar, which until 1917 had been commonly sold by the 25¢, 50¢, or $1.00 sack, was also priced on a per pound basis. Before the substantial postwar changes were made, however, the food price list consisted of the following:

> Potatoes (per pound as of 1918), rice
> Flour, corn meal, bread (all per pound as of 1918)
> Sirloin steak, round steak, rib roast, pork chops, bacon, ham,
>   hens, chuck roast, plate, boiling beef
> Lard, eggs, butter, milk, cheese
> Coffee, sugar, tea.[12]

After the expenditure study of 1918–19, 21 items were added to the food list and descriptions for the remaining items became more precise, referring frequently to "standard

brands," U.S. government grades, or brand names. The addi-
tions and some typical specifications follow:

> Beans ("navy"), onions, cabbage ("Prices are quoted on the
> pound. This method of sale is rapidly replacing the
> sale by the head"), baked beans, canned corn, canned
> peas ("According to size, color, and maturity, peas are
> graded into fancy, standard, and substandard. Prices
> are collected on recognized brands of the standard
> grade"), canned tomatoes, prunes, raisins, bananas,
> oranges
> Canned salmon (both red and pink, one-pound "talls" were
> priced), lamb.
> Rolled oats ("standard brands both in the bulk and in the
> package"), cornflakes, Cream of Wheat, macaroni
> Evaporated milk, oleomargarine, nut margarine, Crisco.[13]

The 1918–19 survey showed a marked rise in average
family income and a substantial drop in the average percentage of income spent on food. Some asserted that this was new
evidence for Engel's law, but the changes discussed here
suggest quite otherwise. A wholly different array of foods
existed for consumption choice, and some of the income increase undoubtedly went to purchase additional quality, if
not quantity, of foods. That such a tendency existed had been
noted earlier:

This is the growing tendency among all classes to demand better
qualities of products . . . the finer cuts, porterhouse, sirloin and
rib roast . . . in part due to the fact that they may be more
readily prepared for the table by boiling or baking than the
cheaper cuts.[14]

"Quality" included some improvement in the nutritional
content of the diet—a matter of great concern to social workers, who tried to educate low-income households about low-
cost, wholesome food. But as the need for vitamins and the
existence of dietary deficiencies were discovered, consumers
needed formal education about the new food values; some of it

was contained in advertising. Significantly, processing did not necessarily mean nutritional improvement: although the vitamin loss from refining flour was known to scientists early in the century, not until World War II were processors required to replace these losses. Quality also meant spending some income to replace labor: when family incomes were high enough for people to become cognizant of the cost of women's kitchen work, the relative cost of canned goods from a mechanized factory dropped sharply. The average housewife could not match the skills of preparation developed by successful food-processing firms.

Most of all, the consumption choices available reflected greater variety. Differences by income levels persisted: in the early twenties low-income consumers ate canned salmon and wealthier families fresh swordfish; "vegetables out of season" were still the prerogative of the well-to-do. But canned salmon was a relief from the salt cod of 1901, and canned fruit and corn offered more variety than dried peas and raisins. While the shifts in food consumption pictured on Figure 1 are important, the changes in meals and menus are more relevant. The disappearance of lard, molasses, dried beans, and "halibut nape"; the increased consumption of butterfat in ice cream and all sorts of cheeses rather than just fluid milk; having salad dressings, mayonnaise, and tomato catsup to use, in addition to vinegar and pickles; sugar in purchased bakery goods, jellies, candies, and soft drinks—all these changes meant that consumers bought not just food stuffs but variety in the diet.

These general attributes of increased variety, stability of quality, and freedom from home preparation continued as later technological developments changed food consumption further. Refrigeration in warehouses and railroad cars lessened the impact of seasonal production; cold-storage eggs and fresh produce were shipped for hundreds of miles. Packaging and processing reduced the number of open bins and weighing or sorting by the store clerk. New types of prepared foods, from canned spaghetti and meatballs through strained baby foods to frozen dinners, accelerated the shift from kitchen to factory. Although the present per capita consumption of food, in pounds, is very close to the quantity estimated for 1909, it is no longer possible to list typical, or even frequent, purchases on one page. The broadening of consumption choice that has taken place can be described only in terms of the supermarkets, with inventories of over six thousand items and new products appearing daily.

Clothing and Shelter

The large-scale surveys at the turn of the century looked to see whether Engel's law of food applied to the other two "basic" items of consumption, housing and clothing. Statistics showed no evidence that, for clothing, expenditures were a smaller percentage of high incomes than of low, but in the pressure for a "fair" wage, budget-makers drew up lists of clothing to define a "necessary" minimum. These reflected differences in climate and consumer habits.

Early in the century, an investigation of Southern wage earners recommended the following minimum wardrobe, based on actual purchases, for adult males:

One suit, two trousers, five colored shirts, two winter underwear, two pairs of shoes, one hat, one pair suspenders, socks;

for adult females:

One shawl, four calico waists, two duck shirts, two drawers, two gingham petticoats, one fascinator, two pairs shoes, stockings.

A study of Northern wage earners suggested adding an overcoat and overalls for men, a wool skirt and flannelette petticoats, plus mittens and winter undershirts, for the women. The reports also described wardrobes slightly above these minima which added variety: a Sunday suit, collars and necktie, and a barbershop haircut for men; dresses, a sateen petticoat, straw hat and gloves for women. Neither level provided for any type of nightwear.[15]

As with food, different income levels produced sharp differences in clothing. Low-income families, which were forced to buy food in small and uneconomical quantities, found it equally difficult to be thrifty with clothing:

Usually there was only enough money on hand each week to buy the cheapest ready-made clothing, which wears out quickly and is not worth repairing.[16]

Because the garment industry was just developing, "ready-made" tended to connote cheap and shoddy. Differences in income also affected the quantity of clothing available; early in the century one social worker noted that, in a poor family, "the mother always wore wrappers at home, and only had one street dress, as she never went anywhere except to church."[17] Deploring this aspect of clothing economy, a 1914 budget-maker insisted:

The stock of clothing should be such as to allow the members of the family to have some social intercourse. The mother should have more than a shawl; she should be equipped with a coat in which to go out in the cold weather, either to church, to settlement club meetings or to gatherings of her friends. Similarly the children should be able to maintain a respectable appearance at school.[18]

At all income levels consumers bought clothing materials and fabric; the minimum lists quoted above assumed that women's and children's garments were made at home, and it was the first step above the minimum that added a purchased suit and coat. But the well-to-do employed tailors and seamstresses for home sewing, while lower-income families made do with the housewife's skill; the prevailing styles of heavy fabrics, voluminous coats and skirts, and numerous layers of clothing emphasized the differences in dressmaking skills and income available for materials.

As with food, early changes in clothing expenditure represented a shift from home production to the factory. Ready-made clothing for men appeared first; changes in style and fabric occurred early in the century:

While the quality of the goods entering into a suit at a given price today might not be equal to that in the same-price suit five years ago, yet the clothing itself would be better . . . in making and in style. A $10 suit today is practically all cotton, but it is stronger. A man who really gets that suit for service will actually get more service out of it than he would have had out of a suit at the same price fifteen years ago.[19]

The National Industrial Conference Board listed, in 1914, 25 articles "in common use by average American families."[20] Seven were yard goods: serge, poplin, broadcloth, percale, gingham, longcloth, fruit of the loom (sic), and voile. By the mid-'20s, only two fabric items remained, Fruit of the Loom and flannelette, and the Board commented: "It appears that more and more clothing is bought ready made . . . in many instances, leaving out quality, the ready made garments are as cheap as material can be purchased."[21]

Some of the income increases over the first two decades were spent to provide more variety in clothing, as lighter, cheaper fabrics and more simply cut clothing appeared:

High shoes . . . are hardly ever carried by New York shoe dealers; shirt waists and skirts are not worn as once they were except as suit combinations, and even the latter are far less popular than the dress and coat; under clothing is reduced to a minimum. On the other hand, it would be a poor family, indeed, which did not provide an occasional pair of silk stockings for its women folk; and fur, of a kind, on coats is well-nigh universal.[22]

The widespread adoption of ready-made clothing lessened the obvious external differences among income classes; if clothing expenditures did not decrease as a percentage of income, it was partly because larger wardrobes were more readily available to all.

As the shift from home to factory brought new alternatives from which to choose items of food and clothing, so it also affected household tasks. The basic utilities of fuel, water, and light governed the housekeeping arrangements of any family by dictating what equipment could be used to prepare food, care for clothing, and keep utensils, tableware, garments, and people clean. It is almost impossible to draw even an impressionistic picture of general housing conditions at the turn of the century. Over half the families lived in rented homes—a ratio that was not changed until late in the '30s. But differences in consumption did not reflect differences in tenure —home ownership or tenancy—as much as location—city or country living. In 1900 almost half the population still lived on farms. In 1910, the first year for which such figures are available, farm *households* numbered 6 million; nonfarm, 14 million.

For the most part, urban slums had grown up without any regulation, but by the late nineteenth century, housing conditions had aroused the social reformers, shocked by the facts turned up in case studies of family living. Their reports emphasize that for city workers privacy was a housing "luxury." The 1901 survey of 25,440 families reported that 21 per cent of them included boarders, and another 3 per cent let out rooms to lodgers. Of the 124,108 persons covered by the study, 11,996 were unrelated boarders and lodgers. Their payments provided almost 10 per cent of average family income, and they usually lived in the "best" rooms of the house or flat. Those social workers who dealt with the "lodging-house problem" for the single individual noted that living in a private home might or might not be a suitable consumption choice. It was certainly the custom for immigrants or for young women who were entering the labor market for the first time. Families with higher incomes "naturally" aspired to a home of their own, and there was much discussion of opportunities for healthful living in the developing suburbs.

In the cities there was little effort to enforce even minimum standards of "healthful living." Both zoning and housing legislation suffered from the lack of clear definition: the minimum standard drawn up in 1912 by the National Conference of Charities and Correction in Cleveland was far superior to the conditions of many homes even 20 years later:

Social welfare demands for every family a safe and sanitary home; healthful surroundings; ample and pure running water inside the house; modern and sanitary toilet conveniences for its exclusive use, located inside the building; adequate sunlight and ventilation; reasonable fire protection; privacy; rooms of sufficient size and number to decently house the members of the family; freedom from dampness; prompt, adequate collection of all waste materials. These fundamental requirements for normal living should be obtainable by every family, reasonably accessible from place of employment, at a rental not exceeding 20% of the family income.[23]

At the turn of the century, only a minority of family dwellings had inside running water, to say nothing of toilets or baths. The New York tenement law, which observers agreed was rarely effective, required running water on each floor and a water closet for every 15 inhabitants. In small towns or rural areas, families relied on hand-pumped wells or on a water tap on the back porch or in the yard. Only one family in ten was a customer of a power plant; kerosene and gas supplied the chief means of lighting. While most city kitchens had an icebox, it was small; the larder or cold cellar on the farms was, by comparison, an advantage. Not all consumers were free to choose what housing to buy; "company houses" in mill towns and mining settlements were common. Those in Homestead in 1910 provided workers with a choice between 4 rooms with no water or light, at $8.50 a month, and 5 rooms with electric lights and two inside faucets, at $12.50 per month.

Coal and wood were the principal domestic fuels used in central heating systems, fireplaces, and stoves. They also stoked the kitchen range, which was frequently the only source of heat. Some houses had gas burners or oil stoves to supplement the kitchen range or to use in the summer, but the slowness with which gas ranges were introduced was deplored by a contemporary writer:

The way in which ignorance on the part of housekeepers blocks social progress is seen in the difference between the development of electric transportation and domestic gas consumption. The use of gas for fuel was proposed before the trolley line was developed, but at each step in the introduction of gas, obstacles due to ignorance of the relations of heat and of the management of mechanical apparatus have so far prevented the extension of this convenient and economical fuel. The manufacturers of domestic utensils have not shown that grasp of scientific principles which is expected of other trades, and small wonder that it is words, not deeds, upon which they rely.[24]

The kitchen stove, however it was fueled, was the source for hot water, although some central heating systems provided hot running water during the colder months. But the teakettle, wash boiler, and scrub pail traveled regularly from faucet to stove. "Set-tubs" installed in the kitchen were a feature of model city flats and suburban homes.

With such limited "conveniences," minimum equipment for housecleaning consisted of brooms, mops, scrub-brushes, a pail, dishpan, dish-drainer, stove polish (26 boxes a year was a reasonable allowance), and insect powder. Kitchen furnishings for the housecleaner-turned-cook included a preserving kettle, jelly glasses and fruit jars, a bread-raising pan, and a long list of utensils, all of which spelled extensive time in food preparation. Finally, the family wash was laundered (frequently in the yard or separate shed) with two tubs, a zinc washboard, a copper-bottom boiler, a wringer, and at least three sadirons, plus bluing, starch, and a reasonable supply (120 half-pound bars) of laundry soap a year.

This recital suggests that the major difference between the well-to-do and the less affluent was not to be found in furnishings and equipment, but in who did the work. The middle-class family of modest means kept "only one maid"; the lower-income family with regular boarders had kitchen help; the large household "with several in the kitchen" might expect to benefit, for "the 'left-overs' are eaten at the second table."[25] While servants did most of the housekeeping in upper-income homes, some domestic help was used by families of the middle- and low-income classes. Even tenement families paid for occasional help with cleaning and the week's washing; more frequently, they kept a daughter out of school to help at home. Almost every "white-collar" family had laundry expenses for the men's detachable collars and cuffs.

In 1920, when the Bureau of Labor Statistics wrote the first "minimum health and decency" standard, it included, somewhat defensively, an allowance for household help:

Expenditure for assistance with laundry work may not be considered possible in the family of an industrial worker. However, from the standpoint of health, it seems that the mother of three children who must do the cooking for the family, the general cleaning of the house, the sewing and mending, the marketing and shopping should be allowed assistance with the family laundry work and scrubbing, amounting to one day per week.[26]

In a revised version the Bureau omitted this recommendation, and differences in household services continued to identify different income levels until the appliance revolution.

Household appliances required, however, that there be electricity in the home; this, as well as fuel and plumbing improvements, was installed in new buildings, rather than in remodeled tenements or houses. After World War I there was little new construction in the rural areas, with their declining population and generally depressed economy: in 1910 there were 6.1 million farm dwellings; in 1930 these numbered 6.6 million. In cities and towns the picture was quite different: the number of nonfarm dwellings increased from 14 million in 1910 to 23.3 million in 1930. The Conference Board included electricity in its cost-of-living index in 1923, with the remark that "the determination of the exact point when that became necessary is, of course, arbitrary."[27] By 1930 approximately half the urban homes used central heating and 85 per cent had electric service. The Board reported, year by year after World War I, the general adoption first of the electric iron, then of the vacuum cleaner, and after these the electric toaster, the mechanical washing machine, the electric range (as early as 1919 the gas stove had become familiar to some families at all income levels), and electric refrigerators. Table 3 gives data on wired homes and appliances from 1925 to 1942, plus a recent year for comparison. The new tools encouraged a greater use of electricity: electrified homes rose from 68 per cent of the total in 1930 to 79 per cent in 1940, but the annual use of electricity per customer almost doubled. The greatest lack still was to be found in the rural areas: only one-third of the farm dwellings had electricity in 1940.

These appliances were a curiously depression-proof example of growth: 18 per cent of all families in the Bureau of Labor Statistics survey of 1934–36 reported some expenditure on electrical equipment, and this form of spending amounted to 35 per cent of the total spent for all home furnishings and equipment. The average expenditure (for all families, whether purchasers or not) of $18.00 for electrical appliances compares with the average of $16.00 for laundry and domestic service. Of the 4 items in Table 3, refrigerators were the most frequently purchased at the time of the survey; among all appliances, electric irons took the lead. The survey reported average prices of $163 for refrigerators, $63 for washing machines, $54 for electric stoves (including hotplates), $44 for vacuum cleaners, and $4 for electric irons; the average family income at

Table 3

**Number of Wired Houses and Percentage of Wired Houses
with Four Household Appliances, 1925–1942**

Year	Number of Wired Houses (in thousands)	Percentage of Dwelling Units with Electricity		Percentage of Wired Houses Owning			
		All	Farm	Mechanical Refrigerators	Washing Machines	Vacuum Cleaners	Ranges
1925	14,965	53.2	3.9	—	21	31	3
1926	16,458	57.9	4.8	2	27	37	—
1927	17,951	63.1	5.9	4	28	39	3
1928	19,090	65.0	7.3	6	30	41	4
1929	19,967	67.9	9.2	9	33	44	4
1930	20,332	68.2	10.4	13	35	44	5
1931	20,151	67.4	10.7	17	41	45	5
1932	19,850	67.0	11.2	22	39	47	6
1933	20,004	66.7	11.8	25	44	49	6
1934	20,694	67.1	12.1	29	46	48	6
1935	21,235	68.0	12.6	34	49	48	7
1936	22,030	70.3	14.5	41	53	49	8
1937	22,939	73.1	18.3	49	56	49	9
1938	23,517	74.9	23.9	52	58	49	10
1939	24,599	77.3	27.4	57	60	51	11

1940	25,638	78.7	32.6	64	63	52	12
1941	27,012	80.0	35.0	73	65	53	13
1942	27,716	81.2	37.8	72	63	51	13
1963				99	72	72	96

SOURCES: Percentages of dwelling units with electricity from U.S. Bureau of the Census, *Historical Statistics of the United States*, Washington, D.C., 1960, Series S-71 and S-72; other figures from G. Frederic Dewhurst and Associates, *America's Needs and Resources*, Twentieth Century Fund, 1947, p. 179, quoting Saul Nelson and Walter G. Keim, *Price Behavior and Business Policy*, TNEC Monograph No. 1, 1940, p. 262. Primary sources for all data are trade publications of the electricity industry.

that time was $1,524. The number of purchasers, but not the price paid, varied by income class; the greatest variation in numbers of buyers occurred in the case of the refrigerator, possibly because it was the newest item, possibly because the price represented a substantial share of income. On this the Bureau commented:

It is striking that a higher percentage of all families surveyed reported purchase of electric refrigerators and electric washing machines than of any item of furniture. . . . The great contribution of these items to lightening the housewife's task and facilitating more pleasant living for the entire family is witnessed by these figures. . . . In purchasing such substantial items, the families tend to pay as much as they think is required to obtain an article of reasonably good durability, and large enough for the family needs, if necessary extending their payments over a longer period of time.[28]

As with clothing, the use of household appliances tended to lessen the obvious differences between income classes. But consumer spending for appliances accelerated only after the major shift from renting to home ownership took place, for housekeeping arrangements reflect patterns of housing. In some ways, appliances introduced an even wider range of consumption choice than did the many changes in food and apparel, for the labor-saving aspects of appliances were less significant than their contribution to household life of flexibility, of some degree of freedom from a rigid dawn-to-dusk schedule. This enabled more married women to hold jobs and thus in turn influenced other consumption choices.

Subsistence and Sundries

At the turn of the century investigators classified household expenses into four broad categories: food, clothing, housing, and "sundries." Not surprisingly, the proportion of income spent on sundries was sharply higher at successively higher income levels. The controversy over the meaning of "sundries" —whether they represent "luxuries"—has persisted, even though the nature of "luxury" expenditure has changed drastically. Nowhere is this clearer than in the case of the automobile. In 1910 the Massachusetts Commission on the Cost of Living remarked:

In the twelve years since the use of self-propelled road vehicles became mechanically perfected and commercially profitable, it is estimated that a million automobiles have been produced, and sold for more than a billion and a half dollars. . . . The great bulk of this output represents pure luxury production, which has taken at least one hundred thousand workers out of employments in which they were producing commodities that were useful and of benefit to all the people, into an occupation in which the product may be termed an economic waste. The machinist building looms or the farmer growing wheat or corn, who goes into automobile making, not only lessens the supply of these necessaries of life, but increases the weight on the demand side of the ratio. So far as these automobiles are useful economically, in that they conserve health or make their owners more productive in their various occupations or professions, this enormous luxury production may be justified; but this is often not the case. While the owner of an automobile is undoubtedly benefited in health by the enjoyment of this sport, the next result of ownership of an automobile may be to make its owner less productive. Frequently he uses it under conditions that take from his business or profession valuable time that would otherwise be given to increase production. This diminution in productivity on the part of the automobile owners must be added to the disturbance of the law of supply and demand in the making of automobiles, while the indirect effect of this show of luxury upon the poor, causing discontent and its consequences, is far-reaching. . . . The progress of civilization has demonstrated that the luxuries of today are considered the necessities of tomorrow. The production of automobiles for commercially economical and purely pleasurable purposes is not likely to diminish, but rather to increase.[29]

35

But in 1927, when automobile registrations came to 172 cars per thousand population, the Commission's prophecy had already come true—for trainmen, at least:

Under the heading "other omitted items of modern living" are grouped certain items which, with the exception of savings, are the things which distinguish life today from the life of previous generations. The radio, telephone and the automobile have ceased to be luxuries. They are essentials of modern life. This is particularly true in the Western states. Automobile registrations show that throughout this section of the country the automobile has come to be regarded as an ordinary necessity.[30]

One of the greatest changes in consumer choices occurred in recreation; at the beginning of the century, social workers noted that nickelodeons and saloons were the chief forms of entertainment for city workers. (That a "free lunch" provided in saloons supplemented the nutritional values available to workers, and that money spent on beer or hard liquor was "wasted," was repeatedly pointed out by the early investigators.) The 1901 survey reported that 70 per cent of the families spent some of their income on amusements and vacations, 51 per cent on intoxicating liquors, and 44 per cent on organizations. Clubs and labor unions sometimes sponsored suppers, picnics, evening "rackets" or dances, but the exigencies of a 10-hour day, 6-day work week limited recreation. In small towns and rural areas, home entertainment was the rule: a piano or victrola in the home, a child taking music lessons—these were mentioned as frequently as vacations away from home or commercial amusements, such as the traveling circus or a theatrical performance.

The motion-picture industry offered the first major change in urban recreation: "It is worthy of note that wherever the 'motion-picture' houses are opened, the patronage of the liquor saloons in the neighborhood shows a falling off."[31] Home entertainment also offered more variety, as first the phonograph and then the radio took the place of the piano. But the greatest variety appeared when paid holidays and shorter working hours became common. The street railway enabled city families to enjoy a day in the country, and some firms began to provide clubhouses, gymnasiums, poolrooms, baseball diamonds, and even, occasionally, golf courses for their workers' newly acquired leisure time.

The second major change was the automobile, which began during the '20s to provide to more and more families holiday excursions, weekend trips, or vacations away from home. Although only 15 per cent of the families surveyed in 1918 reported spending for automobiles, motorcycles, and bicycles combined, in the survey of 1934–36 44 per cent of all families owned cars. Automobile ownership diminished factory workers' interest in team sports sponsored by their employers, by making beaches, golf courses, and tennis courts accessible to them and their families.[32]

The addition of variety, which by now seems to be typical of consumption changes, affected all forms of communication during the first three decades of the century. In the 1901 survey, 95 per cent of the families spent something for books and newspapers; in 1910

the present broader and more general education, even though free from direct expense to the working man, adds to his cost of living by refining his tastes and increasing his desires. For example, the purchase of a morning paper is now his regular habit; an evening paper almost equally so; popular books and magazines are included in the necessities of life.[33]

This same source indicates that about 2,500 magazines existed, whose aggregate circulation amounted to 25 million, almost double that of a decade earlier. Of the 18 thousand newspapers, about three-fourths were country weeklies; but the dailies had doubled their share of total circulation in 20 years, as the population became increasingly concentrated in urban areas.

The number of telephones per thousand population rose from 30 in 1902 to 130 in 1922 and 163 in 1927. Like electricity, telephones were concentrated in urban areas: in 22 cities of 100,000 population or above, 60 per cent of the families had telephones. Radios showed more spectacular gains: from 60,000 homes in 1921 to 7½ million in 1927; four out of five of the families surveyed in 1934–36 reported that they owned radios.

Savings

The first large-scale surveys in this country, Carroll Wright's studies of selected wage-earner groups from 1887 to 1889 and the much wider sample of families in 1901, verified Engel's law of nourishment and posed the problem of saving. From the standpoint of the consumer, two major alternative uses existed for income: consumption and saving. At low-income levels, families had to use most or all of their income in order to obtain the "necessities of life"—those meager living conditions deplored by social workers. At higher-income levels, the "essentials" of food, shelter, and clothing were more easily come by. Although dollar expenditures on these consumption *categories* were larger in every larger-income class, they represented a smaller *percentage* of income at higher-income levels than at lower-income levels. Hence, either "sundries" or savings or both absorbed larger shares of income from upper-income families than from lower-income ones.

Case studies of individual families and early surveys of large groups of consumers attempted to match spending against income for each family and to record the number of consumers who reported a surplus. Sometimes the surplus was calculated as the difference between income and the "necessities" outlined in a minimum budget (expenditures for food, shelter, and clothing). In these cases, the surplus obviously included "sundries" of entertainment, personal care, and so on. In other cases, calculations for total income and total spending on *all* items resulted in actual amounts of either "surplus" or "deficit." The 1901 study contains figures on the disposition of surplus and the financing of deficit. In fact, as later work was to prove more precisely, the number of surplus families and the amount of the surplus were both greater in successively higher-income classes. The alternative to total consumption spending was saving. The amount saved and the fraction of income saved showed the same relationship in every study: in both absolute and percentage terms, saving is larger at higher income levels.

The relationship of saving to income that is exhibited in household budgets or in national economic accounts became a subject of critical interest late in the '30s, after the publication of John Maynard Keynes' classic *General Theory of Employment, Interest and Money*. To the early investigators of working-class families, the very term "saving" seemed frequently inappropriate, so conscious were they of the struggle for a "living" wage. But by the definition that was developed much later, "saving" consists of income that is not spent on consumer goods and services for immediate use. It can be calculated simply, therefore, by subtracting total consumption spending from total income. It is true that some consumers use this "saving" to make purchases, but income "spent" on such assets as real estate, houses, or savings bonds is, nevertheless, not spent on immediate consumption. Income that is used to pay back debts is also not spent on current consumption; debt repayment or a reduction in liabilities constitutes a form of savings. It follows that consumer net worth—the difference between assets and liabilities—represents accumulated savings, and the change in net worth from one date to another equals the saving (or dissaving) over the intervening time period. In the early budget studies and in the observations of social workers, there are scattered clues about the nature of consumer assets and liabilities.

Many of these writers treated saving together with payments for insurance, since both insurance and accumulated savings are able to make up for loss of income. While insurance policies were fairly common at the turn of the century, they differed substantially among families at different income levels. About 15 million life insurance policies were outstanding in 1900, of which 3 million were ordinary life. Sixty-seven per cent of these were whole life policies, with an average face value of $2,250; the remainder were endowment policies, with an average value of $2,057. Only the paid-up value of such policies represents assets. The average premium on such policies, at $18.70 per thousand dollars (male, aged 30) may not seem excessive if it is compared to average annual income figures, but almost 80 per cent of the policies lapsed in 1900, and figures for other years in the same period are roughly comparable.[34] The premium, therefore, did represent a sizable *unit* expenditure, or at least one that it was impossible for low-income families to maintain. Instead, they purchased the 11 million industrial policies outstanding, which had an average value of $131. It was the weekly collection of nickels and dimes by the insurance agent that put the purchase within reach of working-class families,[35] and hence 65 per cent of the families whose detailed expenditures were recorded in 1901 were shown to hold life insurance. It was common to have a policy for each family member, the proceeds being spent entirely for burial expenses. For this reason, social workers saw insurance as being—for the working-class family—a very real "necessity of life":

It is considered by the working class a form of savings. It is an obligation which must be paid before any other. A family is frequently willing to be dispossessed or to go without food or clothing or fuel in order to keep up the insurance.[36]

At the turn of the century, saving occasionally involved home ownership. Of 25,440 working-class families surveyed in 1901, 18.97 per cent owned their homes, over half of which had no mortgage. Only half the mortgagees made any payment on principal, although 95 per cent of them did meet interest payments. For the country as a whole, 37 per cent of the nonfarm houses were owner-occupied, and only one-third of these were mortgaged. Like insurance, home ownership also differed sharply by income class. Contemporary opinion on the value of home ownership was contradictory:

Even on the merely economic side, the possession of money in savings banks, and the ownership of houses to be rented to others, do not compare in profitableness with the ownership of the home in which one lives. . . . The man who owns his own home is always sure of a tenant, always sure of collections, and generally sure to take care of the property. On the side of citizenship the gains that come from home ownership are even greater.[37]

In general we may say that home-buying for the ordinary working man is inadvisable, for usually he will be unable to buy the home outright, and a working man who has a mortgage on his home generally has his body and soul mortgaged with it. In addition to his being bound to one locality when his employment may have been changed to another, he must endure a vast amount of worry incident to the payment, periodically, of interest on the mortgage and usually after buying a house under installment conditions he finds that he has paid too much for it.[38]

Chiefly because of the lack of financing arrangements, the home as a form of savings was far from the reach of the typical consumer. Building and loan societies or cooperative bank arrangements catered to middle-class people, and mortgage

41

payments that represented a regular reduction in principal did not become common until late in the '30s.

The chief form of savings that remained was either a petty hoard of cash or a savings-bank deposit. Of 1,480 families (almost 60 per cent of those with detailed expenditure records) in 1901 who reported a surplus, some 500 held cash on hand and 682 deposited the surplus in a bank. When the postal savings system reported on its first few years of operation, sizable amounts of old bills and coins were deposited, presumably removed from cash hoards.

But while savings-bank deposits increased substantially, the extent to which the "surplus" reported by families at the turn of the century represented saving which led to an increase in net worth is widely open to doubt. As one reporter described the families whose income averaged $815.31 in 1907:

In many cases it seems simply a question of luck whether there will be a surplus or deficit. . . . Unsteady income due to unemployment, illness, or intemperance, with regular pressing daily expenses, left this pitifully small ($15.13) "margin of surplus."[39]

Similarly from a study of 450 women workers in Boston whose weekly wages ranged from $3.00 to over $15.00, and who were concentrated in the annual income groups of less than $500:

Savings deposited in banks are usually drawn out to meet the needs of a less prosperous time, and do not accumulate long. . . . Lowest, in respect to permanence, rank stamp savings, these being used up within a few months, as a general thing. On the whole, savings on any wage below $15 are largely a fictitious, temporary surplus of income over expenses.[40]

All these data make it clear that the relation of saving to income can be measured in different ways. There is, first, the average saving/income ratio, which is higher at higher income levels. Secondly, there is the number (or percentage) of families at each income level who report a surplus of income over expenditures. Finally, there is the level of income at which such "savers" exceed those in a deficit position, or those whose "saving" tends to provide a permanent accumulation of assets. Table 4 shows data from the 1901 survey on the average saving/income ratio; the number of savers by income levels is not available. The "break-even" point appears to be an annual income level of between $500 and $700.

Table 4

Family Expenditure and Saving, by Income Class,
11,156 Normal Families, 1901

| | | | | Average Saving | |
Income Class	Number of Families	Average Income*	Average Total Expenditures	Dollars	Per Cent of Income
Under $200	32		$195.85		
200–299	115	$ 250	312.35	−62	−25
300–399	545	350	388.51	−39	−11
400–499	1,676	450	466.04	−16	−4
500–599	2,264	550	540.02	10	2
600–699	2,336	650	611.58	38	6
700–799	2,094	750	692.65	57	8
800–899	806	850	770.58	79	9
900–999	684	950	816.26	135	14
1,000–1,099	340	1,050	899.74	150	14
1,100–1,200	96	1,150	973.09	177	15

* Average income is taken as the midpoint of the income class; survey data do not include actual income figures.

SOURCE: *Eighteenth Annual Report of the Commissioner of Labor*, Washington, D.C., 1903, Table V, p. 583.

Over the next 30 years, the income of American consumers was to increase steadily. While consumption changed markedly, little innovation was to occur in the forms of savings. The 1918–19 survey by the Bureau of Labor Statistics reported life insurance purchases by 86 per cent of all families, a proportion that did not vary by income classes. The *amounts* spent on insurance by families in the highest-income class were three times those in the lowest-income class. Most families still bought industrial insurance: 45 million policies, with an average value of $133, were in force. Ten years later, the number of such policies had almost doubled: the need to meet burial expenses was still the imperative "form of savings." Ordinary life insurance had also increased, but even in 1929 the average face value of such policies was only approximately $2,500. Saving for a home was the motive of many savings-bank depositors; such regular habits of thrift began to be included in the "American standard of living," if not in minimum budgets:

Except for insurance, these sums make no provision for saving, which is almost a necessity for a single man, in order to permit him to start a home or, having no children on whose support he can count in his later years, to enable him to provide for his old age. It is, therefore, socially desirable that at least $2 a week or $104 a year be added to the actual cost of living of the single man to permit him to provide for the future, which in the case of a married man with children is partially taken care of.[41]

Few families actually purchased houses with this type of saving: a study in 1928 of workers' families found that the first payment for a home was typically made from an inheritance, from income that the wife had earned, or from some other source that was regarded as a "windfall," rather than from regular saving. The ratio of homeowners to renters changed but little: in 1900, 47 per cent of all occupied dwelling units were owner-occupied; in 1930, 48 per cent were. Of nonfarm, owner-occupied homes, 40 per cent were mortgaged, but housing had yet to become the principal form of savings for most consumers.

The most important indicator of the radical change in income and consumption brought by the first 30 years of the century was the surplus-and-deficit position of consumers. By

1930, despite the onslaught of the depression, total personal income in the country had soared from $14 billion to $77 billion. Comparison of two surveys of city workers, for 1901 and for 1934–36, shows that real income per family, after allowing for price changes, had more than doubled. The 1901 expenditures on food, shelter, and clothing—the "necessities of life"—were well within command of the richer families of the '30s. The break-even point for the earlier distribution shown on Table 4 was at the low end of the income scale in 1934–36. If subsistence took a smaller fraction of higher incomes, the share of income saved would be substantially larger in the '30s. The fact is that no such rise in the average saving/income ratio occurred. Instead, the survey showed a change in the division of income between consumption and saving. As incomes increased over time, the percentage saved became smaller at every income level. The same phenomenon appeared in later surveys of the '40s, '50s, and '60s. It can be briefly shown in Table 5, which uses data from the 1935–36 survey.

Table 5

Family Saving and Income, by Income Class,
Nonfarm Families, 1935–1936

Income Class	Average Income	Average Expenditures	Average Saving	
			Dollars	Per Cent
Under $500	$ 292	$ 493	−201	−69
500–999	730	802	−72	−10
1,000–1,499	1,176	1,196	−20	−2
1,500–1,999	1,636	1,598	38	2
2,000–2,999	2,292	2,124	168	7
3,000–3,999	3,243	2,814	429	13
4,000–4,999	4,207	3,467	740	18
5,000–10,000	6,598	4,950	1,648	25

SOURCE: Dorothy S. Brady, "Family Saving, 1888 to 1950," *A Study of Saving in the United States* (Princeton, N.J.: Princeton University Press, 1956), Vol. III, p. 183.

The break-even level of income, that classification in which average saving becomes positive, and families who are savers outnumber those in a deficit position, was between $1,500 and $2,000 in the 1934–36 survey. Deflated for price changes, this amount of income would be roughly equivalent to $900 in the 1901 survey—at which time, consumers of that income level saved, on the average, 14 per cent of their income. For any income class, the saving/income ratio of the '30s was significantly below that of 1900. While saving still remained a larger percentage for high incomes than for low, the shift of income from low to high had not brought about an increase in the percentage of income saved. Most analysts term the phenomenon a shift in the saving function described in terms of income:

The average household must have an ever-increasing nominal or real disposable income per head before it does any saving; or, to put it differently . . . an increasing level of real consumption has been necessary throughout the past half century to elicit the same proportion of saving.[42]

As long as saving and consumption are, however, the two alternatives for the disposition of income, the shift in the saving/income ratio cannot be isolated as a separate function. If, at every income level, today's consumers save a smaller portion of their income than their grandparents did, they must spend a larger portion than their grandparents did on consumption goods and services.

There has been much theoretical discussion of the shift in the saving function and many statistical analyses of it;[43] for the most part they have not been accompanied by much explicit discussion of what changes in consumption have resulted. The brief survey in this chapter has left a number of topics, and a wealth of detail, untouched, yet it allows some tentative conclusions about consumption change during the first half of this century in the United States.

First, a common pattern of consumption emerged. National brands of processed and packaged foodstuffs reduced the regional variations of early menus. Mass-produced automobiles and appliances blurred the sharp distinction between income levels indicated by household servants. Ready-made clothing and the spread of style and fashion through mass media lessened obvious differences in appearance. All these trends continued after interruption by the depression and World War II, but they had their roots in earlier years.

Secondly, within this "typical" consumption pattern, the range of alternatives available to consumers widened enormously. The limitations of the human stomach prevented the increased income from being used to purchase more pounds of food, but it was used to provide a variety that can be appreciated only by a review of the limited lists of food available in 1900. The number and kinds of garments in a city worker's wardrobe or in the wardrobe of the lower-income rural family greatly exceeded, even during the depression of the '30s, the meager supplies of earlier days. The automobile provided a change of scene for commuter and vacationer markedly different from that furnished by the end of the street railway line.

Finally, no rule was developed to define "luxury spending." The words of the Massachusetts Commission in 1910 apply with equal force to all the changes, whether small or revolutionary, that took place after they were written:

The common laborer of today is better housed, fed and clothed, and insists on and receives more comforts and luxuries than the Norman kings who ruled England in the twelfth century. The wage-earner of today lives under conditions that would have been deemed luxurious by a rich Englishman of the fifteenth century.[44]

The growth of the American economy merely speeded up the process. The luxuries of one generation now become the necessities of the next, instead of taking centuries to become established.

The definition of economics with which this book began posed the problem of scarce means which have alternative uses. It is clear that the alternatives confronting the American consumer today differ spectacularly from those of a generation ago; in fact, the range of alternatives has widened so much in every sphere that the problem of consumer choice has been magnified many times over. The next step in following the definition is to examine the scarce means, to learn how individuals and families share in the total income of the economy and how purchasing power is distributed among consumers.

chapter 2 The
Consumer's
Scarce
Means

*T*he growth of the American economy, as the last chapter illustrated, led to striking changes in consumption choice. Equally striking have been the changes in income and purchasing power that it produced. Consumers' income, referring to their "scarce means," is the amount available for spending and saving, and therefore differs somewhat from total, or national, income. Large parts of the total earnings of the economy are not available to consumers to spend or save: corporations, in order to pay for capital goods, often retain profits rather than distribute them to their stockholders; government withholds taxes; and part of the consumers' income is earmarked for direct taxes—the property or income levies of local or state or Federal government.

49

Figure 1. Gross National Product in Constant Dollars (Annually, 1929–1946; quarterly, seasonally adjusted, 1947–)

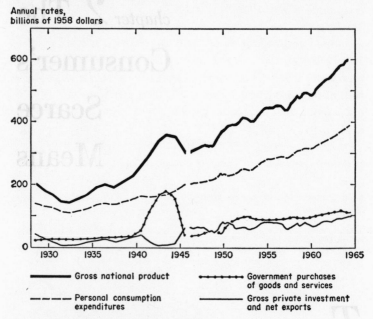

Annual rates,
billions of 1958 dollars

Gross national product
Government purchases of goods and services
Personal consumption expenditures
Gross private investment and net exports

Source: Board of Governors of the Federal Reserve System

The income that consumers are free to spend or save is, in aggregate, Personal Disposable Income,* a sum usually representing between 60 and 80 per cent of Gross National Product. Most of this amount is spent for products and services. Thus, total output for consumers represents, in "normal" times, about two-thirds of total production. This relationship, as well as other data, appears in Figure 1, showing annual aggregates since 1929 for Gross National Product divided into the four

* Because many terms, such as income or consumption, are defined in various ways, capital letters will be used in this book to refer to the statistics and definitions of the Commerce Department's Office of Business Economics, which prepares the aggregate data commonly cited.

familiar sectors of final demand. The use of constant dollars removes the effect of increased prices. It is clear that actual consumption has almost tripled since 1929. (Preliminary figures suggest that Personal Consumption Expenditures in 1965 amounted, in constant dollar terms, to 282 per cent of the 1929 sum.) The current output of consumer goods and services represents at least 8 to 9 times that which was available at the turn of the century, although it is impossible to make accurate allowances for improvements in quality and the greater variety.

To correspond with this picture of total output, Figure 2 presents data for personal or consumer income before taxes.

Figure 2. Components of Personal Income (Annually, 1929–1946; monthly, seasonally adjusted, 1947–)

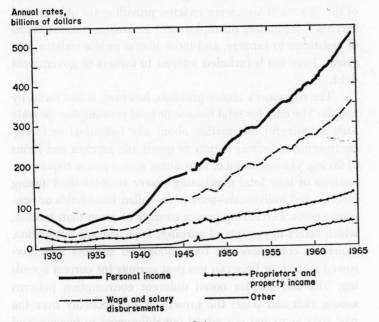

Annual rates, billions of dollars

━━━ Personal income

┅┅┅ Proprietors' and property income

━ ━ ━ Wage and salary disbursements

──── Other

Source: Board of Governors of the Federal Reserve System

These data, in current dollars, cannot be compared directly with those of Figure 1, but the same broad pattern of change appears: the impact of depression, hot war, and cold war can be traced both in the output of consumer goods and services in Figure 1 and in the figures for Personal Income in Figure 2. The latter diagram also shows the chief sources of consumer earnings and consumer receipts. Wages and salaries make up the bulk of income since most consumers sell their services to business firms, to government, or to other consumers. Some income is earned by what consumers themselves own: Proprietors' and Property Income includes dividends, interest, the profits of unincorporated business, and rents. The sums shown on the chart as "Other" represent transfers of income, payments that do not reflect current earnings by the recipients. The dollar amounts involved have grown steadily since the decade of the '30s when laws were enacted providing for old age and survivors' insurance, unemployment insurance, various forms of assistance to farmers, and more liberal public welfare programs. Here too is included interest to owners of government debt.

The consumer's choice problem, however, is one faced by people. The data for total income or total consumption provide little meaningful information about any individual or family confronting an infinite variety of goods and services and forms of saving. The constraint of consumers' scarce means requires an analysis of how total purchasing power is distributed among families and individuals—sometimes called households or consumer units. Purchasing power consists of more than income, which refers to receipts of earnings from current production. American consumers can buy goods and services with borrowed money, or they can use past savings for current spending. The last chapter noted different consumption patterns among rich and poor: the growth of the economy over the past sixty years has not wiped out differences in income, and the ability of particular consumers to borrow or use past savings is closely related to the amount of their income.

The Distribution of Income

There are several methods for analyzing the distribution of income among consumers. First, families and individuals can be classified according to the amount of their income and the number of consumers, or the percentage they represent of the total, calculated for each income class. This approach appears in Table 4 of the previous chapter. Second, the total amount of income received by all the families and individuals within each class can be divided by the number of consumers to obtain a figure for average income—the arithmetic mean; such figures were given in Table 5 in the previous chapter. Calculating median income frequently tells more: half the consumers in a distribution receive more than this amount, and half less. Mean income ordinarily exceeds median income because the few very large incomes are reflected in the first average but not in the second. Third, total income within each class can be computed as a fraction of total income for all classes. In no distribution will the consumers within a given income class receive the share of total income which corresponds to the share of the population they represent. Finally, families and individuals can be ranked in order of the size of their incomes and divided into equal fractions of the population. The total amount of income received by the lowest tenth, second lowest tenth, and so on up to the top tenth can then be computed. Such income deciles provide more detail than dividing the population into larger groups, such as quintiles or fifths. For each of these groups, which contains an equal number of consumers, the lower and upper dollar limits can be shown, and the mean or median income within each class computed. A further calculation shows what percentage of total income goes to each group. Finally, any one of these methods can be applied to data for different years, so that changes over time can be analyzed.

Table 1 presents a distribution of all families and individuals among specific income classes (defined in current dollars), for selected years since the depression of the '30s. The mean income of all consumers has been calculated before and after taxes. Correcting for price changes would reduce the difference in income between 1936 and the most recent year; but in constant dollars even median income is over 50 per cent larger than it was in 1947. So the striking increase of all incomes in all classes, shown in the table, appears whether current or constant dollars are used. The upper end of the distribution—consumers with incomes of over $10,000—contains 15 times the number of such families and individuals in 1935–36. Recent studies of poverty have defined poor families as those with less than $3,000 total money income in 1964 prices and poor individuals as those with less than $1,500 money income. Some 22.5 per cent of all consumers are so identified today, yet this is less than one-half the number in the very lowest income class during the '30s. At that time, 43.5 per cent of all families and individuals were below the $1,000 level, which amounts to $2,083 in 1964 prices.

But the table also emphasizes that the substantial changes have not equalized incomes to any great extent. To note that in 1947 some 4.5 per cent of the consumers received 20 per cent of the total income, while 25 per cent of the families and individuals shared 7 per cent of the total, emphasizes the disparity of incomes among consumers, and such disparity exists in the distribution for each year. Although it is true that more families and individuals have higher incomes today than formerly, the most recent figures show that 12 per cent of all consumers receive less than 2 per cent of total income,

Table 1

Families and Unattached Individuals, Mean Income, Percentage Distribution, and Percentage Distribution of Total Income, by Income Class, in Current Dollars

Income Class	1935–1936		1947		1957		1962	
	Per Cent of Consumer Units	Per Cent of Income	Per Cent of Consumer Units	Per Cent of Income	Per Cent of Consumer Units	Per Cent of Income	Per Cent of Consumer Units	Per Cent of Income
Under $2,000	77.7	45.4	24.9	7.2	14.2	2.6	12.0	1.8
2,000–2,999	13.1	19.5	18.9	11.5	10.0	4.0	8.5	3.0
3,000–3,999	4.4	9.2	19.3	16.3	12.1	6.8	9.8	4.7
4,000–4,999	1.7	4.5	12.8	13.8	12.7	9.1	10.2	6.4
5,000–7,499	1.6	5.8	14.8	21.5	25.7	25.2	24.3	20.7
7,500–9,999	0.6	3.2	4.8	10.0	12.6	17.4	15.7	18.6
10,000 and over	0.9	12.4	4.5	19.7	13.3	34.9	19.5	44.8
Mean Income, before tax	$1,631		$4,126		$6,238		$7,262	
Mean income, after tax	$1,608		$3,719		$5,608		$6,507	

SOURCE: U.S. Bureau of the Census, *Historical Statistics of the United States*, Washington, D.C., 1960, Series G 1–28 and G 120, 122.

while almost 45 per cent of it went to only 20 per cent of all families and individuals. Clearly, the "upper" income class includes some very large sums. Nevertheless, to the extent that "scarce means" have become more abundant, the consumers' freedom of choice has been widened. By the same token, consumption patterns today differ according to income. The distribution used in Table 1 will recur in the next chapter when data on consumer spending according to income are examined.

Table 1 indicates that the distribution changed most between the '30s and the '40s. Rather than resulting from any move to equalize incomes, this change represented the recovery from depression which expanded total production and income in the economy and brought about once-and-for-all gains for low-income families and individuals. In 1935–36, when the 43.5 per cent of all consumers below the $1,000 limit received only 15 per cent of total income, many of them had zero incomes. As unemployment disappeared with wartime production, more families had positive earnings, more workers were paid higher wages, and, at the same time, more families came into the distribution. This last point may be clarified by looking at population figures.

Between 1935–36 and 1947 the population of the country increased 13 per cent, the number of individuals aged 25 to 65 rose by 17 per cent, but the number of families went up by 23 per cent. Average family size diminished sharply during this period; it has been rising since 1955. The conclusion is obvious: the very low family incomes reported in 1935–36 at the bottom of the distribution supported far more people than did the low incomes of 1947. During the depression years, many families doubled up so as to stretch a limited income; many young people had to postpone marriages and their own separate households. When these conditions changed, there was a marked effect on the income distribution. By way of example, imagine two families in 1936, each with an income of $1,784 (the mean amount) and each with two children. The Smiths' grown son has been unable to find work since his graduation from high school; the Joneses' grown daughter is not eligible for a clerk's job with the city because such positions have been restricted to men who "need the job to support their families." The two young people are obviously in no position to marry, nor to become single individuals in their own households. But with the general rise in income, 11 years later two such families with incomes of $4,574 (the mean level) could afford a wedding, the two young people would have jobs, and the newly married couple would join the income distribution. The rise in per capita income, in this instance, dramatizes the impact of the expanding economy. But when the number of families with incomes of less than $2,000 decreased from 74 per cent of the total in 1935–36 to 15 per cent in 1947, the reason was not a redistribution of income but a gain in employment. People became, once more, productive workers able to earn income. Such gains at the low end of the distribution obviously occurred only once; the shift from mass unemployment to almost full employment cannot be repeated.

Since the '40s, the economy has grown with the result that expanded output has led to a continued gain in total income, but its distribution has changed little. The extent of equality—or inequality—in the distribution can better be analyzed with data showing incomes for equal numbers of people, ranked in order from lowest to highest. Table 2 shows the effect of rising total income on the distribution among equal groups—deciles —of the population.

The share of income going to the richest 10 per cent of all consumers has decreased, by some 5 per cent, since 1947. But this loss does not mean any major redistribution from the rich to the poor, since the poorest 20 per cent of all consumers received exactly the same share—4 per cent—of total income

Table 2

Shares of Total Money Income Before Taxes, by Income
Deciles of Spending Units

| Income Decile | Per Cent of Total | | | Mean Income Within Decile | | | | |
| | | | | Current Dollars | | | 1947 Dollars | |
	1947	1955	1962	1947	1955	1962	1955	1962
Lowest tenth	1	1	1	$ 390	$ 470	$ 910	$ 393	$ 672
Second tenth	3	3	3	1,020	1,260	2,020	1,055	1,491
Third tenth	4	4	5	1,450	2,070	2,920	1,734	2,155
Fourth tenth	6	6	6	1,910	2,830	3,910	2,370	2,886
Fifth tenth	7	8	8	2,340	3,590	4,900	3,007	3,617
Sixth tenth	9	9	9	2,800	4,260	5,740	3,568	4,237
Seventh tenth	10	11	11	3,260	5,010	6,780	4,196	5,005
Eighth tenth	12	13	13	3,850	5,910	8,040	4,950	5,934
Ninth tenth	15	16	16	4,870	7,330	9,950	6,139	7,344
Highest	33	30	28	11,020	13,830	17,630	11,583	13,013

SOURCES: "Survey of Consumer Finances," *Federal Reserve Bulletin* (July, 1954), and George Katona, Charles Lininger, and Eva Mueller, *1963 Survey of Consumer Finances* (Ann Arbor: University of Michigan, 1964) for basic data. Calculations of constant dollar income figures use Consumer Price Index.

in each year noted. The rise in mean income in the lower end of the distribution has been quite meager, particularly when constant dollar figures are used. For the most part, gains in income have been concentrated among families and individuals who receive $5,000 to $10,000—exactly what one would expect in a growing economy experiencing prosperity and high-level production. The share of income going to the 7th, 8th, and 9th deciles is larger now than in 1947, and the mean income in each of these classes rose by over 50 per cent between 1947 and 1962. Overall economic growth has also produced a great bunching of consumers at the low end of the top-income decile: not until the late '50s did consumers with incomes of $10,000 or more account for 10 per cent of the population. (Table 1 shows that, in 1957, 12.4 per cent of all families and individuals received more than this dollar sum.)

Consequently, mean income in the top tenth has risen by only 16 per cent in constant dollars. But again, it is clear that this highest group includes some millionaires.

Since only after-tax income can be spent or saved, and since the Federal personal income tax is progressive, the question must be asked whether after-tax figures differ greatly from those of Tables 1 and 2. The mean income before and after taxes, shown in Table 1, dramatizes the stiffer tax bite, the inevitable result of consumers moving into higher income brackets where tax rates are higher.

But the tax alone does not produce any great reduction of inequality; Table 3 shows the distribution of families and

Table 3

Percentage Distribution, Families and Unattached Individuals and Family Personal Income, by Income Level, Before and After Tax, 1962

Income Class	Per Cent of Families		Per Cent of Income	
	Before Tax	After Tax	Before Tax	After Tax
Under $2,000	12.0	12.7	1.8	2.2
2,000–2,999	8.5	9.4	3.0	3.7
3,000–3,999	9.8	10.8	4.7	5.8
4,000–4,999	10.2	11.7	6.4	8.1
5,000–5,999	10.2	11.4	7.7	9.6
6,000–7,499	14.1	14.4	13.0	14.8
7,500–9,999	15.7	13.9	18.6	18.3
10,000–14,999	12.3	10.5	20.2	19.3
15,000 and over	7.2	5.2	24.6	18.2

SOURCE: *Statistical Abstract of the United States, 1964,* p. 338.

individuals, and of their share of total income, among income classes before and after taxes. In 1964 Federal income tax rates were revised to benefit taxpayers in the upper brackets more than those at lower income levels, and the 1966 change in Social Security taxes a smaller percentage of upper incomes than of lower incomes. The slight tendencies toward equaliza-

59

tion shown in Table 3, therefore, overstate the current situation. And the effect of taxes appears slight, indeed. While almost 20 per cent of consumers have before-tax incomes of $10,000 or more, and only 16 per cent exceed this level after taxes, their share of total after-tax income amounts to 37.5 per cent. The impact on the lower half of the distribution is even less perceptible. Mean family income, before taxes, was $7,260; after taxes, it was $6,510. Median income is about $460 higher after taxes than before.

It is also true that the Federal income tax does not now apply to a sizable fraction of income received mostly by those at the top of the distribution, where various types of exemptions exist. The widespread use of stock options, insurance and pension schemes, the investment opportunity of tax free securities and the ability to turn income into capital gains—these mean that much income is received without being subject to tax, and much consumption enjoyed without spending money income.

The Distribution of Consumer Net Worth

The purchasing power, or "scarce means" which consumers choose to spend or save, differs among families and individuals not only because incomes vary widely, but because consumers differ in their ability to use past savings or to borrow. While the distribution of income is highly unequal (a small proportion of consumers receives a large fraction of income, while a large share of the population receives a very small percentage of income), the distribution of net worth, or wealth, is even more unequal. The net worth of any consumer is calculated as the sum of all his assets less his total debts; consumer assets represent accumulated savings. All of the historical data reviewed in the last chapter showed that the amount of saving, by any family or individual, depends chiefly on the amount of income received; the saving/income ratio therefore affects net worth.

First, since high-income consumers can save not only more dollars but a larger fraction of their current income, they can accumulate more assets. When these assets are bequeathed to children or to others, the saving of one generation affects the distribution of wealth in the next. Estate and inheritance taxes have affected the form in which wealth is held, but have not substantially altered its distribution. Second, more families in upper-income classes have income security than those in the middle or low end of the distribution. Regular saving is rarely possible when incomes are both low and fluctuating. The skilled worker with hourly earnings of $3.45 can enjoy a yearly income of over $7,000—well up in the distribution—if his weekly hours of work are steady. But a six weeks' layoff means a 12 per cent drop in his annual income. Any saving out of current income, therefore, may be used up to maintain current consumption in slack periods, just as it was among the poorer workers at the turn of the century. By contrast, the junior executive with a salary of $6,500 a year may be in a much better position to plan for saving and to carry out his plans. Finally, the forms of savings vary markedly among consumers at different levels of income. Upper-income consumers hold more assets whose value may increase with rising market prices; such increases are subject to a capital-gains tax whose rate may be less than the personal income tax rate. Personal trust funds and other means of avoiding estate taxes enable some consumers to have total wealth (all assets that provide income, whether or not these are subject to disposal) which exceeds the value of the assets they personally own.

Table 4 gives 1962 data on specific forms of consumer assets, on one type of debt, and on net worth. The term "family" refers to both families and unattached individuals; net

Table 4

Average Family Net Worth and Family Ownership of Net Worth Components, by Income, 1962

1962 Family Income Before Taxes	Net Worth		Percentage of Families Holding					
	Mean	Median	Own Home	Life Insurance	Liquid Assets	Stocks	Bonds	Personal Debt
Under $3,000	$ 8,875	$ 2,760	44	31	56	9	2	34
3,000–4,999	10,914	3,320	47	53	73	10	1	56
5,000–7,499	15,112	7,450	62	67	86	16	1	58
7,500–9,999	21,243	13,450	74	77	96	21	2	63
10,000–14,999	30,389	20,500	82	82	96	36	6	50
15,000–24,999	74,329	42,750	84	82	97	52	7	41
25,000–49,999	267,996	160,000	92	84	100	78	20	29
50,000–99,999	789,582	470,000	93	84	99	87	36	16
100,000 and over	1,554,152	875,000	97	92	99	98	68	17
Total	22,588	7,550	59	58	78	18	2	50
Mean value			$5,975	$1,376	$2,579	$4,072	$456	$483

SOURCE: Federal Reserve Board of Governors, "Survey of Consumer Finances," *Federal Reserve Bulletin* (March, 1964), pp. 291–93.

worth was calculated as of December 31, 1962. The value of homes represents the consumer's estimate of its market value less the outstanding amount of mortgage debt; the amount of life insurance consists of cash surrender value less secured loans; the value of stocks was figured at market prices and of bonds at par values; liquid assets amount to balances in checking or savings accounts and the face value of United States savings bonds. Other assets entering into net worth included real estate, equity in unincorporated business, and the market value of automobiles less debts secured by automobiles. The liability "Personal Debt" shown on the table refers, for the most part, to short-term installment debt or unpaid bills.

Just as mean income exceeds the median of any income distribution because a few very large incomes influence the mean, so mean and median net worth figures differ—but the disparity is much greater. Furthermore, the difference between the two averages is substantial in each of the income classes shown. The mean net worth figures are heavily weighted by the few very wealthy consumers at each income level. For the lower half of the distribution, median net worth is roughly equal to one year's income; only for consumers with incomes above $25,000 does median net worth represent as much as three years' income. But these families obviously hold a great proportion of the total wealth. A crude calculation from the data in Table 4 suggests that 2 per cent of all consumers—those with incomes above $25,000—receive at least 10 per cent of total income and own about 40 per cent of total net worth.

The forms of savings—the particular assets owned—clearly differ among consumers with different incomes. Consumer ownership of life insurance, annuities and retirement plans has been analyzed in other surveys; they all agree that income is the most important variable determining who buys insurance and in what amount. Table 4 shows that the mean value of family holdings of insurance and annuities was $1,376, but the Survey of Consumer Finance reports that the *median* life insurance premium paid was $170. It follows, therefore, that insurance and retirement plans are concentrated among families in upper-income levels; the Life Insurance Agency Management Association estimates that consumers with incomes of $10,000 or more purchased 32 per cent of the ordinary life insurance sold in 1962. Industrial insurance is still common; with an average value of $430 these policies almost equal ordinary life policies in number. These figures suggest that the need to meet burial expenses still remains in force for low-income consumers. In the 1964 Survey of Consumer Finance more than half the respondents with incomes below $5,000 explained that they purchased life insurance for this reason. The net worth figures of Table 4 indicate that most consumers will rely heavily on social insurance for their retirement income. Only about 30 per cent of all families, in recent years, give "providing for old age" as a reason for saving, but more high-income-level consumers report this than do low-income families.

Home ownership, according to Table 4, appears to be the major form of net worth for most consumers, a fact that is confirmed by other data. This situation represents a striking structural change in the economy over the past thirty years and as such deserves some explanation. The alteration in housing tenure has had more influence on consumer income and consumer choice than any other recent economic development, and its effect on net worth is only one part of its total impact.

From 1900 to the mid-'30s renters outnumbered home owners with very little change in the proportions. Table 4 shows, however, that 60 per cent of all families now own their homes. The cause of this shift was the mortgage terms introduced during the '30s, first for federally insured mortgages and then adopted widely. Loans accounting for the major share of the purchase price of a home and extending over 15 to 30 years permitted lower-income families to become home owners. Monthly payments that provided regular amortization of the principal enabled consumers to save by increasing the equity they possessed in their homes. The greatest growth of home ownership occurred after World War II, when restrictions on construction were lifted, and the value of owned homes has risen steadily since that time. In 1962 the median value of owned homes was estimated at $12,400, ranging from about $8,000 for families with incomes of less than $5,000 to $16,600 for families with incomes from $10,000 to $15,000. Mortgage debt among home owners occurs more frequently at the upper end of the income distribution; 72 per cent of homes owned by families with incomes of less than $3,000 (chiefly elderly couples and individuals) were mortgage-free. The median mortgage debt of $7,500 left the median equity in owned homes at about $4,000.

It follows that for consumers near or below the middle of the income distribution, the most important component of net worth is equity in the homes they live in. A survey in 1960 found that total net worth for one-fifth of the consumers with incomes below $5,000 consisted only of liquid assets and equity in homes; 12 per cent more of them owned their homes, but held no liquid assets. The percentage of consumers owning their homes is greater in each higher income class, but this represents the effect of age and of family composition as well as of purchasing power.

By contrast, income is clearly the chief determinant of consumers' holdings of corporate stock; most of it is owned by a very few people with very high incomes. Table 4 shows that more than half the families with incomes over $15,000 reported stock ownership, but less than 10 per cent of the families below the $5,000 income level did so. Although over one-third of the families with incomes between $10,000 and $15,000 reported stock ownership, the mean value of their holdings was only $7,000; in the next highest income class, the value of stock owned averaged almost 5 times this amount. Median values would show even more concentration of ownership. A rearrangement of the data indicates that upper-income owners, who number about 2 per cent of all consumers, constitute 17 per cent of all stock owners but possess 42 per cent of the total value of all the stock owned. Over half of the families in the top fifth of the income distribution report dividends from stock; this and other property income account for over 8 per cent of the total income received by this group.

Much institutional advertising stresses the notion of "people's capitalism"—which is supposed to imply that ownership of U.S. corporate enterprise is very widely based. The number of stockholders and the percentage of consumers who own corporate stock more than doubled during the '50s—but they represent only 30 per cent of all families, and almost half of them own stock in only one corporation. Furthermore, over one-fifth of the shareowning families own less than $1,000 worth of stock. Concentration of stockholdings among the very high income groups remains a distinguishing feature of the economy. According to an estimate based on a study of estate returns, rather than of living persons, the top one per cent of the adult population owned 77 per cent of the corporate stock in 1953, while slightly over one percent of the total population, with more than $60,000 in wealth, owned 82 per cent of the wealth represented by corporate stock.[1] These and other data are presented in Table 5.

The Lampman study cited in this table gives some details on changes in the distribution of wealth. Like the figures on income distribution, Lampman's data indicate that some reduction in the share of top wealth holders took place up until 1945, but that the movement since then has probably been reversed. Changes in population and in estate law make it

Table 5

Share of Wealth Held by Top 1 Per Cent of Adults, by
Type of Asset (Selected years)

Type of Asset	Per Cent					
	1922	1929	1939	1945	1949	1953
Real estate	18.0	17.3	13.7	11.1	10.5	12.5
U.S. government bonds	45.0	100.0	91.0	32.5	35.8	31.8
Corporate stock	61.5	65.6	69.0	61.7	64.9	76.0
Cash, mortgages, and notes	31.0	34.0	31.5	19.3	20.5	25.8
Pension and retirement funds	8.0	8.0	6.0	5.9	5.5	5.0
Insurance	35.3	27.0	17.4	17.3	15.0	11.5
Economic estate	33.9	38.8	33.8	25.7	22.8	27.4

SOURCE: Robert Lampman, "Changes in the Share of Wealth Held by
Top Wealth-holders, 1922–1956," *Review of Economics and Statistics,*
XLI (November, 1959), Table 8, p. 389.

difficult to establish comparable groups of estate holders, but
Table 5 indicates that, while the ownership of homes, retirement plans, and government securities (with the innovation of
the low-denomination savings bonds during World War II)
has increased among lower incomes and wealth groups, the
total concentration of wealth is still very high. If anything, the
table, which is based on individual holdings, overstates the
decline in wealth concentration among families, particularly in
view of gifts and trust provisions that split individual wealth
among family members.

Though substantial amounts of purchasing power from
accumulated savings exist primarily among the top income and
wealth classes, funds from borrowing are presumably available
to all income groups. How does the distribution of debt among
households compare with the distribution of income and
wealth? This can best be answered by examining the two
major types of consumer debt: mortgages on homes, and short-
term loans, chiefly installment debt.

The significant increase in home ownership resulted directly from changes in mortgage provisions; the amount of home mortgage debt outstanding, therefore, has increased from $18.9 billion in 1930 to $167 billion in 1961 (1- to 4-family houses). The number of nonfarm owned homes that are mortgaged rose from 40 per cent to 60 per cent of the total. Table 4 shows not only that home ownership occurs more frequently among upper-income groups but that the value of the home is greater in each higher income class. Since mortgage debt is a function of home ownership rather than of income, the percentage of families with such debt is also greater in each higher income class. Table 6 gives data on home ownership and mortgage debt, by income classes. The average home owner's equity is a smaller percentage of the average market value of the home now than in earlier years, partly as the result of a shift to larger, more expensive homes, following the trend to larger families. Household formation, which leads to home ownership, has also increased; most families are in the early years of a long-term mortgage, where equity is less than outstanding debt. The figures on mortgage payments in different income classes indicate that the burden of this debt declines sharply with income and is probably less than one-fifth of income for over 90 per cent of all families owning mortgaged homes. Furthermore, since 60 per cent of the total mortgage debt is owed by families with incomes over $7,500, it is worth noting that median mortgage payments by such consumers represent only from 13.6 per cent to less than 10 per cent of their income.

The picture for installment debt and other short-term consumer credit is quite different. Almost half of all spending units owed installment debt in 1964, although less than one-third with incomes under $3,000 were in debt. The median amount of debt, $655, occurred in the income class above $7,500. About the same number of consumers borrow money to purchase automobiles as to purchase other durable goods;

Table 6

Housing Value and Mortgage Debt, Nonfarm Home Owners, by Income Class, 1964

				Family Income Before Taxes				
	All	Under $3,000	$3,000– 4,999	$5,000– 5,999	$6,000– 7,499	$7,500– 9,999	$10,000– 14,999	$15,000 or Over
Percentage of families with mortgage debt	57	20	49	52	66	72	75	71
Median mortgage debt (thousands)	$ 7.1	*	$ 4.7	$ 6.6	$ 6.8	$ 7.4	$ 8.6	$ 9.7
Median monthly mortgage payment	$85	*	$65	$65	$75	$85	$100	
Median house value (thousands)	$13.3	$8.6	$10.9	$11.9	$12.4	$15.0	$ 18.2	$23.0
Share of total mortgage debt (per cent)	100	4	10	7	15	22	30	12

* Too few cases.

SOURCE: George Katona, Charles Lininger, and Eva Mueller, *1964 Survey of Consumer Finances* (Ann Arbor: University of Michigan, 1965), pp. 39–41.

the amounts, however, vary. Automobile paper accounts for about 30 per cent of total short-term debt (including single-payment loans, charge accounts, and service credit). Table 7 gives further data on the burden of installment debt among consumers in different income groups.

Since the end of World War II, three different developments have led to a higher total of short-term consumer debt: the increase in population and household formation, a rise in the average amount of debt owed by borrowers, and a shift in attitudes toward borrowing. Since all of these were accompanied by an increase in incomes, it is not clear that debt has become any greater burden to American families, although the total amount outstanding has grown from $7 billion in 1939 to $76 billion in 1964. Installment debt rose much more sharply; from $4.5 billion in 1939 to about $60 billion in 1964. These aggregate figures, however, cloud the new pattern of income and of consumer choice that has appeared. Data on the distribution of the total debt illustrate the ambiguities in these aggregates.

For some years analysts and forecasters believed in the existence of a ceiling for short-term consumer debt; supposedly, this could be calculated by the ratio of outstanding debt to National Income or to Disposable Personal Income. Figuring total debt repayment as a fraction of total income has also been used in this kind of aggregate analysis. While it is true that consumer debt cannot increase indefinitely, the relevant ceiling is the outstanding debt, or ratio of payment to income, for *families*—not for aggregates and especially not for steadily rising aggregates. Since 53 per cent of the families have no debt, and over 40 per cent of the debtors make payments that amount to less than 10 per cent of their incomes, the pressure of debt on family spending cannot be interpreted from the aggregate figure. Thus, in Table 7, the median ratio, for families, of repayment to disposable income

Table 7
Incidence of Installment Debt Among Families, by Income Class, early 1964

	Total	1963 Family Income Before Taxes					
		Under $3,000	$3,000–4,999	$5,000–7,499	$7,500–9,999	$10,000–14,999	$15,000 and Over
Percentage of families in income class	100	23	17	26	15	14	5
Percentage with debt	47	27	45	59	58	54	29
Median amount of debt for those with debt	$655	$270	$545	$645	$845	$1,045	*
Percentage who‡ never had debt	19	26	18	14	16	19	31
use credit less	29	22	22	28	33	36†	31
Percentage with annual debt payment ratio to disposable income, 1963							
under 5%	8	2	6	11	11	15	4
5–9%	11	5	8	13	12	16	20
10–19%	16	6	12	21	25	18	9
Median debt ratio	12%	20%	16%	12%	12%	10%	*

* Too few cases.
† $10,000 and over.
‡ Based on a survey in May, 1964.

SOURCE: George Katona, Charles Lininger, and Eva Mueller, 1964 Survey of Consumer Finances (Ann Arbor: University of Michigan, 1965), pp. 11, 72–77.

is 12 per cent; the ratio of total repayment to total disposable income is over 13 per cent. In early 1956 only one-third of the debtors had repayment ratios of less than 10 per cent; yet in 1964, 39 per cent of the debtors reported such ratios. What had happened? There was an increase in income that was unaccompanied by an equal increase in short-term debt. The median repayment/income ratio of 20 per cent by consumers in the lowest income class has not increased since 1956, and the number of such low-income consumers whose debt payments took more than 40 per cent of their income has declined.

The concentration of debt in the middle-income classes can also be explained by the changing composition of the debtor category. It was families with incomes between $3,000 and $7,500 that provided the largest number of affirmative replies to the question, "Do you use credit more now than formerly?" Consumers who use credit less now than formerly represent a larger fraction of the total in each higher income class. What this means, of course, is that short-term credit is used by families to purchase consumer durables and to furnish a home at the beginning of a family life-cycle; at later stages in the cycle* short-term debt involves chiefly automobile purchases. This use of debt—some have called it "fractional payment"—for purchases of durable goods reflects a change in consumer attitudes toward debt. In 1950 only half the families who were asked their opinion of installment buying said that it was a "good idea"; 10 years later, such families were 60 per cent of the total. The use of debt will probably increase if total income continues to rise and if the rate of household formation increases.

Up to this point, total consumer purchasing power—the "scarce means"—has been analyzed in terms of its distribution among families and individuals arranged by levels of income.

* Cf. Chap. 3, p. 108.

It is also useful to look at the purchasing power available to consumers in the population, classified in other ways than by their income.

Table 8 follows the same scheme as Tables 1 and 4, but shows the total distribution of Negro and white families among the several income classes. Little comment is needed; the disparity between the races at every income level is immediately apparent and exhibits, perhaps better than any other single measure, the effect of years of discrimination. The income distribution for American Negroes resembles that of an underdeveloped country rather than that of the most productive, wealthiest economy in the world. It is doubtful whether the differences in income noted in Table 8 can be removed in less than a generation, if that soon.

Table 8

Percentage Distribution, All Urban and Rural Families and Single Consumers, by Income Within Race Classifications, 1960–1961

Money Income After Taxes	White	Negro	Other Nonwhite
Under $1,000	3.5%	6.3%	.8%
1,000–1,999	8.8	22.9	10.6
2,000–2,999	10.2	18.9	12.4
3,000–3,999	11.2	17.2	13.7
4,000–4,999	13.4	12.0	15.2
5,000–5,999	13.1	8.8	16.5
6,000–7,499	16.0	7.4	10.5
7,500–9,999	14.4	4.5	11.2
10,000–14,999	7.3	2.0	7.2
15,000 and over	2.2		2.0
Total*	100.0%	100.0%	100.0%
Estimated number of families, thousands	49,393	5,321	593
Average income	$5,772	$3,584	$5,389
Average family size	3.2	3.4	3.8

SOURCE: Bureau of Labor Statistics, *Survey of Consumer Expenditures 1960–61*, Supplement 2 to BLS Report 237–93, June 1966, Tables 22*a–c*.
* Totals have been rounded to the nearest per cent.

Finally, Table 9 shows how consumers in each of several income classes are divided according to age. The last two columns show that over half the families headed by someone aged 65 or over have annual incomes of less than $3,000. And while the median income for the entire population is in the income class between $5,000 and $6,000, that level is exceeded by almost two-thirds of the families whose heads are between 25 and 65 years old, but by only 8 per cent of the oldest age group, and only 14 per cent of those beyond the conventional retirement age of 65. Among elderly consumers, transfer payments account for a large part of income, although the upper income levels include some who receive interest and dividends on invested capital. The distribution also shows the "mass market" of the United States to be clearly identified by age and income: those families headed by a consumer between 35 and 55 years old, and with incomes ranging from $6,000 to $10,000. Other identifications of this market can be made by distributions of income according to family size, family type, and so forth.

Not only income, but consumer choice, can reflect the influence of age, race, occupation—and many other factors. Yet any consumer must choose among abundant alternatives, not because his age or occupation restrict him, but because his purchasing power is limited. Even though his "scarce means" may include savings or borrowing, the sums from these sources are not infinite—but their alternative uses are. The consumer's problem is therefore clear. Its solution is the subject of the next chapter, which turns to an analysis of patterns of consumer choice.

Table 9

Percentage Distribution, All Urban and Rural Families and Single Consumers, by Income Within Age Classes, 1960–1961

Money Income After Taxes	Average Age of Head	Per Cent of Families with Head						
		Under 25	25–34	35–44	45–54	55–64	65–74	75 and Over
Under $1,000	66	0.6%	0.6%	1.0%	1.9%	4.9%	7.4%	20.8%
1,000–1,999	61	9.1	3.1	3.3	5.2	12.1	25.5	36.1
2,000–2,999	54	15.9	7.2	6.0	9.0	12.6	20.9	18.9
3,000–3,999	48	22.5	12.3	8.9	10.0	11.9	16.0	9.1
4,000–4,999	44	20.4	18.7	12.1	11.5	14.6	10.3	3.7
5,000–5,999	43	16.8	18.9	14.2	12.6	10.9	6.3	3.6
6,000–7,499	43	11.3	20.1	20.8	17.1	12.7	5.3	2.9
7,500–9,999	44	2.8	14.5	21.0	18.3	10.6	4.1	2.6
10,000–14,999	47	0.4	4.2	10.5	10.6	7.3	2.6	1.5
15,000 and over	51	0.1	0.5	2.3	3.9	2.4	1.7	0.6
Total*		100.0%	100.0%	100.0%	100.0%	100.0%	100.0%	100.0%
Average income	$5,557	$4,236	$5,730	$6,752	$6,685	$5,340	$3,695	$2,569

SOURCE: Bureau of Labor Statistics, *Survey of Consumer Expenditures 1960–61*, BLS Report No. 237–93, February 1965, Table 1A, and Supplement 2, June 1966, Tables 14a–g. * Totals have been rounded to the nearest per cent.

chapter 3 **Patterns**

of

Consumer

Choice

*E*_{*very*} day families and individuals solve the problem of having limited purchasing power yet unlimited alternatives from which to choose—and their choices help determine production and employment and income in the economy as a whole. But figures for total spending or saving tell little about the process of consumer choice. Just as aggregate income figures mean more when broken down to show data for groups of households, so too consumption spending or consumers' saving can best be analyzed with data for groups of households. One way of grouping families and individuals is by income level—but some people live alone and some are members of a family, some families live in the city and some live in the suburbs, some parents have many children and some few or none at all. These differences, as well, can be used to classify data on consumption expenditures. These household characteristics, and many more, affect consumer choice. Thanks to the abundance of existing data on consumption expenditures, the goods and services and assets that are bought by families and individuals can be analyzed in several ways.

Survey Data: Sources and Methods

In the first large-scale consumer surveys conducted during the great depression of the thirties two quite different approaches were used. In 1934–36, the Bureau of Labor Statistics undertook a study of urban wage earners and clerical workers the results of which appeared in the highly detailed volumes of Bulletins 637–641, *Money Disbursements of Wage Earners and Clerical Workers,* and were used to revise the Bureau's cost-of-living index. A broader sampling of the entire population, *The Study of Consumer Purchases, 1935–36,* conducted jointly by the Bureau of Labor Statistics and the Department of Agriculture's Bureau of Home Economics, covered both urban and rural families. Wide in its geographical spread, this study was confined, however, to certain types of families. Single consumers and families with foreign-born adults were excluded, as were those below a minimum income level. During the early part of World War II, when price rises threatened the economy, the Bureau carried out a limited investigation, which was published in 1945 as *Family Spending and Saving in Wartime.*

The first large-scale investigation of consumer spending that placed no limitations on the type of family to be included was conducted in 1950. A summary report was published by the Bureau of Labor Statistics in 1953, *Family Income, Expenditures, and Savings in 1950,* and detailed reports were published in 1956, with the aid of a grant from the Ford Foundation, by a group at the Wharton School (*Study of Consumer Expenditures, Incomes and Saving*). In 1960–61 another survey designed to lead to a revision of the Consumer Price Index was again extended to include families and single consumers living in both urban and rural areas throughout the United States. Although many informative comparisons can be drawn among the several surveys, they depend on familiarity with the processes of analyzing cross-sectional data, and this means, to begin with, looking closely at one particular study. The one chosen for this chapter is the *Survey of Consumer Expenditures, 1960–61,* which was conducted by the Departments of Labor and Agriculture and published by the Bureau of Labor Statistics in various reports, beginning in 1962. The types of analyses made in the following pages can be applied to many different studies.

Anyone who sets out to use survey data must first study the technical explanations of sampling methods and of how schedules were prepared and edited; for each survey he must know the various ways in which tabulated results can be interpreted. Failure to provide information about the methods used in a survey is a warrant for a strong dose of skepticism about its results.

One problem is common to all analyses of consumer income, spending, and saving: the paucity of reliable statistics about consumer behavior over time, and the temptation to use cross-sectional data as a substitute. Except for some recent work by the Survey Research Center of the University of Michigan,[1] data on consumption and income *for the same family or individual* over any period of time are practically nonexistent. To collect the details of such changes demands enormously costly surveys; only a few such surveys, covering limited areas of information, have been made. The chief methodological difficulty is comparable to the physicist's inability to make certain observations without affecting the behavior of the particles he is observing. Families who keep detailed records of income and expenditure, over a period of time long enough for important changes to occur, necessarily become conscious of their income and expenditure patterns, and may therefore change them. The only conclusions that can be reliably drawn from large-scale surveys result from a comparison of *different* families. For example, the data collected in 1960–61 reveal differences in food consumption between families at high and low income levels, or with young or adolescent children, or living in Atlanta or Chicago. The changes in food consumption patterns that are made by one family, whose income increases, whose babies grow into adolescence, or whose place of residence shifts from Atlanta to Chicago, cannot be learned from these data.

The analyst must be wary of such dynamic terms as "increase," "fall," or "rate of change," when he is referring to consumption among different groups. To say that income "increases" with the level of education means only that aggregate and average incomes are higher, among college graduates, than among equal numbers of junior high school graduates. There is in actuality no measure of a change in income that has taken place over time, as more education has been acquired year by year. This sort of distinction is easy to understand; ambiguities are likely to arise, however, when making statements like "saving, as a proportion of income, increases with the amount of income." The only data that exist show that family saving, as a proportion of family income, is greater among families of upper-income classes than among those of lower ones. Thus the discussion in Chapter 1 of the shift in the saving function referred to different behavior at different time periods, so that it was documented by the experience of different families and individuals. How consumers change their choices about spending or saving *as their incomes rise over time* is not yet fully understood.

80

Differences in consumption and saving choices by families and individuals with different incomes are already familiar from previous chapters; survey data are also tabulated by age of household head, family composition, stage in the life cycle, ethnic origin, geographical location, size of locality, occupation of head of household, and combinations of these variables. Obviously the size of the sample limits the detail of cross-classified tables; some include empty cells, or data with a high sampling error.

Although the categories of consumption spending may differ from one survey to another, standard classifications are also common.* Food expenditures are usually divided into purchases of food for meals at home and spending on meals or snacks away from home. Subclasses of expenditure give data on types of food, such as those listed in Figure 1 of Chapter 1, or even more detailed categories, such as milk and milk products, fresh fluid milk, and whole fresh fluid milk. Categories for clothing expenditures include footwear, materials, clothing care, and sometimes accessories and jewelry. Subclasses sometimes identify the wearer: clothing, men's and boys' 18 years and over; clothing, boys', 2 through 17; and so on. The broad category of housing describes more than the basic "necessity" of shelter: payments by home owners must be distinguished from rent, and both of them from expenses for accommodation away from home. Owner's costs usually refer to current expenditures—taxes, insurance, and interest; any reduction of a mortgage principal is saving. One housing expenditure subclass—home furnishings and equipment—lists appliances, repair services, furniture, linens and drapery, glassware, cutlery, and so on. Some appliances—radios and television, for example—have been shifted between the categories of home furnishings and entertainment. Another subclass—

* Compare the detail of aggregate Personal Consumption Expenditures in any National Income Supplement to the *Survey of Current Business.*

household operation—covers the utilities of gas, fuel, water, and refrigeration, as well as expenditures for maintenance and domestic service.

What earlier surveys frequently lumped together as "sundries" is now fairly well defined. Figures for transportation expenditures separate the current cost of running an automobile plus the purchase of a car from public transit fares and taxi rides. Some surveys classify automobiles and consumer durables as consumer assets, and hence expenditures on these (net of borrowing) represent a form of savings, while the use of these assets, when owned, adds to real income.* Medical care includes payments to hospitals, nursing homes, doctors, dentists, and nurses, as well as for insurance premiums, drugs, and medical equipment. Personal care also comprises both goods and services: cosmetics and toiletries; barbershops, beauty salons, and so on. Details about reading, education, and recreation differ from survey to survey. Gifts and contributions and payments for personal insurance may or may not be counted as consumption spending; the figures are commonly shown separately for the analyst's use.

With so many possible household characteristics and consumption categories, it would be absurd to attempt an exhaustive treatment of empirical data in any one volume, let alone one chapter, but some brief analyses may suggest how survey data can be used. Two quite different approaches—that of consumer choice and that of market competition—are possible for any tabulation of spending. The amounts spent for a given item differ for different classifications of consumers—i.e., at high or low income levels, or of various occupations, or in different areas. First, the amount spent on any one article or category, by any group of consumers, can be calculated as a percentage of their total spending or of their total income; the total consumption pattern of the given group of consumers may be described if such percentages are calculated for all

* See Chap. 6, pp. 243–44.

categories. Secondly, the amounts spent on any one article or category by all the consumers *within each class* can be compared. Each such total can then be calculated as a share of the total purchases of the item by all consumers. Such a proportion shows how large a part a given group of consumers plays in the total market for the product or service. Such a tabulation provides business with a summary of the existing market, as well as with some clues to the future sales potential for which firms will be competing. It reflects the results of two other tabulations—the choices of each class of consumers and the distribution of income among all classes.

An example will clarify these two approaches. The 1960–61 Survey of Consumer Expenditures provides the information given below. The analyst of consumer choice notes

Characteristics	Total	Urban Families and Single Consumers Inside SMSA's	Rural Nonfarm Families and Single Consumers Outside SMSA's
Estimated number in universe (000)	51,795	31,804	8,569
Per cent of families	100	61.4	16.5
Average annual money income after taxes	$5,634	$6,170	$4,150
expenditures for current consumption	$5,154	$5,635	$3,806
expenditures for fuel, light, refrigeration, water	$ 250	$ 241	$ 254

that household utilities take 4.3 per cent of total expenditures for current consumption by urban families, but 6.7 per cent of the total for rural nonfarm families. This higher percentage represents a greater number of dollars from a significantly lower average of both income and total consumption expenditures. Rearranging the data, the market analyst is able to show that firms that sell fuel, light, refrigeration, and water to consumers are dealing in a billion-dollar market. Urban families, despite their smaller average family expenditure, spend 56 per cent of all the dollars that buy these items. Rural nonfarm families, on the other hand, account for only 16 per cent of the total consumer purchases in this category. When spending data are available in detail for both products and areas, such an analysis can describe the potential market for a firm that is competing with other sellers to consumers. For example, the total spending on food purchased away from home in the city of St. Louis gives a prospective restaurant-operator in that city a figure which, modified and amplified, can enter into his estimate of possible sales.

In one sense, firms that sell to consumers compete for the entire dollar spent—e.g., autos compete in this way against appliances—and therefore such firms need data on aggregate income and the total of potential consumption spending. But how that total spending will be divided among alternatives is still a matter of consumer choice and is influenced by a host of variables, some of which will be explored in this chapter. Competition among particular *firms* is more intense, and has more effect on the process of consumer choice, in market areas such as the men's clothing business, the furniture trade, or drug stores. But since each of these has a counterpart in consumption expenditures, survey data can provide quantitative estimates of the size of the market.*

Income

The familiar differences in consumption spending by families at different income levels can be analyzed in great detail, if need be; Table 1, the first of many tables to be drawn from

* But see Chap. 6, pp. 215–23.

the 1960–61 BLS Survey of Consumer Expenditures, shows the well-known effects of income in terms of 19 major categories of goods and services.

In order to avoid the difficulties of dealing implicitly with saving as well as with income, expenditures on these goods and services are shown as percentages of *total current consumption spending*. For at low income levels, such total spending frequently exceeded total income, since consumers used past savings or borrowing to augment current income in order to spend. For example, the 10 per cent of all families and single consumers whose incomes ranged between one and two thousand dollars spent, for food, amounts that represented 35 per cent of their after-tax income. For this group of consumers the average decrease in assets was $510; the average increase in liabilities was $106. At high income levels, on the other hand, the categories of spending sometimes represent much smaller shares of the consumers' total command over resources: expenditures for food, for example, are 19 per cent of total *spending* by the top income class, but only 12 per cent of average money income after taxes. Such a reminder of the impact of *income* upon total consumption spending, as opposed to saving, is implicit in all the analyses made here. Since consumption takes a smaller share of high incomes than of low, given forms of expenditure, as a percentage of *consumption*, will be lower at low incomes, and higher at high incomes, than the corresponding percentages of expenditures in relation to *income*.

The table demonstrates the continued validity of Engel's first law: percentage expenditures for food and shelter are consistently less at successively higher income levels. "Shelter" includes rental expenditures for dwellings, payment for accommodations away from home and, for home owners, the operating costs of taxes, insurance, interest, and repairs. The growth in home ownership discussed previously is apparent: 57 per

Table 1

Expenditures on Current Consumption as a Per Cent of Total Consumption Expenditures, All Urban and Rural Families and Single Consumers, by Income Class, 1960–1961

Income Classes
(Money income after taxes)

Characteristics	Under $1,000	$1,000–1,999	$2,000–2,999	$3,000–3,999	$4,000–4,999	$5,000–5,999	$6,000–7,499	$7,500–9,999	$10,000–14,999	$15,000 and Over
Per cent of families	3.7	10.2	11.1	11.8	13.3	12.7	15.1	13.4	6.8	2.0
Average family size	1.6	2.0	2.6	2.9	3.2	3.6	3.7	3.9	4.1	3.8
money income before taxes	$573	$1,545	$2,618	$3,746	$4,922	$6,045	$7,499	$9,716	$13,583	$27,753
age of family head	66	61	54	48	44	43	43	44	47	51
number of children under 18	.3	.5	.9	1.1	1.3	1.6	1.6	1.6	1.5	1.2
Per cent home owners, all year	51.0	46.0	46.0	45.0	47.0	56.0	67.0	71.0	78.0	87.0
auto owners	25.0	33.0	53.0	71.0	82.0	89.0	92.0	95.0	96.0	96.0
Total expenditures for current consumption	100.0	100.0	100.0	100.0	100.0	100.0	100.0	100.0	100.0	100.0
Food, total	29.0	29.9	28.2	26.2	25.4	25.0	24.2	23.8	22.1	19.1
food at home	24.2	26.1	23.5	21.5	20.8	20.8	19.6	18.6	16.4	13.0
food away	4.8	3.8	4.7	4.7	4.6	4.1	4.6	5.2	5.7	6.1
Tobacco	1.7	2.0	2.2	2.2	2.1	2.0	1.9	1.7	1.3	1.0
Alcoholic beverages	.5	1.0	1.1	1.3	1.5	1.5	1.6	1.6	1.8	1.8

Shelter	12.5	11.6	12.2	12.9	13.2	13.1	13.9	15.3	17.1	17.6
rented dwelling	1.7	2.4	3.4	4.1	6.1	7.6	8.7	9.7	11.5	10.3
owned dwelling	8.8	8.1	8.0	8.1	6.6	5.1	4.8	5.3	5.3	6.7
other	2.0	1.1	.7	.7	.5	.4	.4	.3	.3	.6
Fuel, light, refrigeration, water	3.4	4.0	4.4	4.8	5.1	5.1	5.5	6.5	8.1	9.2
Household operation	8.3	6.0	5.5	5.5	5.4	5.4	5.6	5.5	5.9	5.6
House furnishings, equipment	5.4	5.5	5.5	5.5	5.5	5.1	4.9	4.4	4.0	3.8
Clothing, material, services	12.3	11.9	11.2	10.5	9.8	9.5	9.0	8.3	6.7	6.2
Personal care	2.4	2.7	2.9	2.9	3.0	2.9	3.1	3.2	2.9	2.5
Medical care	6.2	6.3	6.3	6.5	6.6	6.6	7.3	8.2	8.8	10.2
Recreation	4.7	4.9	4.4	4.1	3.7	3.6	3.3	2.7	2.1	2.1
Reading	.9	.9	.9	.9	.9	.8	.9	.9	.9	.9
Auto transportation	11.2	14.6	15.1	14.6	14.8	15.0	12.8	9.4	6.3	5.3
Other transportation	3.2	1.9	1.4	1.2	1.1	1.4	1.5	1.6	1.5	1.4
Education	2.8	1.9	1.1	1.0	.8	.6	.6	.4	.3	1.1

SOURCE: U.S. Department of Labor, Bureau of Labor Statistics, *Survey of Consumer Expenditures, 1960–61*, BLS Report 237–93, Table 1A.

cent of the families and single consumers in this survey owned their homes. Although the "necessities of life" require a smaller *share* of high-income spending, they represent much larger amounts: average expenditure for food by consumers with incomes between $10,000 and $15,000 amounted to $2,100, four times as much as the money spent for food by consumers with average incomes of less than $2,000. The average amounts spent for rent by the median income class and by the class two steps below ($5,000 to $5,999 and $3,000 to $3,999) are almost identical: $316 and $318. Yet they represent almost 9 per cent of total spending for the lower income class, and only 6 per cent for the upper group. Expenditures for clothing are consistently larger at each income level; for other categories no clear pattern of differences by income classes seems to exist.

Much of the data on the table is interrelated. The percentage of families who own their homes is larger in each successively higher income class, yet the percentage of total spending for "owned dwelling" changes very little above the median income class. Since expenditures include payments of interest on a mortgage, and for new home owners the proportion of interest to principal in each payment is substantial, average housing expenditures reflect the number of home owners rather than their income. Rent expenditures, on the other hand, drop fairly precipitately, and show an absolute decline at higher income levels. Spending for "other" shelter is substantially greater beyond the $10,000 income level; a similar pattern occurs for "other" transportation expenditures. Both reflect the more frequent use of hotels and vacation accommodations by upper-income consumers. Expenditures for food away from home takes a larger percentage of total expenditures in both lower and upper income classes than in the middle income group, where the number of children under 18 is largest and food is chiefly prepared at home. At all levels of income, food purchased away from home includes meals at school or on the job; upper-income families also dine out for entertainment and recreation. These observations raise questions about family size, age of head, and number of children, and such factors are also relevant to Table 2, which rearranges the data from which Table 1 was prepared.

Because of differences in income and consumption choice, as well as in the number of consumers in each class, the distribution among income classes of total spending (or of the shares of the total market for each spending category that are represented by each income class) contrasts sharply with the analysis in Table 1. Engel's law does not appear directly, yet a closer look at the expenditures for the "necessities of life" is rewarding. The two highest income classes, which contain far fewer consumers than the two lowest, do well over twice as much spending on food as these poorer families, despite the fact that food takes a far greater share of low-income families' total consumption. The share of the clothing market attributable to each income class accentuates the effect of income on consumption, as shown in Table 1. Total rent expenditures, on the other hand, are almost identical for the top and bottom income groups: each of the smaller number of consumers in the well-to-do group spends a larger enough number of dollars on rent so that their total spending equals the large number of small expenditures by low-income families and individuals. That income is the primary constraint on consumption appears from the fact that the upper-income groups account for a larger share of the market than they do of the population in every spending category but one; below the $3,000 income level, no group's share of spending matches its proportion of the total population.

Some of the analysis of Table 1 is reinforced. The impact on the housing market of middle-income families, headed by a person in his early 40s, shows up clearly. Although higher-income families spend a slightly larger share of their total

Table 2

The Market Distribution of Consumers' Choices:
Shares of Total Spending by All Families and Single Consumers,
by Income Class, 1960–1961

	Money Income After Taxes										Total Spending, All Families and Single Individuals
	Under $1,000	$1,000–1,999	$2,000–2,999	$3,000–3,999	$4,000–4,999	$5,000–5,999	$6,000–7,499	$7,500–9,999	$10,000–14,999	$15,000 and Over	
Per cent of consumers	3.7	10.2	11.1	11.8	13.3	12.7	15.1	13.4	6.8	2.0	
Average family size	1.6	2.0	2.6	2.9	3.2	3.6	3.7	3.9	4.1	3.8	
Share of total spending on											
food, prepared at home	1.2	4.8	7.0	9.3	12.3	13.8	18.3	18.7	10.7	3.7	100
food, away	.9	2.8	5.6	8.2	11.1	11.0	17.2	20.9	14.9	7.2	100
tobacco	.9	4.0	7.3	10.2	13.7	14.3	19.1	18.4	9.0	3.1	100
alcohol	—	2.2	4.1	7.4	11.4	12.4	19.4	20.8	15.0	6.7	100
rent of home	1.8	7.7	10.6	14.0	16.6	14.9	14.1	12.7	5.7	1.8	100
home ownership	.9	2.7	4.4	5.8	8.4	12.3	21.1	22.5	14.8	7.1	100
shelter, away from home	.8	1.7	2.5	4.7	6.8	9.0	17.3	20.7	20.5	16.4	100
fuel, light, refrigeration, water	1.8	5.9	7.7	9.5	12.1	13.4	17.8	17.6	10.4	4.0	100
household operations	.9	3.7	5.7	8.4	11.0	12.2	17.6	19.0	13.4	8.3	100
household furnishings	.7	2.8	4.9	7.9	11.2	13.5	19.3	20.5	13.3	5.8	100

clothing and clothing care	.6	2.3	4.7	7.5	10.7	12.4	18.7	21.5	14.8	6.8	100
personal care	.8	3.7	6.5	9.3	11.9	13.5	18.2	19.6	11.9	4.7	100
recreation	.5	1.9	4.0	7.1	10.7	12.0	19.2	21.9	15.9	6.7	100
reading	.9	3.6	5.7	8.1	10.9	12.7	18.5	19.4	13.5	5.4	100
education	1.0	1.0	2.1	4.5	6.5	9.3	16.8	21.0	23.4	15.1	100
automobile purchase and upkeep	—	1.6	4.0	7.9	12.7	14.1	19.4	21.6	13.6	4.6	100
other transportation	.9	3.4	6.2	8.3	10.7	9.5	14.7	18.3	15.9	12.0	100
medical care	1.4	4.7	7.1	9.3	11.4	12.7	17.7	18.5	11.9	5.2	100

SOURCE: Calculated from data in U.S. Department of Labor, Bureau of Labor Statistics, *Survey of Consumer Expenditures, 1960–61*, BLS Report 237–93, Table IA.

consumption expenditures on home ownership, they play a much smaller role in the total spending for homes by all consumers. On the other hand, the families above the $7,500 income level clearly make up the bulk of the market for hotels, motels, and other lodging away from home, just as they do for food purchases away from home, and for transportation other than automobiles. The table also lends support to the concept of a mass market: 41 per cent of the families, with incomes ranging from $5,000 to $10,000, account for from 49 to 56 per cent of total spending in all the categories except the three just mentioned and education, in which their share dips to 47 per cent.

The previous chapter showed how the distribution of income among consumers produces a mass market of families and single consumers within this middle-income range; their patterns of consumption choice, nevertheless, come to involve more than incomes. The mass market contains the largest number of families with young children and, on the average, the family head is significantly younger than in the income classes above or below. These and other family characteristics influence the consumer's choices among the available alternatives. It would be useful to isolate these characteristics and to measure their specific effects on different kinds of consumption spending. What makes consumers differ in their buying of major appliances—their income or family size or home ownership or age? A partial answer can be given by way of the concept of *elasticity,* which is frequently applied to income. With this tool, survey data can provide some measure of the effect of income differences on consumption differences.

All survey data show that family consumption expenditures vary according to level of income; for most items, more money is spent at high than at low levels of income. Average family spending may be very similar in two income classes or it may be very different, depending on the specific product, its price and the quantity that is purchased. For example, spending on personal care by urban families and single consumers in the 1960–61 study averaged $158.17 for the median income group, but $177 for the next higher income class. Within this category of spending, women's and girls' haircuts also took different sums from families in the two income classes: average expenditure was $4.35 in the median income class and $6.01 in the next higher.

Although the dollar difference in spending by the two sets of families is $1.66 for haircuts and $19.00 for personal care, it is obviously incorrect to conclude that income differences are more important to the latter category of expenditure than to the former. The absolute difference in expenditure between two income classes must be related to the absolute amount spent by each income class: the difference in consumption calculated as a percentage of consumption. For haircuts, for example, the difference amounts to 38.2 per cent of spending on haircuts by the median income class, and 27.6 per cent of spending on haircuts by the next higher income class. The conventional formula calculates any spending differences between classes as a percentage of expenditures in both classes, thus, $\dfrac{C_1 - C_0}{C_1 + C_0}$. Applying this rule to the data for personal care and haircuts, let C_0 represent spending in the median income group and C_1 spending in the next higher income class. The data for haircuts, $\dfrac{\$6.01 - \$4.35}{\$6.01 + \$4.35}$, produce a calculated ratio of .16, which proves to be larger than that for total personal care, $\dfrac{\$177 - \$158}{\$177 + \$158} = .057$. The *percentage* change of spending from a lower to a higher income class is greater for women's and girls' haircuts than it is for total personal care, although the *dollar* difference in spending was exactly the opposite.

If data on expenditures are used to represent consumption,

they must be further adjusted to calculate the effects of income, for just as dollar expenditures form quite different percentages of different incomes, so the differences between dollar expenditures may represent a large or a small percentage of income. And figures for income must be treated in the same way as spending differences were—i.e., a difference of $1,000 between two income classes must be represented as a percentage of the absolute dollar incomes in both classes, $\frac{Y_1 - Y_0}{Y_1 + Y_0}$. The same reasoning holds: a $1,000 difference between $4,000 and $5,000 is 25 per cent of the lower income and 20 per cent of the higher income. The complete formula for income elasticity, therefore, is this:

$$\frac{C_1 - C_0}{C_1 + C_0} \div \frac{Y_1 - Y_0}{Y_1 + Y_0}$$

Most consumption surveys offer a choice of data representing income: Table 1 lists money income before taxes and average money income after taxes; the complete data also show other money receipts, including net change in assets and liabilities, gifts, and so on. In calculating income elasticity here, the figure for total expenditures on current consumption will be used instead of any "income" data: this total was used in Tables 1 and 2. The following example is drawn from Table 1.

Characteristics	Income Class (Money income after taxes)	
	$5,000– 5,999	$6,000– 7,499
Average money income	$5,491	$6,707
Size of family	3.6	3.7
Expenditures for consumption	$5,172 (100%)	$6,125 (100%)
Expenditures for food	1,291 (25%)	1,480 (24.2%)
Expenditures for clothing	508 (9.8%)	641 (10.5%)

Substituting the data, therefore, results in the following elasticity calculation:

$$\text{Food:} \quad \frac{C_1 - C_0}{C_1 + C_0} \div \frac{Y_1 - Y_0}{Y_1 + Y_0} = \frac{\$1,480 - \$1,291}{\$1,480 + \$1,291} \div \frac{\$6,125 - \$5,172}{\$6,125 + \$5,172} = .85$$

$$\text{Clothing:} \quad \frac{C_1 - C_0}{C + C} \div \frac{Y_1 - Y_0}{Y + Y} = \frac{\$641 - \$508}{\$641 + \$508} \div \frac{\$6,125 - \$5,172}{\$6,125 + \$5,172} = 1.37$$

The two measures, .85 for food and 1.37 for clothing, are pure numbers. For this particular range of total consumption spending, the measures of elasticity mean that a one per cent change in income (represented by total current consumption expenditure) is accompanied by a less than one per cent change in food spending but by a change in clothing expenditure of more than one per cent. Elasticities can be greater or less than one, or they can be negative. In the latter case, expenditures move in a direction opposite to that of income, being less at high incomes and greater at low incomes. A number that is less than one means that the product or service is "income-inelastic"; values above one refer to consumption categories that are "elastic with respect to income." Such measures permit consumption expenditures for a variety of items, over a wide range of incomes, to be meaningfully compared.

Highly sophisticated techniques have been developed for calculating elasticity, and, given the basic data, the measure can be computed for very specific items and groups of consumers. Typical of such work is the exhaustive analysis of the 1955 Household Food Consumption Study, published in 1959 by the Department of Agriculture under the title *Income and Household Size.*[2] It presents 6 household classifications and 16 major food groups; the income elasticity for bread, for example, was .14 for low-income nonfarm families, .10 for farm families, −.05 for high-income nonfarm families, and .08 for high-income farm families. These figures, like those in the example worked out above, refer to consumption expenditures at different income levels.

All figures on spending are the products of two variables: the price of the item and the amount purchased. It is possible to collect data on the physical quantities of a specific product that consumers buy and to show how consumption, as defined in terms of pounds or quarts or units or dozens, appears at different income levels, sizes of family, regions of the country, and so on. Such facts would also permit income elasticity to be computed—measuring, for example, the difference in the average pounds of bread purchased by families at two different income levels. The Department of Agriculture study includes such calculations based on quantities as well as those based on expenditures: income elasticities for bread range from .12 in low-income to −.08 in high-income nonfarm families, and from .10 in low-income to .04 in high-income farm families. These figures indicate that a change in income affects the total *expenditure* for bread more than it does the total *quantity* of bread purchased. For example, among low-income nonfarm families a one per cent increase in income is accompanied by a .12 per cent increase in the quantity of bread bought, but by a .14 per cent increase in the amount spent on bread. In short, consumers at higher income levels spend money on higher-priced items as well as more of the same items. And if income elasticities seem a tortuous way to make such a simple statement, they do have the advantage of being precise and unambiguous.

They have the further advantage of providing a technical definition to supersede the ambiguous terms "necessity" and "luxury." If income elasticities are computed from data on physical quantities consumed, then both salt and cigarettes have the distinction of being income-inelastic. There are those who are offended to hear both items referred to as "necessities." And these technical measures of income elasticity can locate the minimum levels of consumption in a factually neutral fashion which would have been the envy of the budget-makers of the early 1900s.

Despite the variety of alternatives now available, the total quantity of food consumed today is close to what it was 60 years ago. At any one time, moreover, upper- and lower-income families buy about the same number of pounds of food. The difference in total expenditures represents in part different foods—meat and vegetables, instead of bread and potatoes—and in part higher-priced items within the general food category, such as tenderloin instead of chuck, and frozen instead of canned vegetables. The same pattern exists in other categories of consumption. But if larger expenditures for the same physical volume represent some consumer estimate of quality, then income elasticities based on expenditure will differ from those based on quantity insofar as consumers seek to buy quality rather than quantity. The consumption level at which this takes place lies beyond the minimum. It is defined by consumers themselves, and obviously changes over time with changes in custom and social behavior. The Bureau of Labor Statistics terms this point the level at which the struggle for "more and more" gives way to the search for "better and better."

The Bureau has used this reasoning to compile the "City Worker's Family Budget"[3] from data on family consumption choices. This list of goods and services describes a "modest but adequate level of living." Its recommendations for food make use of survey data so as to supplement technical definitions of minimum standards in terms of nutritional requirements. Food is unique among consumer goods in that it has an objective basis, established by the sciences of medicine and nutrition, for that slippery word "necessity." A minimum amount of food is necessary to sustain not only life but also health and growth. Recommended dietary allowances of calories, proteins, fats, and other nutritional elements have been calculated for human beings of different ages, sexes, types of body build and physical activity. A nutritionally satisfactory diet can be obtained at very low cost—but would not be acceptable to many consumers. Even though an objective, scientific definition of "need" exists, consumers demand more than this. Using food consumption studies to determine the choice of foods, the Department of Agriculture has worked out menus that incorporate the recommended dietary allowances. Such menus exist for low-cost, moderate-cost, and liberal diets.[4]

For other categories of spending, the survey data provide more direct evidence of a "modest but adequate level of living." In the process of being revised, the "City Worker's Family Budget" has been adapted to estimate poverty in the United States. But as a typical attempt at drawing up a standard for consumption, the budget deserves careful consideration.

The "representative list of goods and services considered necessary applies only to a city family, assumed to consist of an employed husband, aged thirty-eight, whose wife is not in the labor force, with a daughter eight and a twelve-year-old son." It begins with a 5-room dwelling, in which most of the furniture is expected to last about 20 years, the kitchen range and the refrigerator even longer. A pair of sheets can be replaced every 16 months, a wool blanket every 4 years, a clock every 5 years, and dishes every 7 years. The husband has a haircut every 2 weeks, the boy less frequently and the daughter not at all; the wife uses a refill for her home permanent set every 9 months or so. Clothing allowed includes 1 skirt, 2 blouses, and 3 cotton dresses for the little girl; a wool suit, a rayon suit, and 3 dresses for her mother, who can buy a new suit every 4 or 5 years, but can replace the dresses—1 cotton, 1 rayon, and 1 housedress—yearly. The husband is allotted 2 business shirts a year, and a bathrobe every 25 years.

The fact that this budget defines the family quite carefully: how many and how old its members are, where it is located, what the adults do, reminds the analyst that elements of family life other than income influence consumption choice.

Family Size and Composition

Most broad spending categories must be analyzed in terms of the size and composition of the spending unit. The number of family members affects income: the same money total provides a smaller per capita amount for 5 persons than for 3.* The composition of the family affects income: per capita real income for a family with 2 adults and 3 children under 6 will be larger than for a 5-adult family, even though both are at the same money income level. Both size and composition affect consumption per person: some economies of scale exist, particularly in housing and home furnishings and equipment, but also in food consumption.

Since both income and family size affect expenditures for many items, they must somehow be disentangled. Table 3, which uses 1960–61 data for urban families and single consumers, shows average food spending as a percentage of total consumption expenditure for families of different size but at the same level of income. It serves to elaborate the summary of Table 1, which merely showed average family size for each income class. Unlike Table 1, it omits rural families and single individuals; the column of food expenditures by all consumers, therefore, differs from similar data on Table 1.

That table, and the first column of Table 3, show clearly that average food expenditures represent smaller percentages of average total consumption at successively higher income

* In the example used above to calculate income elasticity, the two income classes selected were chosen partly because the average family size in both was roughly the same.

Table 3

Expenditures on Food as a Per Cent of Total Consumption
Expenditures, Urban Families and Single Consumers,
by Income and Family Size, 1960–1961

		Family Size					
Income Class	All	One	Two	Three	Four	Five	Six or More
Under $1,000	27.8	28.7	26.5	40.4	—	—	—
1,000–1,999	29.8	28.9	30.3	31.4	29.1	37.0	36.3
2,000–2,999	28.4	26.0	28.2	28.7	29.3	32.9	35.9
3,000–3,999	25.9	22.7	25.1	26.7	27.1	27.5	34.4
4,000–4,999	25.3	21.6	23.5	25.1	26.5	29.0	31.4
5,000–5,999	25.0	18.3	23.6	24.2	25.6	26.7	31.0
6,000–7,499	24.2	20.5	21.6	22.9	25.0	26.8	29.4
7,500–9,999	24.0	20.3	20.8	23.2	24.4	26.5	27.3
10,000–14,999	22.2	13.3	20.4	20.8	22.1	23.1	26.6
15,000 and over	19.1	26.4	17.1	18.1	19.2	21.0	21.2
Total	24.3	23.6	22.8	23.2	24.4	25.8	28.6

SOURCE: U.S. Department of Labor, Bureau of Labor Statistics, *Survey of Consumer Expenditures, 1960–61*, BLS Report 237–38, and Supplement 2, Part A, Tables 11a–11g.

levels. For any particular family size, however, this effect is not so pronounced, and in some cases it does not exist. Average food expenditures make up a larger and larger portion of the total in successively larger families, as shown in the Total row. The data for single individuals, and to a lesser extent two-person families, are least indicative of Engel's law: the effect of higher income does not seem either strong or consistent. In both cases, the explanation lies in a subdivision of the expenditure category. Food purchased for home preparation follows the classical pattern, forming a consistently smaller share of total consumption at successively higher incomes. But food purchased away from home, by two-person families, accounts for almost as large a share of spending, no matter what the income class. And for single consumers, the expense of dining out equals or exceeds the share of total consumption spent on food prepared at home.

Table 4 shows a market analysis for these two subdivisions of food expenditures in terms of three variables: what per cent

Table 4

The Market for Food: Shares of Total Spending,
Urban Families and Single Consumers, by Income Class,
by Size of Family, by Location, 1960–1961

Income Class	Per Cent of Total Families	*Per Cent of Total Spending for*		Average Family Size
		Food for Home Preparation	Food Purchased Away	
Under $1,000	3.7	1.2	.9	1.6
1,000–1,999	10.2	4.8	2.8	2.0
2,000–2,999	11.1	7.0	5.6	2.6
3,000–3,999	11.8	9.3	8.2	2.9
4,000–4,999	13.3	12.3	11.1	3.2
5,000–5,999	12.7	13.8	11.0	3.6
6,000–7,499	15.1	18.3	17.2	3.7
7,500–9,999	13.4	18.7	20.9	3.9
10,000–14,999	6.8	10.7	14.9	4.1
15,000 and over	2.0	3.7	7.2	3.8
Number of Persons in Family				Average Family Income
1	15.2	5.5	14.1	$3,070
2	30.1	24.5	24.4	5,676
3	17.9	19.7	19.6	7,198
4	16.2	20.6	18.6	7,792
5	10.5	14.9	12.4	7,872
6 or more	10.2	15.3	10.7	6,863
Location				
Urban	72.6	76	81	$6,691 (3.1 persons)
Rural nonfarm	21.1	19	15	5,168 (3.5 persons)

SOURCE: Calculated from data in U.S. Department of Labor, Bureau of Labor Statistics, *Survey of Consumer Expenditures, 1960–61*, BLS Reports 237–38 and 237–93.

of total spending occurs in each income class? in each family-size category? in each type of location? The income class data duplicate those on Table 2 so as to facilitate the comparisons with the other classifications. Note first that the mass market (40 per cent of the consumers, with incomes between $5,000 and $10,000) accounts for half the spending on food prepared at home and almost half the total spending on food away from home. While upper-income families spend a larger share of the total food dollars than their proportion of the population, their effect on the market for home-prepared food is far smaller than on the market for food purchased away from home. Family size has a direct bearing on the restaurant and dining-out market, for families without children eat out more frequently. Table 4 shows that single consumers, who amount to 15 per cent of all families, buy only 5 per cent of the total food purchased for home preparation; two-person families also account for a smaller share of this type of food expenditures than their share of the total population. Despite the smaller average income of these two family-size groups, they account for almost as large a share of the total spending on food purchased away from home as they do of the population.

The last two rows of figures show the importance to market analysis of another variable, that of location. Urban consumers account for a greater share of total food spending, especially for food purchased away, than their proportion of the population. The total spending of rural nonfarm families reflects their lower income, and they do not, therefore, make up as significant a part of the food market as they do of the population, despite the fact that the average family size is larger so that there are more mouths to feed. Similar market analyses, showing the effects of both income and family size, can be prepared for housing, clothing, and so on.

Larger families can achieve some economies of scale in consumption, as can be seen in Table 3. Families of different sizes within the same income class show only slight differences in food expenditures as a percentage of total spending. At the $4,000–$4,999 level, for example, the change from a single consumer to a two-person family results in additional food spending of $203, but each additional person thereafter represents additional food spending of much less than this. The Department of Agriculture has calculated the cost of its various food plans for various types of families, and for individuals defined by age and sex. Assuming a 4-person family, the Department explains, "For individuals in other size families, the following adjustments are suggested: one-person—add 20 per cent; 2-person—add 10 per cent; 3-person—add 5 per cent; 5-person—subtract 5 per cent; 6-or-more-person—subtract 10 per cent."[5] Such a recommendation quantifies the economies of scale, at least for the menus of these plans.

Comparison of the changes in average expenditure in different sizes of families leads to another analysis of elasticity, this time a measure that shows the change in food consumption (as a percentage of total food consumption) in relation to the change in family size (also on a percentage basis). The study mentioned above, *Income and Household Size,* presents such measures computed on the basis of the value of food consumed per person, so as to allow for the effect of income. Economies of scale make household-size elasticity measures negative; that is, the value of food per person is less in larger families. Again, such elasticity measures will differ for particular consumption items: the study estimates the elasticity of potatoes, with respect to household size, at −.18 for low income and −.13 for high income nonfarm households. Comparable elasticities for soups were −.49 and −.32. There are not many economies of scale available in preparing potatoes, but such economies do exist with soup.

Although Table 3 presents a cross-classification of data, the simplest way to disentangle income from family size is to divide both income and consumption figures by the number of persons in the family. Such per capita data most frequently appear in comparisons of living levels between large groups, such as the populations of different countries. For surveys of families and single consumers within a fairly homogeneous economy like that of the United States, this process of division is too crude to be helpful. It conceals the fact that family members differ in age and sex, and therefore in their consumption choices.

Family composition, apart from size, can be analyzed in a number of different ways. Engel recognized this problem in his early studies of food consumption and devised a basic food consumption unit, "quet" (named to commemorate a Belgian social philosopher, Quetelet). The quet was defined as the value of the food that was consumed by a child less than one year old; an adult male then represented 3.5 quets, an adult female 3.1. Today, similar calculations achieve greater accuracy by using the recommended daily allowances of nutrients: they are usually based on an adult male equivalent. For even greater precision, food consumption data can be computed in terms of the number of meals taken at home by each family member and guests.

Such a technique demands an objective standard for requirements which can be used in calculations for various family members.[6] Other types of consumption—clothing, housing, utilities, transportation—cannot be handled in this fashion because, in simple terms, the clothing "requirements" of a teen-age girl are not some fraction (or multiple) of her father's. Another technique that allows for differences in family composition therefore classifies consumers according to the family members present. *The Study of Consumer Purchases* in the '30s set up 9 family types; the latest BLS survey in 1960–61 uses 7 types classified

. . . on the basis of the relationship of family members and the age of the children of the head of the family. Five types consisted of consumer units in which both the husband and wife were present. One of these was composed of a husband and wife only; husband and wife families with their own children (including adopted and stepchildren) but with no other persons in the family were classified in three types according to the age of the oldest child (under 6 years, 6–17 years, 18 years and over); and the fifth type, "other husband-wife" families, included those with or without their own children but with other persons in the family. A sixth type included families with children and only one parent (the head) present and no other persons in the family. The remaining type covered all other consumer units, including one-person families.[7]

Table 5 presents summary data for 4 types of consumption spending—food, clothing, shelter, and automobiles—by these 7 family types. Most noticeable is the jump in the percentage of home owners between the classes of families with young children and those whose oldest child is over 6. Average spending for shelter, not only in percentages but also in dollars, is lower for home-owning families than for the large number of renters among families with small children. Average income and family size are greater among families with older children, and these families devote a larger share of their income to the clothing and food needs of their children. The difference between the husband-wife family and that with children under 6 is less than two people (1.5 in statistical terms), but it requires that the latter type of family spend more for shelter and, as a result, have lower spending for food. The data of this table show that family composition, like family size, affects income: on a per person basis both income and potential consumption are less, the larger the family and the older the children.

To indicate the effects of family composition separately from those of income, Table 6 presents 4 major types of urban

Table 5

Spending on Food, Shelter, Clothing, and Automobiles, by Family Type, All Urban Families and Single Consumers, 1960–1961

	Total	Husband-Wife Only	Husband-Wife; Oldest Child			Other Husband-Wife	One Parent; Children	All Other
			Under 6 years	6–16 Years	18 Years and Over			
Per cent of families	100	22.0	12.0	24.1	9.6	5.7	5.7	21.0
Average family size	3.1	2.0	3.5	4.6	4.2	4.6	3.0	1.4
Money income after taxes	$5,906	$5,529	$5,766	$7,154	$9,455	$7,388	$4,426	$3,327
Per cent of total consumption								
food	24.3	23.0	22.3	25.8	23.4	25.8	25.5	24.3
clothing	10.4	8.5	8.8	11.3	12.1	11.8	11.7	9.2
shelter	13.9	14.2	15.9	12.9	10.8	11.3	14.7	18.7
automobile	13.0	14.0	15.3	12.3	14.6	12.4	10.2	9.8
Per cent of families								
home owners, all year	53	58	31	67	75	64	35	36
auto owners, end of year	73	76	89	90	88	85	46	36

SOURCE: Bureau of Labor Statistics, Survey of Consumer Expenditures, 1960–61, Supplement 1 to BLS Report 237–38.

Table 6

Clothing Expenditures as a Per Cent of Total Consumption
Expenditures, Urban Consumers, by Family Type
and Income, 1960–1961

Income Class	All	Husband-Wife	Husband-Wife, Children Under 6	Husband-Wife, Oldest Child 6–17 Years	Husband-Wife, Oldest Child 18 and Over
Under $1,000	4.7	4.2	3.6	10.5	5.0
1,000–1,999	6.1	5.0	7.7	8.1	5.5
2,000–2,999	8.2	5.3	8.6	7.9	10.5
3,000–3,999	9.0	7.4	8.8	10.0	7.3
4,000–4,999	9.7	7.4	8.6	11.0	11.9
5,000–5,999	9.9	8.4	8.9	10.7	10.9
6,000–7,499	10.3	9.1	8.8	10.9	12.0
7,500–9,999	11.1	9.4	9.2	11.6	12.0
10,000–14,999	11.9	10.6	7.7	12.0	12.5
15,000 and over	12.3	11.1	10.7	13.8	12.7
Total	10.4	8.5	8.8	11.3	12.1

SOURCE: Bureau of Labor Statistics, *Survey of Consumer Expenditures, 1960–61*, BLS Report 237–38, and Supplement 2, Part A, Tables 26a–26g.

families arranged by income class, with average clothing expenditures as a percentage of total consumption spending for each. For all urban consumers, clothing accounts for 10.4 per cent of total expenditures. Disregarding family composition, this percentage varies from 4.7 in the lowest income class to 12.3 in the highest. And the upper-income classes (consumers above $7,500) weight the average heavily. From income data alone, given in the first column, it appears that more than three-quarters of all families and individuals show a smaller share of total expenditures devoted to clothing than the arithmetic mean of 10.4 per cent.

Classifications by family type furnish more details. On the average, clothing expenditures move from 8.5 per cent of the total for the husband-wife family to 12.1 per cent for the family whose oldest child is over 18. This same pattern exists within each income class. The average percentage of clothing expenditures derived from data for all urban consumers, 10.4 per cent, appears in quite different income classes, but for different family types. It is exceeded, for example, by all families with incomes above $4,000, if they also have children over 6. Both family composition and family size are implicit in these data, for in every income class the family type with an oldest child between 6 and 17 also shows the largest average family size. Because at any given income level the amount of income per person is less, while there are more to be clothed, the simple income effect shown on Table 1 is paralleled on Table 6 only by the two-person, husband-wife family.

Another way of analyzing family composition arranges consumers in a life-cycle pattern. The Survey of Consumer Finance[8] uses classifications that modify those suggested by Paul C. Glick in "The Family Cycle."[9] Table 7, which uses the latest versions of life-cycle stages, presents data for the same years of 1960 and 1961 and should be compared with the last two rows of Table 5. Although the latter suggests that over half the childless couples own their homes, Table 7 distinguishes sharply between younger and older couples. The former class contains the most renters; the incentive to buy a home comes from both increasing years and the presence of children. Automobile ownership, according to Table 5, is most frequent among families with children from 6 to 17, but Table 7 suggests that two-car ownership occurs not only in such families but also with childless couples, almost one-quarter of whom report two or more cars.

Finally, Table 7 differentiates the young single consumer from the older individual who is approaching the end of the family life cycle. Less than one-fifth of the former group own homes, while about half the older individuals do. Widows and

Table 7

Ownership of Automobiles and Houses, by Life-Cycle Stages, 1960, 1961

Group	Percentage Total Sample 1961	Percentage Owning Autos Jan.–Feb. 1961			Percentage with Homes 1960			Percentage Total Sample 1960
		None	One	Two or more	Owned	Rented	Other	
All spending units	100	26	59	15	58	36	6	100
Aged 18–44								
single	10	52	48	—	18	58	24	5
married, childless	5	15	62	23	35	62	3	5
youngest child under 6	} 34	10	74	16	56	41	3	22
youngest over 6		7	67	26	72	27	1	9
Aged 45 and over								
with children	14	13	64	23	72	24	4	13
childless, in labor force	} 19	19	59	22	75	22	3	12
childless, retired		28	65	7	69	25	6	6
single, in labor force	} 14	51	45	4	43	40	17	6
single, retired		71	29	—	53	36	11	7
Other	4	51	43	6	—	—	—	—

SOURCE: *1961 Survey of Consumer Finances* (Ann Arbor: University of Michigan, 1962), pp. 39, 141; *1960 Survey of Consumer Finances* (Ann Arbor: University of Michigan, 1963), p. 62.

widowers tend to maintain the family home, although there are more varied housing patterns for households over 65 than for any other age group. Table 9 in Chapter 2 showed that wide disparities of income also exist among the older consumers. Automobile ownership, on the other hand, clearly reflects employment: about half the single consumers who are in the labor force own cars, while less than one-third of the older, retired individuals do so.

The life-cycle classification helps to analyze data on housing, automobiles, and other assets as well as on the incidence of debt. But the stages identified assume a fairly typical pattern of family formation, based on the sociology of the United States and not necessarily applicable to spending patterns in other countries. Furthermore, even though the life-cycle classifications form a coherent progression, descriptive of many family histories, the spending or ownership data that they present refer to different families, not to the same family as it progresses from one stage to another. The caution expressed earlier* about the static nature of survey data also applies here; while differences between spending patterns of different families at different stages of the life cycle are illuminating, they tell nothing about consumption changes by the same family or group of families.

The life-cycle analysis includes employment status: both the number of employed family members and their occupations affect consumption choices. Table 8 uses clothing expenditures as an example, although occupational differences are revealed in many other types of family spending. In all income classes the average share of total expenditures devoted to clothing is less for retired consumers than for any other group; the "need" for clothing on the job appears to be decisive here. The use of income for clothing rather than for some other consumption choice is less clearly defined among

* Cf. above, pp. 79–81.

Table 8

Clothing Expenditures as a Per Cent of All Consumption Expenditures, by Income and Occupation, All Urban Families and Single Consumers, 1960–1961

Income Class	All	Self-Employed	Salaried Professionals, Officials	Clerical and Sales	Skilled Wage Earners	Semi-Skilled Wage Earners	Unskilled Wage Earners	Retired	Not Working
Under $1,000	4.7	8.6	5.4	9.5	4.8	2.6	6.5	3.3	3.2
1,000–1,999	6.1	7.4	8.7	8.1	6.4	8.1	9.4	4.3	6.2
2,000–2,999	8.2	8.5	7.2	10.6	8.5	8.8	9.2	5.6	9.9
3,000–3,999	9.0	9.0	9.4	10.8	7.9	9.4	10.0	6.4	10.3
4,000–4,999	9.5	9.8	9.6	11.0	8.5	9.8	10.3	7.6	11.1
5,000–5,999	9.9	10.6	9.0	10.3	10.0	10.0	10.6	7.8	10.0
6,000–7,499	10.3	10.8	9.7	11.4	10.0	10.7	10.5	8.4	10.1
7,500–9,999	11.1	10.7	10.7	11.8	11.2	11.9	11.1	10.3	10.1
10,000–14,999	11.9	12.3	10.9	12.7	12.2	14.1	12.3	10.3	16.5
15,000 and over	12.3	13.2	11.9	13.6	12.1	10.6	21.3	9.2	11.5
Total	10.4	11.3	10.5	11.4	10.3	10.7	10.4	6.8	9.5

SOURCE: Bureau of Labor Statistics, *Survey of Consumer Expenditures, 1960–61*, BLS Report 237–38, and Supplement 2, Part A, Tables 17a–17i.

occupational groups. Higher incomes produce perhaps the smallest increases in clothing expenditures for the salaried professional and official group. This occupational class has the highest mean and median income; it also shows the highest average expenditures for housing and home furnishings, education, reading, and recreation. Wage-earning families that fall into income classes above $7,500 generally have more than one full-time worker; consequently, employment requirements for clothing apply to more people.

Employment status and the number of family earners also influences the *market* for clothing, as shown on Table 9. The

Table 9

The Market for Clothing and Personal Care: Shares of Total Spending by All Urban and Rural Families and Single Consumers, by Number of Full-Time Earners in Family

Number of Earners	Per Cent of All Families	Per Cent of All Expenditures on Clothing	Per Cent of All Expenditures on Personal Care
None	30.8	15.7	19.3
1	57.5	64.6	63.9
2	10.8	17.5	15.6
3 or more	0.8	1.9	—

SOURCE: Calculated from U.S. Department of Labor, Bureau of Labor Statistics, *Survey of Consumer Expenditures, 1960–61*, BLS Report 237–93, Table 9A.

indication in Table 8 that retired consumers have smaller clothing expenditures than employed people recurs even more sharply in Table 9, where the 30 per cent of all families that have no full-time earner account for less than half this percentage of total clothing spending. Families with only one jobholder are most frequent and, therefore, account for almost two-thirds of total consumer purchases of clothing and personal care. Yet the 11 per cent of the families with two full-time earners account for almost twice this proportion of the market for clothing, although the effect on personal care is not as great. When such analysis is coupled with the fact that employment is increasing among married women, it gives business a clue to future markets and sales potential.

Location and Housing Tenure

Consumption choices differ according to the living arrangements of the family or individual: in what region of the country consumers live—North, South, West, East—or in what subdivision of these broad areas; whether in highly urban areas, large cities, small cities, towns or villages in rural areas, or on farms; whether home owners or renters or neither. The latter category includes those families that receive housing as part of their compensation, and those that share housing— most frequently younger couples or single individuals of any age.

Regional variations in consumption sometimes reflect physical geography: almost 20 per cent of the households in the Pacific and South Atlantic states owned portable heaters in 1961, as contrasted with only 3.4 per cent of the households in the Mountain states. Sometimes spending patterns demonstrate regional customs, habits, or tastes: the New England market pays a premium for brown-shell eggs. Consumption data report such differences among geographical areas, but they do not disclose the causes for dissimilarity: do Southern consumers eat more pork than Northerners because they prefer it to beef or because pork is more plentiful? Is pork more plentiful in the South as a result of regional consumers' preference or because costs of production are lower than for beef? Since no definite answers, it seems, can be found for such questions, it is fortunate that marked regional variations in consumption patterns are steadily lessening, so that such questions will eventually become irrelevant. Variations by location remain: household expenditures differ in large cities, in small cities, in rural nonfarm areas, and on farms.

Urban or rural location and size of city or town have frequently been used to prepare market analyses, based on different spending patterns, such as those in Table 10. The family characteristics of consumers in New York City, Washington, D.C., and rural nonfarm areas in the Northeast were found to be fairly similar: average family size was between 3.0 and 3.5; average family income ranged from $6,339 to $7,800. Total expenditures for current consumption, and the percentage of this total devoted to each major category nevertheless vary among the three groups much more widely than these differences in income and family size would suggest. Spending on food away from home and on alcoholic beverages is significantly larger in the two cities than in rural nonfarm areas; total food expenditures by the country consumers are larger than those in Washington. The expenditure for shelter by the three groups also shows wide variation: consumers in Washington spend on housing a fractionally larger share of total expenditures than does either of the other two groups, but the percentage spent for rentals, as opposed to owned dwellings, is highest in New York City. Families in the rural areas averaged about two-thirds of the expenditures of city consumers for all shelter, while the percentage of their total consumption that was used to pay rent amounted to less than one-fourth the size of their home-ownership expenses; the two were almost equal in Washington, but in New York City the average rent expense was almost double that for home ownership. Spending for utilities and home care reflects this difference in tenure arrangements. The other two areas of significant variation are clothing and automobile expenses. In both dollar and percentage terms the amount spent on clothing in New York is highest, in rural areas lowest. But in rural areas the share of

Table 10

Summary of Family Expenditures and Income, Three
Selected Places, 1960, 1961

Characteristics	New York City, 1960	Washing- ton, D.C., 1960	Rural Nonfarm Areas in the Northeast, 1961
Average			
money income, before taxes	$7,800	$7,777	$6,339
family size	3.0	3.1	3.5
age of head	48	45	48
expenditures for current			
consumption	$6,336	$5,813	$5,342
Per cent of total			
food prepared at home	19.4	17.5	20.6
food away from home	6.2	5.7	3.7
tobacco	1.9	1.4	2.0
alcoholic beverages	2.2	1.8	1.6
rented dwelling	9.7	8.0	2.3
owned dwelling	5.8	8.5	9.0
other shelter	.9	.4	.7
fuel, light, refrigeration,			
water	3.0	4.0	6.8
household operations	6.1	6.4	5.0
house furnishings and			
equipment	5.0	4.9	5.3
clothing, materials, services	11.0	10.4	9.1
personal care	2.5	2.8	2.5
medical care	6.8	5.8	6.2
recreation	3.6	3.8	4.3
reading	1.0	.9	.9
education	1.1	1.2	.9
automobile	8.3	11.3	16.0
other travel and transportation	2.8	2.7	1.0

SOURCE: Bureau of Labor Statistics, *Survey of Consumer Expenditures,
1960–61*, BLS Reports 237– 3, 237– 4, 237–84.

expenditures that goes to automobile purchases and care is
almost double that in New York, and well above the share in
Washington, D.C.

This type of analysis provokes two comments: first, that

many of the differences that appear when consumers are classified by location also appear when other classifications—for example, income and family composition, or employment among family members—are used. Family characteristics are interrelated. Secondly, a percentage distribution requires that the total of all figures equal 100 per cent. While this may seem obvious, analysts sometimes overlook its implications for specific categories of spending. For example, among country families spending on automobiles took 16 per cent of the total consumption expenditures; in New York City the comparable figure was 8.3 per cent. The difference in this item means that spending on other items must also differ. Consequently, while it is tempting to say that country living "requires" an automobile and city living "requires" a lot of dining out, it is also possible to say that it is because New Yorkers do not have the automobile expenses of their country cousins, that they have "extra" income to devote to dining out.

The third variation in living arrangements, the housing tenure of consumers, appears most clearly in figures on spending for household operation, home furnishings, and equipment. The 1960–61 BLS survey distinguished three classes of families: owners all year, renters all year, and those who were owners part of the year and renters part of the year. Families who received "free" rent were included with renters. These three types of urban families and single consumers, classified by income, had expenditures for home furnishings and equipment as shown in Table 11, which also includes the average family size for each subclass. For urban United States, which has an average family size of 3.1, the average expenditure on home furnishings and equipment of 5.1 per cent of total consumption reflects variations both in income and in housing tenure.

Comparing family size and expenditure within the same income class helps to allow for the income variable. Table 1

Table 11

Expenditures for House Furnishings and Equipment as a Per Cent of Total Current Consumption Expenditures, Urban Families and Single Consumers, by Tenure and Income Class, 1960–1961

	Total		Owners All Year		Renters All Year		Other	
Income Class	Average Family Size	Per Cent of Expenditure	Average Family Size	Average Expenditure	Average Family Size	Average Expenditure	Average Family Size	Average Expenditure
Under $1,000	1.3	3.1	1.4	4.5	1.3	2.0	1.2	.2
1,000–1,999	1.7	3.6	1.6	3.8	1.7	3.2	1.8	9.6
2,000–2,999	2.3	3.9	2.1	3.6	2.3	3.8	3.5	7.1
3,000–3,999	2.6	4.7	2.5	4.6	2.7	4.7	3.2	5.7
4,000–4,999	3.1	4.9	3.0	4.9	3.1	4.7	3.8	6.9
5,000–5,999	3.4	5.3	3.6	4.8	3.3	5.3	3.6	9.2
6,000–7,499	3.6	5.5	3.7	5.3	3.2	5.2	3.6	9.3
7,500–9,999	3.8	5.4	3.9	5.2	3.3	5.3	4.1	7.6
10,000–14,999	4.0	5.4	4.1	5.3	3.8	4.9	4.1	11.1
15,000 and over	3.7	5.3	3.8	5.1	2.7	6.5	4.6	7.8
Total	3.1	5.1	3.3	5.1	2.8	4.9	3.6	8.4

SOURCE: Bureau of Labor Statistics, *Survey of Consumer Expenditures, 1960–61*, BLS Report 237–38, and Supplement 2, Part A, Tables 25a–c.

provides a reminder that more than half the families with incomes of less than $5,000 are renters all year; below this income level, there is little difference between year-round renters and owners, either in family size or in percentage spent for home furnishings. Above it, however, the average home owner's family is larger than that of the average renter, so that even though the home-furnishings expenditures are closely similar in the two groups, they represent a larger drain on the resources, per person, of the home-owning families. What stands out from Table 11 is the strikingly high percentage of total consumption devoted to home furnishings by families who both rented and owned during the year. These sums, which exceed the average for all consumers at every income level except the lowest, represented purchases accompanying a new home. Presumably, if the figures for those who moved from rented to owned homes could be segregated, their expenditures would be even higher. The effect of tenure is clearly stronger there than that of income: note that in the two income classes immediately above $5,000, families whose tenure changed spent more than double the percentage of year-round owners.

Again not surprisingly, those families whose tenure changed form a most important part of the market for home furnishings, particularly for some items. The data of this survey are too few to do more than hint at this market, but the last columns of Table 12 show its implications. Although the "other" families and single individuals amount to only 3.9 per cent of all consumers, they account for 7.5 per cent of total spending. Because of their sheer number, year-round home owners make up the bulk of the market. Renters, even though their home-furnishings expenditures were almost the same percentage of their total spending as they were for owners, amount to only one-third of the total market. The 1964 *Surveys of Consumer Finance* emphasizes the same breakdown for the

Table 12

The Market for Home Furnishings and Equipment: Per Cent of All Families and Share of Total Spending, Urban Families and Single Consumers, by Tenure and Income Class

Income Class	Owners All Year		Renters All Year		Other	
	Per Cent of Families	Per Cent of Spending	Per Cent of Families	Per Cent of Spending	Per Cent of Families	Per Cent of Spending
Under $1,000	1.0	—	1.4	—	—	—
1,000–1,999	3.2	1.0	5.4	1.0	—	—
2,000–2,999	3.7	1.2	5.9	2.2	—	—
3,000–3,999	4.2	2.5	6.8	4.3	—	—
4,000–4,999	5.4	4.2	7.3	5.5	—	0.6
5,000–5,999	6.7	5.9	5.8	5.8	.6	1.3
6,000–7,499	10.6	12.3	4.9	5.6	.9	2.2
7,500–9,999	10.4	14.5	3.8	5.5	.7	3.4
10,000–14,999	5.9	10.7	1.5	2.7	—	1.0
15,000 and over	2.0	5.4	—	.9	—	—
Total	53.0	58.5	43.0	34.1	3.9	7.5

SOURCE: Calculated from United States Department of Labor, Bureau of Labor Statistics, *Survey of Consumer Expenditures, 1960–61*, BLS Report 237–38, and Supplement 2, Part A, Tables 25a–c.

market. Sixty-nine per cent of owners who had purchased homes between 1963 and 1964 spent over $100 on automobiles and household durables during 1963; two-thirds of them spent over $500, and expenditures of $1,000 or more were reported by almost half. By contrast, among the renters who moved during this period, only 54 out of 100 families made such purchases. Because automobiles are included in these totals, and the number of automobile purchasers within three years is substantial, the effect of home ownership on furnishings is imprecise, but it is clearly present. For specific products, especially major appliances, the market is even more heavily weighted toward owners, and especially new owners.

Other Variables

Other household characteristics are used to classify consumers, with different problems involved in defining, measuring, and appraising each characteristic. In some cases (as has already become apparent), two or more are correlated: income differences are associated with both occupational and educational differences; both home ownership and mortgage debt follow life-cycle stages; family size and composition affect all figures on family spending. To analyze consumption choice by way of cross-classified tables, such as those used in this chapter, becomes an extremely complicated task.

The goal of dealing with all the important family characteristics at once has been approached by multiple correlation techniques that are beyond the scope of this book,[10] but the method involved can be appreciated if some of the data in this chapter are reexamined. Table 1 shows that average food-consumption expenditures for all families and single consumers in rural and urban United States in 1960–61 amounted to 25 per cent of current consumption, or $1,235. How many families there were with expenditures of precisely this figure cannot be known: $1,235 is a calculated mean from which spending by particular families and individuals differs. The statistician can compute the significance of these differences by the measure of standard deviation, which is merely a shorthand indication of how representative the average, $1,235, is of all the original data. When the standard deviation is very large, the analyst knows that the average is less applicable to the cases it describes than when it is very small. By rearranging data for various classes of consumers, multivariate analysis can help explain what family characteristics are associated with deviations from the mean.

For example, the figure for average food expenditures in Table 3 was 24.3 per cent or $1,311. This mean was calculated from data for only urban consumers, and is, therefore, more representative of that group than the figure in Table 1. But urban consumers in the income class between $5,000 and $6,000 averaged food expenditures of 25 per cent of their total spending, or $1,291. The deviation of this figure from $1,311 may be said to occur because of income differences. Within that income class, families are of different sizes. The calculated mean for food expenditures by 4-person families, for example, was 25.6 per cent or $1,437; this deviation from $1,311 occurs because of the size of family. This sort of reasoning can be continued, for Table 5 shows 6 family types, all of which include 4 persons, and average food expenditure will be different for each of these groups. Statistical methods of multiple correlation are used to establish the relative impact of these different characteristics on the grand mean, for all types of families of all sizes (including single consumers) in all income classes living in the entire United States. Hypothetically, such analysis might show that family size accounts for 45 per cent of the deviations from the mean, income for 32 per cent, location for 5 per cent, and so on.

Although this explanation is made in terms of an average

of spending, the technique can obviously be applied to other measures of consumption and to many family characteristics. The Survey Research Center, using data from its extensive *Surveys of Consumer Finance,* has worked out such multi-variate analyses for some consumption choices; of these, education is a good example. Their findings substantiate other indications that the educational level of parents or their aspirations have an exceptionally strong influence. Using the number of grades completed by children as data for education obtained or "consumed," Morgan, David, Cohen, and Brazer find the following characteristics of families explanatory factors, in order of importance: education of family head, difference in education of heads and wives, occupation of head, number of living children, movement out of the Deep South, attitude toward hard work, highest income ever earned, and other sociological characteristics.[11] This primary importance of the education of the family head is confirmed by expenditure data from the BLS 1960–61 survey, even though these do not altogether measure the amount of education "consumed."

Table 13 shows that the average share of total spending allocated to education is greater, the more the years of school completed by the family head. For all consumers, education accounted for 1.1 per cent of total spending. This figure was exceeded by families with less than 8 years of school in only the two top-income classes, but in all income classes it was exceeded by families whose head had completed 12 years of school. The percentages in the very lowest income and highest education classes refer to students who are themselves family heads, and should, therefore, be disregarded. In the middle-income classes, from $4,000 to $10,000, there is striking evidence that education takes a larger share of total spending by the educated. Although among those with 12 years of school or less, there is a substantial jump in education expenditures as incomes exceed $10,000, it is still significantly less than the

Table 13

Expenditures on Education as a Per Cent of Total Current Consumption Expenditures, by Education of Family Head and Income Class, Urban Families and Single Consumers, 1960–1961

| | Years of Education, Family Head | | | | | | | | | |
| | Total | | 8 Years or Less | | 9-12 Years | | 13-16 Years | | 16 Years or More | |
Income Class	Average Family Size	Per Cent of Total Expended	Average Family Size	Per Cent of Total Expended	Average Family Size	Per Cent of Total Expended	Average Family Size	Per Cent of Total Expended	Average Family Size	Per Cent of Total Expended
Under $1,000	1.3	1.7	1.3	.0	1.2	.1	1.7	4.7	2.5	21.1
1,000–1,999	1.7	.3	1.7	.1	1.6	.1	1.3	1.9	2.0	17.9
2,000–2,999	2.3	.4	2.3	.3	2.3	.3	1.7	2.1	1.4	2.8
3,000–3,999	2.6	.6	2.8	.3	2.7	.4	2.0	1.5	2.4	3.6
4,000–4,999	3.1	.6	3.2	.3	3.1	.5	2.5	1.0	2.3	2.8
5,000–5,999	3.4	.7	3.7	.6	3.5	.5	3.0	1.2	3.2	2.5
6,000–7,499	3.6	.9	3.6	.9	3.6	.7	3.6	1.3	2.8	1.8
7,500–9,999	3.8	1.1	3.7	.8	3.8	1.1	3.8	1.3	3.2	1.4
10,000–14,999	4.0	2.0	4.1	1.4	4.0	1.8	4.0	2.2	4.0	2.6
15,000 and over	3.7	2.9	3.6	1.2	3.6	1.9	3.7	3.3	3.8	3.2
Total	3.1	1.1	2.8	.6	3.2	.9	3.2	1.7	3.3	2.6

SOURCE: Bureau of Labor Statistics, *Survey of Consumer Expenditures, 1960–61,* BLS Report 237–38, and Supplement 2, Part A, Tables 20a–20d.

proportion spent by the two more educated groups whose families are the same size. The classification by income in this table avoids the complication that income itself is highly correlated with the educational level of the family head.

Consumer spending data do not satisfy the analyst's questions about education; they exclude taxes that support public education and they bear little relation to the quantity or "quality" of education obtained. Knottiest of all is the problem of separating out the consumption and investment aspects of education[12] and, therefore, of determining the role of public and private expenditure.* The interrelationship of education and income has a twofold meaning: the education attained by one generation will affect the distribution of income in the next. Insofar as high-income families are able to start their children on the road to high incomes more easily than low-income families, the inequality of income distribution is built in. And since higher-income families are the ones more likely to have a higher education, this primary influence is reinforced by the ability to purchase education.

This brief glimpse at the use of survey data to learn what characteristics of consumers affect their choices may leave the analyst convinced of the overriding importance of income—which may very well be conceded. What has yet to be understood, however, is the process of consumer choice. Families and individuals may be described in terms of certain characteristics, but it is incorrect to think of these as causal factors. Choices are made by consumers, both families and individuals. Users of cross-sectional survey data may implicitly assume that, as families move from one income level to another, their spending patterns change accordingly. But there is nothing in a money income of $7,500 that forces consumers to make specific choices, and the analysis of families in the same income class, but with differing occupations or housing ar-

* Cf. Chap. 9, pp. 323–24.

rangements or other characteristics, provides a strong warning against thinking in causal terms.[13] It may be convenient and even helpful to speak of "the influence of family size on food expenditures," but it is a particular family, of whatever size, that faces the basic economic problem of allocating income to food and to all other goods and services. It may be illuminating to discern a common pattern of consumption, but its existence and the existence of variations from it reflect choices by consumers.

While these opening chapters have concentrated on empirical data, the *process* of consumer choice requires a different type of analysis from that used so far. Chapter 4 develops a model of the consumer's basic economic problem—that of allocating limited income among alternatives—and offers possible solutions to this problem.

chapter 4 A Model

of

Consumer

Choice

The empirical details in the previous three chapters describe consumption choices that have already been made. The data record incomes that have been received, expenditures that families or individuals have made, and housing arrangements as they have come to exist. They do not explain *how* consumers chose their housing, or *how* families or individuals decided how much to spend on what. A model of consumer choice or decision-making has been developed in economic theory, which helps to explain the process of consumption choice. This model assumes that consumers seek maximum satisfaction by spending their income for goods and services, or by saving it for future consumption. The concept of maximum satisfaction has a distinguished history.

Value and Utility

Adam Smith discussed satisfaction in terms of utility, which gave value to goods and services. He distinguished two kinds of value—value in use and value in exchange—and noted the famous paradox that

The things which have the greatest value in use have frequently little or no value in exchange; and on the contrary, those which have the greatest value in exchange have frequently little or no value in use. Nothing is more useful than water; but it will purchase scarce anything; scarce anything can be had in exchange for it. A diamond, on the contrary, has scarce any value in use; but a very great quantity of other goods may frequently be had in exchange for it.[1]

Value in use was further clarified by the work of McCulloch and Senior who made it clear that when the consumer buys anything, whether it be a "consumable commodity" or services, he does so in order to purchase utility. This utility may be provided just as much by the servant who lays the fire as by the coal which burns. In short, goods and services must be *consumed* for man to obtain their utility, and man chooses consumer goods and services in order to gain their utility.

When this point had been established, economists concentrated on the problem of value in exchange. Their preoccupation with the relation of costs to prices, and with the labor theory of value, cast utility in a minor role, as noted by John Stuart Mill:

Happily, there is nothing in the laws of value which remains for the present or any future writer to clear up; the theory of the subject is complete. . . . The use of a thing . . . means its capacity to satisfy a desire or serve a purpose. Diamonds have this capacity in a high degree, and unless they had it, would not bear any price. Value in use . . . is the extreme limit of value in exchange. The exchange value of a thing may fall short, to any amount, of its value in use; but that it can ever exceed the value in use implies a contradiction.[2]

And utility was rarely needed as a limit; in most cases value in exchange reflected the "difficulty of attainment" of any economic good, whether from limitation of supply or in terms of the labor and expenditure needed to produce it.

The concept of utility was revived by Jevons in England, Menger in Austria, and Walras in Switzerland, who developed value theory and originated marginal analysis. Their predecessors, the Frenchmen Cournot and Dupuit, and the German Gossens, were rescued by Jevons from the oblivion into which they had fallen. Declaring that economics was a science of quantities, Jevons urged that economic theory be stated in mathematical terms. He wrote with a precision that contrasted sharply with the comparative looseness of earlier language in economic writing:

Pleasure and pain are undoubtedly the ultimate objects of the Calculus of Economics. To satisfy our wants to the utmost with the least effort—to procure the greatest amount of what is desirable at the expense of the least that is undesirable—in other words, *to maximise pleasure,* is the problem of Economics. But it is convenient to transfer our attention as soon as possible to the physical objects or actions which are the source to us of pleasures and pains. A very large part of the labour of any community is spent upon the production of the ordinary necessaries and conveniences of life, such as food, clothing, buildings, utensils, furniture, ornaments, etc.; and the aggregate of these things, therefore, is the immediate object of our attention . . . the term *utility* [will] denote the abstract quality whereby an object serves our purposes. Whatever can produce pleasure and prevent pain *may* possess utility. . . . The food which prevents the pangs of hunger, the clothes which fend off the cold of winter, possess incontestable utility; but we must beware of restricting the meaning of the word by any moral considerations. Anything which an individual is found to desire and to labour for must be assumed to possess for him utility.[3]

From there, Jevons went on to distinguish between the total utility of any commodity and the utility from various portions, or "increments," of a commodity. Adam Smith's paradox had existed partly because he had not specified the *quantities* of diamonds and water: in speaking of value in exchange, Smith could have been referring to a single diamond, while in extolling the value of water in use, he obviously meant more than a single, diamond-sized drop. It was important, therefore, to specify the number of units in the commodity: water, for instance, might have a value in use because the amount was sufficient to supply drinking and toilet facilities for a city. Different kinds of uses for a commodity could be distinguished: water, for example, might be available for drinking, bathing, irrigation, landscaping, and so on. Thus both the quantity and the type of use would have to be specified so as to separate total utility from the *increase* in utility provided by an increase in consumption.

Jevons, who was primarily interested in successive quantities of the same product with the same use, invented the term "final degree of utility . . . the degree of utility of the last addition, or the next possible addition of a very small, or infinitely small quantity to the existing stock."[4] This introduced the law of diminishing utility, which states in brief that the "final degree of utility" decreases as the commodity increases in quantity. Successive analyses have refined these two ideas, yet they remain central to the process of consumer choice. For, if people receive decreasing amounts of utility or satisfaction from an item as they increase their consumption of it, they will look to other alternatives, which may provide more utility. This reasoning calls to mind the empirical evidence of the preceding chapter, which showed the levels at which consumers shift from seeking "more and more" to seeking "better and better." Furthermore, the law of diminishing utility can be generalized to provide a complete solution of the problem of economic choice and thereby to show how a consumer disposes of his total income. Jevons reached only a first approximation in his observation that "a person distributes his income in such a way as to equalize the utility of the final increments of all the commodities consumed."[5] That statement is insufficient in that it does not refer to income: it is not the utility of equal increments of a commodity, but of equal sums spent on a commodity or service, that matters to the consumer.

Jevons' "final degree of utility" was a forerunner of the concept of marginal utility, which was developed by Carl Menger. He surpassed Jevons in his appreciation of all the implications of utility; he also went beyond Smith, who had called consumption the sole end and purpose of all production. For Menger showed that the value of *every* economic thing—including raw materials, capital, patents, and human services—depends on the utility it can produce for the consumer.[6] He pointed out that the same good might supply different consumer wants (the various uses for water given above, for example), that such wants differ in importance, and that, in any case, the amount of satisfaction varies with the amount of consumption. "Not only do our specific kinds of wants, and accordingly their satisfactions, differ in importance, but our satisfaction of a particular want will be more or less complete as the quantity of goods available to meet it is greater or smaller. A little food preserves life, more food insures health, and additional quantities bring amenities, but to a decreasing extent, until a point of satiation is reached."[7]

Although he had stated the law of diminishing utility, Menger did not expand it into a complete solution of the consumer's economic problem, but instead remarked that man's economic behavior consisted of "weighing of the different importances of wants, the choice between those which remain unsatisfied and those which, *according to the available means,* get satisfied, and the determination of the degree to which these latter wants get satisfied."[8]

Like Menger, the American economist John Bates Clark recognized different types of wants and their relative importance. Calling the concept of final utility too narrow, Clark pointed out that most strictly defined commodities have so few uses that the utility of successive quantities of the identical product approaches zero almost immediately. If, he reasoned, the *type* of product can be varied, the notion of a diminishing, but still positive, utility becomes more reasonable:

Coats of one kind bestowed on a man, one after another, soon lose their power to benefit him. The fourth may be of so little use that a tramp can have it for the asking. Duplicate copies of the same book or of the same picture encumber the shelves and walls, and their room is better than their presence. Very abrupt, in short, is the descent of the "utility curve" which, in graphic representation, expresses the lessening services that successive units of things of exactly the same kind are capable of rendering. Vary the articles in kind, and you have a different result. Change the weight, the color and the cut of successive coats, and the man will be glad to have more than four of them. . . . Clothing in general, not confined to garments of any kind, shows a utility curve descending gradually. . . . The first generalization to be made [of the law of diminishing utility] consists in applying the law, not to single articles, but to consumers' wealth in all its forms.[9]

With this argument, Clark distinguished *marginal* from *final* utility, "the last increment which has been consumed, or . . . the next increment which is about to be consumed," as Jevons had put it.[10] The concept of final utility seems to imply that there are successive quantities which the consumer adds, over time, to what he already has. But the difference in consumers' choices is rarely purely additive: a wealthy man does not own ten shanties and the poor man one; the rich man's house contains the same element of shelter as does the shanty, and much more beyond, up to "the final increment of his consumers' wealth":

It is clear that what is called a "final" unit of consumers' wealth is not the one secured last in point of time. In the case of the house in our illustration, the first and the last increments of consumers' wealth were bought at the same time, and so were all the intermediate increments. This, moreover, is the usual rule.[11]

Since nearly all commodities contain a "bundle" of utilities—different characteristics, which fulfill different wants—each of these might appeal to a separate consumer. In that case, the utility that actually rules is not "final," in Jevons' sense, but "marginal," in the sense that some quality in the commodity will appeal to the marginal purchaser.

Make watches dearer than they are, and the man who pays a hundred dollars for a watch will not go without one. He will buy one that formerly sold for ninety dollars, and will forego something in the way of ornamentation. Another class will take the grade that lately sold for eighty dollars, and will forego something in the way of accuracy. Each class will give up, not watches, but something in watches. A certain class that formerly bought dollar watches will, however, give them up altogether, since there is no cheaper pocket timepiece to be had. To these men the lowest grade of watches, taken in their entirety, may be rated as final utilities.[12]

Clark emphasized that the law of diminishing utility was one example of the general law of diminishing returns, which he elevated to a principle of transcendent importance, but his discussion confused the precise statement of this law with an explanation of why it holds.

The idea that successive units of the same commodity provide less utility may seem intuitively acceptable to most people, after they have been contemplating an endless parade of identical pairs of shoes, copies of the dictionary, or pieces of pie. But many people just as intuitively dismiss the law as simply irrelevant to a world in which no such monotonous increase in limited fare appears. The historical development of a common consumption pattern in this country has stressed the broadening of choice: more variety available in food, clothing, house furnishings, recreation, and so on. And the increase in variety has been eagerly welcomed by consumers. Economists recognized almost immediately a pervasive human want for variety: not for more and more of the same thing, but for better quality and for different products. The same choice of variety helps establish the minimum quantities for a "modest but acceptable" consumption level, the point at which, as the BLS puts it, the drive for more and more gives way to a drive for better and better. "Better," to both nineteenth-century theorists and twentieth-century statisticians, means "different." Adam Smith wrote that economic development would increase consumption above a subsistence level, but with *different* articles, either manufactured in cities or imported from abroad. Senior wrote of one of the "most powerful principles of human nature, the love of variety."

> The mere necessaries of life are few and simple. . . . But no man is satisfied with so limited a range of enjoyment. His first object is to vary his food; but this desire, though urgent at first, is more easily satisfied than any other, except perhaps that of dress. . . . Last come the desire to build, to ornament, and to furnish: tastes which are absolutely insatiable where they exist, and seem to increase with every improvement in civilization. . . . It is obvious . . . that our desires do not aim so much at quantity as at diversity. . . .[13]

It follows from this law, of course, that any *one* "taste" or want, or desire, can be fully satisfied. So the Law of Satiable Wants (so christened by Marshall, but sometimes called Gossens' First Law, after its original formulator) is the proof for the law of diminishing utility.

This insatiable craving for variety and differences in quality interested Clark more than the differences in quantity that could be analyzed with the theory of marginal utility. He did not provide a complete solution to the consumer's economic problem. But he insisted that only the individual consumer could judge utility to himself, and stressed that consumers continually compared utilities in coming to a decision on choice:

It is the users of an article who can best gauge the well-being that it gives them, and they make this estimate continually. Shall I buy this article? Will the paying for it trench on my income and make me go without something that is of greater importance? Is this article or some other of equal cost the more desirable? Such comparisons of services rendered by different articles are going on in the minds of the many consumers who constitute the purchasing public.[14]

Other economists helped to develop the marginal utility theory, and it may be that Edgeworth, Wicksteed, and Walras actually deserve more attention on that account than that which has been given here to Jevons and Clark. An exhaustive history of economic thought is not needed to realize how early significant concepts originated: utility, incremental or marginal, and the inviolability of an individual's estimate of utility or compared benefits. The utility solution was most completely stated in Alfred Marshall's *Principles of Economics,* which secured for it widespread acceptance. But Marshall, like his predecessors, was not specializing in consumption analysis; he needed a theory of consumer choice in order to explain market demand and to develop equilibrium analysis, which would show how resources were allocated and production carried on. In his *Principles,* Marshall began with the law of diminishing utility, translated it into market demand, discussed price elasticity, and posed various statistical problems before stating either the central problem of consumer's choice or its solution.

Eventually, it appears. "If a person has a thing which he can put to several uses, he will distribute it among these uses in such a way that it has the same marginal utility in all."[15] This succinct phrasing is then elaborated into a specific description of the choices a consumer has in spending his income:

When commodities have become very numerous and highly specialized, there is an urgent need for the free use of money, or general purchasing power; for that alone can be applied easily in an unlimited variety of purchases. And in a money economy, good management is shown by so adjusting the margins of suspense on each line of expenditure that the marginal utility of a shilling's worth of goods on each line shall be the same. And this result each one will attain by constantly watching to see whether there is anything on which he is spending so much that he would gain by taking a little away from that line of expenditure and putting it on some other line.

Thus, for instance, the clerk who is in doubt whether to ride to town, or to walk and have some little extra indulgence at his lunch, is weighing against one another the (marginal) utilities of two different modes of spending his money. And when an experienced housekeeper urges on a young couple the importance of keeping accounts carefully, a chief motive of the advice is that they may avoid spending impulsively a great deal of money on furniture and other things; for though some quantity of these is really needful, yet when bought lavishly they do not give high (marginal) utilities in proportion to their cost. And when the young pair look over their year's budget at the end of the year, and find perhaps that it is necessary to curtail their expenditure somewhere, they compare the (marginal) utilities of different items, weighing the loss of utility that would result from taking away a pound's expenditure here, with that which they would lose by taking it away there: they strive to adjust their pairings down so that the aggregate loss of utility may be a minimum, and the aggregate of utility that remains to them may be a maximum.[16]

Note that this explanation, simply if not indeed laconically worded, relies on the law of diminishing utility and assumes that utility can be measured. The young couple has first to compare the utility potential of one item costing £ 1–0–0 with the utility of another. Since most consumer goods have different prices, the pair have further to calculate the weighted marginal utility of each purchase, multiplying the amount of satisfaction it offers by its price. Only in this way can the total utility of various consumption choices be compared to total income. Almost immediately, economists agreed that utility could not be measured in such terms, and worked out a second type of solution. Despite some recent experimental success, the problem of measurability still remains.

Marshall, however, used marginal utility analysis to derive an equilibrium solution to the consumer's basic economic problem: the question of choice. Lord Robbins' definition, quoted in the Introduction, can be restated in the three conditions that frame this problem for the consumer: the limits of his income, or "scarce means," the prices he must pay for each of the unlimited variety of goods and services and assets he can buy, and his own estimate of the utility to be gained from different quantities of each. These three conditions provide the most general statement of the consumer's economic problem. The empirical data in the previous chapter documented for various groups of families the actual spending and saving that disposed of their limited income. Whether or not such consumption patterns represented an equilibrium, however, is another question. A restatement of the last condition, that of estimating utility, leads to a different type of analysis, which also solves the problem of allocating income.

Maximizing Consumer Satisfaction

At the heart of this solution to the consumer's economic problem lies the freedom of consumer choice. Jevons had pointed out that anything the individual desired possessed utility to him, and Menger and Clark had reiterated that only the consumer could weigh one alternative against another. Although Marshall did not hesitate to dictate what people "ought" to spend money for, he recognized that the task of estimating the marginal utilities of two different kinds of spending could be performed only by the spender. The model of consumer choice assumes that the consumer knows what he wants, what is best for him, what is useful, what will bring him satisfaction.

The modern statement that consumers have such knowledge avoids the problem of measuring the amount of satisfaction or utility involved, by assuming that consumers know which of two situations they would prefer. Given two choices —for example, going to the theater or playing bridge—each individual could state whether he prefers bridge to the theater, or theater to bridge, or finds them equally attractive. In the last case, he is indifferent between the two choices. Such preferences can then be graphed by means of *indifference curves*, which illuminate the consumer's economic problem and its various solutions.

When the analysis is applied to consumer choices, the model assumes two commodities whose quantities can be so varied as to provide different combinations of both. Figures 1 through 4 use indifference curves for frozen corn and frozen beans; a housewife planning family meals for a week is the consumer whose choice problem will be analyzed. Figure 1 shows the family preferences—of which the housewife is aware—for different quantities of the two vegetables measured along the two axes. Lines I^1, I^2, I^3, and I^4 represent successively "better," more preferable, situations; each line taken separately describes combinations among which the family has no preference, to which the housewife is *indifferent*. The lowest indifference curve, I^1, discloses that 4 boxes of corn and 2 of beans would be "just as good as" 2 boxes of corn and 4½ of beans and the family "would just as soon have" 7 boxes of corn and 1 of beans as either of the other two combinations. These points occur on a curve, I^1, which also locates a number of other combinations which the family likes equally well, or is equally indifferent to: 12 packages of corn and half a package

Figure 1. Indifference Curves

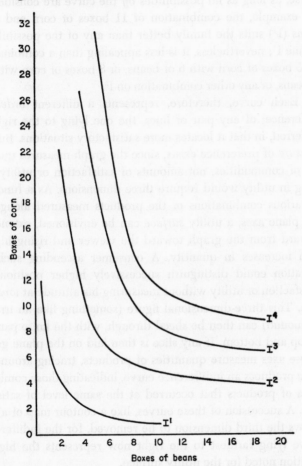

of beans, 3 boxes of corn and 3 of beans. All these possibilities, however, are less preferred than any in the set described by line I², a "higher" indifference curve. And any combination shown on I³ is preferable to any possibility on I². The various combinations *on* each I curve are equally satisfactory, of course, as long as no possibilities *off* the curve are considered. For example, the combination of 11 boxes of corn and 4 of beans (I^2) suits the family better than any of the possibilities on line I^1; nevertheless, it is less appealing than a combination of 15 boxes of corn with 6 of beans, or 8 boxes of corn with 11 of beans, or any other combination on I^3.

Each curve, therefore, represents a different *order* of preference; of any pair of lines, the one lying to the right is preferred, in that it locates more satisfactory situations. But no *measure* of preference exists, since the graph measures quantities of commodities, not amounts of satisfaction or utility. To bring in utility would require three dimensions. As a function of various combinations of the products measured along the two plane axes, a utility *surface* can be envisioned, extending upward from the graph toward the viewer and rising higher with increases in quantity. A consumer ascending such an elevation could distinguish successively higher positions of satisfaction or utility without measuring his altitude at any one spot. This three-dimensional figure (something like an irregular mound) can then be sliced through, with the knife parallel to top and bottom. If any slice is then laid on the plane graph whose axes measure quantities of products, tracing around its edge produces an indifference curve, indicating those combinations of products that occurred at the same level of satisfaction. A succession of these curves, like a contour map of a hill, allows the third dimension to be removed, for the indifference curve lying farthest to the right now represents the highest position noted for the utility surface.

Indifference curves are easily understood when they describe two items that can be substituted for each other; in the examples, corn and beans are both vegetables in the general category of food, theater and bridge both offer recreation. Expenditure data show that consumers do shift choices within such general categories. The shape of the curve traces the extent to which the consumer finds the two products substitutable; since this is a separate decision for each individual, indifference curves may vary in shape from person to person. They depend on the consumer's individual tastes and preferences.

The curves on Figures 1 through 4 are concave to the origin, meaning that the family's willingness to substitute corn for beans depends on the quantities of each product involved. Each combination on any one curve is equally satisfactory to any other combination on the same curve, for changing from point to point means substituting a quantity of one vegetable for a quantity of the other. The *rate* at which corn is substituted for beans (and vice versa) changes along the length of any one curve. In general, the larger the quantity of one product, the more of it the consumer is willing to give up in order to gain an increase in another product.

For example, Curve I[1] shows that, if the family is offered 4 boxes of corn and 2 of beans, it will be equally pleased with 3 boxes of corn and 3 of beans. In this case, the consumer substitutes corn for beans in a 1 to 1 ratio: getting one extra package of beans is worth giving up one box of corn and vice versa. But such a 1 to 1 ratio of substitution does not prove equally satisfactory everywhere along the curve, where different quantities of the two products are at stake. When only 2 boxes of corn and 5 of beans are contemplated, the family will not substitute the two products in this 1 to 1 ratio: getting one extra package of beans is not worth giving up a box of corn, when this box represents half the total corn consumption possible. While 9 boxes of beans and 1 of corn are "just as good as" 2 of corn and 5 of beans, this means that 4 extra packages of beans have been substituted for a single box of corn. Curve I[2] provides more examples of the same phenomenon. The family is indifferent between a combination of 5 boxes of beans with 8 of corn and 7 packages of beans with 6 of corn: getting 2 extra boxes of beans is worth giving up 2 boxes of corn and vice versa. But when only 4 boxes of beans are in view, accompanied by 11 of corn, it takes more corn to compensate for the loss of beans: a position of equal satisfaction on Curve I^2 calls for 16 packages of corn and 3 of beans, since the two products are not substituted in a 1 to 1 ratio.

Substitution ratios can be calculated for successive points on any indifference curve: the amount of corn the family is willing to give up for a given quantity of beans is small when the combination involves small amounts of corn, and much greater when the amount of corn relative to beans is larger. The ratios change as the slope of the indifference curve changes; Table 1 locates some points on the four indifference curves and gives calculated substitution ratios for both corn and beans between these points. Note that these are not ratios of the absolute quantities involved: the first rate shows that 3 boxes of corn (the difference between 7 and 4) will be substituted for 1 of beans (the difference between 1 and 2), giving a ratio of 3:1 or 1:3. These are, therefore, *marginal rates of substitution*. They enable a quantitative measure of consumer tastes and preferences.

Whatever the products or absolute amounts involved, consumer preferences generally indicate marginal rates of substitution which decrease as the amount of one product increases. The explanation is the desire for variety—just as the Law of Satiable Wants explains diminishing marginal utility. For example, curve I^4 suggests that a combination of 24 packages of corn and 6 of beans is equally satisfactory to one of 18 boxes of corn and 7 of beans because giving up 6 boxes of corn to obtain the increase in variety offered by an extra package of beans is not a great sacrifice. Exactly the reverse is true, however, when the combination contains many packages of beans and only a few of corn.

Table 1

Points of Equal Satisfaction and the Substitution Rates
Between Them

| Curve | Combination | | Substitution Ratio | |
	Corn	Beans	Corn for Beans	Beans for Corn
	7	1		
			3:1	1:3
	4	2		
			1:1	1:1
I¹	3	3		
			1:3	3:1
	1	9		
	16	3		
			5:1	1:5
	11	4		
			3:1	1:3
	8	5		
			1:1	1:1
I²	6	7		
			1:3	3:1
	5	10		
	15	6		
			2:1	1:2
	9	9		
			1:2	2:1
I³	8	11		
			1:4	4:2
	7	15		
	24	6		
			6:1	1:6
	18	7		
			4:1	1:4
I⁴	14	8		
			2:1	1:2
	9	17		

143

Given the consumer's tastes and preferences, plotted by indifference curves, the other conditions framing the consumer choice problem are income, which is limited, and market prices, which must be paid. In a two commodity example, the data on prices and income have to be translated into quantities of the two products. Figure 2 superimposes an expenditure or outlay curve, which provides price and income data, on the indifference curves of Figure 1. "Income" in this case refers to the amount of purchasing power available for the two items. If beans cost 16¢ per package and corn 8¢ while the housewife has a total of $1.44 per week to spend on frozen vegetables, these data define a *consumption possibility*, plotted as CC on the graph. It shows all the different combinations of frozen corn and beans that any given sum, representing the same expenditure or outlay, can buy. The slope of any such curve equals the ratio of the two prices—which reflects the consumer's position in the market, because prices to the individual are fixed no matter what quantities he buys. The intersection of the curve with the two axes measures the available income in "real" terms: $1.44 will buy *either* 9 packages of beans *or* 18 boxes of corn.

The consumer's problem is now completely stated in graphic terms; the object is to choose that combination of frozen corn and frozen beans which the family most prefers and is at the same time able to purchase.

To set out the problem this way is also to solve it. Five packages of beans and 8 of corn, at point E, is the consumer's choice. Here the outlay curve, CC, is tangent to I^2, which is the highest level of satisfaction within reach. This choice is preferable to any other combination within the housewife's means: all other points on CC lie below this indifference curve, I^2. And although the family would be more satisfied at any point on I^3, which is a higher indifference curve, its limited income, and the prices existing, described by the consumption-

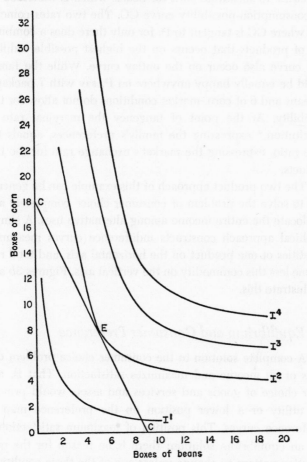

Figure 2. Consumption Possibilities

possibility curve CC, prevent the housewife from buying these larger quantities. The point can also be defined by the equality of two rates: the rate at which the family is willing to substitute corn for beans, which is described by the indifference curves, and the rate at which the family is able by purchases, to substitute corn for beans, which is described by the consumption-possibility curve CC. The two rates coincide only where CC is tangent to I², for only there does a combination of products that occurs on the highest possible indifference curve also occur on the outlay curve. While the family would be equally happy anywhere on I², say with 7 packages of beans and 6 of corn, market conditions do not allow for this possibility. At the point of tangency the marginal rate of substitution,* expressing the family's preferences, equals the price ratio, expressing the market's exchange rate for the two products.

The two-product approach of this example can be generalized to solve the problem of consumer choice completely and to allocate the entire income among alternative uses. A simple graphical approach constructs indifference curves measuring quantities of one product on the horizontal axis, and total real income less this commodity on the vertical axis. Figures 3*b* and 4*b* illustrate this.

Equilibrium and Consumer Preference

A complete solution to the consumer choice problem disposes of all income and maximizes satisfaction. That is, any other choice of goods and services and assets would provide less utility or a lower position on the preference map of indifference curves. This position of maximum satisfaction is also an equilibrium solution: there is no reason for the consumption pattern to change unless one of the three conditions

---

* Note that Table 1 does not give the marginal rate of substitution *at* the point where 5 boxes of beans and 8 of corn are chosen: the rates shown are for quantities larger and smaller than these amounts. Thus the marginal rate of substitution between a choice of 4 beans, 11 corn and a combination of 5 beans, 8 corn, is 1:3, while the marginal rate of substitution between the combination 5 beans, 8 corn and a choice of 7 beans, 6 corn is 1:1. Obviously, therefore, the market's rate of substitution, 1:2, lies *between* these points.

Figure 3. Income Changes

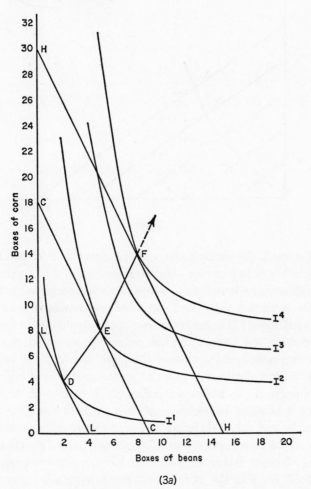

(3a)

that frame the original problem of choice changes. Indifference curves provide considerable insight into the effects of income changes and price changes on consumer choice.

Figure 3*a* reproduces the equilibrium solution developed

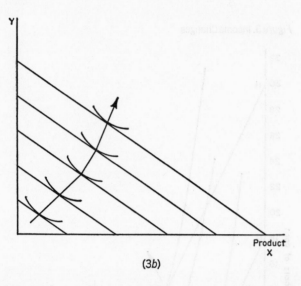

(3b)

in Figure 2; the outlay curve CC is tangent to I^2 at point E. Two other outlay curves are drawn on Figure 3 to represent two situations where income differs from that portrayed in CC, although market prices and consumer preferences remain unchanged. Line LL assumes that only 64¢ is available for frozen vegetables; the housewife must reduce consumption of corn and/or beans, but she chooses the point at which the family will be least displeased: point D on the next lowest indifference curve, I^1, to which the outlay curve is tangent. At that point, 2 boxes of beans and 4 of corn are both desirable and possible, and this is therefore preferred to any other combination on the consumption-possibility curve LL. In a situation of higher income, where the housewife has more money to spend on food, the sum she earmarks for frozen vegetables may rise to $2.40, as described by HH. How should she spend this new amount to best satisfy the family's preferences between corn and beans? By investigating indifference curve I^4, which shows that the family prefers 14 boxes of corn and 8 of beans, point F, to any other combination allowed by the line HH.

148

The 3 outlay curves are parallel because the price ratio of corn and beans does not change; it is differences in consumer *income* that make different quantities of consumption possible. Joining the 3 equilibrium points, D E F, traces an income-consumption curve which slopes upward from left to right: increased income makes possible increased quantities of frozen-vegetable consumption. The more general case is plotted on Figure 3*b*, where the horizontal axis represents quantities of one product, the vertical axis quantities of everything else. The income-consumption curve for most commodities slopes upward from left to right—provided the product has been carefully defined.

The theory jibes with the empirical findings of consumption studies: at higher incomes larger quantities will be purchased. The *amount* of consumption increase with increase of income varies among income levels. On Figure 3*a*, the income increase from LL to CC results in a greater rise in corn consumption than in beans; when income rises from CC to HH, the increase in corn consumption is even more marked. Figure 3*b* shows that higher incomes lead to more of X (hypothetical product), but that consumption increases at a decreasing rate, as compared to increases in the quantity of Y. Since the vertical axis and the quantities of Y represent all other goods and services available, this figure is actually another way of showing the principle of diminishing utility or the Law of Satiable Wants.

The movement along an income-consumption curve of this analytical model expresses a change from one equilibrium position to another, as the circumstances influencing the choice problem change. The same indifference map remains, since it records the preferences of the same consumer. It follows, therefore, that this analysis is conceptually quite different from the empirical findings of consumption studies, which can show choices at different income levels only by using data on the decisions of *different* consumers. For Figure 3, it is quite

Figure 4. Price Changes

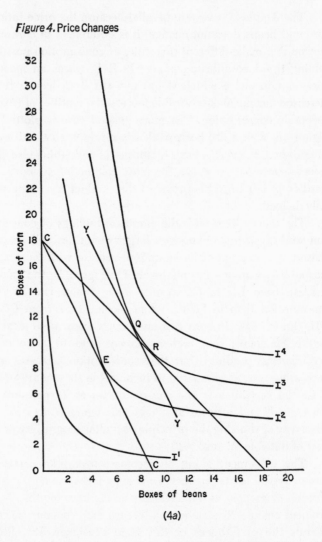

(4a)

proper to use dynamic terms: income *does* rise from LL to CC to HH, consumption *does* increase. But the figure uses only hypothetical data; to substitute figures obtained from survey

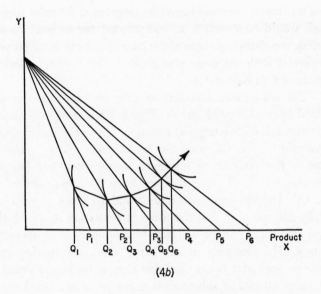

(4b)

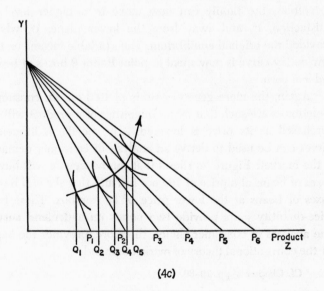

(4c)

151

data for frozen corn and bean consumption at different income levels would be incorrect, as was pointed out earlier.* Nevertheless, the changing slope of the income-consumption curve is concerned with the same phenomenon that income elasticity measures with survey data.

The consumer's equilibrium solution may also be disturbed by a change in prices. Figure 4 superimposes such a circumstance on the original situation. Given the consumption possibility curve CC and the indifference curves, point E remains the position of maximum satisfaction, but line CP describes a ratio of prices different from the one described by line CC. Income remains the same and 18 boxes of corn will totally dispose of it. But the price of beans has dropped; this same amount of income will now buy 18 boxes of beans rather than 9. The decrease in the price alters the market ratio between corn and beans, and this ratio is no longer equal to the marginal rate of substitution at the point described in the earlier choice. With the same $1.44 weekly allotted for frozen vegetables, the family can now move to a higher level of satisfaction, I^3, and away from the lower plane, I^2, which provided the original equilibrium. The available income on the new outlay curve is now spent at point R—for 9 boxes of beans and 9 of corn.

Again, the more general case is plotted on 4b; consumer preferences are such that larger quantities of a product will be purchased as its price is lowered. Any specific indifference curves can be used to derive an analysis of consumer demand in the market: Figure 4a shows that the housewife will buy 5 boxes of beans at a price of 16¢ per box and that she will buy 9 boxes of beans at the lower price of 8¢ per box. These two price-quantity pairs provide two points on a demand curve. The analysis of consumer choice, therefore, provides the basis for the conventional theory of market demand.

* Cf. Chapter 3, pp. 79–80.

In particular, it helps to explain price elasticity of demand. Figure 4c contrasts with 4b; both show the same income and the same price ratios. When the price of X is lowered, the new equilibrium positions involve larger quantities of X; when the price of Z is lowered, the new equilibrium positions involve larger quantities of Z. But the same decrease in price results in a greater increase of consumption of X than of Z. The demand curve for Z will be less elastic than for X.

This is the same notion of elasticity that was introduced in Chapter 3, but it now refers to price rather than to income. Price elasticity measures the change in consumption (as a percentage of total consumption) compared to the change in price (as a percentage of price). Indifference-curve analysis measures consumption in terms of quantities of products. When the increase in quantity consumed, as a percentage of the total quantity of the product consumed, exceeds the decrease in price, as a percentage of the price, elasticity will be greater than 1. A price elasticity of less than 1, or an inelastic demand, means that a price change will be accompanied by a smaller change in quantity consumed or demanded. Elasticity is often explained in terms of luxuries and necessities: salt is a "necessity," and therefore consumers will buy it even if there is a large increase in price; perfume is a luxury and therefore, if prices rise, consumers will decide they don't "need" it. But the previous chapters have emphasized the ambiguity of these terms; it is uncommon, perhaps, to think of cigarettes as a necessity like salt, yet the demand for each is highly inelastic with respect to price.

The explanation for price elasticity that is suggested by comparing Figures 4b and 4c depends completely on the tastes and preferences of the individual consumer: the indifference curves for product Z are not identical with those for product X. But price elasticity can be further analyzed.

A change in price where income and preferences do not

change resembles a change in consumer income. In Figure 4a, when the price of beans drops the housewife can buy as many beans as she did in the first case defined by CC, but with less money. (Note that the equilibrium on CC represents 5 boxes of beans; at the lower price of 8¢ a box, this takes only 40¢ of the housewife's food budget, not 80¢.) She has, therefore "extra" income, which she may or may not decide to spend on "extra" beans. The *income effect* of the price change is shown by line YY. The change in price, represented by the new consumption possibility curve PC, enabled the family to reach a higher indifference curve, I³, from that allowed by the former price ratio. This plane of satisfaction might also have been reached with an increase of income, as shown on Figure 3. If so, the outlay curve, parallel to the original CC, would have included the segment YY which is tangent to I³. If, therefore, the new level of satisfaction had been reached with increased income, a combination of corn and beans would have been chosen which would be different from the choice that was made when the price of beans decreased. For YY is tangent to I³ at point Q; PC is tangent at point R. What does this mean?

At the original equilibrium solution, E, the housewife chose 8 packages of corn and 5 of beans; at R, 9 packages of each. But if there had been more money to spend—the hypothetical income increase of YY—the family would have asked for fewer beans and more corn: point Q represents a choice of 11 boxes of corn, not 9, and only 7½ boxes of beans. The income effect of the price change, therefore, increases bean consumption by 2½ boxes: at point Q, 7½ boxes of beans are chosen, rather than the 5 purchased at point E. The total increase in bean consumption which results from the price change is, however, greater than this. With a change in price ratio a marginal rate of substitution holds that is different from the one that would have been obtained with a change in income, and beans are substituted for corn. The combination of 9 boxes of each is equally satisfactory to the family as the combination of 11 corn and 7½ beans—both points, R and Q, lie on the same indifference curve. The *substitution effect* of the price change, therefore, increases bean consumption by 1½ boxes—the shift from point Q, allowing 7½ boxes of beans, to point R, calling for 9 boxes of beans, represents the family's willingness to substitute beans for corn.

Because any price change contains an income effect, and because, in general, consumption increases as income increases, a drop in price will allow the consumer to choose more of the product. The income-effect of a price change will, of course, differ for various products; it can be predicted when the income-consumption curve for a product is known, as in Figure 3, or if empirical studies of income elasticity exist. Empirical findings tell much about income effects: for instance, Chapter 3 noted that expenditures at higher incomes were greater for both food and clothing, but the increase in spending for clothing exceeded that for food. The income-elasticity measure calculated for clothing was greater than that for food. It follows that, *other things being equal,* a given percentage price change in clothing will affect clothing expenditure more than a like price change in food will affect food expenditure.

The substitution effect of a price change also differs among products. Consumers' preferences are not such that consumers will exchange one product for a second in the same ratio as they will exchange that same product for a third. Consequently, the two impacts—the income effect and the substitution effect—may lead to quite different increases in consumption for two products whose prices change in exactly the same way—as Figures 4b and 4c demonstrate. In short, consumer preferences for spending increased income, and for substituting one product for another, determine the elasticity of demand with respect to price.

This type of analysis also adds to the understanding of

CONSUMER CHOICE IN THE AMERICAN ECONOMY

necessities. The Bureau of Labor Statistics' "adequate" level of subsistence* (the real-income level beyond which an increase in income goes to quality and variety rather than to larger quantities) occurs on an income-consumption diagram when the curve begins to slope upward; in Figure 3b, this is after the third outlay curve shown. On the other hand, necessities may also imply a lack of substitutability: a change in the price ratio between two products may not lead to any substitution of one for the other. A decrease in the price of drugs will not cause consumers to use drugs instead of food, even though the income effect may enable more consumers to use drugs. Again, it is consumer preferences that determine the amount of substitutability, and therefore an objective definition of necessities is impossible. Only from consumer behavior, from consumer preference as revealed in their spending patterns, can clues to the nature of necessity and luxury be gleaned. No data have yet been found to "plug into" the model, and therefore consumer choices can be described only after they have taken place. It is this that justifies the use of expenditure data to calculate income and price elasticity of demand.

Changes in Consumer Preferences

There is no "preference-consumption curve" that shows how, with given income and prices, changes in preferences cause different consumption choices. But during the years when economists were gradually developing the formal analysis of consumer choice, they made some scattered observations about consumer tastes and preferences, some of which are surprisingly relevant to current thinking.

The terms "luxury" and "necessity" caused just as much

* Cf. Chap. 3, pp. 97–99.

trouble to early theorists as they did to the social workers who tried to define minimum needs, and the power of custom and tradition was recognized by Adam Smith as well as by LePlay and Engel. In *The Wealth of Nations,* Smith wrote, "Every man is rich or poor according to the degree in which he can afford to enjoy the necessaries, conveniences, and amusements of human life,"[17] and in discussing taxation he distinguished luxuries from these "necessaries," which he said included "not only the commodities which are indispensably necessary for the support of life, but whatever the custom of the country renders it indecent for creditable people, even of the lowest order, to be without."[18] He did not give a similar definition for luxuries, and was careful to say that tobacco, liquor, coffee, chocolate, tea, and sugar were only what *he* called luxuries.

John Rae, a Canadian whose first work was published in 1834, looked to human behavior for an understanding of luxury, and found it in vanity. He defined luxury as

the expenditure occasioned by the passion of vanity . . . the mere desire of superiority over others, without any reference to the merit of that superiority. . . . The things to which vanity seems most readily to apply itself are those to which the use or consumption is most apparent, and of which the effects are most difficult to discriminate. Articles of which the consumption is not conspicuous, are incapable of gratifying this passion.[19]

Vanity, Rae thought, was such a powerful influence that consumers whose income increased would spend more money on luxuries so that their total expenditures would still take the same share of their greater wealth.

The quotation clearly foreshadows Thorstein Veblen, the coiner of such discomfortingly critical terms as "pecuniary emulation" and "vicarious leisure." These, he thought, rather than "needs," formed consumer choice (and were also responsible for the position of women, the study of dead languages, and the pervading influence of fashion). But Veblen was always careful to isolate his discussion of consumer tastes from the analysis of consumer choice:

Throughout the entire evolution of conspicuous expenditure, whether of goods or of services or human life, runs the obvious implication that in order to effectually mend the consumer's good fame it must be an expenditure of superfluities. In order to be reputable it must be wasteful. No merit would accrue from the consumption of the bare necessaries of life, except by comparison with the abjectly poor who fall short even of the subsistence minimum; and no standard of expenditure could result from such a comparison, except the most prosaic and unattractive level of decency. . . .

The use of the term "waste" . . . is not to be taken in an odious sense, as implying an illegitimate expenditure of human products or of human life. In the view of economic theory the expenditure in question is no more and no less legitimate than any other expenditure. . . . Whatever form of expenditure the consumer chooses, or whatever end he seeks in making his choice, has utility to him by virtue of his preference. As seen from the point of view of the individual consumer, the question of wastefulness does not arise within the scope of economic theory proper.[20]

Oddly enough, this conscientious distinction of analysis from value judgments was ignored by Alfred Marshall, despite the fact that he wrote perhaps the most complete and careful exposition of the theory of consumer choice. He larded his technical analysis with opinions, not a few of which unabashedly explained how consumers *should* spend their income. Thus:

When the necessaries of life are once provided, everyone should seek to increase the beauty of things in his possession rather than their number or magnificence. An improvement in the artistic character of furniture and clothing trains the higher faculties of those who make them, and is a source of growing happiness to those who use them.[21]

Marshall's followers were more careful with their admonitions, and modern expositions of the theory of consumer choice make it clear that "the economist *studies* the choices, he does not judge them."[22] Although the economist uses consumer preferences as basic data, the preferences themselves "he cannot question and must accept as given."[23] Contemporary economists also admit the powerful influence of custom and social usage. "It is impossible to understand the wants of the individual without knowing the society within which he lives, for all of his specific wants are determined by that society. One wears a necktie because that is done in his society. Even the iconoclast has his images chosen for him."[24]

But the traditional theory of consumer choice includes implicit assumptions about the formation of wants. One of these involves the unit of analysis. The examples presented in this chapter describe the choice problem that confronts a housewife as she makes decisions on behalf of her family. The conventional unit of analysis in survey data is either the household or the single individual, but in theoretical analysis the economist has not attempted to identify whether "the consumer" is husband, wife, child, or family. The identity of the consumer, however, clearly affects the shape and position of the indifference curves—those indications of wants and preferences that are basic to the choice problem. For obvious reasons, the question of "who decides" is vital to firms that compete in consumer markets, and research on this point depends more on their empirical investigations than on theoretical analysis.

A more troubling problem arises from the model's assumption of freedom of choice. However "the consumer" is defined, the problem of choice remains an individual, particular one for each choice-maker. Preference maps may be influenced by society, but the formation of wants, whether influenced or not, occurs outside economic activity. Each consumer is free to make his own economic decisions, to allocate his specific income as he chooses among goods and services. Implicit in this reasoning is the idea that consumer preference is independent of the *economic* behavior of others, although it may be subject to social custom or usage.

James Duesenberry, in *Income, Saving, and the Theory of Consumer Behavior,* argues that most observation leads to exactly the opposite conclusion and that consumer preferences are interdependent. Such a statement does more than reinforce the homage paid to custom and social usage by all the writers from Smith to Stigler. For Duesenberry claims that there is general agreement in a society, not only on the specific things used to fulfill consumers' needs, but also on the relative desirability of these things:

(1) Physical needs and the activities required by the culture require the consumption of certain kinds of goods . . . ; (2) each of the needs, whether physically or socially generated, can be satisfied by any of a number of qualitatively different types of goods; (3) these different types of goods, or, in the broader sense, ways of doing things, are regarded as superior or inferior to one another; (4) there is a generally agreed-upon scale of ranks for the goods which can be used for any specific purpose.[25]

A severe limitation on the freedom of consumer choice here appears: the individual consumer can vary only the *quality* of the goods and services he uses.

In terms of indifference-curve analysis, this means that there are not as many preference maps as there are consumer units, since people resemble one another in their tastes and preferences. The same preference map will exist for large groups of people, who can be described in terms of age, occupation, social status, family size, education, and so on. These, of course, are the familiar household characteristics referred to in consumption surveys. Because spending habits have been learned from the behavior of such groups, the decision-making process set out by the formal analysis simply does not apply to a large part of the consumption pattern.

Figure 5 helps to clarify the issues here. 5*a* describes

A Model of Consumer Choice

Figure 5. Preference Changes

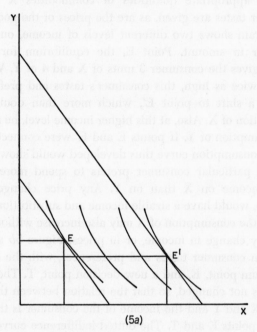

(5a)

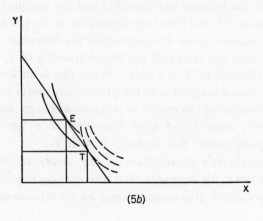

(5b)

two equilibrium situations for a consumer who is faced with choosing appropriate quantities of commodities X and Y. Consumer tastes are given, as are the prices of the goods, but the diagram shows two different levels of income, one twice the other in amount. Point E, the equilibrium for a low income, gives the consumer 3 units of X and 4 of Y. With an income twice as high, this consumer's tastes and preferences indicate a shift to point E', which more than doubles his consumption of X. Also, at this higher income level, he reduces his consumption of Y. If points E and E' were connected, the income-consumption curve thus developed would show clearly that this particular consumer prefers to spend more of his higher income on X than on Y. Any price change in X, therefore, would have a sizable income and substitution effect.

But the consumption of X may also increase without there being any change in income, or in prices. Figure 5b shows a change in consumer tastes and preferences, with the original equilibrium point, E, and a new decision point, T. The outlay curve has not changed, so that the relation between the price ratio of X and Y and the income of the consumer is the same for both points E and T. The dotted indifference curves show an alteration in the consumer's preference map. For some reason, Y has become less desirable and the marginal rate of substitution of X and Y no longer conforms to the price ratio at point E. Instead, point T indicates that the consumer is better satisfied with less than half the former quantity of Y, and his income diverted to X as a result. While this is an interesting exercise, such a diagram does not provide any useful analytical tool for predicting the results of preference change, insofar as, in general, there is no clear indication of a "preference-consumption curve" that connects E with T.

Duesenberry's contribution to the theory of consumer behavior lies in his suggestion that such changes in preferences can be predicted. If consumers agree on the relative desirability of goods to fulfill the same purpose, then there does exist a clear ranking of different goods. Thus, in 5a, when the consumer more than doubles his consumption of X as his income doubles, he reflects the consensus of society that more of X is preferable to more of Y. Now if 5b represents a different consumer, it is possible to predict that he too, *without* any change in income, will consume more of X. For this to happen requires only that he be exposed to a new consumption pattern, and gain direct knowledge of the ranking generally given to different goods:

For any particular family the frequency of contact with superior goods will increase primarily as the consumption expenditures of others increase. . . . We might call this the "demonstration effect." People believe that the consumption of high-quality goods for any purpose is desirable and important. If they habitually use one set of goods, they can be made dissatisfied with them by a demonstration of the superiority of others.[26]

The reason for the shift of indifference curves shown in 5b now becomes clear: it resulted from the exposure to consumption expenditures at a higher income level, which demonstrate the preferability of X to Y. These may be choices of a neighbor, a fellow-employee, another member of the Couples' Club, or a familiar frequenter of the same store. Any of these social groupings, and many others, provide the areas in which the demonstration effect can take place.

The argument implies that consumer income plays two roles. Along with past savings and the ability to contract new debt, money income provides the purchasing power of "scarce means" that the consumer uses to carry through his choices. In relative terms, as compared with the incomes of other consumers, income describes social status. Consumption expenditures can be analyzed for different families classified by their rank in an income distribution, and this then becomes a useful tool for predicting consumption choices. The indifference

curves that were drawn as basic data on Figure 1 thereafter fit into this part of the analysis. The choice combinations
lying to the right of the diagram are said to be preferable to
those lying to the left because they include more of both
possible choices—larger quantities of both X and Y, whatever
these represent. The income-consumption curve slopes to the
right because with higher incomes consumers seek more. The
historical developments reviewed in Chapter 1 provide the
facts on what this "more" means in the United States economy:
the emergence of a common pattern of consumption with less
regional variation and fewer obvious differences between income classes seems to lend support to the Duesenberry hypothesis that there is an accepted "ranking" of goods and
services.

But survey data show that wide variations in consumption
choice persist, and even multivariate analysis, after sorting out
all the influences of family size, education, occupation, and so
on, still leaves a large unexplained area, labeled "consumer
tastes and preferences." And the warnings in the previous
chapter about the pitfalls in using cross-sectional data to
predict consumption choice bear reiteration. The demonstration effect undoubtedly exists, but so does the craving for
variety. The effects of market competition have been to spread
more and more alternatives before the individual consumer,
making it less and less likely that identical, or even similar,
patterns of choice will occur.

chapter 5 The
Consumer
in the
Market

The formal analysis of the last chapter dealt with consumer choice, the decisions that allocate income among goods and services and forms of saving. Goods and services must be purchased before they can be consumed, and consumption expenditure is therefore different from consumption choice. In essence, the consumer must go to the market with his consumption choices; there they are the object of intense competition among sellers, each of whom wishes to convert the consumer's choice into expenditure.

Most relevant to consumer choice is the retail market. Most consumers buy the greatest part of their goods and services from retail outlets. Retailing is part of the distribution industry, which performs the function, in this context, of getting goods from producers to consumers. Such a specialized function exists only in a complex economy; where families live on what they themselves produce, or in a small, almost self-sufficient community, it is a simple matter for the consumer to obtain and use the output of farmland, mill, bake-oven, and loom. But most countries have organized markets for production and distribution; the United States is one instance of a "market economy." In retail stores, consumer choices become consumption expenditures: consumers make purchases. Defining distribution or retailing simply as an *industry*, therefore, overlooks the two-way relationship between sellers and consumer-buyers; what industry sells, consumers buy. If distribution is defined as the process of getting goods from producers to consumers, it may equally well be defined as the process of enabling consumers to receive goods from producers. To the consumer, shopping and buying is a process, and considering distribution in terms of this process is more enlightening than trying to fit it into a model for the analysis of industry. The link between consumers' choices and the market in which choices become expenditures consists of a process of distribution, or its mirror-image, the consumer buying-and-shopping process.

In this process, several distinct activities take place; they require distinct functions to be performed. Most analyses of consumer choice, such as the one in the previous chapter, assume that the individual knows the existing alternatives and their prices, as well as his own preferences. But acquiring information about the goods and services available is usually an important part of the shopping process. Sellers take active steps to provide such information; advertising, for example, is part of the distribution process. Once a decision to purchase has been reached, the consumer must inform the distributor; if he is to receive the particular product or service he must give an order in some way or other. If the seller is to distribute the particular product or service, he must learn of the consumer's choice; he takes an order. The consumer chooses, however, not only the item he has decided to buy, but also the seller he has decided to buy it from. Although in some cases (a particular "make" of automobile or cosmetics, an individual doctor or barber) the choice of *what* to buy may not be altogether separable from *where* to buy it, for broader types of choice and for myriad specific items the two are in fact different decisions. Another part of the consumer's buying process consists of paying for his purchase: the seller must arrange to receive payment. The consumer must take possession of the item, whether it is delivered to his person or to some location, including his home. The seller may provide transportation or assume responsibility for installation, but in any case he must give over the article to the buyer. Finally, an important part of the consumer's buying or shopping process appears *after* purchase, when the buyer refuses to keep the item or demands some recompense for his lack of satisfaction, and the seller carries out a warranty or evades responsibility.

For each part of the consumer shopping process, therefore, there is a corresponding function of distribution. These functions are basic to any system of distribution, however it is defined, but the task of performing them in the United States today is shared by manufacturers, retailers, and consumers in different ways for different goods. Economists have run into difficulties in the past in trying to analyze distribution as an industry that provides services—for example, defining retailing in terms of services to consumers such as credit, delivery, or installation. With such a definition retail margins are then compared to the costs of providing various services. But over the past 60 years the distribution process has evolved so many variations that it can no longer be described in such simple terms. Some of the "services" formerly provided by retailers have now been taken over by either the manufacturers or the consumers, and new "services" on the part of both retailers and manufacturers have allowed the consumer to escape some household chores. As new and different ways have appeared for the consumer to shop and to buy, they have changed the nature of competition among sellers in the market for consumption choices.

"The Merchandising Revolution"

At the turn of the century, 29 million workers were employed in the United States; 2½ million of them were in wholesale and retail trade. The goods these latter moved sold to consumers for $8.4 billion, and amounted to slightly over half the Gross National Product. In 1965, Personal Consumption Expenditures on goods totaled $254 billion and 12.6 million people, 17.5 per cent of total civilian employment, worked in wholesaling and retailing. Adjusting for price changes,[1] the output of consumer goods today is 7 times that of the earlier date; employment in distribution has also increased, but the volume of goods handled per worker has risen much more. Harold Barger's more refined calculations suggest that output per man hour in distribution rose 78 per cent from 1899 to 1949.[2] With the growth of employment and productivity came changes in the ways consumers shopped and purchased, as radical as the changes in the goods they bought. Manufacturing, transportation, and wholesaling also altered dramatically over this period, but consumers are chiefly concerned with retailing.

Sixty-five years ago the typical retailer was a small independent store: the general store, in a small town or in the country; more specialized retailers, in urban areas. The number of stores and the particular lines of goods they carried were a direct function of population and the size of the market. In scattered areas of the country, particularly in the Midwestern and South Central states, the mail-order catalogue offered some alternative choices to those found in isolated general stores. In a few large cities, pioneering department stores threatened the existence of the small shops; in smaller localities at the same time, the local dry-goods merchant might be experimenting with the metamorphosis into a department store. Stores that had been organized into chains sold groceries, drugs, jewelry, and variety goods, but only in a few areas.

To analyze retailing requires basic data: the number, size, and type of stores for different market areas, and the different numbers of consumers or families they contain. No such information was collected prior to the early '30s; the dearth of earlier statistics on retail trade was deplored by contemporary observers.[3] The data on consumer spending patterns reviewed in Chapter 1 seem oddly flat without any parallel information on where, and how, consumers obtained the goods they did. The early history of retailing relies on anecdotal reminiscences, a few scholarly monographs analyzing the growth of a handful of firms that prospered sufficiently for the details of their survival to be recorded, and descriptive material culled from biographies, town reports, and trade papers.

It is generally accepted that colonial America was served by peddlers, general stores, and the shops of craftsmen and importers. During the nineteenth century, the growth in population and industrial production led to the development of rapidly growing centers of trade, in the new settlements as well as in the older-established areas along the Eastern seaboard. The larger markets encouraged increased specialization; in distribution, this took two forms. First, firms selling both at wholesale and retail gave up one or the other operation; individual sellers became identified as importers, or as jobbers, or as retailers. Second, many retail firms became specialty shops instead of general merchants. They carried fewer lines of goods, but a larger inventory in each. Thus, dealers in dry goods began to specialize in men's furnishings or in millinery, and in the food line butchers, bakers, fruit stores, fish stores, fancy grocers, tea and coffee merchants made their appearance, to supply the consumer with greater variety.

For the country as a whole, quantitative data illustrating these trends are nonexistent. But local evidence of a pattern that later on developed generally can be found in the earliest census of retail trade ever taken: that of Massachusetts in 1905. In that period, the country as a whole was shifting from an economy based primarily on agriculture to one based on industry. In Massachusetts, industrial development was more advanced, yet the shift from a farm economy was far from complete. The Commonwealth's population of 3 million lived in 33 incorporated cities and 326 towns. The cities and larger towns were concentrated in the manufacturing centers of the east and in the Springfield-Holyoke area along the Connecticut River in the west. Throughout the state there were isolated rural areas, small towns and country villages that were built around farms. The details for different areas are sufficient to document the effects of urbanization and growing markets on retailing.

The Census of Trade for 1905 counted some 29,000 "establishments" in Massachusetts, with a total invested capital of $288,000,000. Of these, 24,522 were retailers, whose sales totaled $445,000,000, and 3,315 were wholesalers, with sales of $510,000,000. The remainder were classified as jobbers, commission dealers, or in export-import trade. Many firms combined retail operations with one or more types of wholesaling, so that much of the census data fails to distinguish between the two levels of sales.

With some adjustments, most of the wholesale sales can

be excluded from the data. Thirty-three cities accounted for 97 per cent of the wholesale trade in the state, and in half the counties the cities included 90 to 100 per cent of wholesale sales. In 4 of the remaining counties there were no cities; wholesale trade here amounted to less than one-half of 1 per cent of the state's total. In each of the other three counties, there was only one city, and several towns as large; wholesale trade for the county as a whole amounted to less than 5 per cent of the figure for the state. Exporters, importers, and export-importers were listed only in Boston, while 98 per cent of the jobbing sales occurred in only 14 cities and 99 per cent of the commission business was confined to 12. It is safe to assume, therefore, that most of the "establishments" in the *towns* were retail stores.

Census data for towns can be easily summed up: retail stores were miniscule in size and offered no great choice. In some villages they did not even exist, yet in urban areas the small, poorly stocked, high-cost retail outlet was all too frequent. Owner management was common, although the sales volume could scarcely have provided a living wage in many cases, let alone a return on investment.

Table 1 lists the number of towns with different numbers of retail stores: 6 reported "no mercantile establishment." Without attempting to derive "average" sales figures, a simple comparison of total sales, total employees, and the number of firms shows the extremely small size of the typical retail store. In Clarksburg, for example, combined sales of 4 separate establishments totalled $26,680 annually; 4 partners and 2 stockholders had invested (among all 4) $3,200, and employed 2 workers who earned (between them) $16.00 per week. Sixteen towns reported no employees in mercantile establishments; Table 2 lists data for other towns with 3 stores.

The general store played a large part in the consumer's shopping process, even in as highly developed a state as

Table 1

Number of Mercantile Establishments by Towns,
Massachusetts, 1905

Number of Establishments	Number of Towns
0	6
1 or 2	45
3	17
4	9
5–9	55
10–14	38
15–19	25
20–24	16
25–29	20
30–34	13
35–39	5
40–44	8
45–49	10
50 and over	49

SOURCE: Census of the Commonwealth of Massachusetts, 1905, Vol. III, *Manufactures and Trade* (Boston: 1908), pp. 169–74.

Massachusetts. Ninety-nine per cent of all cities and towns reported at least one general store, and two-thirds of the towns had 3 or more such outlets. For the United States as a whole, Barger's estimates suggest that sales of *country* general stores represented about 14 per cent of total retail sales (excluding sales in bars and restaurants) until about 1890, when the percentage dropped to 12; by 1909, they accounted for only 10 per cent of total sales. These figures conceal the overall impact of the general store on rural consumption patterns. The store's general manager played several roles that affected his customer's income: he bought fresh produce or butter and eggs for his own inventory from local farmers and their wives; he sometimes acted as packer and shipper of farm products to merchants in larger towns; and his occasional duties as freight

Table 2
Population and Establishments in Trade, All Towns with Three Establishments, Massachusetts, 1905

Town	Number of People	Families	Total of Partners	Wage Earners	Invested Capital	Total Value of Annual Sales	Weekly Wages
Berkeley	931	243	3	4	$ 5,600	$34,900	$30
Berlin	906	238	3	3	4,000	10,000	25
Blandford	746	185*	3	6	9,000	26,800	55
Chesterfield	563	159*	4	3	11,100	44,000	26
Granville	865	226*	5	3	12,000	50,000	26
Hadley	1,895	420*†	3	5	8,500	40,000	38
Heath	356	93	3	0	3,100	17,500	0
Lancaster	2,406	514*†	3	0	3,600	7,400	0
Lanesborough	845	208	3	6	16,050	45,323	67
Lincoln	1,122	240	4	5	9,200	72,284	60
Plympton	514	163	3	0	6,200	46,000	0
Rowe	533	113	5	0	6,200	46,000	0
Royalston	903	256*†	3	5	10,000	41,930	37
Sterling	1,315	356†	3	6	10,300	40,900	64
Sunderland	910	202*	4	4	8,000	55,000	33
Westhampton	466	113	3	0	1,400	13,600	0

* Hotel.
† Institution.

SOURCE: Census of the Commonwealth of Massachusetts, 1905, Vol. I, *Population and Social Statistics*, pp. 61–216, and Vol. III, *Manufactures and Trade* (Boston: 1908), pp. 169–82.

agent put him in a position to assist local craftsmen or processors who were trying to sell their output in a larger market. From extending credit to farm families to tide them over seasonal production and income, the owner-manager might develop a banking business or dealings in real estate; he frequently became a partner in local industry—a tannery, sawmill, or mine. Because he traveled to cities on buying trips and was called on by occasional jobbers, he provided firsthand reports to supplement the weekly periodical or days-old county newspaper; he was a central source of local news.

Along with wholesale price lists and flyers from city merchants, the general store also provided some descriptive material for consumers' special orders; for the most part, however, there were few alternatives from which to choose. The general store stocked staple foods: flour, meal, sugar, rice, as well as grain and other animal feed. Molasses and syrup, dried fish and salt pork, dried beans, a few canned goods, spices, vinegar, tubs of lard, crates of dried fruit, and the "old-fashioned" hard candy so often associated with country stores, made up the bulk of the inventory of foodstuffs. Although the general store occasionally supplied butter and eggs or fresh produce, these were also sold directly to consumers by the farmer or his wife. Nearly all of the items described in Chapter 1 as typical of consumption patterns at the turn of the century could be found at the general store: bolts of cloth, lace and ribbon trimmings, bonnets and "fascinators," washtubs and stove polish. Furnishings for both home and farm were on hand: leather goods, nails and hardware, medicines for humans and animals, horse collars, shirt collars, saddles, and suitcases. For the storekeeper to have to buy such a wide variety of items in small quantities may seem to have required skill and expert judgment of consumer preferences, but in fact it took little effort. If none of the materials spread before the housewife seemed quite appropriate for the dress or coat, little other opportunity for choice existed. If cobwebs and dust did accumulate on inventory for which there was no demand, it remained in stock; eventually it would be sold, or else the storekeeper's family would use it. More often it happened that each trip to the store made the pocket watch, the penknife, the embroidery silks, or dress patterns seem more desirable to the customer, and frequently a substantial period of time would elapse between the consumer's choice and his subsequent purchase.

The combination of limited inventory, slow turnover, extensive credit and small sales volume meant high costs passed on to the consumer, and little return to the proprietor. Four towns listed in the Massachusetts Census each reported three general stores: total annual sales in each town ranged from less than $100 to just over $200 per family. Annual sales per store of less than $10,000 were common.

In urban areas general stores persisted, although other kinds of retail outlets were appearing rapidly. The growth of specialization can be traced by comparing the number of towns with particular types of stores: while nearly every town reported at least one general store, 80 per cent of them had at least one grocery store, two-thirds had a drug store, and 60 per cent at least one dry-goods retailer. Table 3 gives the total number of establishments in 25 selected lines of trade; it shows how frequently such specialized stores occurred in cities and towns within the Commonwealth. It is also clear from the last column of this table that food stores were among the very first to specialize, for grocers, meat markets, provisioners, fruit stores and confectioners were significant subdivisions.

The specialized retailers who dealt in dry goods, drugs, hardware, or a particular type of foodstuffs resembled the general stores in country areas in their extremely small sales volume, limited inventory, and high costs. Total sales of less than $10,000 annually were reported by many establishments

Table 3
Distribution of Establishments, by Kind of Business, Massachusetts, 1905

Merchandise Line	Total Number of Establishments	Per Cent Found In				Per Cent of All Cities and Towns with 1 or More
		Boston	Cities with 3 or More	Towns with 3 or More	Other Cities and Towns	
Books, periodicals	592	35	38	6	21	45
Boots, shoes, rubbers	1,166	29	41	22	91	51
Butter, cheese, eggs	138	47	20	4	28	14
Cigars, tobacco	603	37	34	14	14	35
Clocks, watches, jewelry	609	32	36	11	21	49
Clothing	836	28	47	15	10	37
Coal, wood	575	22	37	12	28	59
Drugs, medicines	1,443	21	53	17	9	66
Dry, fancy goods	1,297	26	42	23	9	61
Fruits, confectionery	828	16	39	44	14	55
Furniture, carpets	537	29	46	5	20	40
General	811	2	8	63	27	99
Groceries	4,306	28	44	25	3	80
Groceries, provisions	2,761	20	63	14	4	56
Hardware	472	27	41	12	20	39

Liquors, beverages	1,598	42	47	9	2	22
Lumber	253	40	24	1	35	29
Meats, provisions	1,425	32	32	25	11	72
Men's furnishings	263	45	42	0	17	17
Restaurants, lunch rooms	1,292	40	39	15	7	44
Saddlery, harness	143	27	22	0	51	24
Stationery, school supplies	114	50	10	0	40	14
Stoves, hardware, tinware	373	18	35	13	34	47
Tea, coffee	167	44	38	2	17	12
Varieties, small wares	1,029	26	55	10	9	41

SOURCE: Calculated from Census of the Commonwealth of Massachusetts, 1905, Vol. III, *Manufactures and Trade* (Boston: 1908), pp. 249–79.

in all lines of trade. It is not clear how the Census listed the drivers of the wagons and carts that brought goods to consumers: some of these were independent peddlers, who today would be counted as separate "establishments," but others were the routemen for bakeries, dairies, ice and coal companies, and grocers. In either case, the choices they offered consumers were limited, and their sales were low. It is probable that, considering family income and expenditure at the time, more retail outlets existed than could efficiently provide goods to consumers. This was suggested at the time:

On an average in all of our cities there are at least ten times as many middlemen or retail dealers as there should be. To illustrate: in a recent walk in New York City I counted twenty retail shops, where groceries, vegetables and meat were sold, in one block. I live in an apartment house which has about forty apartments, and from observation I should judge that at least twenty different grocers and butchers, each maintaining delivery wagons with drivers, deliver goods at this one apartment building,—not once, but several times each day. Nothing could be more wasteful or extravagant than this. Four good, up-to-date concerns, selling groceries, vegetables and meats, in each block, would be ample.[4]

Contemporary estimates for the country as a whole support this picture of small-volume operators; one estimate was that the average annual sales figure for all retailers was between $25,000 and $30,000. It seems clear that the buying patterns of most families were shaped more by the goods available in meagerly stocked outlets than by their own tastes and preferences.

Two different types of retailing—the mail-order house and the department store—served to widen the consumer's range of choice of products and to develop a new form of buying process. They introduced both diversification and integration into the structure of distribution.

In 1900, 6 out of 10 Americans lived in rural areas, and only one-fifth of these inhabited a recognized "place," whether it be village or small town. Even their visits to a country store, with its limited supplies, required a journey. Larger towns provided some variety: a 1901 study of retail stores in 4 Massachusetts cities shows that sales of dry goods, fancy goods, and notions were made to out-of-town customers, while food stores sold chiefly to the local population.[5] Highly specialized stores could be found in Boston, which listed at least 3 establishments for each of 19 different types of food store (e.g., bakery products, cream and milk, delicatessen, fruit, etc.) and many subdivisions of the dry-goods line (e.g., linen and home-furnishings shops, milliners, men's furnishings, etc.). For many consumers such a shopping process as this was out of the question. The post office provided the substitute: after rural free delivery service was introduced in 1896, magazine advertisements and sellers' catalogues acquainted consumers with shopping by mail. During the latter part of the nineteenth century, wholesalers, importers, and an occasional manufacturer of jewelry, patent medicines, books or toys would advertise mail-order sales in farm magazines; in fact, many periodicals appeared that depended chiefly on such advertising revenue. The first specialist in mail-order sales, Montgomery Ward, was founded in 1872; it was followed rapidly by Spiegel May, the Stern Company, the Larkin Company, and Richard Sears' various companies.

These firms diversified and grew by adding more and more lines of merchandise. Originally concentrating on promotional goods—such as Sears' watches, sewing machines and cream separators, or Spiegel May's jewelry, or Montgomery Ward's notions and trimmings—the catalogues show the gradual evolution of lines of dry goods, ready-to-wear clothing, groceries, farm machinery, household furniture and furnishings, drugs and patent medicines, automobiles and even savings deposits. By 1895 the Sears, Roebuck catalogue, for example, listed the following complete departments:

crockery, bicycles, guns, revolvers, fishing tackle, sporting goods, baby carriages, furniture, agricultural implements, buggies, harness, saddlery, sewing machines, boots, shoes, clothing, pianos, organs, musical instruments, optical goods, watches, jewelry, diamonds, silverware, and clocks.[6]

Mail-order firms added to and changed their merchandise offerings continually. Not all lines were successful: groceries did not survive; drugs and patent medicines declined in importance after the enactment of the Pure Food and Drug Law; home-building supplies proved less than spectacular. But sales of clothing, dry goods, farm and home furnishings continued to grow, and with a continually widening range of items.

Firms vied with each other in preparing lavish catalogues. Within each department a great variety of choices appeared: 9 pages on curtains and floor coverings of different patterns, materials, and colors; several models of sewing machines, with different cabinets and different prices; couches priced from $5.45 to $49.50; women's underwear—plain, lace-trimmed, with ruffles or ribbons, of cotton or cambric; 6 fashions in silk hose (colored, bright clocked, plated, black dropstitch, bright silk, and black spun silk dropstitch). Not only did such variety far exceed the limited lines of the country stores, where any unwise choice of the manager might be doomed to remain in stock, but the catalogues displayed new fashions and products from year to year.

Catalogue prices were dramatically low, even though they included express charges before parcel post was introduced in 1913. The connection between price and quality (at least for Sears, Roebuck) is best summarized by the authoritative account in *Catalogues and Counters:*

"Quality" was a word and a concept with connotations peculiar to rural residents. Quality meant serviceability and value; a piece of merchandise had to be good enough to perform the functions the catalogue said it would perform, and the price had to be low enough for them to afford it. That meant really low, and low prices often enabled them to buy goods which, even though perhaps shoddy, could not otherwise have been bought at all. It apparently meant little or nothing to the farmer that the ghastly, standardized furniture sold by Sears, Roebuck was almost utterly devoid of aesthetic quality. . . . As far as the customers . . . were concerned, if a dresser held clothes and if a bed offered a relatively comfortable night's sleep to a man who had plowed all day, that was sufficient—provided the price was "right." . . . Sears offered men's suits at $4.98, when the general market price was often twice that figure. True, they were made of shoddy wool . . . they were ill-fitting; and they did not wear long in every case. But where else could the farmer buy a Sunday suit for $4.98? . . . Sears guaranteed his $11.96 cookstove to cook. It cooked. And it cooked for years and years. Sears' plows would plow, and Sears' washing machines would wash. That was what farm families wanted.[7]

Like chain stores and department stores, the other large retailers, mail-order firms, as they grew, integrated back along the supply line, contracting with manufacturers to take all or a large part of the factory output, investing capital in firms that would produce to the retailer's specifications, in some cases taking over outright the ownership of producing firms. Such large-scale buying by powerful retailers forced prices to consumers to go still lower and helped to establish consistent product standards. The mail-order catalogues retained their best-selling models from year to year, while different firms vied with each other to offer recompense to the dissatisfied customer. To counteract the overt hostility of local stores, the mail-order firms wooed the consumer in a friendly, "folksy" manner —not merely with crass appeals that emphasized lower prices and better services. Catalogues and their use became an important part of life, as well as a buying method, for millions of customers. Barger's estimates suggest that mail-order sales, in 1909, accounted for between 1 and 2 per cent of all non-food retail sales. Sears, Roebuck, with over 100,000 items in its catalogue in 1908, sold one-quarter of this total; Montgomery Ward sold about one-eighth, and National Bella Hess less than 5 per cent. By 1919, mail-order sales accounted for 2 per cent of all retail sales (excluding food, automobiles, and coal and lumber yards).

The importance of mail-order firms to a major share of American consumers in the early years of this century cannot be overestimated. Yet the population growth of the twentieth century and the shift from farming to industrial occupations came to mean that more and more consumers were living in towns and cities. While catalogues were still making an increasing variety of goods available, rural customers dwindled as a fraction of the total population. In the cities and towns, department stores and chain stores offered new consumption choices and different shopping methods to the growing urban population.

The first department stores—A. T. Stewart, John Wanamaker, Marshall Field, Macy's, Jordan Marsh, and others—appeared in the largest cities; other firms were quick to follow their example, however, in a town or city whose expanding population, it was hoped, would support this type of operation. Barger's estimates show a growth of department-store sales from 1 to 4 per cent of total retail sales between 1899 and 1909. The Massachusetts Census, taken at the midpoint of this 10-year period, lists 129 department stores, which accounted for almost 10 per cent of the state's total retail sales. Seventy-one of these were located in 11 cities and did 87 per cent of the total department-store business. The others were probably located in the remaining 22 cities and in the few large towns of equal size. By 1915 it was estimated that 8,000 department stores existed in the country, and some 1,100 were thought to account for 40 per cent of the sales of dry goods and women's ready-to-wear articles. If sales of food, automobiles and their accessories, coal, farm implements, restaurants and bars are excluded, sales through department stores in 1919 amounted to 11 per cent of total retail sales, and by the early '20s a contemporary observer was commenting that the department store existed "in practically all towns of over five thousand population."[8]

To the consumer, the department store offered the convenience of one-stop shopping and the luxury of an inventory stocked in depth for each of the specialized lines carried elsewhere in separate stores. The stores experimented with merchandise, offering such lines as groceries, chinaware, furniture, automobiles, shoes, as well as personal service departments—hairdressing, cleaning and repair—whose success depended as much on consumers' adopting a new shopping process as on the operating costs and efficiency with which such departments might be managed.[*] Some, welcomed by customers, remained; other lines or departments were dropped. The store's fortunes depended on its reputation; at the same time that consumers were learning to ask for name brands of foods, fabrics, and drugs, they began to refer to the department store itself for information and a standard of quality. The "big stores," finally, provided luxurious surroundings to make shopping a pleasurable experience.

Marshall Field opened its new building with a grand three-day celebration in 1902; it was

an imposing, dignified structure of white granite and steel. . . . Behind its doors was placed a sumptuous vestibule with mahogany-paneled walls, red marble floors and specially designed chandeliers weighing over twelve hundred pounds apiece. It was as large in itself as many a store. . . . To a new visitor, after viewing the plain, straight lines of the outer walls, the interior of the store must have been a pleasant surprise. Entering the building at Randolph near State Street, there stretched before him for the entire length of the building a spacious central arcade formed by parallel rows of classic white Grecian columns. At the same time, symbolic of a

* Cf. Chap. 6, pp. 237–40.

new age, was the total absence for the first time of unattractive gas jets and the substitution of completely electric Tiffany chandeliers. These reflected a much more brilliant light than heretofore on the wares encased in polished mahogany and French glass counters. Aisles were comfortably wide, and all floors above the first were covered with thick pile carpeting or Oriental rugs. . . . Wood-paneled library and writing rooms fitted with deep, luxurious Oriental rugs and comfortable mahogany and green leather furniture provided the latest thing in comfort. Tired patrons found an unlimited supply of popular magazines and daily newspapers to while away the time; or the maid in constant attendance would, on request, pass out literature and poetry from the large catalogued library. Desks were supplied with an abundance of stationery for writing notes to one's friends. . . . In the inner recesses of [the rest room] were three maids who were in charge of the lavatory, one of thirty-nine identical such rooms located throughout the building. These maids supplied free of charge to the guests of the store, "soap, face and talcum powder, individual flannel cloths for powdering, hair pins, safety pins, needles, thread, tape, shoe laces, shoe buttons, pearl buttons, button hooks, scissors, sewing silk and hooks and eyes." The floors were of white marble, the fittings of porcelain, the walls lined with mirrors; and the furniture and dressing tables were of white enamel. Each dressing table was provided with an electric curling iron, and combs. Also to be found here were scales and "measuring machines"—another convenience for the feminine shopper. As a final touch, the surroundings were sometimes enhanced by bouquets of fresh flowers.[9]

Although this kind of sumptuous service was wholly denied to the rural customer with his mail-order catalogue, it was also not available to most urban consumers for their routine purchases. But the large sales volume and the centralized buying practices of the department stores were also typical of the chain organization, which appeared in the latter part of the nineteenth century and developed with accelerated growth after 1910.

Importers, wholesalers, and manufacturers originated the chain form of retailing. The tea and coffee importers who added staple groceries to their inventories gained substantial economies of scale and introduced standard weights and packaging in many lines. Merchants of drugs and variety goods found equal opportunities for central buying and for central administration of their heterogeneous inventories. Clothing and shoe manufacturers opened their own retail shops, so as to take advantage of the profit inherent in close control of inventory. Numerous small retail outlets located in neighborhood districts of cities and towns became typical for the chain stores.

The chain could vary margins on different items more profitably than could the independent storekeeper. Early estimates of retail gross profit in the grocery field suggest that many staples must have sold at extremely narrow margins. A prominent retail grocer in 1910 wrote that:

Sixty per cent of our business pays only from ten per cent to twelve per cent, while the majority need seventeen per cent. In most cases there is a large loss, i.e., from five per cent to eight per cent, hence a large profit must be added to other goods. We practically rob customers on teas and coffees to make up the balance.[10]

A shoe manufacturer described a similar situation in his retail stores:

The actual cost to the retailer in disposing of his goods will average thirty per cent . . . on the shoe I have mentioned . . . you find that the retailer does not get thirty per cent,—not over twenty-six or twenty-seven per cent; so the leading lines of the shoes that sell, he may sell for nothing. You make the money on the intermediate shoes, or women's shoes.[11]

Chain stores were able to charge lower prices because of their close connections with sources of supply. The economies of centralized accounting and management, or "cash-and-carry" policies, also reduced their expenses. An executive of one of the earliest chains, specializing in foods, explained it clearly:

185

We sell no goods on credit, and we do no delivering, and we keep no books except at headquarters. We are cutting the very finest of butter that we can have from the tub at thirty-four cents today. That has been our price for more than two months. I presume that the ordinary grocery man, where he sells a person on time and loses a bill now and then, and has to go to a good deal of expense for keeping delivery wagons and bookkeepers for keeping his accounts, would get thirty-eight or forty cents,—and he ought to. . . . Now we buy our coffee and our teas direct. All of our teas are imported to us. Our coffees we buy right from the importers, and we put that coffee right out direct to retail. . . . In buying our goods we arrange with packers in Maine or in the west, who ship us those goods direct. . . . There is no intermediate profit between the goods that we buy from the producer and our prices. . . . And by buying our goods in quantities, and buying them at first hand and cutting out the middle price, it enables us to make a price that ordinarily cannot be made where a grocery man goes into a jobbing house and is trusted thirty or sixty days, and then has to send those goods out to his customers. He has to have a little better price.[12]

The net effect on independent competitors was often disastrous: the death rate of retail stores was estimated at between 96 and 100 per cent. Early attempts at cooperative buying were unsuccessful, and small grocers, shoe stores, clothing establishments, and druggists diminished in importance. Again, no reliable data on chain-store growth exists: an estimate in 1915 counted 2,800 chains with 30,000 stores, of which 500 firms operated 8,000 grocery stores. Chains varied in importance from city to city: in Philadelphia and Chicago the chains were thought to account for over half the sales of groceries and drugs.

The first two decades of the twentieth century brought striking changes, as new types of stores came into being that offered wider assortments of stock. In 1914 the Bureau of Labor Statistics was collecting retail prices almost entirely from "neighborhood stores"; a few "downtown stores" were included, but chain stores only rarely. By 1921 wage-earner families were patronizing a wide variety of retailers—"the neighborhood stores, the downtown store, the department store, and the chain stores."[13] During the '20s and '30s, these forms of organization continued to spread, and new retail specialists appeared, as automobiles and appliances entered the consumer's range of choice. From the consumer's point of view, however, a major transformation had already taken place and, as more alternatives for goods and services became available, the shopping process could be carried out in a variety of ways.

This transition is sometimes called "the merchandising revolution." At the turn of the century, distribution had been analyzed in terms of technical "services"—assembling, storage, the assumption of risk, financing, rearrangement, selling, transportation, and the like.[14] But the changes in distribution so far described brought new dimensions to consumer decisions about what and where to buy. The purely technical view of distribution gave way to a concept of merchandising, or meeting consumer choice, a far more complex activity defined by the American Marketing Association as "the planning involved in marketing the right merchandise or service at the right place, at the right time, in the right quantities, and at the right price."[15] Under the conditions existing earlier, consumer choice was so limited that such planning was irrelevant; with a vast increase in production and with new forms of retailing, it became imperative. The change from distribution to merchandising can be clearly seen in the consumer's shopping process.

Shopping and Selecting

In making his decisions to purchase, the consumer finds a range of information, presented by producers and sellers* in display, advertising, and demonstration. From the medieval fair, where goods were spread out before the strolling buyer, to the free samples sent to homes or thrust on shoppers in stores, products themselves have served to enlighten consumers about the possibilities available. Innovations in display introduced by department stores and chains have spread rapidly to other retailers. In 1910 the effects were already apparent:

Sixty years ago there was probably not a light of plate glass in any retail store in the United States. Today no store is up-to-date without plate glass windows. Elaborate cabinet work must now be provided in the city shops. A department store with fixtures costing a quarter of a million dollars must obtain a continuous return on the investment. Of course, the customer pays it.[16]

That the consumer was probably happy to pay for light, ventilation, refrigerated equipment for foods, closed cabinets, and clean interiors may be surmised from a contemporary description of a grocery store in the neighborhood of Boston:

The oatmeal or rolled oats, Indian meal, etc., are in open barrels just beneath shelves that serve as boulevards for countless rats and mice both day and night, as they journey to their "ratskeller." Dried codfish may be found, as in ye olden days, whole and on the skin, lying exposed to all the dust for weeks and sometimes seasons. When one enters the door a bell rings, which calls the attendant from the barn, where he has been unharnessing or brushing the

* Today, "word-of-mouth" information from satisfied or dissatisfied customers supplements the efforts of sellers and is probably crucial for determining the success or failure of a new product. (Cf. Chaps. 8 and 10.)

horses. Accordingly as one article or another is desired, he plunges his unwashed hands into the pork or pickle barrel, cuts cheese or butter, often drawing kerosene and molasses in the meantime, and wiping the overflow on his coat sleeve or jumper. In summer no attempt is made to keep out flies, and much of the merchandise is open to them for food. The maple syrup bottles stand nearby, and the keeper himself has been seen to take a swallow from them at different times, when his sweet tooth called. Prices are the same as in a well-kept store, both for articles in bulk and in packages. Here and in many other stores the question resolves itself into bulk *vs.* packages; uncleanliness, liability to disease and fairly high prices *vs.* cleanliness, health and but small increase in cost.[17]

As late as 1928 consumers were reporting that cleanliness was one reason for their buying in chain stores rather than from independents.

With packaged goods, store interiors as display spaces changed in appearance; boxes and cans were arranged to show off the brand names, and the barrels and crates on the floor vanished when inventory could be stacked high on shelves or under glass-topped counters. As ready-to-wear garments took more of the consumer's dollar, clothing racks and fitting rooms became standard fixtures in stores. Arranging windows with models, mannequins, and forms, lighting and decorating open counters, stacking tables with neat piles of merchandise, keeping inventory clean and polished, designing wide aisles and open spaces, inviting consumers to browse at leisure—all these were ways of allowing and encouraging the shopper to see for himself and sometimes to handle the merchandise, to receive its message.

When the customer cannot "see for himself" but must have the article shown, the sales clerk represents another source of information—along with explanations, answers to specific questions, and testimony from previous purchasers, the salesman usually included some degree of persuasion and encouragement. Early in the century the specialty shop emphasized the need for personal services:

You take a high-class retail store today, and the customer demands a great deal better attention. If a gentleman walks into that store and every clerk is busy, and he has to stand around a moment or two, he walks out and goes down to a store on the other side of the street.[18]

A skilled sales staff could catch and hold the attention of the shopper. Department stores that offered decentralized selling claimed the expertise of specialized shops: the general storekeeper's knowledge of both fabrics and millinery fashions could scarcely rival that of two clerks, each in his separate department. Early guides for retail clerks wrote painstakingly about how to approach the customer, and what was implied in knowing the merchandise:

Opinions differ as to the best manner of approaching customers, and the approach must, of course, vary according to conditions. For example, a spacious suit department affords greater opportunity for a gracious approach, perhaps necessitates the exercise of more judgment, the possession of more poise, than a small compact small-wares section. But . . . it is the first duty of a salesman to learn all that he can about the stock he is given to sell, not simply its arrangement in drawers or on shelves and its price, but also its history or manufacture and its essential characteristics or *selling points*.[19]

Customers who bought from mail-order firms had to do without both the salesclerk's attention and the attractions of the merchandise. On the other hand, they spent far more time poring over what information was available than did the shopper in a store. So the catalogue and its "copy" was vital to both consumer and seller; as mail-order firms gained in size and experience, their managers were increasingly concerned with the content and distribution of their paperback salesclerk.

Clear pictures showed the important details of the goods for sale, and descriptions were highly specific:

Our $5.98 trousseau outfit. A trousseau fit for an American queen made of fine cambric, of four pieces, gown, skirt, drawers and corset cover. All made with matched point de Paris lace. Sizes, 32, 34, 36, 38, 40, 42, inches bust measure. Gown is made Empire style, fine grade of cambric, fancy revers, which are trimmed all around with fine point de Paris insertion and lace four inches wide. Bosom has one row of insertion and one row of fancy ribbon insertion, also with a four inch lace. Sleeves have an insertion of ribbon and four inch lace.[20]

The salesman's ability to instruct and persuade inspired the catalogue composers: the copy quoted referred to a woodcut of a winsome young woman wearing the gown and displaying the skirt, with the other two pieces in careful detail at her side. More pointed selling effort frequently appeared:

Our special $12.50 Overcoat Kitchener Style Overcoat, Made of Dark Mixed Goods, the Very latest style. $12.50 Kitchener Overcoat. Sizes 35 to 44 chest measure. Very Fine Quality Fancy Dark Mixed Vicuna Overcoat. The fabric is a regular overcoating Vicuna, heavy in weight and not too soft to wear well. The ground is black with a very fine mixture of bluish gray, and just a tinge of red, giving it a rich effect. A firm but soft finished overcoating in one of the new shades. Coat is made in Kitchener style as shown in cut, with peaked lapels and vertical pockets cut through to trousers. Has outside breast pocket, cuffs of same goods, and silk velvet collar. Body of coat lined with heavy leather cloth Italian, and sleeves have Skinner's fine quality satin lining. Edges are ⅜ inch single stitched and seams are raised and stitched to match. This is a fine coat and very genteel in appearance. In ordering give chest measure. Measure around the body just below the arms, over vest but under coat. Style 12. $12.50.[21]

Pictures abounded in the catalogues; both consumers and the mail-order firms benefited when technical developments in printing permitted woodcuts to be replaced first with halftones, then with photographs, and later by increasingly realistic colors.

Used to relying on the retailer, consumers during the early years of the century found themselves the object of solicitude by manufacturers and producers, who began to take on the functions of informing and selling. Branded merchandise, and packaging to display the brand, could succeed only if the consumer "recognized, preferred, insisted on" the brand. Advertising reiterated the brand names in periodicals, flyers, posters, and in display material for shop windows, trolley cars, and railway stations. Gradually, the correct dosage of information and persuasion was calculated.

At the turn of the century, about 600 firms placed national advertising in magazines; the newspapers provided space for retailers to announce their wares, and many advertisements were little more than lists of goods for sale. Makers of drugs and patent medicines were the first heavy advertisers, for reasons closely associated with the consumer's buying process. Such items could not be sold in bulk to retailers, for prepackaging—whether of pills or of a bottled elixir—was part of the product. The name of the remedy was essential information for the consumer; it was displayed prominently on labels and given wide publicity by advertising, frequently along with wildly exaggerated claims about ingredients and efficacy. Drugs were among the first items sold by mail order—a result of the close relation between advertising, brand names, and packaging. In other lines, packaged goods and brands soon replaced sales in bulk: staple foods and household supplies, such as soap and stove blacking. As processed foods became more common, consumers learned more brand names—Royal baking powder, Gold Medal flour, Crisco, Campbell's soup, Kellogg's corn flakes, Uneeda biscuit.* Because the basic food

* Cf. Chap. 1, pp. 18–22.

items were familiar to the consumer, such advertising concentrated on slogans, trademarks, and other brand identifying features. W. H. Underwood claims the earliest use of a trademark: its Red Devil on canned deviled ham appeared in 1824. The "Campbell Kids" were first displayed on streetcar cards in 1904; "It Floats" was famous at the turn of the century; the Gold Medal slogan, "Eventually—why not now?" dates from 1907. Manufacturers who operated retail outlets displayed advertising as well as merchandise. Some textile products were labeled—Fruit-of-the-Loom, Skinner satin, J. P. Coats' thread —and some new products added new words to the language as generic rather than brand names: Kodak, Saltines, Vaseline.

The distinction between the informational and selling aspects of advertising was clear to observers in the first decades of the century, and today's controversy over the "wastes" of advertising appeared in early writings:

Modern industrial conditions have radically changed the character of advertising and the part it plays in the modern economy of a people. To advertise is no longer strictly synonymous with to inform. Much of the advertising of today, especially in the daily newspapers, voices the rivalry of sellers of identical goods. Knowledge of the character and quality of these goods is nowadays obtained by the buying public through other means, and the advertisements are merely intended to draw the buyer from tradesman A to tradesman B, or *vice versa*.[22]

This emphasis on rivalry overlooks the function played by advertising in establishing brand names. To the consumer, branded products brought better quality, with sanitary conditions in the factory and packaging to prevent spoilage and filth in the stores. To the seller, establishing such conditions was profitable only if consumers recognized the products and asked for them by name.

It is impossible, of course, to determine the precise point at which advertising achieved consumer recognition. But its effect on the consumer's buying process was clear from the start. Manufacturers began to inform the consumer and influence his choice-decision early in the century. The impact of their advertising activities lessened the need for retail salesmanship:

Today the petty retailer does not have more than five or ten barrels of flour, but he will have as many brands as he has barrels, simply to suit the whim of the customer who comes in. He is a man who does not try to sell what he finds to be best; he is no longer an expert;—does not pretend to be. Customers come in and ask for the thing they see advertised, and he passes it out without a word.[23]

But manufacturers' advertising did not entirely replace the selling efforts of retailers. Dealers and manufacturers were both needed in order to introduce new products with both information and persuasion; once they were accepted as part of the consumption pattern, the retailers' influence diminished. Such was the course of events with automobiles, electric refrigerators and washing machines, radios, and the host of minor innovations in the consumption pattern.* On the other hand, consumers continued to want personal information about some products with which they were perfectly familiar. Meat and produce, for example, needed no explanation, but shoppers relied on the butcher to recommend a particular grade or cut of meat and on the produce merchant to guarantee fresh fruits and vegetables. Not until after World War II did prepackaging and branding for such items become common, while the expert and his advice retired behind the scenes. Apparel retailers assisted consumers in choosing among new materials with unfamiliar qualities or new colors and styles. And there were many other examples: a knowledgeable furniture salesman, for example, could show details of construction or design, or give advice about decoration. Such items were

* See also Chap. 8.

manufactured by many small firms, and brand names were not representative of the major portion of the industry output.

In general, however, the shopping process has developed a wider range of sources of information to the consumer, and the decision-making process has become more complex.

Paying for the Goods

When consumers buy, they must pay for their choice; sellers, therefore, must have some way of receiving payment. The new forms of retailing led to new policies and techniques for receiving consumers' payments. Credit sales had been typical of the small store, whether urban specialty shop or general store, and had imposed higher costs on both consumer and retailer:

The growth of retail credit must be set down as one of the causes for the excessive costs of distribution.

In the past fifteen years there has been a notable change in the attitude of retail establishments in this matter. . . . The credit system was formerly used almost entirely by the well-to-do, the poor being given but slight opportunity to use it. Of late there has been a large extension of it by the installment stores, where furniture, clothing, jewelry, household goods, in fact, almost every needed article except food, can be procured by the payment down of a small part of the price, the balance being paid in installments.[24]

When this observation was made, in 1910, cash sales at lower prices were beginning to appear, introduced by chains and mail-order firms and then taken up by some department stores.

Mail-order firms gave consumers careful instructions about writing orders and sending payments. "If you live on a rural mail route, just give the letter and money to the mail carrier and he will get the money order at the post office and mail it in the letter for you."[25] The use of C.O.D. sales had to be limited, after Sears, Roebuck's famous slogan "Send No

Money" had increased total sales by 50 per cent within two years but had also piled up almost a million dollars of merchandise refused. Although smaller firms sold special items through the mail on a C.O.D. or "pay later" basis, the general mail-order firms adopted a strict policy of cash payment in full with the order. For the most part, "cash" meant money orders, which had been inaugurated by the postal service in 1864, although customers' letters frequently contained currency and even silver. In stores, the problem of controlling cash receipts where several clerks or departments were involved was solved in different ways. One system of overhead wires carried cash boxes to and from a central desk which collected payments and made change; larger stores introduced pneumatic tubes for the rapid transit of containers holding the customer's money together with the sales slip describing the purchase. When cash registers came on the scene, the department that made the sale could receive payment itself, while the receipts of separate outlets of the chain stores became subject to centralized control. To the consumer, such technological changes brought convenience in the shortening of the time required to complete the purchase.

The use of credit evolved along two lines: installment sales for goods with a high unit price, and various charge-account systems which formalized "open credit." Installment selling first appeared in the mid-nineteenth century for sewing machines, pianos, and encyclopedias and other sets of books. The mail-order firms had adopted installment selling for a few durable items prior to World War I, but the great growth of this kind of credit occurred during the '20s with the burgeoning of the automobile industry.

Over the same period, the growth in family incomes and the expanded production of low-priced clothing items lessened the market of the "installment stores." A store that offered charge accounts became a distinct type of retailer, and credit was gradually recognized as a service for which consumers paid. Nowhere was this clearer than in the battle between chain stores and independents: the Federal Trade Commission investigation of chains in the late '20s documented what everyone knew—that chain stores meant cash sales. Cash sales of 95–100 per cent of their total volume were reported by chains in the groceries, dry goods, drugs, tobacco, and variety lines; credit sales were more important for department store chains and independent specialty stores in all lines. Among all the reasons for buying at independent stores rather than at chains, consumers mentioned most frequently the availability of credit. The charge customer also used other services, particularly telephone orders and return privileges, which distinguished this entire buying process from that of the anonymous cash purchaser. Before the introduction of revolving credit and similar systems designed to attract lower-income customers, charge accounts and the services that they involved served to differentiate not only stores, but the consumers to whom they catered. A retailer's steady customers became a "clientele," when these customers developed shopping habits that made them loyal to one particular store, and the use of charge accounts came to be important among these shopping habits.

Getting the Goods

The third part of the consumer buying process—taking possession of the product—evolved along with the other changes in shopping and retailing. Early in the century some observers became concerned about the increase of delivery expense. Stable costs for boarding teams were rising, and more and more labor had to be used to get goods to consumers. Stores hired delivery clerks, drivers, and messengers to call regularly for the consumer's order.

Some department stores and grocery stores carry their delivery service to an almost absurd degree—a situation brought about by the unreasonable demands of shoppers and by keen competition among the stores for business.[26]

Every city retailer of any size complains of this. Nobody now wants to carry bundles. . . . Frank Tilford of Park & Tilford, New York, testified that . . . "In Boston . . . they do not require the prompt deliveries that they do in New York; we have to make deliveries every hour."[27]

But consumers, particularly those in low-income groups, transported most of their purchases themselves. The chains spread the practice of deliberately limiting delivery in order thereby to reduce costs and prices; the specialty shops and department stores that continued to accept telephone orders (replacing the messenger service) and to make deliveries became identified by these services. "Cash and carry" now became one buying method; "charge and send," another.

A direct link between farm and home was an early dream of the twentieth century. The street railway had seemed to be a potential economical delivery system to urban consumers; perhaps farmers could also use parcel post. Such direct delivery from producer to consumer never did materialize, but parcel post was used increasingly by large retailers, both department stores and specialty shops, and urban transit contributed to the growth of large-scale retailing. Streetcars took consumers to the downtown stores, and car cards provided suggestions of what to buy when they arrived. "Cash and carry" won more supporters when there was also a cheap ride home for the buyer laden with packages. As urbanization continued, early in the '20s the larger mail-order firms began to open retail stores to aid their declining sales. The catalogue augmented the store's inventory; some ordering centers, set up with only a few display pieces, made city consumers more conscious of mail-order catalogues. This shift to retail stores altered the nature of the business substantially, but by the early '30s Sears' and Ward's volume of store sales exceeded that of their mail-order sales.

Beginning in the late '20s, consumers gradually learned to shop by automobile and thus to take on more and more of the delivery function themselves. It remained only for retailing to design stores especially for mobile customers; supermarkets, which appeared in the mid-'30s, were the first to capitalize on the advantages of parking lots. The phenomenon of the shopping center, which had a spectacular growth after World War II, owes its success to the willing acceptance by consumers of the delivery functions that had been performed by many retailers at the turn of the century.

Over the same period consumers found equally striking changes in the way they received their purchases from the stores. The first shift from bulk sales to packaging provided boxes and cartons, which carried advertising messages as well as products. The development of transparent materials altered not only packaging but the whole shopping process. Cellophane, prior to World War II, and the host of plastics introduced after the war let consumers see what they were buying and reduced the need for a clerk to display it. Store personnel lost other functions—weighing out, measuring, cutting up, picking out, and doing up parcels with paper and twine. The salesman's functions of suggesting merchandise or picking out a specific article were even less essential when "factory-wrapped and inspected" became a mark of quality. The end result was self-service, which combines two steps in the shopping process—giving an order and receiving the merchandise. Both retailers and consumers are still experimenting with self-selection and various forms of self-service over a wide range of goods.

Delivery and Returns

Sales returns were an inevitable development of the large-scale retail organizations that came into existence at the turn of the century. Department stores and mail-order firms found that increased sales sent the ratio of returns to sales steadily higher. Partly, this reflected the inefficiencies of rapid growth. The function of receiving the customer's order was imperfectly performed when it was done by a clerk who did not know how to fit clothing properly, or a mail-order packer who was careless about stock numbers. But sales returns also reflected the sheer increase in the number and variety of goods. The consumer, realizing that his range of choice was constantly widening, no longer felt committed to one decision if he found a later reason to change his mind. As ready-made clothing became common, the possibilities of returning it increased. If the garment did not mix, match, or fit, unlike a length of cut fabric it could be resold without charge to another customer. Originally, the retailer accepted returned goods only when there were justifiable grounds for complaint, but very soon stores began to vie with one another in their liberal treatment of customers who returned goods. The result was that accepting returned merchandise, like charge accounts and delivery, became recognized as a distinguishing characteristic of certain stores rather than an essential part of all retailing.

As the manufacturer assumed more prominence in the distribution process—making a sales appeal to the consumer over the retailer's head, or packing and branding the goods for the consumer's "protection"—he met with a reverse flow of complaints by consumers addressed directly to the factory. Within the factory, systems of inspection and quality control were one way of reducing the costs of complaints and returns; outside it, the location of repair and maintenance facilities to provide consumers with proper servicing became a major concern. Fewer manufacturers left the whole problem to retailing; some even set up their own service centers. To the consumer, this was one more evidence of the retailer's having turned into a passive channel through which goods flowed: the store might or might not provide "services," but it was no longer solely responsible for the merchandise.

Against the background of economic growth in the American economy, this chapter has explored the merchandising revolution and its effect upon consumers. The dramatic shifts in income and in goods and services available, previously discussed, have been accompanied by equally striking changes in the shopping process. The increase in income and in available alternatives did not do away with the consumer's problem —if anything, it has become more complicated. And the merchandising revolution has not removed any of the activities necessary for getting goods from producers to consumers—the order must still be given, payment must be made, physical transfer completed, and unhappy choices rectified; if anything, the proliferation of ways to carry out the shopping process has further complicated the problem of consumer choice.

The merchandising revolution has also changed the nature of competition among sellers. In today's economy, sellers appeal to consumers not only with their wares, but also with the various shopping opportunities they offer. The answer to how competition in the market affects consumer choice—and vice versa—requires an exploration of the contemporary scene. In the next chapter, a model for market competition will be developed that will guide this exploration by linking the model of consumer choice to the competitive activities of sellers, via the consumer's shopping process.

201

chapter 6 A Model of Market Competition

*I*n the markets in which consumers buy, competition takes many forms. Most models of economic theory analyze markets using a conventional definition of demand framed in terms of prices and quantities, which shows that buyers choose smaller or larger quantities, at higher or lower prices, of the same product or service. To the business firms that sell to consumers, however, this aspect of demand is less important than consumer preferences, for it has been shown that families and individuals seek variety in goods and services and in shopping methods. The consumer-buyer and his decisions are central to any market analysis that seeks to explore the relationship between forms of competition and consumption choice.

Consumer Markets

It is the existence of consumer choice that justifies the description of consumer markets as "competitive." Such a market exists where two or more sellers compete, where consumers are able to buy from more than one firm. Competition is in contrast with monopoly, which by definition refers to a single seller controlling the entire supply of a product or service. If consumers want what a monopolist is selling, they must either buy from him or go without. To cite a specific example of an existing monopoly, however, requires an extremely precise definition of the product or service. For example, in most urban areas public utilities are monopolies: there is only one telephone company, water company, gas company, electricity supplier. But if telephone service is defined as a form of communication, more than one supplier of such facilities exists: telegraph, mail and face-to-face conversation are among the other forms communication can take. Only insofar as the consumers find telephone service unique and are unwilling to substitute for it another form of communication does the company have a monopoly. The strength of the monopolist's power, therefore, is a reflection of consumer preference.

In the familiar statement, the monopolist is said to charge "what the traffic will bear," but this also implies that he cannot charge more. No monopolist can force larger quantities of his product on consumers than they are willing to buy at his dictated price. It is consumer demand that determines whether or not the traffic will bear *any* burden; if consumers come to regard another supplier as equally satisfactory, the monopoly situation no longer holds. In many localities consumers are free to choose between gas and electricity for cooking: the two

204

"monopolists" are competitive so long as consumers are willing to substitute their products one for the other. For many consumers, a preference map could reasonably be drawn with electric ranges on one axis and gas ranges on the other. In short, competition exists wherever consumers are willing to substitute one product for another, or one seller for another. If consumers regard one firm as unique, that firm has a monopoly; consumer preferences have established that there is no acceptable substitute, and there are therefore no competing sellers. So determining which markets are competitive and analyzing the nature of competition are, in essence, questions of investigating consumer preferences.

In the model of *pure* and *perfect* competition, each seller's product or service is defined as identical with that of every other seller, and a sufficient number of sellers exists so that each supplies only a fraction of the total quantity of goods or services available to buyers. Sellers thus differ only in the quantities they offer at a given price; buyers differ only in the amount they are willing to purchase at a given price. Competition in such a market is price competition: many buyers and many sellers, each a minor part of the whole market, help to establish the *equilibrium price* that results. As in the case of monopoly, a specific example of the competitive model can be found only with an extremely narrow definition of the product.

The nature of the product in the model of perfect competition—the fact that it is *what* it is—is somehow preordained; whether or not it is a homogeneous product depends upon the buyers. In the model, it is demand that finds the goods or services of different sellers to be identical. In a consumer market, therefore, it is consumer preference that must determine homogeneity: for pure competition can exist only if consumers are *indifferent* among sellers and their products, and responsive solely to different prices and quantities. But such a situation of indifference does not describe the actual consumer choices among the widely varying products and services and shopping processes in the American economy.

Two commonly used examples of near-perfect competitive markets refer to corporation stock and agricultural products. Yet in neither case is the consumer indifferent to the sellers from whom he buys. It is true that one share of General Motors common stock is identical with another share; but the consumer is not only buying General Motors common stock, he is also shopping at his broker's. Similarly, the consumer may well be indifferent as between the milk from one farm and that from another—but not if the first farmer sells to White Creamery and the second to Johnson Brothers. Brokers differ in the abundance (and relevance) of the information they offer and in their provision of credit; retail dairies may have different delivery schedules and will surely have nonidentical routemen. So the consumer's preference for one seller over another exists; because the shopping or buying process cannot be separated from consumer choice, there is no possibility of finding identical sellers to consumers, and the model of pure or perfect competition is irrelevant to an analysis of consumer markets.

Since it is only the individual consumer who can decide whether or not a product or service or shopping process is unique, a model must be found that allows for differences—and also for substitutions—among goods and services and sellers. Such a model exists in the theory of monopolistic competition—which, in fact, is the general case, for elements of both monopoly and competition enter into *all* markets, not just those in which consumers buy. But monopolistic competition will be applied here only to consumer markets and to the activities of buyers and sellers there.

In this model, each market consists of a group of firms that sell a general class of product or service. Each firm in the market offers a unique product or service, which is differentiated from that of the others, and it therefore enjoys the

206

monopolist's power over supply and its price. But all of the firms are *competing* sellers, in that to some degree the product of one can be substituted for that of the others. The actual degree of monopoly power is determined by the buyers, and depends on the extent to which they actually do regard the products as substitutes for one another. Chamberlin's classic, *The Theory of Monopolistic Competition,* makes this explicit (italics added):

A general class of product is differentiated if any significant basis exists for distinguishing the goods (or services) of one seller from those of another. Such a basis may be real or fancied, *as long as it is of any importance whatever to buyers, and leads to a preference* for one variety of the product over another.[1]

Sellers differ, therefore, not only in the quantity of output they will offer at a given price, but also in the type of output: each firm does not offer a product or service identical with that of others but one which is differentiated from the others. Competition, in such a market, consists of *nonprice* competition: sellers offer competing products; they may or may not compete in terms of price.

For consumer markets, the model has other implications. If sellers offer differentiated, but substitutable products, buyers differ also, not only in the amount, but also in the *kind* of product, they are willing to purchase at a given price. Consumers, as buyers, differ not only in their incomes and their sensitivity to prices but also in their preferences. Market demand cannot be framed solely in terms of prices and quantities, with buyers choosing more or less of what is essentially the same product or service. Therefore, manufacturers and distributors use nonprice competition in attempting to fulfill consumer preferences. The model helps to explain the historical changes in consumption, for these reflect variations in products and services as well as the effects of price competition. Innovations and deliberate changes in production and distribution occur when sellers compete for consumer choice; they remain if consumers choose to accept them.* The influence of consumer preferences on monopolistic competition deserves more analysis.

First, the very existence of product differentiation depends on consumers as well as producers. The general class of product—say frozen beans—is differentiated because Birdseye frozen beans are not identical with Snowcrop frozen beans. Each processor has taken steps to ensure this—by his selection of particular ingredients and the specific details of his freezing technology; by the use of distinctive packaging and a brand name to identify his product; by his advertising of its superior quality or its appeal to gourmet tastes. But all such attempts are worthless unless the potential buyers—the consumers—are willing to recognize significant differences between Birdseye and Snowcrop frozen beans. If a firm competes by changing its output—for example, by introducing a product variation—its competitive position will be improved only if consumers accept the change, and prefer it to what is offered by others.

This reasoning about monopolistic competition and differentiation applies to sellers, themselves, not only to the products and services they sell. It applies particularly to retailers. It is true that every retail outlet does have a monopoly—a complete control of a unique supply—in its location.[2] One, and only one, filling station can sell gasoline at a particular corner of Main Street and State Avenue. But if consumers are indifferent between this location and that occupied by another filling station, the monopoly aspects of location per se are irrelevant. Much more important, as a means of differentiation, are the various aspects of the consumer's buying process that were reviewed in the last chapter. How the consumer can shop and select—what alternatives the retailer stocks in his inventory;

* See Chaps. 1 and 5, especially pp. 47 and 183.

208

how the retailer accepts payment—whether the customer pays cash or uses a charge account or an installment plan; how the consumer's choice arrives at his home—whether the store delivers it or allows the buyer to pick it up from an open case or shelf; how the complaint of a dissatisfied customer is handled—whether the retailer replaces or repairs the article: these are the identifying characteristics that differentiate one seller from another. And each variation introduced into the shopping process will actually serve to differentiate only when consumers accept it as a means of distinguishing one retailer from another.

Secondly, the relation between nonprice competition and consumers' preferences makes information, on both sides of the market, critically important. As buyers of a general class of product, consumers confront many sellers of products that are closely equivalent: the consumer's taste for variety is satisfied by the existence of a wide range of differentiated articles. Given information about the differences in products and prices, an astute buyer could select the particular item that best fits his set of tastes and preferences; his choice would reflect not only the availability of substitutes but the degree of closeness to which they are equivalent. The more information they have about the product and shopping process offered by each of the existing alternative sellers, therefore, the better off are the consumers. Exactly parallel reasoning applies to firms. As sellers of a general class of product or service or shopping process, firms face many buyers, who have closely similar, yet different, preferences. Given adequate information about consumer preferences as well as estimates of the quantities that buyers will take at different prices, the profit-maximizing firm could produce the particular item that best fits its available resources of technology and knowhow. The seller can differentiate his output from that of competitors most successfully by incorporating in his product or service the differences that

209

consumers will find significant—by giving consumers, in short, what they want. The more information he has about consumer preferences, therefore, the better off is the supplier.

Efforts to improve consumer information have been carried through as a government responsibility in certain areas and recognized as a worthy objective by some independent organizations, such as, for example, the nonprofitmaking Consumer's Union. But efforts to improve seller information have depended on the decision of the firm to improve its understanding of what people want to buy. Firms' activities in this area, broadly described as market research, are subject, like any other business operation, to the guide of profitability—and payoff estimates for any kind of research are notoriously imprecise. Both types of information, however—that which is sought by consumers and that which is sought by producers— have an important bearing on consumer choice; they will be discussed in later chapters.

The market model of monopolistic competition is clearly relevant to consumer purchases; the characteristics of this model—competing sellers who offer differentiated products or services or shopping processes—are evident to a greater or less degree in different areas of consumption expenditures.

Competing Sellers

To analyze those markets in which consumer choices are carried through, Table 1 provides a useful reminder of the broad categories of consumption. The first column reviews the results of the 1960–61 Survey of Consumer Expenditures, analyzed in some detail in Chapter 3. It shows the percentage of total current consumption expenditures represented by the average spending of all families and single consumers for particular types of goods and services. The second column

Table 1

Percentage Distribution of Consumption Spending, 1960–1961

Category	Average for All Familes and Single Consumers, 1960–1961	Aggregate Personal Consumption Expenditure, 1961
Total	100	100
Food prepared at home	19.6	16.4
Food away from home	4.9	3.8
Tobacco	1.8	2.2
Alcoholic beverages	1.5	3.5
Rental dwelling	5.3	4.0
Owned dwelling	7.0	10.1
Other dwelling expense	.7	.5
Fuel, light, refrigeration, water	4.9	4.3
Household operation	5.7	3.5
House furnishings and equipment	5.3	6.6
Clothing, materials, service	10.3	10.1
Personal care	2.9	1.7
Medical care	6.7	6.1
Recreation	4.0	4.7
Reading	.9	1.1
Education	1.0	1.2
Automobile	13.7	11.4
Other travel and transportation	1.5	1.6
Other	2.2	7.3

SOURCE: Calculated from data in Bureau of Labor Statistics, *Survey of Consumer Expenditures, 1960–61*, p. 2, and U.S. Office of Business Economics, "Personal Consumption Expenditures by Type," *Survey of Current Business* (November, 1965), pp. 20–23.

reviews the aggregate approach discussed in Chapter 2 and shows the percentage of the total, Personal Consumption Expenditures, represented by total consumption expenditures in each category. The basic data used to derive these figures are not completely comparable because of differences in statistical methodology, but the proportions of the totals for each item are strikingly similar. Where do consumers spend these sums? who are the competing sellers? how are their products differentiated? how do people shop and buy in order to fulfill their tastes and preferences?

The model of monopolistic competition describes markets in which there are numerous buyers and sellers. For nearly all types of consumption spending, the individual household is one of many buyers; the model of monopsony, in which one buyer confronts many sellers, is irrelevant to the problem of consumer choice. The number of sellers for each category of consumption spending cannot be counted: markets are not classified in this way. However, most of the durable and nondurable goods listed are bought from retailers; most of the services are supplied by firms. Are there in fact numerous competing sellers?

Total retail sales of $244 billion in 1963 represented 65 per cent of Personal Consumption Expenditures, a fraction that has not varied widely over the years since 1929. Table 2 presents selected data on consumption and retailing for those years in which the Census of Business was taken, plus 1964 and 1965. The high percentage of retail sales to total consumption expenditures in 1948 marks the postwar catching-up period, when all kinds of goods in short supply during the previous years were reappearing in the stores. The table also repeats the familiar rise in real income; per capita retail sales in 1965, after allowing for price changes, were more than double the 1929 figure. The number of outlets has not changed very much since 1939, so retailing has become a more concentrated "industry." In 1963, 8 per cent of all establishments accounted for over 57 per cent of total sales. But there are still thousands of small businesses: almost half the establishments sold less than $50,000. For the most part these were individual proprietorships; they constituted two-thirds of the total number, but made only 27 per cent of the total sales. But the corporate form itself does not account for the concentration, for while 21 per cent of all retail establishments were incorporated, one-

Table 2
Consumption and Retailing, Selected Data, 1929–1965

	1929	1939	1948	1954	1958	1963	1964	1965
Gross National Product (billions)	$ 103.1	$ 90.5	$ 257.6	$ 364.8	$ 447.3	$ 589.2	$ 628.7	$ 675.6
Personal Consumption Expenditures (billions)	77.2	66.8	173.6	236.5	290.1	373.8	398.9	428.5
Retail sales (billions)	47.8	41.4	128.8	169.9	199.6	244.2	261.6	
Sales, as a per cent of Personal Consumption Expenditures	61.9	62.0	74.2	71.8	68.8	65.3	65.6	
Population (thousands)	121,767	130,880	146,631	163,026	174,882	189,417	192,119	194,583
Consumer Price Index, commodities 1957–1959 = 100	$ 59.7	$ 44.7	$ 89.4	$ 95.5	$ 100.8	$ 104.1	$ 105.2	$ 106.4
Sales per capita, current dollars	393.0	316.0	879.0	1,042.0	1,141.0	1,289.0	1,362.0	
Sales per capita, constant dollars	658.0	707.0	983.0	1,091.0	1,132.0	1,238.0	1,295.0	
Number of retail establishments (thousands)	1,476	1,770	1,668* 1,769	1,728	1,795	1,708		
Number of families per store	244.6		275.8* 265.7	300.0	307.0	343.0		

* The lower figure is comparable with later years; the higher figure, with earlier years.

sources: Retail sales and number of establishments from *Census of Business*, various years, U.S. Department of Commerce, Bureau of the Census; other basic data from *Economic Report of the President*, January, 1966.

third of them sold less than $100,000, and probably represented the same type of one- or two-man management as the proprietorships or partnerships. At first glance, this increase in concentration since 1929 may seem like a decrease in the number of sellers to consumers, for in 1929 there were 245 families per store, and in 1963, 343. But closer analysis diminishes the validity of this conclusion.

The pattern of concentration differs sharply for various kinds of retail stores. For selected types of retailing, Table 3 presents two crude measures of concentration. First, data for those establishments with annual sales of over $300,000 have been calculated to show the number of such stores as a percentage of the total, and the combined sales of such establishments as a percentage of total sales. In each line of business, a small percentage of large establishments accounts for a much larger share of total sales. Yet the discrepancy between percentage of establishments and percentage of sales by such outlets differs markedly in different kinds of retail trade. The calculation for nonstore retailers was based on establishments selling more than $1,000,000 annually; if a similar calculation had been made for department stores it would have shown that 83 per cent of the establishments, with sales above $1,000,000, accounted for 95 per cent of total sales. Second, the sales class that includes the median sales figure has been located for each kind of business. Fifty per cent of all the establishments in that area of retailing have annual sales less than the dollar figure which is the upper limit of this median sales class, while fifty per cent of the establishments have annual sales greater than the lower class limit. This calculation emphasizes the large number of sellers with small sales volume in each kind of business. In most categories, more than half the stores sell less than $100,000 annually. The individual consumer finds many more sellers among grocery stores, apparel shops, and automobile service stations than among passenger-

Table 3

Number of Establishments and Sales, Retail Trade by
Kind of Business, 1963

| | | | Establishments with Annual Sales Over $300,000 | | |
| | Number of Establish- ments | Sales (000's omitted) | Per Cent of Num- ber | Per Cent of Total Sales | Median Sales Class |
Kind of Business					
Total retail	1,707,931	244,202	8.03	57.78	—
Lumber, build- ing materials	92,703	14,606	12.97	52.04	$ 50,000–99,000
General mer- chandise	62,063	30,003	20.16	85.08	50,000–99,000
Food stores	319,443	57,079	11.28	67.67	30,000–49,000
Grocery stores	244,838	52,566	14.48	72.23	30,000–49,000
Passenger car dealers, franchised	33,349	37,375	70.16	93.56	500,000–999,000
Gasoline service stations	211,473	17,760	1.80	9.28	50,000–99,000
Apparel, acces- sory	116,223	14,040	7.15	42.07	50,000–99,000
Furniture, home furnishings	93,649	10,926	8.12	42.57	50,000–99,000
Eating, drink- ing places	334,481	18,412	2.02	20.31	30,000–49,000
Drug stores, proprietary stores	54,732	8,487	9.84	35.84	100,000–299,000
Mail-order houses	4,206	2,379	1.76	64.73*	100,000–299,000
Vending machines	9,363	1,452	3.07	40.84*	30,000–49,000
House-to-house	66,223	2,373	3.19	23.94*	less than 5,000

* Refers to establishments with annual sales over $1,000,000.

SOURCE: U.S. Bureau of the Census, *Census of Business 1963, Retail Trade: Sales Size, BC 63–RS 2*, U.S. Government Printing Office, Washington, D.C., 1965, Table 1.

car dealers or bookstores. But for the consumer to have access to many sellers requires the physical presence of many retail establishments, and this table does not show the distribution of outlets among the population. Two recent developments in retailing suggest that, despite the decrease in the ratio of stores to population, the number of competing sellers and shopping alternatives has increased.

First is the continuous shifting of product lines among different types of sellers. The "kinds of business" categories used by Census data and presented in Table 3 are misleading in that each establishment is classified according to the product line that makes up the greatest share of its total sales. As each Census has explained:

It should be noted that kind-of-business classifications are not interchangeable with commodity classifications. Most businesses sell a number of kinds of commodities. The kind-of-business code assigned generally reflects either the individual commodity or commodity group which is the primary source of the establishment's receipts or some mixture of different commodities which characterize the establishment's business. Thus, the classification of establishments by kind of business generally does not make it possible to determine either the number of establishments handling a particular commodity or the sales of that commodity.[3]

Since World War II, many retailers have been innovating by offering different assortments of goods to consumers. In the 1963 Census, establishments accounting for some 80 per cent of total retail sales provided a breakdown by merchandise lines of all their sales, and these data show much about the extent of retail diversification or "scrambled merchandising." To a greater or less extent, the variations in products offered by different retailers has made the kind-of-business classification a less meaningful indication of the sources of supply to consumers, and has caused considerable alteration in consumer shopping patterns.

Most familiar to household shoppers are the nonfood departments of food stores, which date from the early '50s. In a recent survey, supermarkets reported an average of about 2,000 items stocked in health and beauty, housewares, soft goods, and toy lines—in 1958 the figure was 915. Table 4 lists some specific examples, with the percentage of supermarkets that carry each product. In supermarkets alone, nonfood sales

Table 4

Per Cent of Supermarkets Carrying Specific
Nonfood Items, 1963

Item	Per Cent Carrying
Flashlights	99%
Toiletries	99
Stationery	98
Christmas decorations	95
Thread	93
Nylon hosiery	92
Socks	88
Dolls	85
Work gloves	81
Electrical appliances	68
Towels	66
Greeting cards	63
Camera film	60
Garden tools	58
House plants	55
Beach toys	42
Diapers	40
Motor oil	40
Anti-freeze	38
Hardware	34
Boy's dungarees	30
Blouses	24
Sporting goods	22
Men's dungarees	15
Small appliances	15
Major appliances	3

SOURCE: *Super Market Merchandising, Nonfood Buyer's Guide* (January, 1964), p. 88.

now amount to about $3 billion, or 5 to 6 per cent of total sales. The Census data, including all food stores rather than just supermarkets, show nonfood sales amounting to about 15 per cent of total sales. With higher markups than those on grocery products, such items produce a larger share of profit than of sales. To a great extent, the wider inventory offered by the supermarket in both food and nonfood lines offsets the substantial decrease in the number of food stores. Although in 1948 there were 351,000 grocery stores, the 1963 Census reported only 245,000. But it does not follow that these figures record a loss for the consumer of accessibility to competing products and sellers.

Similar shifts in inventory, or products offered, have been introduced (partly in reaction to the supermarket's competition) by druggists, variety stores, and others. The departmentalized drug store far outnumbers the specialized pharmacy, and sales of books, household supplies, toys, appliances, and stationery amount to almost as much as the sale of drugs and medical supplies. Some specific examples are given in Table 5, with the proportion of all drug stores that carry these items.

Perhaps most responsible for these changes was the appearance and rapid growth of discount stores, which are said to have two origins. New England supermarkets experimented early in the '50s by adding soft goods to their self-service operations; on the West Coast, so-called "closed-door" discount houses offered a much wider range of goods to customers who were limited to certain broad groups: government employees, clerical and office workers, or residents of a particular area. The discount house emerged so rapidly that no adequate definition could be devised for it, before growth and expansion began to change its characteristics. The basic features of a discount operation were its large size, its minimal furnishings and sales personnel, its limited inventory and services, and its

Table 5

Per Cent of Drug Stores Carrying Specific Items

Item	Per Cent of Stores
Electric heating pads	98%
Hair combs	97
Men's wallets	90
Ladies' wallets	88
Ink	87
Lighters	87
Crayons	83
Notebooks	83
Shoe polish	82
Carbon paper	78
Pipes	78
Rubber bands	78
Electric hair dryers	61
Staplers	56
Convalescent aids	51
Fuses, cords, electrical supplies	51
School lunch boxes	51
Typewriter ribbons	50
Needles, thread, sewing accessories	32
Camera repair service	24
Electric blankets	22
Cooking utensils	13
Kitchen cutlery	10

SOURCE: *Drug Topics* (New York: Topics Publishing Co., February 24, 1964, and June 29, 1964).

very high rate of turnover. Such methods of operation enabled discounters to sell at dramatically lower prices than conventional retailers, whose higher margins reflected higher costs. Originally, these stores could be identified by such "discounting" from list or minimum prices, but department stores and specialized dealers began to meet their competition, while discounters' costs and prices crept upwards as they offered more and more services.

The Census of Distribution has never offered data on discount stores, because the problem of working out a satisfactory definition proved insoluble. But their existence can be clearly seen in Census data, in the steady growth of the number of establishments classified as limited price variety stores (20,917 in 1954; 22,378 in 1963) and in figures for department stores. These outlets, numbering 2,761 in 1954, and 4,251 in 1963, include not only "conventional" department stores, but their new branches—and some unknown number of discount stores. A trade association for discounters has collected figures for the number of establishments and their sales, showing a growth of discount retailers from 1,329 in 1960 to 2,951 in 1964. This source defines a discounter as "a departmentalized retail establishment utilizing mostly self-service techniques and operating at a lower margin than conventional stores selling the same type of merchandise."[4] (Neither discount store nor conventional retailer seem able to define their business without referring to the other.) As sales of such stores have grown from an estimated $2 billion in 1960 to $11 billion in 1964 a pattern of concentration has emerged, with a few giants accounting for the major part of total sales.

With new types of stores continually appearing and new lines of products continually being introduced by established retailers, the consumer finds continual change in the number and type of sellers for any one item. One observer has characterized the constant shift in product lines as the spread of "the department store concept, embracing a great range, selection, and variety of goods all under one roof . . . Almost all sizable stores today are department stores in this sense."[5] Table 6 summarizes, for four types of stores, 1963 Census data showing the percentage of establishments carrying various lines of merchandise, and sales of each line as a percentage of total sales. From the consumer's point of view, it is the first calculation which is important, for it illustrates the number of competing sellers available to him. The table suggests, for example, that women's and girls' clothing other than footwear can be found in 7,000 drug, food, and auto-supply stores. There are approximately 28,000 apparel shops which handle this kind of clothing, as well as 26,000 general merchandise stores, including department stores and limited price variety shops. From the retailer's point of view, the second calculation, that of merchandise sales in a particular category as a percentage of total sales, is useful, as an indication of how consumers respond to this scrambled merchandising, and how much of a particular store's sales can be attributed to new lines of business.

Experiments with changing product lines have extended to services as well; some supermarkets have a registered pharmacist on their staff, the number of checks cashed daily is second only to those cashed by banks, 6 per cent of these stores have luncheonettes, and 11 per cent offer a food catering service.[6] The service of traveler's checks is no longer confined to a few specialized companies, as more banks and credit-card companies have introduced them. Department stores offer "Christmas Club" plans, in which customers pay a fixed sum weekly and then receive a merchandise certificate in mid-November, with a bonus ranging from 5 to 10 per cent. "An 8% bonus really costs the store only about 5%—which is a small price to pay to bring the customer into the store every week for 46 weeks. And most stores, knowing what it costs in advertising to bring a person into the store, charge the bonus cost to advertising."[7] It seems clear, therefore, that the department-store concept or "scrambled merchandising" has actually multiplied the numbers of sellers available to consumers.

While there may be no typical example, the case of appliances illustrates possible developments. Each of the appliances introduced during the '20s and '30s offered new alternatives for consumer choice.

Table 6

Establishments and Sales, by Merchandise Line, Four Kinds of Retail Business, 1963

Merchandise Lines	Number of Establishments by Kinds of Business				Total Sales by Kinds of Business (In millions)			
	Food Stores	Drug Stores	Limited Price Variety Stores	Home and Auto Supply Stores	Food Stores	Drug Stores	Limited Price Variety Stores	Home and Auto Supply Stores
Total†	133,941	37,766	15,161	3,630	$47,470	$6,593	$4,081	$671.2
Groceries, other foods	100.0%	29.0%	72.5%	1.1%	85.2%	1.9%	4.7%	0.2%
Meals, snacks	4.4	33.3	28.2	—	0.2	4.3	4.8	—*
Alcoholic drinks	0.9	—*	—*	—	0.1	—*	0.1	—†
Packaged alcoholic beverages	20.0	12.9	1.2	—	1.4	2.7	0.1	—†
Cigars, cigarettes, tobacco	62.8	75.7	8.1	0.8	4.1	8.8	0.4	—*
Cosmetics, drugs, health needs, cleaners	55.5	100.0	90.5	4.9	4.1	71.8	5.9	0.3
Men's, boys' clothing, etc., footwear	4.2	2.6	80.9	3.3	0.1	0.3	6.4	0.2
Women's, girls' clothing, etc., footwear	6.6	4.6	88.7	0.7	0.2	0.4	19.9	0.1
All footwear	2.8	1.5	71.8	2.7	—*	0.1	2.9	0.1
Curtain, draperies, dry goods	1.9	2.2	89.5	2.5	0.1	0.2	11.8	0.1

Major appliances, radio, TV	1.7	6.2	45.9	95.5	0.1	0.5	1.9	24.9
Furniture, sleep equipment, floor coverings	—*	2.0	38.6	30.4	—*	0.1	1.3	2.6
Kitchenware, home furnishings	8.1	10.2	89.4	86.4	0.3	1.1	7.4	7.4
Jewelry, optical goods	0.9	26.0	72.6	25.2	—*	1.0	1.8	0.5
Sporting, recreation equipment	1.1	5.3	46.6	86.5	—*	0.7	1.1	9.6
Hardware	4.6	5.3	81.5	86.5	0.2	0.5	5.1	8.3
Lumber, building materials	0.8	1.3	14.5	37.6	—*	0.1	0.3	1.4
Automobiles, trucks	—*	—*	—*	1.4	—*	—†	—*	0.2
Auto fuels, lubricants	3.7	0.7	1.1	26.5	0.1	0.1	0.1	1.7
Tires, batteries, accessories	0.5	0.6	2.2	100.0	—*	—*	0.1	29.6
Farm equipment, machinery	—*	—*	—*	2.5	—†	—†	—*	0.5
Hay, grain, feed, farm supplies	2.1	—*	—*	1.0	0.1	—*	—*	0.1
Household fuels, ice	0.9	—*	—*	1.2	—*	—*	—*	0.2
All other	54.6	46.4	93.0	63.3	3.0	4.7	21.0	4.8

* Less than .05%.
† Not available to prevent disclosure.
‡ Total number of establishments and reported sales based on only those establishments which provided data by merchandise line.

SOURCE: U.S. Department of Commerce, Bureau of the Census, "United States Summary, Merchandise Line Sales of Retail Establishments, 1963," *1963 Census of Business*, Washington, D.C., 1965.

In order for the consumer to decide on the purchase of an electric iron, a toaster, or a vacuum cleaner, she had to learn not only that these were available but also how to operate them, how to make use of them in her own household, how to care for them and store them when they were not in use. The simple price-quantity decision was far from enough; what was needed was an entirely new "preference" on the part of consumers. Sellers played a major part in informing consumers, not only through the manufactures' massive advertising, but also the retailers' displays and demonstrations, the detailed explanations and advice by a knowledgeable salesperson, and visits to groups of consumers and individual households in order to show off the new appliance. These functions were the province of specialized dealers or of particular departments of larger stores. Such activities bulked even larger in the selling efforts that introduced automobiles and major appliances—the refrigerators and washing machines that were sold more and more widely during the '30s. Installment plans and other methods of deferred payments became an important part of the shopping process, and again these were introduced by specialized dealers and the larger stores. But as each appliance became an accepted part of the consumption pattern, and replacement sales came to be common, the retail functions of persuading and selling first-time owners slackened off. The burden of unfamiliarity grew less with each new appliance: the consumer who had grown up with an electric toaster took the electric coffee pot in stride. Not *whether* to buy an appliance, but *which* model and *which* brand was now the major consumer choice; manufacturers' advertising of product differentiation enabled consumers to form preferences. Retailers who lacked the specialized knowledge that was needed in order to persuade a new customer to buy an unfamiliar appliance could take orders, receive payment, and transfer title to everyday items in common use.

Small appliances are found at jewelry stores, gift shops, drug stores and radio-television stores. In 1963 almost 6 per cent of all retail establishments carried some major appliances, including radios, TV, and musical instruments; sellers included retailers classified as lumberyards, hardware stores, automotive dealers, and jewelry stores. The construction industry also helps to distribute major appliances: new homes are commonly built already equipped with ranges, dishwashers, disposals, refrigerators, and laundry equipment, while kitchen remodeling has become a specialized building service. From the consumer's point of view, a hint of this multiplication of sellers can be found in Table 7.

The second development in retailing that has increased the consumer's accessibility to competing sellers encompasses changes in location and hours of operation. Many changes in shopping habits have had their origin in the increasing use of automobiles; this process culminated in the development of shopping centers, which succeeded by extending the techniques of large parking lots and a location away from "downtown" that had been first introduced by the supermarkets. Shopping centers are a special example of the department-store concept, since they unite in a central location one or more large department stores with a surrounding assortment of specialty shops. Here too there is continuous experimentation with goods and services offered: nonstore facilities to be found among the 7,500 existing shopping centers include offices, medical centers, theaters, bowling lanes, community centers, and churches. "One developer suggests that regional centers surrounding large cities are really the 'downtowns' for their suburban areas, and should include space for civic functions and offices for branches of the city administration."[8]

Accessibility is also a matter of timing; recent changes in store hours and remaining open at nights and on Sundays offer more shopping alternatives to consumers. In June, 1961, a

Table 7

Purchases of Selected Appliances, by Place of Purchase, All Households Purchasing, 1959–1960

Appliance	Depart-ment Store	Jewelry Store	Radio-TV Store	Appli-ance Store	Furniture Store	Auto Supply	Mail Order	Discount Store	Other
				Per Cent Purchased In					
Toaster	28.7	2.9	.3	23.7	3.3	2.9	.6	10.1	27.5
Portable phonograph	24.1	2.3	17.3	16.2	7.9	4.1	3.0	11.6	13.5
Portable radio	20.6	10.1	14.0	22.7	4.8	4.2	4.2	12.5	10.1
Electric clock	26.9	7.1	1.0	23.7	3.7	.6	3.1	9.5	24.4
Electric range	9.9	—	1.2	48.6	13.7	1.8	6.0	2.1	16.7
Black and white TV	17.8	—	21.8	31.3	13.0	1.7	3.3	6.4	4.7
Electric refrigerator	21.2	—	—	43.9	16.5	—	3.5	5.2	9.7

SOURCE: *Look National Appliance Survey* (New York: Cowles Magazine and Broadcasting, Inc., 1961).

Supreme Court decision upheld the "Blue Laws" of Maryland, Pennsylvania, and Massachusetts, which require Sunday closing for most types of retailers; yet little settled policy emerged, even in these states. Some 25 states have Sunday laws that apply specifically to retailing, but most of them, written early in the country's history, had been completely forgotten until Sunday openings became a competitive weapon for discounters, supermarkets, and roadside stores. Opposed to Sunday hours are city retailers "downtown" (although they themselves do a sizable volume of telephone business on Sundays), some suburban retailers, organized workers, and churches. The National Association of Discount Merchants found that 80 per cent of its members disagreed with Sunday openings "in principle," yet they estimated that Sunday sales accounted for 15 to 30 per cent of the week's volume. Shopping at night is equally important to retailers and to consumers. A recent survey suggests that over half the country's retailers are open 5 or 6 nights a week, while stores that stay open 4 or more nights report that these night hours account for 50 per cent of their week's sales. Longer hours also appear in consumer services: a substantial fraction of the banks that have been chartered in recent years advertise: "Open from 8 to 8," and self-service laundry and dry-cleaning machines are available 24 hours a day. Again, the success of these changes reflects consumer preference and acceptance. "The Sunday sellers believe the shoppers themselves are their trumps. 'It's up to the consumer,' Sunday sellers say. 'If people don't want to shop on Sunday, why do they come?' "[9]

Finally, accessibility can also mean bringing the store to the customer; house-to-house selling and mail-order retailing have also developed innovations.

Between 1954 and 1958, the number of mail-order establishments increased by 26 per cent, while average sales dropped slightly. This development intensified during the next few years; 1963 data show a two-thirds gain in the number of establishments over 1958; average sales in 1963 were less than three-quarters of the 1958 average. The latest Census gives separate figures for different types of mail-order business, which show clearly that the few large establishments (153) providing department store merchandise maintain an appropriately large sales volume (1963 average $1.4 million).* Some new mail-order establishments represent diversification by existing firms—the magazine publishers and insurance firms who base their mailings on ready-made lists of customers. But many new firms have entered the field, starting with a small list of specialties and finding opportunities to add to their offerings. Their small size is indicated by figures on the number of establishments with and without paid employees; 48 per cent of the mail-order outlets selling furniture, 42 per cent of those dealing in apparel other than women's wear, 60 per cent of those dealing in books, and 52 per cent of those carrying other types of merchandise have no payroll. In the last catch-all classification, the average sales of establishments with paid employees amounted to almost $400,000, while the average sales of those with no payroll amounted to only $12,000. Another form of mail-order business, the book-club scheme, has spread so that the consumer may now receive the record-of-the-month, the fruit-of-the-month, the fabric-of-the-month, and even the mystery-package-of-the-month. Bank-by-mail plans accentuate the importance of the post office, for consumers can now choose either to spend or to save by mail order.

House-to-house selling amounts to only 1 per cent of total retail sales, but has strategic importance in certain lines. The overall sales figure has not expanded greatly during the past decade, but the kinds of door-to-door sales have shifted somewhat. Census data report several thousand establishments with no paid employees which sell groceries, fruits and vege-

* See also Table 3.

tables, milk, bakery products, and other foods—many of these are local producers of such foodstuffs who have an established route of customers. It is the larger firms, fewer in number but accounting for the bulk of the sales, that do house-to-house selling of manufactured goods. For example, in 1963 some 920 establishments selling household appliances averaged sales of $176,000. The *Look Appliance Survey,* quoted in Table 7, found that door-to-door sales meant household purchases of 1 per cent of the washing machines and unit air conditioners bought in 1961, 4 per cent of the freezers, 7 per cent of the sewing machines, and 26 per cent of the vacuum cleaners. House-to-house sales have amounted to 20 per cent of the cosmetics market for over 10 years, during a period when total sales of perfume, cosmetics, and toilet preparations were doubling and both department stores and drug stores were losing volume to supermarkets and discount houses. The leading firm in the cosmetics industry, Avon, uses house-to-house distribution exclusively: its average sale per customer is 5 times the corresponding average in retail outlets, while Avon's advertising budget as a per cent of sales is about one-fifth the industry average. Like other retailers, house-to-house sellers have varied the lines of merchandise they carry, with the aid of manufacturers who plan particular styles of dinnerware, kitchen gadgets, curtains, and the like especially for this market. Prepackaging and plastics have made the salesman's task less burdensome and his goods more attractive to the customer. Finally, nonstore sales include the use of party plans, selling a variety of housewares and apparel to consumers in their homes. These combine shopping and social entertainment; to a certain extent consumers become both buyers and "retailers."

These developments—a change in the inventory assortment and a growing accessibility of consumers to retailers—suggest that at least one aspect of the model of monopolistic competition, that of numerous competing sellers, is present with regard to most products that consumers buy. For services, however, the picture is quite different: here, most consumers typically face one or a few sellers.

In the first place, firms that sell services are far more specialized than retail stores, so that the department-store concept or scrambled merchandising has not had much influence on them. Aside from the fact that most services cannot be shipped but must be rendered directly to the consumer or his possessions, services by their very nature depend on the supplier's personal skill and ability.* As a result, few economies of scale have been developed by chains or by the single large firm. (The major exception is probably service outlets operating under a franchise system, which will be discussed in the next chapter.) The preponderance of small firms is again apparent from Census data on employment: the number of proprietors (sole owners or partners) exceeds the number of paid employees in many of the service trades and is almost equal to the number of paid workers in others. Among suppliers of personal services, for example, self-service laundries, barber shops, shoe and hat repair shops, cleaners and pressers, and clothing repair shops fall into the first category; among automobile services, general repair shops, radiator repair, muffler shops, and house-trailer rental services appear in the second category. Establishments with no paid employees account for the majority of sellers of all types of specialized repair services—radio and televisions, watches and jewelry, furniture and upholstery, knife and tool sharpening, sewer and septic tank cleaning.

The small firm is therefore typical of many service industries; the number of sellers in any given area depends on the size of the market in that area; and the existence of local monopolies is more pronounced. The one-bank town, the one or two pharmacists who serve an area; the single hospital

* See Chap. 8, pp. 289–91.

within reach; the only golf course, theater, or racetrack for miles around—all these tend to make the consumer keenly aware of the differences between many sellers and only one.

On the other hand, consumers have become more mobile and local firms in all kinds of business feel the competition of sellers at greater distances. One-third of the shoppers in supermarkets, for example, travel more than two miles to reach their "favorite" store, although half of them live closer to other supermarkets. Such a threat of potential competition has considerable effect on many "pocket monopolies." In some cases, the local banker, druggist, or jeweler may have a monopoly simply because he has emerged as the sole survivor of what was a highly competitive struggle—but it may break out again, if a new firm decides that the market is big enough to share. Consumer mobility has been highly important to the category of "food purchased away from home." In 1935, 153,000 eating and drinking places had total sales of about $1.66 billion; in 1963, there were 264,000 such establishments, with sales of $17 billion. A great variety exists—restaurants, cafeterias, drive-ins, roadside ice-cream stands, pizza palaces, and pancake houses.

Some services, such as public utilities, depend on the economies of scale. The single large firm, which is technically superior in this field to many smaller competitors, is granted a local monopoly under government regulation of prices and output. The relative strength of the monopoly reflects consumer preference: the householder may buy either gas or electricity for cooking; he may choose to travel by either bus or railroad or airplane. But not all consumers find competing sellers available: while gas and oil may be alternatives for heating in some regions, they may not be so in others; railroad transportation is nonexistent in many places and is rapidly disappearing elsewhere. It is true that public utility commissions theoretically exercise their control on behalf of the consumer interest; actually their performance varies widely, and depends on the level of government that possesses the authority, as well as on the skill of the regulatory personnel.

Differentiation and Close Substitutes

In monopolistic competition, each competing seller offers a unique output, but one that is closely similar to the output of others. The amount of differentiation depends on consumer preferences: the long-standing and acrimonious debate over "real" or "imagined" differences and "rational" or "irrational" preferences is quite beside the point.

Chamberlin's original explanation of differentiation distinguished two possibilities: the first is "based upon certain characteristics of the product itself, such as exclusive patented features; trade-marks; trade names; peculiarities of the package or container, if any; or singularity in quality, design, color, or style."[10] Such differentiation is the prerogative of the producer, and clearly the production of manufactured consumer goods fits this description. American industry is engaged in turning out close substitutes within a general class of consumption choice: automobiles come from four large domestic firms and a number of smaller foreign manufacturers, but the range of models, optional features, and colors makes thousands of alternatives available; appliances come from an industry that has few producers but hundreds of products; about 300 processors ship many more hundreds of brands of frozen foods. The list can be continued indefinitely. Trademarks and brand names serve to reinforce, in the consumer's mind, product differences of design or patented features. The historical development of such differentiation, as reviewed in Chapter 1, suggests that consumers did benefit from improvements in quality and standardization and that brand names were essential to the process. It is clear that such differentiation also exists in the service trades, if only because human labor is involved, and human beings are not identical.

Chamberlin's second type of differentiation has to do with the conditions of sale; specifically, for retailers, "such factors as the convenience of the seller's location, the general tone or character of his establishment, his way of doing business, his reputation for fair dealing, courtesy, efficiency, and all those personal links which attach his customers either to himself or to those employed by him."[11] Here, obviously, all the variations in the consumer's shopping process serve to differentiate sellers: the retailer's "way of doing business" is the counterpart of the consumer's way of receiving goods from producers. Economists are given to listing different "services" as examples of output differentiation by retailers: credit, delivery, self-selection, store furnishings, repair and installation, and hours of operation. More important than any of these is the retailer's choice of inventory: the particular alternatives he groups for the customer's shopping. The expansion of "scrambled merchandising" in the past few years reinforces the idea of distribution as a process rather than a service industry.

Abandoning the industry concept in favor of the process viewpoint helps to clear up an untenable distinction in the theory of monopolistic competition, between product differentiation and selling costs. Clearly, it is consumer preferences that establish the existence and the extent of product differentiation. Chamberlin introduced the term "selling costs" to describe the firm's means of *changing* consumer preferences; among these, advertising has since occupied most of the discussion. The purpose for making this distinction was originally to define two different types of competitive activity by sellers. First, competition takes place through product variation, the dynamic aspect of differentiation. When a product is changed, its cost of production is affected. Second, sellers compete by attempting to change consumer preferences for the same product, and now selling costs are added to production costs. Chamberlin suggests that the consumer can choose, however, to "contract" or to buy the product without receiving the selling effort.[12] A housewife can purchase soap and yet refuse to look at television; the TV commercial is therefore a selling cost to the firm. But the housewife (unless she is blind or illiterate or unfamiliar with the language) cannot avoid the advertisement on the soap wrapper; the package and its message are therefore product variations and, as such, represent production costs to the firm.

If, however, consumer choices require a process of shopping and buying in order to become consumer purchases, this distinction loses its importance. The opposite of selling is buying; the "selling costs" of the firm have a counterpart in the "buying costs" of the household.

The first step in the buying process requires that information be available for a consumer decision; selling efforts provide such information. It is impossible to separate those activities that acquaint the consumer with a product, and result in his *forming* a preference for it, from those that *change* his preference. Furthermore, firms that actively vary their products make some efforts to fulfill consumer preferences,* not just to change them. For no new product can improve the firm's position unless consumers know about it, accept it, and change their buying habits accordingly. It is impossible to separate the impact made on consumer preference by the advertising of a product change from that made by the product change itself. Granted that advertising cannot be equated with unbiased information, which enables the consumer to choose what best fits his tastes and preferences, it does contain some information, if only the fact that a product or seller exists.

It is not wholly for its own selfish reasons that the

* These efforts are worth some analysis, which will be given in Chap. 10.

advertising profession deplores the saying that is so often quoted, "Build a better mousetrap and the world will beat a path to your door." It is rather in recognition of the power of consumer demand, a recognition established in economic analysis by the statement that a product variation exists, "as long as it is of any importance whatever to buyers." A product difference may, in fact, be completely ignored; adding a chemical food coloring to make frozen beans greener will not impress the color-blind consumer. On the other hand, the informational content of an advertising message may itself change the product in the eyes of the consumer, as Chamberlin's most recent article recognizes:

There is certainly an adverse "value judgment" in the general discussion of information as afforded by advertising. Although generally defended within limits and with qualifications, what seems to be in mind is purely technical information. Yet the fact that a certain prominent athlete or movie star smokes a certain brand of cigarettes is just as much *information* as statements about the quality of the tobacco—and it may be much more important to the buyer.[13]

Many costs of production, or product differences, also provide information, in the same way that selling efforts and costs do. A small manufacturer of hand tools, unable to demonstrate his product's "technical" superiority or to differentiate its design, printed two words on the handle of each tool in his line and thereupon found his sales shooting upwards. It was clearly the information contained in the two words that changed consumer preference. But the two words happened to be "Lifetime Guarantee"—and this, of course, made the tools a different product. The firm incurred additional production costs in making the guarantee good, but such a guarantee, unadvertised, would not affect consumers' preferences.

The interdependence of product differences and selling effort is perhaps clearest in packaging, which cannot be successfully distinguished from the product itself, and which was included in Chamberlin's list of possible product variations. Yet packaging also serves to sell, or assists the consumer to buy. Some of this is the result of an increase in information: the consumer can observe and judge through transparent wrapping. Some represents pure advertising: a better surface for brand names, trademarks, or slogans. But how is one to define advertising whose message proclaims the absence of advertising? Cigarettes, cosmetics, and household supplies can now be purchased with an outside cover, which can be removed to reveal a "lovely container with no ugly advertising" to mar its surface. The appeal of such a so-called product difference would not exist unless there had been previous consumer experience with so-called selling costs. And, of course, some packaging has an immediate impact on consumer taste and preference:

Three motivating factors for a successful packaging program are consumer needs, desires, and weaknesses. "Consumer weakness includes the embellishments assigned to a package. . . . They add little or nothing to the factual aspect of the package, nothing to the product, but to a large measure they create the impulse for purchasing."[14]

The firm's activities in providing a differentiated product cannot be easily untangled from the activities which result in selling costs, because they both may provide information about products and thereby lead to the establishment of consumer preferences.

The difficulties involved in trying to separate selling costs from variations in the product arise from the implicit assumption that selling, like distribution, consists of a separate service function. Insisting upon this assumption leads to the paradox that, while the model of monopolistic competition, which describes competing sellers of a general class of service, applies readily to retailers, the model of monopolistic competition, describing product or service differentiation separately from selling costs, does not apply at all to retailers. For Chamberlin's original definition of product differentiation suggests that differences may occur in the "conditions surrounding its sale" and lists various ways in which retailers differ from one another. But these are exactly the characteristics which retailers vary in order to differentiate their stores, and so there is nothing left to account for the retailer's "selling efforts."

A specific example may make this clear. Chamberlin suggests that "selling costs" are incurred for those activities that can be distributed separately from the "product." If so, a consumer does not pay for these costs as a necessary part of the "package" he purchases. According to this reasoning, a store that offers both credit and delivery and at the same time charges a lower price with cash payment is offering, in effect, two different "packages"; a store that offers credit *without* giving a discount for cash incurs a selling cost, which is presumably covered by the prices charged. However, this ignores the dual relation between selling costs and buying costs. From the consumer's point of view, some means must exist for him to make payment. In the second case, the cash customer who does not obtain a discount in a credit store may have to pay for the store's selling cost, but in the first case, a cash customer who does receive a discount incurs a buying cost. The nature of this buying cost is clear: the cash customer must have ready access to liquid assets. For in either case, the medium of exchange must exist—either in the hands of the consumer who pays it to the retailer or in the retailer's credit which is extended to the consumer.

The definition of selling and distribution as "services" poses the further problem that retailers provide many services that are not paid for by a consumer's purchase. The casual shopper who wanders through a dress or furniture store in order to get new ideas; the passerby who is reminded by a window display about something he needs to buy; the avid bargain hunter who gets advice, technical information, and even the make and model number from a specialized dealer— yet does his buying in a discount house—all these are receiving the retailer's services without making any payment. Are they enjoying the benefits of his selling costs or of his product? Exactly the same "services" are sought by purchasers. Is the salary of a windowdresser to be apportioned between production and selling costs according to the proportion of viewers who buy to those who do not? And what of those customers who are attracted by the display to enter the store, yet find their readiness to buy thwarted by a gap in inventory?

All these difficulties arise when distribution or selling is regarded as an economic function performed solely by sellers. The distinction between product differentiation and selling costs implies that consumers choose a product separately from the way in which it is sold, and ignores the consumer's choice of a shopping process. But when distribution is seen as a process, the problems disappear. This process consists of an assortment of functions, and these may be variously performed by manufacturer, retailer, and consumer. In terms of the consumer's shopping process, each retailer is a unique seller because each outlet offers a slightly different way for these functions to be performed by all three participants. Consumers must under any conditions select their purchase, inform the seller of their choice, make payment, and take possession of the goods or services, but these same tasks may be accomplished in quite different ways.

If manufacturers' attempts to change consumer preferences via selling costs are successful, consumers are "presold," and the retailer's responsibilities for informing, advising, and persuading disappear. But these responsibilities are the retailer's product: his costs of doing business are less to "presold" consumers because he need not employ specialized sales people. It is clear that if retailers vary their product—their way of doing business—by offering self-selection, their production costs decline, yet this may only be possible because manufacturers have incurred additional selling costs in advertising in order to enable consumers to help themselves. They may be assisted in this task not only by the selling costs of the manufacturer but by product variation, for household supplies are sold in protective transparent wrapping, clothing is prepackaged, and appliances come in factory-sealed cartons, with informative labels or instruction booklets. Since all the functions of distribution remain, no matter what the shopping process, there seems little point in trying to allocate costs between product variation and selling effort.

If consumers use credit for an increasing number of purchases, both retailers and manufacturers may vary their product: the former by offering a variety of revolving credit systems, the latter by setting up subsidiary finance corporations to handle installment paper. If the shopping process shifts the delivery function from retailers to consumers, manufacturers may vary their product by packing toys and furniture for assembly at home, turning out a "handi-size" packet for a car's glove compartment or a "giant economy size" carton with convenient carrying handles. The process of consumer shopping is capable of just as much variation as any product or service. One article describes such developments as continuing innovation:

In each period of innovation established retailers have failed to realize that the new type of store was finding consumer acceptance on other than a price basis . . . Major retail innovations involve an "invention" of new means of performing the retailing function. They may be dependent on concomitant developments in products, in physical handling technology, and in organization at the wholesale supply level; *but most important of all, they are dependent on changes in the income, location, and style of life of the consumer.*[15]

239

Although these writers recognize that consumers must accept changes in distribution, they see the phenomenon too narrowly because they are focusing chiefly upon retailing. Manufacturers, retailers, and consumers all have a share in the innovating, just as they do in the distribution process.

The model of monopolistic competition places its emphasis on sellers' attempts to differentiate their offerings via variations in the product or service or shipping process rather than price competition. All the empirical data so far presented support this analysis for the markets in which consumers buy. This is not to say that pricing is never used as a competitive weapon, or that these characteristics of monopolistic competition apply with equal strength to all consumer purchases. But to analyze market competition and consumer choice means analyzing nonprice competition and its various appeals to consumer tastes and preferences.

Extra-Market Competition

The validity of this approach is even verified by examining those areas of consumption expenditure that take place outside the market's framework of purchase and sale. Voluntary contributions and gifts are, obviously, not market transactions: they involve social as well as economic benefits and costs. But the notion of "competing sellers" is not completely far-fetched when applied to such organizations as the Red Cross, the Community Chest, the local hospital or political party, one's church, or one's alma mater. From the consumer's point of view they all offer opportunities to dispose of his income; expenditures in one area must be weighed against the appeal not only of alternative charitable organizations but of goods and services in the market. The satisfaction that the consumer receives from his donation, however, cannot very satisfactorily be evaluated against price. One can readily say to a retailer that a suit, or desk, or bunch of asparagus "isn't worth the money," but such a remark is rarely applicable to the fund-raiser for a worthy cause who will accept any contribution, no matter how small. Clearly, therefore, the consumer's decision as to how much of his income he will contribute, and to what organizations, turns on nonprice considerations and his own tastes and preferences.

Aside from voluntary contributions and gifts, another area of extra-market consumption exists which is of greater or less importance to particular consumers. *Income in kind* consists of extra-market consumption—goods and services made available to the consumer in place of money income. The national income accounts note two different types of income in kind: that which represents payment of wages and that provided by assets which the consumer owns. The 1960–61 Survey of Consumer Expenditures reviewed in Chapter 3 does not distinguish either of these from the value of goods and services received as gifts or from welfare agencies—still another form of extra-market consumption, to be discussed in Chapter 9.

The first type—income in kind representing wages—includes such things as meals furnished to employees of restaurants and hotels, board and room provided to boarding-school teachers or hospital staff, uniforms issued to personnel in many occupations, and so on. These provide utility or satisfactions, and the consumer's "real income" is obviously increased, over his money income, by the value of such items. But while he is relieved from any demands on his money income for these things, he is also relieved—or rather prevented—from making his own consumption choice. It is not his preferences as a consumer that determine the style of uniform, the size of room, the menu of the meal that he receives.

This limitation of consumer choice which is inherent in payment in kind should be recognized in any discussion of nonmonetary payments—sometimes called fringe benefits. Employees' discounts, company-subsidized recreation or entertainment, paid vacations, stock option plans, medical and health insurance, company-provided trips or cars, and similar goods and services furnished to employees as part of their compensation have become far more numerous since World War II—some estimate that nonwage compensation amounts to 20 per cent of total labor income. To the extent that these substitute for money payments, they reduce the freedom of consumer choice and the exercise of consumer preference. It should be clear that consumers can gain maximum satisfaction only if they are free to select their own patterns of spending and saving. Whenever income is paid in kind, that freedom disappears.

For example, the faculty member who lives in university-subsidized housing has given up some measure of choice: his actual housing has been limited to the area selected by the university, the architectural and decorating styles approved by the university, the maintenance and furnishing conditions set by the university. The fact that he pays less than the market rental for such housing may or may not be sufficient compensation for the loss of choice. But it is incorrect for the recipient to calculate the entire subsidy as real income (or consumption). For the subsidy must also cover the cost of his restriction, his inability to shift income from one type of spending to another, his limited choice of alternatives. The uncommitted consumer can generally succeed in finding a little money for an unexpected emergency by cutting down on housing expenditure— letting the utility bill go unpaid for two months, postponing a needed repair, in short, reducing his consumption of housing in order to increase consumption elsewhere. No such opportunity exists for the dweller in faculty housing: his housing consumption is fixed; the portion of his income that is represented by subsidized housing is committed to housing and cannot be

242

switched, at the consumer's behest, to any other preference. The same reasoning applies to any form of income payment in kind; in so far as consumption is bestowed, rather than bought with money income, the consumer's freedom of choice is thereby narrowed. It is ironic that the acceleration of nonprice competition with its use of variations in products and in shopping processes to fulfill consumer preferences should have occurred during the same period of time that the proportion of income paid in nonmonetary form should have risen. Presumably the personal income tax structure now existing has been more than a little responsible.

The second type of income in kind—services provided by land or capital goods which the consumer owns—poses all sorts of problems if any sort of quantitative measure is desired.[16] In an underdeveloped economy, much consumption is closely tied to production, without the intervention of a market. As the United States changed from an agricultural economy to an industrial country, the value of farm production consumed on the farm diminished steadily as a proportion of total consumption. Most consumption in a developed economy requires expenditures in the market; the major exception today is the value of homes owned by consumers not only on farms but in metropolitan, suburban, and rural areas.

The national income statistics list the "net rent of owner-occupied farm and nonfarm dwellings" as part of both income and consumption. A home-owning consumer is his own landlord; his real income is higher than that of a tenant with the same money income. To some extent, his consumption is locked into his receipt of this income, but the limitation of choice is not a result of employment, as is the nonmonetary compensation of employees. The choice of housing can be changed; it merely requires a longer period of time and more complex decisions than for the type of expenditure that is central to most market analysis. The market for homes is a capital market as well as one for consumption. Consumers are similarly locked in by any purchase involving contractual payments. Most renters do not consider their expenditures for shelter on a short-term basis, as they do the weekly food bill or the fall clothing assortment. Payments of insurance premiums are not reviewed for possible change each time income is received, nor are monthly payments of installment debt, school or college tuition charges, and so on.

Both income in kind and contractual payments take the consumer out of the market: but in all cases, except that of fringe benefits to labor, the consumer is free to return to the market at any time, solely on the basis of his income and preferences. It is to an analysis of the effects of these tastes and preferences on sellers in the market that most attention must be given.

chapter **7 Price**

Competition

in the

Market

*W*hen sellers compete for consumer purchases, they do so with a variety of weapons: merchandise assortment and quality, product variation and its advertising, brand names and guarantees, salesmanship and services and all the devices gathered under the head of nonprice competition. Price competition, far from being a general practice, is rarely used as the primary weapon to attract consumer choice. Not only do prices on similar products fall very close to one another, when they are not identical, but they also change rather infrequently, at both the manufacturing and retail levels. The major exception is probably food; prices for fresh produce reflect short-run and seasonal changes in supply, and processors' prices reflect both seasonal and trend shifts in supply. Retail sellers of food, however, exhibit remarkable similarity in the level of their prices and in the timing of their price changes.

The special terminology which exists for price change seems to verify this generalization. At retail, prices "deteriorate" from being "kicked around," and even a "price war" can break out; manufacturers' prices are "shaded," "firmed up," "hesitant," or "off"; at either level, the term "price-cutter" is an epithet of contempt. Outside forces, such as the 1965 excise tax cut or freight rate increases, are said to "necessitate" price change. Firms that suffer ailing sales or profit conditions may have succumbed to "overemphasis on competitive pricing"; a new model of a well-known product is advertised this way to the trade: "You don't have to sell on price!" The implication of all this is clear: not only is business quite familiar with the theory and practice of nonprice competition, but businessmen themselves offer considerable justification for concentrating on it:

Does competition depend on the price alone? . . . The producer of goods does compete in efficiency of service, in style of the article being sold, in design, in advertising his lines of merchandise to the retailer and to the consumer. These are all elements of competition. Salesmanship is an element of competition. These are the things that we are competing with. . . . Do you think there is competition between the Arrow shirt people and the Manhattan, Jayson, and Van Heusen people? I tell you there is plenty of competition between them. Where does that competition lie? In price? No, their price lines are about the same. Each of them makes a $4.50 shirt, each one makes a $5 shirt, and each one makes a $6 shirt. But they are competing in the quality of their product and in their design and advertising to get consumer acceptance. These are the areas of legitimate competition.[1]

Similar statements abound in the trade press, in afterdinner speeches and in testimony before Congressional committees; the ideas are taken for granted by most businessmen.

Some consumer transactions that do involve substantial

price competition occur in real estate, automobiles, and major appliances. In each of these areas, consumer choice is courted with nonprice competition, yet both buyers and sellers remain extremely price-conscious, nevertheless. Consumers boast of where they can get the "best price," and retailers advertise "the best deal in town" or "rock-bottom prices always." The market for these goods differs from those for other consumer purchases in which there are many buyers and many sellers. The sale of a house, or the purchase of an automobile or of a large appliance, in which a trade-in may be involved, allows for bargaining between the individual buyer and seller. The one-price system does not exist: different buyers may have different prices quoted to them. Whether or not a purchase results, and on what terms, depends on the bargaining skills on both sides—on the knowledge, preferences, persuasiveness, and bluff demonstrated by both buyer and seller. Even such transactions, however, also reflect the existence of price conformity among sellers and price stability over time, for the bargaining process generally consists of discussing discounts from a stated price, and it is such "base-point" prices that are subject to the terms quoted above.

These pricing aspects of nonprice competition raise several questions. What institutional forces promote relative price conformity and price stability? what are the implications for consumer choice? finally, how can price itself be used as a form of nonprice competition?

The model of consumer choice presented in Chapter 4 is basically a static model: it provides an equilibrium solution for the consumer who faces well-defined given conditions. Real-world consumers, however, have to make their choices while all sorts of conditions are constantly changing: the availability of substitutes, the quality of product or service, their own tastes and preferences, and so on. In such circumstances, if prices are relatively stable over time and generally uniform among sellers, then consumers have one less variable to deal with, yet the process of consumer choice still differs from that described by the model.

In that analysis, each choice depends on the consumer's weighing all the possible alternatives of spending and saving, but the array of alternatives is too great for consumers to make such an evaluation with every purchase. The number of transactions needed in order to provide goods and services to an average family for one year has been estimated to be in the thousands; in supermarkets alone, the average shopper buys 20 to 40 items twice weekly. But if prices are generally stable, the consumer's choice, once made, will remain valid; if prices are generally uniform, the consumer can consider other differences among sellers.

Such an interpretation of the theory of consumer choice enhances its realism. The mental gymnastics involved in calculating the marginal rate of substitution between a given product and all the other goods and services that are available with a total given income seem an improbable exercise for consumers to indulge in regularly. But if marginal analysis need not be applied in every case, its calculations can be more readily used, either wholly or in part, for *some* purchase decisions— —with illuminating results. The consumer who is contemplating the purchase of a new pair of shoes need not review or revise her entire consumption pattern, but she will very likely consider the satisfaction to be derived from $19.95's worth of new shoes as opposed to $19.95's worth of new hat. One of the commonest uses of such "opportunity cost analysis" occurs when consumers weigh one possible purchase against another item that will have to be foregone if this one is purchased. Other real-world situations provide evidence for the realism of the theoretical analysis. The statement "It's certainly worth the extra money" implies direct measurement of a marginal rate of substitution against a price ratio; the verdict delivered by a customer, "Thank you, they're not quite what I'm looking for," means that none of the alternatives offered will maximize satisfaction.

A second implication of relative price stability and general price conformity among sellers is that it allows more detailed elaboration of that catch-all category "consumer tastes and preferences" in the theory of consumer choice. That model analyzes changes in prices, while the monopolistic-competition model of consumer markets stresses the *lack* of price change. In the market model, sellers concentrate on nonprice competition and confront the consumer with variations in product, design, quality, terms of sale, and so on. The model of consumer choice has little room for the impact of these nonprice variations; the framework of indifference curves and levels of satisfaction is unenlightening. It follows that for the most part the analysis of consumer tastes and preferences has been of theoretical interest to psychologists and sociologists, but it has been of keenly practical interest to marketing businessmen.

Finally, where price competition is lacking, the seller may use price itself as a form of nonprice competition. Price lines or price endings serve to identify a particular producer; price comparisons can be used to differentiate a particular model or product. There is the "top-of-the-line" model or the "promotional number"—both terms being meaningful in relation to some average or normal (and relatively fixed) price. There are also "high-price" stores and "bargain outlets"; the implications as to quality may or may not be justified.

None of this argument implies that price competition cannot exist anywhere, but rather that it is not typical of consumer markets. It follows, therefore, that the individual seller who does compete on a price basis has made a deliberate choice of policy. Furthermore, this policy will serve to identify the particular seller, to distinguish his output by his way of doing business.

In general, price competition as a means of differentiation occurs less frequently among manufacturers than it does among retailers. As Professor Oxenfeldt has pointed out, it is Macy's or Gimbel's that claims not to be undersold, rather than General Electric or General Motors.[2] And the producer's concentration on nonprice considerations tends to minimize price change, with resultant stabilizing effects on resale prices. The consumer is generally unaware of price changes at the manufacturing level, but does react to a retailer's use of price competition, for such a practice sometimes characterizes certain stores, which differ from other outlets where prices are not of primary importance. But if one store (or a type of retail operation) can use price competition in this way, as a differentiating characteristic, it must be because there is relative price conformity among other sellers. Much of what exists can be traced to the strength of custom and tradition.

The Role of Convention and Custom

Any consumer with some experience in shopping can predict what the prices for many goods and services will be on his next buying expedition, whether or not he expects the products themselves to change. The price to consumers, whether computed by retailers or manufacturers, is frequently a matter of routine calculation based on long-standing trade practice. A single observed price may represent the force of conventional price endings, customary price lines or price points, or a traditional markup. Each of these deserves some consideration.

First of all, "customary" prices frequently depend on established price endings. "In dresses . . . for some reason, wholesale prices usually have $.75 tacked on, while retail tags add $.95 or $.98."[3] "In the candy business the 9's—19¢, or 29¢, and 39¢—are considered the most acceptable consumer-pricing range."⁴ Many numbers are thus in effect prevented from ever occurring as retail prices. The way in which prices are quoted reflects two facets of the monetary system in any economy: the monetary unit and its subdivisions, and the kinds of "token money" (whether small bills or coins) that represent small denominations carried for the sake of convenience in completing transactions. The first facet accounts for the fact that, in the United States, prices end in cents as well as dollars and more sales take place at $7.95 than at $8.00, while in Great Britain prices end in pennies as well as shillings and pounds. The second means that pay-station telephone calls and chocolate bars have been priced in multiples of five, since nickels, dimes, and quarters are all "small change" in the United States. Both odd-cents pricing and payment in fractional currency reflect custom and convention, frequently reinforced by spectacularly unsuccessful attempts to change.

There are many references to consumer psychology, or consumer preferences, in causal explanations for the existence of these price endings. "Note that today, most food products sell at 19¢, 29¢, 39¢ and so forth. This is what is called a psychological price, and people will buy items at 29¢ when they won't buy at 28¢, 38¢, etc., even if the price is cheaper."⁵ One elaboration of this consumer "psychology" suggests that $2.98 can lure the buyer who would not spend $3.00. But it is difficult to give any credence to the notion that the consumer is so massively ignorant of the difference between 19/6 and £1, or between $7.95 and $8.00. It is true that price endings that are fractionally lower than the next whole dollar occur far more frequently among low-priced articles than they do among high-priced goods. It can be argued, of course, that consumers with low incomes are the chief buyers of low-priced merchandise, and that such buyers are in fact and with reason sensitive to the gain or loss of a few pennies. But it may also mean merely that pricing per se, as a tactic or policy in competition, may be a more successful strategy for low-income buyers than for high-income ones.[6]

A slightly more sophisticated reason for the existence of odd-cents endings notes that such prices expand the possibilities of advertising appeals. The seller can say "Under $3.00" as well as "Only $2.98." This argument seems more reasonable than the first in explaining fractional price endings on furniture or clothing or appliances that sell for hundreds of dollars. Pricing a refrigerator at $199.95 allows the seller to claim, truthfully, "Less than $200," while it is hard to believe that a consumer, in contemplating that price tag, would feel the nickel saving to be a real bargain.

In some areas the impact of sales taxes has an obvious effect on price endings: a 5 per cent tax on restaurant meals over a dollar means that a luncheon special that is priced at 99¢ is more than just a penny cheaper. On the other hand, a general sales tax will make saving by way of fractional price endings much more difficult to achieve.

A corollary to the notion that fractional price endings occur most frequently on low-priced goods for low-income consumers is that *not* using fractional price endings may have a certain snob appeal. Pricing a fur-trimmed suit or an easy chair at $145 rather than at $139.95 suggests that the slight difference in expense is more than compensated for by the selling process offered by the retailer. Other price endings may be used to identify sellers in quite an opposite way. In the garment or appliance industry, where price endings of $.50, $.95, or $.98 are extremely rigid, unfamiliar endings, such as $.31 or $.73, carry a strong implication of discounting and of genuine bargains. Once a customary price has been established, the retailer can differentiate his offerings precisely by failing to observe it.

Price endings, of course, determine only a fraction of the

total price. Price points have an equally strong influence in many lines: "A portable television set that has been selling at around $150 could be reduced either to $140 or $130, depending on just what the manufacturer wants or needs to accomplish. . . . The set [could] be priced at $135, but this is off-point pricing and most companies do not go in for that."[7] "Popular price points in promotional offerings were $6.98, $7.98 and $8.98 a square yard."[8] Such customary prices also reflect the influence of a price line or price range:

Retailers will see new "fill-in" price points emphasized in all classifications of floor care products . . . as manufacturers strive to provide logical step-ups from promotional models.[9]

Like price endings, a price range can serve to differentiate a product or seller. The terms "big ticket" or "low-end" describe merchandise by their rank in the distribution of prices. For many years automobiles were divided into high-priced, medium-priced, and low-priced cars. More specifically, manufacturers of furniture, clothing, jewelry, and other consumer goods may be identified by the price range in which they sell their products:

In dresses, the top price range is considered to start at $39.75, which means a retail price of about $69.95. . . . The firm making $6.75's, for example, which retail for $10.95 or $11.98, may go as high as $12.75, which costs a woman $21.95 to $22.95.[10]

The company [Clairol] is just starting to ship its cosmetics. . . . Prices, Gelb says, are at the Max Factor–Revlon level: $1.10 for lipstick, $1.50 for powder and liquid make-up, 85¢ for nail polish.[11]

At retail, price lines sometimes serve to describe the type of outlet:

Formerly known as Big Red, the Evans firm has transformed and upgraded over a 5-year period from a "low-end furniture" company to a "top-price" level. . . . This autumn the firm plans to open a high prestige salon . . . featuring custom interiors, high styling with gold-lettered delivery vans and white uniformed servicemen.[12]

The same is true of price points; saying that one store's best sellers are at $69 while another's are around $99 provides a clear distinction between two different types of stores, even when they carry the same product line.

While similar examples of customary prices and established price lines can be accumulated easily, explanations of the phenomenon are not easy to come by. The persistence of price lines and customary prices reflects the strength of the conventional markups that are used in pricing by both manufacturers and retailers. Where the manufacturer quotes prices on a list basis with varying trade discounts, the list prices are frequently quoted at the retail level, if only as the base from which the retailer is to discount. If the manufacturer does not publish list prices, he must nevertheless calculate some approximation to retail prices in order to estimate consumer demand for his product. In either case, there must be an allowance for the distributors' margin—wholesale and retail markups over factory cost. The retailer also uses a markup over factory cost in order to calculate price to the consumer, if he does not accept the manufacturer's suggested price. The force of custom and tradition is even stronger in markups than in price endings or price points: "At $99.50 this would show over 60 percent gross, as compared to the traditional 41 percent to 43 percent gross. In the men's wear field, 60 percent gross is an unheard-of markup."[13] "Fixed margins would appear to have been a factor in maintaining some of the traditional distinctions between trades."[14] "The recommended markup on ethical drugs was 66⅔%."[15] Just as with customary prices, traditional retail margins may be noted chiefly by their absence, as individual dealers set out to distinguish their operations from their competitors' by using price competition and a lower markup. But

254

also just as with list prices, it is the historically established markup that serves as the base from which to depart.

All these pricing practices exist for sound business reasons. The theory of the firm, which has not been dealt with in this work, presents a model of price determination by sellers which closely parallels the theory of consumer choice. In particular, it shows that each seller is faced with an array of alternative possibilities that are as multitudinous as those facing the consumer. Hence, the model does not describe every pricing decision taken by a real-world retailer any more than the theory of consumer choice describes every purchase decision made by a real-life consumer. The retailer reserves marginal analysis for strategic decisions, and uses "rule-of-thumb" pricing practice generally, in order to economize time and energy.

The "nonprice" aspect of price—the use of prices and price lines to distinguish, or differentiate products and sellers—has significant implications. Insofar as prices to consumers are preselected by manufacturers and retailers, the cause-and-effect relations that are generally accepted as determining prices in the market must be reversed. Economic analysis views market competition in terms of supply and demand which, between them, determine price: products are supplied, these supplies come to the market, and it is the meeting between these supplies and consumer demands that shapes prices. But the widespread use of familiar price endings and price points, as well as of customary margins, suggests that events do not take place in that order. Instead, prices are actually determined before production; the manufacturer designs his output to meet a price. This is widely recognized in various trades and helps to explain the business insistence on nonprice competition mentioned above.

Now, if we are going to try to price in a way that the retailer can finally come out to 29¢ or whatever, we can only put so much product into the package. In short, as a manufacturer, we begin by

255

figuring what kind of a retail price we can get, and we work back from that point to determine what weight of product we can put in the package. Not only do we do this, but every other company in the grocery business does the same.[16]

With few exceptions every designer is ruled by the price tag. His working method and the materials he uses are rigidly limited by the firm's price range. A designer of dresses retailing at $29 to $49 points out, "I have to watch the cost of the fabrics I use, keeping in mind how much yardage goes into a sheath and how much into a full-skirted style. . . . I can't make too many that sell at $49, but if I have a sheath at $29, I can't have another too much like it at $49, even if the higher priced one is made of more expensive fabric."[17]

In a sense, "packaging to price" is moreover a form of adaptation to modern prepacked, self-service merchandising of yesteryear's customer request to "give me 15 cents' worth of rice, please!"[18]

The situations described here obviously do not invalidate the usefulness of conventional supply-demand analysis, for the market still remains powerful. If consumer demand at a chosen price was gauged incorrectly, either price or supply must change; if costs of production were inaccurately estimated, price or output must alter. In most manufactured consumer goods, the adjustment takes place in output: the manufacturer or retailer drops the model that is a slow seller, or else redesigns the product to compensate for rising costs. The *ability* to make such changes in output is an indication of the monopoly power of the seller; the *necessity* for such changes stems from the competition that limits any such power. Furthermore, even when prices, rather than output, change, the effect of predetermined prices still remains. Price changes that are expected to be permanent usually consist of a move to the next familiar price point.

The manufacturer's production decision includes not only prices and price lines but also a choice of distribution channels. To work back from any retail price to its factory cost requires the calculation of a margin to allow distributors, and the margin chosen may define the type of retail outlet. For retailers, also, it is the decision on price that comes first:

It is a maxim of good merchandising that goods should be sold before they are bought. This means that the merchant should be sure of the saleability of the merchandise at specific retail prices before he makes a purchase.[19]

When the retailer decides what prices he will sell at (and buys accordingly), he helps to identify the store's assortment of offerings. Prices in a shop window carry information to the consumer about the entire retail operation, not just the particular items displayed:

The good merchant's two great watchwords are "assortments" and "presentation." These are the "what" and "how." Determining what assortments of goods are to be offered comes first, what classifications, styles, materials, colors, prices, sizes. . . .[20]

It is clear from this quotation that price is only one of many characteristics (of not unequal importance) by which a seller differentiates his business.

To the consumer, this aspect of pricing is also important. The retailer's inventory provides an important source of information—the opportunity to compare goods as well as to make a choice. The assortments and price lines that are carried often determine a shopper's preference for one store rather than another.[21] In order for prices and price lines to hold this informational content for consumers, they must be relatively stable over time. Custom and convention make prices recognizable. They may be used to identify sellers who operate in closely similar ways, or to distinguish the individual retailer, who is using odd prices as a "product" differentiation.

Price is far more than a rationing device that determines which potential customer will be able to afford to make a purchase. Generally it is one of the most important actions in creating an impres-

257

sion of the firm among potential customers. Especially as tangible differences among rival products shrink, these intangibles will grow in significance for marketing success.[22]

To preserve customary prices and traditional markups requires some reinforcement of conventional pricing practices, particularly that of discouraging retailers from using overt price competition as a marketing weapon. In the case of a branded or trademarked item, the manufacturer has considerable potential influence over retail prices. Most controversial of the ways in which such influence is exerted are the resale price maintenance laws.

Resale Price Maintenance

Resale price maintenance in this country has evolved along with the changing nature of competition. By their introduction of trademarks and brand names in the late nineteenth century, manufacturers made it easier for consumers to buy. Standardized goods quickened the growth of the one-price system, for bargaining between retailer and consumer began to decrease when clerks and assistants staffed the larger stores. With some products, therefore, manufacturers had succeeded in "preselling" consumers, and a retail store appeared to be almost an outlet or agent of the producer. Brand-name manufacturers then took a decided interest in what retailers were doing with their products. As Justice Brandeis was to put it, in a classic article:

If a dealer is selling unknown goods or goods under his own name, he alone should set the price, but when a dealer has to use somebody else's name or brand in order to sell goods, then the owner of that name or brand has an interest which should be respected. The transaction is essentially one between the two principals—the maker and the user. All others are middlemen or agents; for the product is not really sold until it has been bought by the consumer.[23]

If it was the manufacturer who determined the resale price of his product, he could protect* his "interest which should be respected" and also be responsible for the entire transaction—"essentially one between two principals." If the price so determined also respected the customary margins of wholesaler and retailer, then price competition was effectively eliminated, and the manufacturer's entire efforts could be concentrated on advertising his trademark, using the brand name to differentiate his product, and maintaining the standard of quality associated with his presold, mass-produced, nationally distributed item. The only drawback in such an arrangement was that it was illegal.

Section 1 of the Sherman Anti-Trust Act of 1890 declared every "contract, combination in the form of trust or otherwise, or conspiracy in restraint of trade or commerce among the several States" to be illegal; in three decisions rendered during a 3-year period, the Supreme Court held that the Act applied to contracts written to maintain resale prices. The last of these cases, Dr. Miles Medical Co. v. Park and Sons Co. 220 U.S. 409, made it clear that statutory exemption from the antitrust law would be needed in order to legalize resale price maintenance contracts. Although bills were introduced in Congress almost yearly from then on, and a few states passed enabling legislation, it was not until the depression of the '30s that sufficient economic pressures were felt to bring resale price maintenance contracts into common use.

By that time, the impetus to restrict price competition came from the retailers, not from manufacturers who were seeking respect for their "interest." What the retailers sought was protection for their income, and in some cases for their

* See the observation by the Bureau of Labor Statistics on "protected" prices for flour (1890–1910) as quoted in Chap. 1, p. 21.

very existence in business. The competition, early in the century, from department stores and mail-order houses seemed only a minor irritation to established forms of retailing when it was compared with the plague of chain stores, whose sales and share of the market grew in accelerated fashion during the twenties.

Barger's estimates,[24] for example, show that in 1909, when 77 per cent of all manufactured food products were sold to wholesalers and 23 per cent to retailers, grocery independents accounted for 31 per cent of producers' sales, and grocery chains for 13 per cent. By 1929, it is true, independent stores had increased their share to 35 per cent, but chain stores now sold 21 per cent of manufactured food products. Furthermore, they purchased 18 per cent of it direct from the producer, while the independent stores bought only 5 per cent from the manufacturer. During the '20s, the independent stores declined absolutely, as well as relatively, in retail sales and volume. A similar trend occurred in other lines: in 1909, independent shoe stores distributed 40 per cent of the total shoe output and chains 10 per cent, but 20 years later the chain share had doubled, while independent shoe stores had dropped to 33 per cent of the total. Between 1919 and 1929, independents' total retail sales declined as well. Furniture, drug, and variety chains were equally successful in cutting into the markets of established, independent retailers. This growth accompanied intense price competition by the chains.* Their operating methods realized lower costs than the "historical" margin, and their lower prices were calculated on the basis of cost rather than by convention. Consumers changed their shopping habits in order to buy at chains, where the increased volume enabled even further economies of scale.

The loss of sales volume by independent retailers repre-

* Cf. Chap. 5, pp. 184–86 and the Federal Trade Commission's *Report on Chain Stores*, 1934.

sented an absolute loss of income. Any competitive attempt to meet chain-store prices worsened their position, for the typically small independent operation was not able to cut costs, as the chains were. The owner-manager of such a retail store knew that the connection between prices and his income was clear-cut and direct. In the '30s, the drastic drop of national income produced a decline of consumption spending from $79 billion to $46 billion between 1929 and 1933, and the decline of independent retailers' income was even greater. Not only were people spending less; with lower incomes, they were also becoming more price-conscious, and shifting what spending they did, away from the high-cost, high-priced retail outlets. The independent retailer, seeing bankruptcy ahead, joined the drive to protect and restore income to the established way of doing business.

Independent retailers saw their cause as a drive for Fair Trade, rather than fair income. Many of the economic measures taken during the depression were couched in terms of a similar idea of justice: the "Fair Labor Standards Act," for example, was the title for legislation that fixed minimum wages and maximum hours. Presumably, government interference with freedom would be tolerated only in the name of justice. There was also a strong overtone of equal treatment for various sectors of the economy; the term "parity" was used for farm legislation, and implied in other areas.

Resale price maintenance, by allowing prices to be fixed at a level that would provide a "fair trade" of goods for money, could improve retailers' income in two ways. First, even though sales had been hit hard by the depression, if conventional margins were restored, income would be improved. Second (and more important in the long run), if manufacturers set minimum retail prices, the chain stores could no longer threaten the livelihood of conventional retailers with price competition. Elsewhere in the economy similar arrangements for price-fixing, along with reduction of output, were quite generally sought as remedies for the depressed conditions of the early '30s; the NRA retail codes encouraged the fixing of retail margins. But such provisions ran counter to the antitrust laws and led to the Supreme Court decision that voided NRA.

An attempt to tax the chainstore out of existence with the chainstore tax . . . did not work. Next came the NRA, and the codes of fair competition. Looking back, these were basically an attempt to preserve the status quo in merchandising and sales, to protect business as it then existed in its existing channels of distribution. The attempt was protective of the small businessman and other businessmen to an extent wholly inconsistent with the hard competition concept of the Sherman Act.[25]

The failure of NRA led to renewed efforts to use resale price maintenance contracts for income protection and to remove fair trade from the shadow of restraint of trade. State legislatures were more cooperative than Congress in the drive to exempt such contracts from antitrust law. A law passed in California in 1931 was imitated in several other states after intense lobbying, particularly by the drug industry. This was enabling legislation: each law applied only within the state it was passed in, and merely permitted the manufacturer to sign up retailers in a general agreement on prices. These laws safeguarded such agreements from the charge of restraint of trade, and allowed the law of contract to be used when the manufacturer wished to enforce resale price maintenance.

Participation in such programs remained voluntary, however, so that the problem of reseller compliance arose almost immediately. Any restrictive agreement by an industry or a group with numerous members offers potential gains to one uncooperative unit: the fruits of violating the agreement may be so substantial as to constitute an irresistible form of temptation. If minimum retail prices provided reasonable (and possibly generous) margins, the "chiseler" who shaded his prices slightly and increased sales greatly was bound to appear. The same problem arose with manufacturers' codes under NRA and with voluntary agreements among farmers. The income protection offered by depression programs was jeopardized unless full compliance could be assured. Both farmers and labor turned to Federal legislation as a way to replace voluntary compliance and were successful in obtaining Federal support for their aims; big business, for obvious reasons, did not try the same. In the meantime, small retailers worked, first in the state legislatures and then in Congress, to improve their lot.

The original structure of resale price maintenance was incomplete in that no retailer could be forced to sign a contract, and thereby give up his right to compete by lowering prices. The remedy for this defect was to make the minimum prices set by the manufacturer binding on all retailers, whether or not they signed an agreement. The "nonsigner clause" was first enacted in California in 1933 and then rapidly imitated in other states. It provided that an agreement or contract on resale prices between a manufacturer and any one retailer within a state also became binding on all other retailers, upon their being notified of the terms of the contract. While theoretically this allowed the manufacturer to fix minimum resale prices for his products whether or not his buyers approved, in practice this rarely happened. Most fair-trade prices reflected historical or traditional retail margins and represented, therefore, the kind of income protection that most retailers actually sought.

After the initial passage of the nonsigner clause, 14 state legislatures responded to retail pressure with laws enabling resale price maintenance contracts. In 1936 the Supreme Court held the Illinois Fair Trade Act (which included a nonsigner clause) to be constitutional. Shortly thereafter, Congress passed the Miller-Tydings bill, which was the first successful action to approve resale price maintenance in interstate commerce. This bill amended the Sherman Act and the Federal Trade Commission Act so as to exempt from antitrust laws resale price maintenance contracts that were applied in states whose laws permitted such contracts. Naturally enough, in the year following the passage of the Miller-Tydings Act, 28 states enacted resale price maintenance laws. The amendment provided that resale price maintenance contracts could be written only for commodities that had been trade-marked or branded by the producer or distributor and were "in free and open competition with commodities of the same general class."

Like a good deal of antitrust legislation, the amendment does not stand up under economic analysis. A brand or trade-mark differentiates one product from others that are close substitutes, and in that respect has already abolished "free and open competition." The meaning of "the same general class" of commodity has never been satisfactorily defined, either in economic theory or in judicial interpretation. Finally, the existence of "free and open competition" is somewhat dubious when one essential form of competition, varying prices, is prohibited. But this legislation was not written to settle such general questions; its quite specific purpose was to allow manufacturers to adopt a price maintenance policy without danger of violating the Sherman Act. By 1941, 45 states had enacted fair-trade laws, and resale price maintenance had become part of the institutional framework of consumer markets.

The period during World War II and immediately thereafter brought relative scarcities of consumer goods and services, which meant a strong seller's market and rising prices. There was little advantage in cutting prices at a time when there was a limited quantity of merchandise and also consumer willingness, backed up with rising incomes, to pay higher prices. Fair-trade prices were not particularly thought about, and it was not until the late '40s, when consumer supplies finally caught up with the backlog of demand, that there was any consumer resistance to price rises. At this point, however, innovators began to experiment with new methods of cutting costs and abandoning traditional margins and discovered that consumers were price-conscious after all—when they were given the opportunity. The development of the discount house, which ignored conventional markups as well as customary prices, led to a recurrence of open price competition. Where fair-trade contracts prohibited this, the retailers retaliated by violating the contracts and then appealing the court action that was brought by the manufacturers. During the past 20 years, the status of resale price maintenance as a barrier to open price competition by retailers has been debated in the courts and legislatures, as well as in the markets.

In 1951 the Supreme Court nullified the use of the nonsigner clause. Technically, the decision in Schwegman Bros. v. Calvert Distillers Corp. held that the Miller-Tydings amendment did not make resale prices that had been established under state fair-trade legislation binding upon nonsigners. Within days, price cutting on fair-traded items spread over the country; full-scale price wars occurred in New York City and in other large cities. Consumers found prices on well-known electrical appliances, drugs, cosmetics, films, and housewares plummeting from day to day. Congress found fair-trade supporters pleading for help, and responded with the McGuire Act, which was passed in 1952 as a direct answer to the Supreme Court. This provided exemption from Federal antitrust action to the nonsigner clause of state laws, and the Supreme Court has refused to review several cases challenging its constitutionality. In June, 1964, however, it upheld the applicability of the act to a Fair Trade Act that had been passed in Ohio, and recognized the intent of Congress to legalize such price-fixing, specifically with respect to non-signers (Hudson Distributors, Inc., v. Eli Lilly & Co.).

For the individual retailer, refusal to sign a fair-trade agreement was no longer adequate justification for ignoring manufacturers' established prices. But the fact that state legislation did not everywhere exist could be turned to account. In 1952, after General Electric had obtained an injunction preventing Masters, Inc., from violating resale price maintenance agreements on small appliances, the New York City retailer set up a subsidiary to provide mail-order service from Washington, D.C., where no fair-trade law existed. The New York store distributed advertising and order blanks to prospective customers and then shipped G.E. products to Washington for mailing. Since some appliances went to New York consumers, General Electric obtained an injunction against Masters' selling at less than the prices established under the New York State fair-trade law. But in May, 1957, the U.S. Circuit Court of Appeals upheld the retailer's case, and the Supreme Court has refused to review this decision or its parallel, Bissell Carpet Co. v. Masters.

The three retailers involved in these cases, Schwegman Bros., Hudson Distributors, and Masters, Inc., are of course discount houses. This type of retail operation was characterized by its insistence on price competition as a choice of policy. It benefited by the very existence of resale price maintenance laws, for fair-trade prices could then be used to show how cheaply goods were offered. Consumers would scarcely have been receptive to the advertising of discounts unless they had been familiar with stable and uniform prices. The success of the discount house intensified price competition, as established retailers sought to match the lower prices.

At the same time that Congress had moved to make fair trade legal in interstate commerce, various states moved to make it illegal in intrastate commerce. The Schwegman decision, holding that resale price maintenance laws could not be applied to nonsigning "recalcitrants . . . dragged in by the heels and compelled to submit to price fixing" was followed in 19 states, where the courts ruled the nonsigner clause invalid. Five other state Supreme Courts declared their entire fair-trade laws to be unconstitutional. Most of the decisions have ruled that such laws constitute price fixing and hence are an unconstitutional delegation of legislative power. And some have referred specifically to the use of price competition:

The Unfair Practices Act (sec. 325.04) is designed to protect the public from predatory or below-cost trade practices. On the other hand, under the apparent purpose of protecting the goodwill of the manufacturer of the brand commodity, the nonsigner provision (sec. 325.12), in reality, eliminates competition in price honestly based on differences in selling costs as between merchants whose costs of business may differ as a result of normal and natural competitive practices.[26]

As we have stated before, the real effect of the nonsigner clause is anticompetitive price fixing. . . . Except in times of economic emergency such inflexible price arrangements which the act sanctions are not in line with our traditional concepts of free competition, which have traditionally been the "yardstick" for protection of the consuming public.[27]

The position of large and small retailers on the use of price competition as a deliberate policy is quite different. It was the small retailer who sought to protect his normal or conventional markup against the encroachment of the chain stores in the '20s and '30s, and it was the small retailer who has been threatened by the competition of discounting. Most proponents of resale price maintenance legislation argue that it is needed to protect small business and to prevent its extinction. Typically, the small retailer will offer as evidence a product that is being sold by a large competitor at a price below the wholesale cost to the small firm. For example:

We carry a famous make high chair. The best possible price we can buy that for is $7.50. This famous make high chair was advertised by a local giant for $6.88. I sent my girl up to buy some, because I could buy them from him cheaper. The doors opened at 10 o'clock and she was in at 10:05, and there were no high chairs. This, in my opinion, is not competition, this is stupidity, that we permit in a country such as this things to go on like that.[28]

It is doubtful whether this type of "predatory price-cutting"* has actually been as responsible for the troubles of small retailers as the more widespread price reductions that represent lower margins and reflect the lower cost of doing business on the part of the large store. The two previous chapters have discussed the many different ways in which the total distribution process can be carried out; there are thus many different forms of retailing, each with a different level of costs. Certain types of cost savings, those associated with the reduction of "services," are open to both large and small firms. Others, which are closely associated with large sales volumes, are less readily available to small firms. Furthermore, not all manufacturers seek to "protect" the small retailer or to preserve his "traditional" margin, either in resale price maintenance contracts or by means of the less binding suggested list prices. As the Assistant Attorney General for Anti-Trust pointed out, in recent testimony:

National manufacturers of branded commodities set their price levels to please their principal customers and maximize their own profits, quite properly. . . . On commodities which can most advantageously be sold by the chains at a low margin, the price set by the manufacturer is low. On commodities in which it is advantageous to retail at a high margin, the retail price is set high.[29]

If, on the other hand, the manufacturer does respect traditional retail margins, which enable the small outlet to

---

* Further protection of the small businessman from this type of "unfair" price competition could be afforded by tightening existing legislation. Cf. *Price Discrimination* Hearings, 1964, esp. pp. 127–145.

cover its higher costs or more complete services, then the inducement for other types of retail operation to take advantage of these "shelter" margins is very great indeed. One of the best statements of the ensuing predicament for manufacturer and traditional retailer is that offered by R. Lee Waterman, of the Corning Glass Works, in support of Federal fair-trade legislation:

Corning Glass Works manufactures and sells glass cooking ware under the trade name "Pyrex Ware." I shall present the views of a manufacturer whose line of product is purchased relatively infrequently by any one family unit, and who must therefore depend on wide distribution in all parts of the country to obtain sufficient volume on which to base efficient manufacturing methods. In such a line, the price which a consumer must pay is determined primarily by volume of production rather than by distribution costs. . . . From a retail point of view, housewares is not a low cost line to handle if the retailer accepts his responsibility to stock and sell the things which his customers want and need. Using "Pyrex Ware" as an example, a minimum assortment would include at least 26 different sizes and shapes. . . . Such an assortment necessarily includes some items which would be rather slow turnover items, but the neighborhood retailer carries them because he is responsive to the needs of his customers, and has built his business on rendering a complete service. . . . So-called discounters have asserted a right . . . to pick two or three of the best known and fastest selling items, which they advertise that they can sell, because of their efficiency, at from 2- to 5-percent below the prices charged by the poor old inefficient neighborhood store. They accept no responsibility for service in terms of assortment and will cheerfully abandon the line when it has served their publicity purposes.

The point with which we are concerned is whether a manufacturer . . . who believes that his ability to serve the public efficiently can be best promoted by choosing a particular plan of distribution, may take the necessary steps to control it.[30]

Aside from the rise of the discount house, or discounting as a general practice, it seems clear that the margins prevailing in fair-traded goods, or those where list prices were generally respected, were responsible for much of the reshuffling of products among different types of retailers that was discussed in Chapter 6. Certainly the supermarkets' addition of drugs and toiletries, which they sold at "traditional" or "fair-trade" markups, added substantially to their profits. That these traditional markups were in some sense "too high" has been pointed out by both analysts and businessmen:

The fundamental cause of the amazing return of our economy to haggling, to price flexibility, is not list pricing—nor advertising either—but too much spread in margins through the chain of distribution to the consumer—and sometimes even at the manufacturing level.[31]

The whole incentive for establishment of discount houses resulted because of the abnormally high markup on many appliances and other products. This gave the discounters a chance to step in and easily substantially undersell established dealers.[32]

A more specific (but not necessarily accurate) estimate of "too high" suggested:

The traditional 50 percent above cost retail markup under price-fixing fair trade gave the discount houses a great margin to play with, especially since their operating cost is only about 12 percent.[33]

The manufacturer who truly wishes to preserve his small dealers and their traditional markup by using resale price maintenance must also enforce it. Here, too, the problem of large and small firms arises. The small retailer who violates a resale price maintenance contract is less likely to be prosecuted than the large firm. Indeed, the violation may not even be recognized and, if it is, it may not seem to warrant the costs of legal action against its continuance. (Of course, such violations have also been one route by which "small retailers" have grown to be "large firms.") The large retailer is more likely to have lower operating costs, which permits him to adopt price competition as a deliberate policy. The large firm is also likely to occupy a prominent position for both consumer and supplier. It is understandable, therefore, that fair-trade violations by firms such as Hudson and Masters have received widespread attention. But courts have held fair-trade agreements invalid when manufacturers have unduly concentrated their enforcement activities on large firms. "It is more correct to say that the fair trade fracas is one between big retailers or price stores on the one hand, and big manufacturers or quality stores on the other, rather than one between big or little retailers."[34] Consequently, compliance programs have been extremely costly. A New York court outlined the essentials for enforcement as follows:

General Electric, as any other manufacturer or producer, should

1. Keep itself informed as to price-cutting activities and other trends generally known in the industry or trade.

2. Close scrutiny should be kept over prior violators and appropriate action taken where indicated.

3. Investigate and follow up complaints vigorously.

4. Enforce fair-trade prices by repeated legal action if necessary.

5. The enforcement program must be a continuing and sustained one.[35]

In the light of these stipulations, it is understandable that 5 years of an enforcement program, which involved 3,000 suits, cost General Electric some $5,000,000.

With the increased costs of securing compliance and the difficulties of operating a resale price maintenance program under widely varying conditions of legality in the several states, many large manufacturers have abandoned the use of fair trade. G.E.'s announcement of a change in policy in 1958 explained that:

An effective fair-trade enforcement program is no longer available in the marketing of the products of the housewares and radio receiver division of General Electric Co. . . . 18 vast and commercially important non-fair-trade areas . . . adjoin fair-trade States and greatly compound the difficulties of equitable enforcement at their borders . . . in some fair-trade States it has become increasingly difficult to secure prompt injunctive relief or, once obtained, to secure adequate penalties to enforce compliance. . . . Despite the magnitude of these continuous efforts, we can no longer uniformly establish and effectively protect our fair-trade price structure in the manner originally contemplated by the fair-trade laws.[36]

An increase in the effectiveness of resale price maintenance requires some easier method of dealing with the problem of compliance. Such an approach has been taken in bills introduced in Congress regularly since 1957 after the decision in the Masters case. In the early '60s the sponsors of such legislation found a new title, "Quality Stabilization" to replace the former, more accurate, "National Fair Trade Legislation." The successive bills include specific recognition of continuing property rights by the owner of a name, brand, or trademark, and therefore the owner's right to establish resale prices on such goods. To assure compliance with such prices, the firm may prohibit the use of its name, brand, or trademark by any reseller who does not observe the established prices. A violator of this prohibition would be liable in a suit in a Federal court.

These bills take a much more positive stand in favor of resale price maintenance than the existing Federal and state legislation, which merely exempts such contracts from the provisions of antitrust law. Despite the attempts of proponents of the bills introduced to differentiate their product by use of the name "Quality Stabilization," it is clear that price maintenance is their chief goal; much has been made of the fact that, aside from the title, the word "quality" or its equivalent is not mentioned in the legislative draft. The House Committee, reporting favorably in 1963, specifically acknowledged this:

The reported bill is of the same general pattern as the Miller-Tydings and McGuire Fair Trade Acts. Both the quality stabilization and the fair trade approaches say, in effect, that resale price maintenance practices are not inherently illegal.[37]

The crucial difference between the proposed Federal legislation and the patchwork of laws and court decisions that now exists is the method of securing compliance. The present system allows a manufacturer to sign a contract which establishes resale prices that are binding on all retailers duly notified thereof. If a reseller cuts prices below the stated minimum, he may be charged with violating a contract and the manufacturer may seek redress. But it takes a court decision to establish the fact that violation has occurred, as well as the amount of damages, if any, with which to compensate the manufacturer. The quality stabilization bills make the retailer who cuts prices a violator, not of a civil contract, but of Federal law. Furthermore, the determination of the violation would be made, in the first instance, not by a court but by the manufacturer, who would have the further right to apply penalties to such an offender. The Federal Trade Commission referred to these measures as "a private measure of law," and at least one supporter of the bill finds this wholly desirable:

The beauty of the quality stabilization bill is that it does not rely upon a Government agency for the enforcement of the law, but relies upon the initiative of the people being hurt, the manufacturer of the brand name and the retailer who builds his business by dealing legitimately in the brand name.[38]

It seems fairly obvious that, if such compliance programs were available, the number of price maintenance agreements would increase.

Aside from the objections raised by executive agencies, economists, lawyers, and businessmen on both legal and economic grounds, effective political opposition to such legislation comes from the supporters of states' rights. A Federal law would, of course, establish a uniform price maintenance rule throughout the country. Since some state legislatures have never passed fair-trade laws, some have repealed them, and some have had their laws judged unconstitutional by the state Supreme Courts, there are good arguments to show that Federal legislation in this area would override the expressed judgment of a large part of the population. One solution to this problem provides that any state may nullify the provisions of the Federal law by prohibiting resale price maintenance within the state. But this would greatly diminish the advantage of resale price maintenance to the manufacturer, and hence would also diminish the likelihood that manufacturers would adopt the practice.

Retail price stability and the influence of manufacturers on retail price levels do not depend merely on resale price maintenance contracts. In fact, one of the chief arguments of supporters of Federal legislation is that other methods of price maintenance are so much more effective that the criticism of "price-fixing" should not in all fairness be levied against fair-trade agreements or "quality stabilization" efforts.

Manufacturers' Prices at Retail

The distribution policies employed by manufacturers can exercise a substantial influence over retail prices. The most complete control is to be found in direct selling by producers to consumers. Many variations exist: direct mail and house-to-house selling were discussed earlier. Such methods generally prevent any price difference from appearing among sellers, while the distribution method provides a particular form of product variation. Stanley home products, which are sold at parties, and Electrolux vacuum cleaners, which are sold door-to-door, compete with close substitutes not only by their brand name and product differences but also by the personal service involved in home salesmanship and delivery. As differentiating or identifying characteristics of the seller, such distribution channels are probably epitomized by the familiar "Fuller Brush Man" or "Avon Calling." Price competition is likely, nevertheless, where a manufacturer sells direct to consumers as well as through dealers. Prospective members of a record or book club are offered substantial savings from "regular" prices as an incentive to join; the buyer's commitment to purchase a given number of items may or may not make such lower prices reflect lower costs. Another form of direct selling consists of retail outlets owned by the producer: the oil industry's experience in this respect covers all aspects of price and nonprice competition. Manufacturers' retail outlets are common in certain lines of food and clothing, and may also involve the same problems of price competition with independent retailers as are found in direct selling.[39]

If manufacturers prefer to stay out of retailing enterprise, they can still influence the conditions of sale to consumers by limiting the number of distributors or franchising their dealers; the automobile industry provides a familiar example. Here, as with some other merchandise lines, the dealer is not permitted to carry closely competing brands. But selective distribution is used without such a proviso by some manufacturers of cosmetics, clothing, house furnishings, and other articles for which the number of brand names far exceeds that of the automotive industry. The twofold relationship between manufacturer and dealer is designed to improve the competitive position of each. The dealer, assured of some monopoly power within a given area, has less incentive to lower price. The manufacturer looks for efficient distribution and extra effort on the part of the dealer to increase sales at the expense of competitive products. For the consumer, however, the use of selected distribution may cut two ways. If the consumer has not been presold on the brand as well as on the product itself, the shopping inconvenience of having only one dealer in the area may be overriding. On the other hand, the consumer's decision may be influenced by the dealer–monopolist's powers of persuasive selling.

Even without these controls, manufacturers' list prices for branded products have a considerable effect on prices to consumers. Advertising accustoms people to the notion of a prevailing price, but denoting these prices as "suggested" allows for the actual variety of prices that consumers will meet from a variety of retail outlets. Some list prices, on the other hand, are fairly rigidly observed without their existence being advertised to consumers; the conventional markups on which they are based continue to prevail. And some, particularly in automobiles and appliances, serve as the base from which an individual bargain can be struck.[40]

Widespread use of list prices, even to discount from, have an important effect on the process of price increase. Manufacturers who are faced with rising costs frequently seek to compensate for such rises by economies rather than move to the next price point. Retailers who are faced with rising costs will seek to "trade up"—sell the next highest-priced item—rather than adjust away from the familiar list price. Low-enu or low-margin merchandise may be dropped entirely. On the other hand, innovators may find a source of profit in abandoning familiar price endings or even price points. The removal of excise taxes in mid-'65 may result in a sizable realignment of familiar price lines, as the opportunity occurs for price competition.

Although the emphasis so far has been on manufactured goods,[41] price stability also exists generally throughout consumer services. Rent and insurance expenditures, fixed contractually, enable both consumer and seller to plan ahead with a considerable degree of certainty. Public utility and transportation rates are fixed by legal regulation. Both stability and general uniformity among sellers characterize service charges, such as barbershop prices and physicians' fees for house calls. With or without benefit of legality, these are set on an agreed level within a given area.[42] Finally, the growth of franchising in many service industries has spread the pattern of price conformity and nonprice competition.

In service operations, the franchisor is not necessarily a producer, but merely the owner of a copyright, a patent, a trademark, or a brand name covering some specific form of business operation. In some cases the franchised retail outlet may handle only one or two products: drive-ins, selling a specialty food product, such as doughnuts or pancakes or soft ice cream, for example, or the swimming-pool installation companies. In others, the individual retailer may handle a substantial number of goods and services: Howard Johnson's, the Holiday Inns, the Western Auto Supply Company. Purely service operations include specialized dry-cleaning establishments and equipment rental. Industry groups in which franchising plays a leading role include the following:

Auto, truck, and trailer rentals
Automobile and truck dealers
Candy and confectioneries
Carpet and upholstery cleaning services
Coin-operated and regular laundries and dry-cleaning services
Drug stores
Gasoline and oil service stations
Grocery stores
Hardware stores
Hearing aids
Moving companies
Roadside food, beverage, and soft ice cream
    dispensing restaurants
Soft drink bottlers
Swimming pools

Temporary help services
Tires and auto accessories
Tool and equipment rentals
Variety stores
Water-conditioning systems and services

Estimates of total sales or consumer purchases from franchised outlets are imprecise because Census data define retailers by the product lines they carry rather than by the contractual arrangements of the owners. Franchising has been described in glowing terms:

Franchising offers an opportunity for people to "be their own boss" or "have my own business." . . . This Nation has been built on the desire for independence, individual accomplishment, and becoming one's own boss. The rate of new business formation in this country is eloquent testimony to this desire. Franchising offers a convenient and economic means for the fulfilling of such a drive or desire with a minimum of risk and investment and maximum opportunities for success.[43]

The "independent businessman" of this description has little leeway for determining the operating methods for his firm, since the franchise spells out such conditions in great detail. In particular, price competition is relegated to a minor place, although the price line or price range offered may serve to identify all the franchised sellers. The contract frequently specifies the physical arrangement and decoration of the outlet, so as to secure prominent display of the brand name in order to appeal to the consumer. But since the brand guarantees standardized merchandise or service, the franchise agreement also specifies exactly how the dealer is to carry on his "independent" business:

The franchise system sets up an interrelationship between the franchisor and the franchisee in which a proven package is sold to the franchisee. This package usually includes goods or services, training, promotional techniques, standard management techniques, continued management aid and assistance, together with the right

278

to distribute or sell products and/or services for which the franchisor will receive such consideration as a franchise fee and/or royalty on sales or a profit from the sale of equipment or products to the franchisee.[44]

A formula for the franchised service, specifications of cleanliness and speed in service, minimum orders for materials and supplies, how customer complaints are to be handled and accounts kept, what advertising claims may be made in what media—these and other provisions of the "package" effectively control the nature of the franchised operation. Price is a minor detail in such an arrangement: the franchised outlet seeks the nonprice advantages of large firms:

Franchising is about the only method remaining in this country by which an individual can avail himself of chainstore advantages such as trade mark and trade name acceptance, customer acceptance, advertising and advertising materials, merchandising, publicity, training research, product improvements, new products, and general market information pertaining to his business, similar to that used by the large chains.[45]

Although this statement uses the term "chainstore advantages," it is in fact referring to a market power that the seller seeks to establish through nonprice competition.

From the point of view of the consumer, the franchised dealer may or may not differ from the wholly independent retailer. In theory, when a reliable, standardized quality of service or product associated with an established brand name is provided by a franchised outlet, consumers will purchase there rather than from other, nonbranded, sellers. In fact, aside from the assurance of uniform prices, franchised outlets are not always standardized. Most consumers can distinguish quite clearly between the satisfaction offered by one Howard Johnson's and that offered by another some two states away, despite the identical surroundings, menu, decoration, and so on. Service operations allow infinite room for differentiation, intentionally or not.* It may or may not be true, as well, that the existence of an independent businessman is more conducive to a nonprice competition that fulfills consumer preferences than are the efforts of a salaried manager:

Americans prefer to do business with those to whom they can talk, and if necessary, complain. The paid manager, unless he rises to the occasion, invariably strikes the customer as a subordinate person "who follows orders." Just how subordinate can be seen in a remark overheard the other day in a well-known restaurant. A woman customer turned to her friend to complain about the service. "Why tell me?" she was told. "Speak to the manager." "What's the use? He doesn't care. He doesn't own the place."

There's the rub. The manager who is *really* the owner does "own the place." Thus he is quite likely to act on the complaint as well as perform a myriad of functions a non-owner-manager would pay others to do. The result, assuming a franchisee follows the business principles established for him, is a shop which generates more sales, has less expense, and turns in a larger profit than any comparable company owned and operated unit.

Franchising thus is the ultimate in serving the public.[46]

Strict economic analysis cannot share this sanguine conclusion. Granted that the drive for independence and the willingness to work hard are necessary conditions for success in the franchised operation, but these factors alone do not ensure that this type of dealer is more attentive to consumer satisfaction than the manager of a chain store outlet or a department store buyer.

What is clear, is that all types of sellers rely on various forms of nonprice competition in order to attract the consumer. Institutional arrangements tend to create a situation of relative price conformity and stability that makes it possible for marketing strategy to concentrate on nonprice competition. Inevitably, then the consumer wishing to fulfill his tastes and preferences will base his decisions largely on nonprice considerations.

* Cf. Chap. 6, pp. 230–33.

chapter 8 Nonprice Competition and Consumer Choice

*W*hile previous chapters have argued that nonprice competition is the norm in consumer markets, there is little reason to investigate all the forms of such competition. If this study were primarily concerned with the firm, it would be useful to investigate product differentiation, brand names, guarantees, terms of sale, packaging, delivery, and the host of other variations open to manufacturers and retailers. Suffice it to say that all such tactics employed by sellers competing for consumers' choices appeal to consumers' tastes and preferences. From the point of view of the consumer, such market competition represents attempts—sometimes futile or inept, sometimes ingenious and welcomed—to fulfill his wants.

Typically, any seller's appeal to a consumer's tastes and preferences suggests that he alter or reinforce his shopping habits. Just as custom and convention play a major role in determining sellers' activities—although only their pricing decisions have been discussed here—so do they in determining consumer activities. While the model of consumer choice analyzes purchase decisions, the ways in which consumers behave in real situations reflect purchasing habits. Sellers use non-price competition to influence such habits and to promote consumer loyalty—to a product, a brand name, or a particular retail store.

The Satisfied Customer

In the theory of consumer choice, the equilibrium solution represents maximum satisfaction because all the alternatives—all the goods and services and forms of savings that might be purchased with a given income—have been considered. In real life, this peak of satisfaction is out of reach because consumers cannot investigate every such possibility. A good deal of the technical data about structure, performance, and quality of goods and services is incomprehensible to them. Much information about the availability of substitute products or services or sellers is lacking. Even if these conditions did not exist, the task of assimilating all the information possible about all the alternatives would still be an unbearable one. In a dynamic world, furthermore, consumers would have to review or revise each choice-decision whenever any change occurred in the market, thus setting in motion an equally impossible information-gathering process. What types of information form the basis of actual consumer choices?

The sources of information available to the consumer include: objective, but somewhat general, reports from governments or academic organizations, less objective analyses by service publications and current periodicals, more specific recommendations from consumer testing organizations, and particular experiences recounted by other consumers.* None of these classes of data is systematically gathered or presented in terms of the tastes and preferences of the individual consumer; furthermore, they are widely scattered over the whole range of products and services in the normal consumption pattern. Once the consumer considers a specific purchase, he can obtain more or less detailed information from both manufacturers and retailers. The degree of expertise represented by all these sources varies widely, as does their objectivity.

For the individual consumer, the most reliable and informative source is his own experience with a given product or service. His own tastes and preferences cannot be disputed by logical arguments from others, nor can the amount of satisfaction he will receive from a given consumption item be predicted by any outside source of information. The importance of freedom of consumer choice cannot be overemphasized: while it is commonly accepted that interpersonal comparisons of utility are invalid, the corollary is often glossed over—that there is no arguing with individual choice that is based on experience. This is not to say that the individual's experience necessarily provides him with the *maximum* utility that might be available.

But here the solution to the consumer's information problem comes from abandoning the notion of maximizing in favor of what Professor Simon has called "satisficing." That is, the consumer may be satisfied with an acceptable choice, one that is "good enough"; this represents the "kind of rational behavior that is compatible with the access to information and the computational capacities that are actually possessed by organisms, including man, in the kinds of environments in which such organisms exist."[1] This view of consumer behavior also differs from the conventional model in that the alternatives are

* These are discussed in more detail in the following chapter.

283

* Please note term *logical arguments*

not all evaluated before making a choice which is final, for "in actual human decision-making alternatives are often examined sequentially,"[2] with the possibility of improving the situation by later moves. The consumer's own experience now becomes critical.

If a specific choice provides an acceptable level of satisfaction after purchase, this experience may be sufficiently decisive for the consumer to make the same choice again. If it is not, then the consumer may seek further information, but the purchase experience has taught him something and he can carry on his search within the narrower range of choice defined by his own tastes and preferences. For example, if purchase of notepaper proved useful in size, shape, and surface, but somewhat flimsy in weight, the consumer's subsequent shopping process would emphasize the investigation of this characteristic of the alternative stationery products available. Once a satisfactory product or service has been found, it will tend to be repurchased. Consumers' repeat purchases often grow into habits. In the many cases in which specific items of consumption expenditure are not frequently repeated, the same analysis may nevertheless apply to sellers, so that a consumer who has found a "satisficing" experience with a particular seller tends to return to that seller.[3] From the consumer's point of view, such repeat purchases make his problems of shopping and choosing and spending and saving manageable. They may economize on time and energy sufficiently that, for marginal consumption choices, the consumer can devote a much larger share of the decision-making process to acquiring more information and considering all available alternatives.

It is obviously to the seller's interest to have such repeat purchases lead to the establishment of a consumer's habit, especially one that cannot easily be broken; at its strongest, this represents a bond of loyalty. The seller's attempts to form such habits influence the kind of information he provides to the consumer.

The Ignorant Consumer

When the consumer, on becoming aware of his lack of information, attributes it to his own inability to comprehend technical data, the seller who is also an expert occupies a special position. Besides being a supplier of goods or services, he is a consultant as well, someone to whom the buyer turns for advice. If the gap between the ignorance of the consumer and the technical knowledge of the seller is sufficiently emphasized, the consumer's quest for useful information may be reduced to the query, "Which shall I buy?" Here the seller actually chooses for the buyer. Beyond this question lies the even more extreme case in which the consumer says to the expert not "Which shall I buy?" but "What shall I do?" In this situation, the buyer is willing to give up a large part of his consumption choice, including some degree of control over the disposition of his income. Such a process occurs most frequently when the consumer discovers that he has a critical lack of technical information. The problem of medical services provides a good illustration of this, for most consumers.

The medical profession stresses the differences between the information possessed by the consumer and that of the physician, thus adding to the layman's awareness of his own ignorance.[4] It takes education and training to produce a skilled physician, and the emphasis on the investment required highlights the consumer's lack of such resources. To a greater or lesser degree, the aura of mystery that surrounds medicine intensifies the consumer's consciousness of being uninitiated in the general field of medical knowledge. And for specific medical services, consumers typically lack information from their previous experience: few patients have their appendixes removed twice; for few does an operation prove so satisfactory that a repeat purchase of that same operation is in order.

As a result, the consumer seeks chiefly to buy technical

information and expert advice, as against some particular medical service. In many cases, he consults the physician not so much to purchase his skill at setting a broken bone or his remedy for a specific affliction, as in order to obtain a solution to his choice-problem. And the physician stands ready to supply not only advice and information, but such a decision, ready-made, for the consumer to adopt. On occasion the consumer asks the physician, too, not "Which shall I buy?" but "What shall I do?" The physician then undertakes to make such a decision for him. Assured of access to a host of potential services embodied in the physician's skill, the consumer is urged to let the doctor select the appropriate procedure, and to turn his choice-problem over to the expert.

To take a simple example: the purchase of drugs and medicine differs substantially from other consumer expenditures. The conventional model, which assumes given conditions of income, prices, and preferences, does not apply to drug purchases, for the relevant preferences are actually those of the physician, while only the income is the consumer's.* The consumer abdicates control over his decision-making process when he has a prescription filled. Other purchases of medical services may imply the same shifting of choice-decisions. The routine checkup at the doctor's or dentist's is not routine in the same sense as a routine order for milk given by the housewife. The consumer knows what he is buying in the routine checkup; but he does not know what further purchases he may be asked to make as a result. He thus gives up not only his preferences but also some control over the disposition of his income.

Typically, the consumer's lack of useful technical information is replaced by a feeling of trust in the doctor to whom

* Prices are presumably fixed in the market, although the proposal that prescriptions be written for generic, rather than brand, names of drugs suggests that prices to the consumer may differ, depending on the physician's exercise of his "preferences."

decisions are transferred in this way. This stems in part from the highly emotional content of the consumer's choice. His lack of information about medical care and about his own needs involves much more awesome questions than his lack of technical expertise about an automobile engine. The preservation of human life may be involved in both cases, but it is the primary consideration in the first, whether the consumer chooses to keep this in the forefront of his thinking or relegates it to his subconscious.

The profession uses two arguments for substituting trust for information. First, the patient who trusts his doctor will increase the efficiency of medical services: he will be ready to provide the factual details needed for an expert decision, and he will follow the instructions needed to ensure expert care. Secondly, the ethics of the medical profession recognize the doctor's responsibility in acting for the consumer's best interest. Hence, dependence on the expert is clearly superior to uninformed choice. The consumer's substitution of trust for information is most complete when a general practitioner recommends a specialist. Here the consumer trusts not only the immediate skills of the physician, but also his decision as to what further sources of information to seek. The consumer's question "What shall I do?" has already implied his willingness to accept an expert's answer.* But it has also included his willingness to accept referral, to be told, "Don't ask me, let Dr. Expert decide."

This same notion of substituting trust for information applies in many other areas of consumption expenditure. It may occur whenever the consumer knows that he lacks such technical information as is possessed by an expert. It may also be the result of experience, since the consumer who accepts

---

* This reasoning implies, of course, that charlatans and quacks, despite their lack of knowledge or skill, render a real satisfaction to the consumer in making decisions and providing a solution to his problems of choice. Surely it is this satisfaction that enables quackery to persist.

the expert's advice and makes his purchase accordingly, gains firsthand knowledge of the product or service. And provides him with much more immediate and relevant information than has the counsel of the expert. If the expert's advice produces an acceptable level of satisfaction, the consumer will tend to return for more advice—and it is this sort of "repeat purchase" that establishes trust or loyalty, just as the repeat purchase of a particular brand of soap establishes a habit. Since the expert and the seller are identical in fields other than medicine, many consumption expenditures actually represent trust in an expert who is also a supplier.

In varying degrees, consumer purchases of services resemble the patient-doctor relationship. Closest in this respect, perhaps, are the other professions—for example, the law, accounting, or architecture. The expert's knowledge represents an accumulated investment in formal education and training; the consumer buys access to a service potential. Consumer trust not only increases the likelihood that all relevant details are supplied for proper counsel; it also means that the consumer will accept referral to another specialist within the profession. In some cases, the consumer's initial question verges on the simple "What shall I do?" A satisfactory solution to that one choice-problem then tends to build up repeat consultations, or trust. There are obvious differences, of course: for the most part, legal or financial or building problems lack the emotional overtones of life and death, nor is there the repeated assertion that the professional knows best*—which implies that the consumer would be better off to surrender his entire decision-making function.

On the other hand, the purchase of funeral services exemplifies just this idea of permitting the expert to make the entire

---

* For an extreme example of the medical profession's assertion of its superior knowledge, and therefore authority, see the exhortation of Dr. Ennis, former President of the AMA, to trust the doctor's decision on Medicare, *New York Times*, June 25, 1962, p. 54.

choice. In this case, there are infrequent transactions, and so consumer loyalty to the same expert is not as likely, yet the emotional content of a decision may be much stronger. It is not certain, however, that the technical information involved represents a sizable investment in formal education and training, nor is it certain that the funeral industry accepts the professional ethic of acting in the consumer's best interest. Significantly, most suggestions for increasing consumer utility in this field recommend that a family decide its own funeral arrangements ahead of time. In effect, this means taking back the consumer's choice function from the expert who so frequently exercises it. Aside from this, reformers urge the industry to provide more information to the buyer at the time of purchase: the simplest factual details of price, product, and quality of service are, in many cases, lacking.

In the category of personal services—barbers, beauty parlors, masseurs, and so on—consumer purchases clearly represent a search for technical skill. Unlike the patient visiting the doctor, the consumer here normally expects a specific service to be performed. The physician who says, "You don't need treatment," or the lawyer who advises, "Don't do anything," provides utility solely with this advice; the barber who says "Let it grow" will probably not entirely satisfy the customer who wants a haircut. But although the consumer may purchase merely technical skill—in the simplest terms, he does not know how to cut hair—he also buys access to a number of potential services, and to advice and information as well. The supplier's investment in education and training is much less than that of the professional, so that the consumer's ignorance seems less crucial. On the other hand, since most personal services must be repeated regularly, the sheer frequency of transactions encourages habit formation, once the consumer has attained an acceptable level of satisfaction. And the interpersonal relation between supplier and customer may build, if not trust, then a form of loyalty—a man to his tailor, a woman to her hairdresser.

Repair and maintenance services, particularly for consumer durable goods, also combine the expert with the supplier. The consumer expects the serviceman to diagnose the ailing appliance in much the same way as he looks to the physician to diagnose his own ailment, and repair work, like medicine, often involves more spending than the consumer had anticipated. The service trades as a whole do not attempt to command consumer respect or confidence by invoking a professional ethic of acting in the consumer's best interest, yet it is for that very reason that the opportunity for an *individual* supplier to create consumer loyalty may be greater. The serviceman has invested in his own training, and offers a pool of potential skills. If one repair job proves satisfactory, the consumer does have some reason to repeat purchases from the same supplier. But purchasing repair services does not always provide the consumer with sufficient informational experience, because performance after repair depends on the durable good itself, as well as on the skill with which it was serviced. To some extent, therefore, the consumer is asked to trust the supplier, rather than his own judgment, about whether the job was satisfactory.* It is probably for this reason that dissatisfaction with appliance servicing runs high on the list of consumer problems: "doing as well as can be expected" seems to be a reasonable comment after a bodily operation but not after a mechanical one. The consumer's lack of technical information can lead to frustration rather than to trust.

The professions and most service trades provide the clearest illustration of the consumer's inability to comprehend technical information. Many consumption purchases do not even represent independent consumer choice, for trust in an expert

---

* This point has an important bearing on the manufacturer's choice between providing service facilities or leaving this function to retailers.

is substituted for informed tastes and preferences. But the consumer's own experience after purchasing provides an independent test of the expert's competence. If the consumer receives an acceptable amount of satisfaction, he has a strong incentive to repeat his purchase, for his only alternative is to shop around for another expert rather than to attempt to acquire technical competence himself. Much of this analysis also applies to producers and retailers of consumer goods.

The Manufacturer and Consumer Purchasing

Even where technical expertise is not at issue, the sheer bulk of information that theoretically requires attention may be impossible to assimilate. A businessman describes the problem in these terms:

A buyer must make a number of choices when she goes to the store—service, quality, convenience, size of the package, the guarantee, the repairs, who supplies the replacement parts, and so on. We can call these the hitching post of price. If she did not have a hitching post, she would have to correlate one against the other, and by means of price, she has six to eight correlations to make. But when we add the question of premiums, she not only has to correlate all of this information in relation to price, but she has the added questions as to the worth of the premium, the integrity of the premium giver, and so on, so you compound the problem of choice. . . .[5]

Again, the notion of "satisficing" suggests that, once the consumer has found a satisfactory choice, he will tend to repeat it rather than undertake the costs of amassing information that may or may not bring an increase in utility. Repeat purchases lead to habit, based on the most important source of information available to the individual consumer—his own satisfactory experience.

For most sellers, repeat purchases pose a twofold challenge. The individual firm attempts to break the consumer's habit of purchasing from existing competitors and to help consumers to form and maintain habits of buying its own products or services. Various means of nonprice competition are used, including product differences and alternative means of carrying out the shopping process.* Among the most important of these means for manufacturers engaged in monopolistic competition are brand names and advertising.

In the theory of monopolistic competition, brand names serve to differentiate sellers. Each manufacturer has a monopoly of the particular brand he sells; competition comes from other brands which are close substitutes. Even if two products are technically so similar that they could not be distinguished by the "blindfolded" consumer, they still differ because of their distinctive labels. But no product differentiation succeeds unless consumers recognize and appreciate it; hence advertising in order to increase consumer awareness of product differences necessarily accompanies the use of brand names. Both advertising and brand names represent a kind of consumer information.

First, through advertising the seller may emphasize the importance of technical information and lay claim to special competence as an expert. In some cases, this means referring to the skilled personnel of the company or its scientific research; in others, it means urging consumers to trust the manufacturer as an expert. Critics of advertising have claimed that some producers deliberately stress technicalities in an attempt to prevent the consumer from acquiring information:

Descriptions and illustrations of highly technical manufacturing processes and explanations or the spelling-out of the scientific name or formula of chemical ingredients . . . make little or no

* Cf. Chap. 6, pp. 237–40.

sense to the layman and are intended only to impress and overawe him.

The same intention to impress the buyer is also present in advertisements that stress the scientific research engaged in and the elaborate testing equipment used by the producer to maintain high standards of quality. Besides impressing the buyer, much advertising in effect also tells him that he, a mere layman, would be unwise to judge quality standards by mere inspection, and that he should rely instead on the guarantees offered by the manufacturer's reputation.[6]

Such attempts to establish between buyer and seller the same relation that exists (in varying degrees) between the consumer and the supplier of professional or technical services are less successful because a similar type of advertising appeal is voiced by many competing manufacturers.

An illuminating example of the similarities and differences between professional expertise and that claimed by manufacturers arose with the certification given "Crest" toothpaste by the American Dental Association in 1960. The profession worded its statement extremely carefully:

Crest has been shown to be an effective decay-preventing dentifrice that can be of significant value when used in a conscientiously applied program of oral hygiene and regular professional care.[7]

It was obviously not the *information* contained in this sentence that would affect the consumer's choice-decision, since the company itself had been making similar (and more exaggerated) claims for some years. The impact lay in the source of the information; because consumers have trust in the medical and dental profession, the words of such professional spokesmen about a specific product carried considerable weight.

To the company, however, the certification was valuable because "Crest" was the only toothpaste so recognized by the American Dental Association; Proctor and Gamble held, as it were, a monopoly on this type of information. The product differentiation* paid off handsomely: "Crest" sales zoomed, until the toothpaste was the market leader. At first, competing sellers countered with advertising appeals that focused on areas completely different from the prevention of decay. But as clinical evidence on other toothpastes accumulated, claims similar to that made for "Crest" were made. The monopoly position held by Proctor and Gamble diminished substantially when ADA certification was extended to Colgate-Palmolive's "Cue" toothpaste, and professional approval no longer dominated advertising competition. Presumably the quality of the toothpaste had not changed and its decay-preventing characteristics remained; what is important to the seller, however, is *differentiation.* The firm seeks to publicize technical information or expertise that applies solely to the particular brand, not to its competitors.

Secondly, the seller may use advertising to reinforce consumer habits and to encourage repeat purchases that will lead to habit formation. Sheer reiteration of the brand name—visually through advertising media and on the product or package itself, aurally over radio and television—remains important, especially when a profusion of alternative consumption choices become available, each assaulting the consumer with a barrage of information. Repetition of an identifying theme serves the same purpose—a trademark, slogan, or symbol. The value to the seller of such advertising was empirically demonstrated during World War II when many consumer goods disappeared entirely from the markets, and manufacturers invested heavily

---

* The profession's endorsement provides another example of the irrelevance of the distinction between product differentiation and "selling costs." The *informational* content of the message could be avoided by consumers who chose not to listen to its repetition on television or to read its presentation in magazine advertising. Such selling efforts would, according to Professor Chamberlin, give rise to selling costs. Yet "Crest" held a monopoly of the dental profession's approval; it was therefore different, as a product, from all other toothpastes. Whether or not consumers absorbed the news about this difference, it existed.

in advertising in order to keep brand names alive in consumers' memories.

Repeat purchases are the consumer's way of avoiding the burden of seeking additional information that may not produce additional utility. The extent of the data to be garnered is substantial.

The shopper today must be an expert in every field. Each item must be judged for quality and price after it is all assembled and made pretty with paint and wrapped in cellophane which defeats every sensory test except sight. She must judge quality described as—fancy, prime, best, hennery—in combination with grade A, AA, B and #1, 2 or 3. Nowhere will she find an explanation of such common terms or anyone to explain their exact meaning—if any. She must quickly compute the relative value in the "regular, family and jumbo sizes"—finding a common denominator for the incongruous fractions in which their contents are stated. Without training in food additives, she must judge whether they contain harmful ingredients, in harmless amounts. Seldom is she informed if the use of certain chemicals has been tested at all. She must judge the engineering skill of the appliance maker and the integrity of the guarantor. What of the integrity of the retailer, his service policies, repairs, replacement parts and their cost?[8]

Once having made a choice, the consumer finds that advertising serves as reassurance that his original choice was correct, that he cannot improve his position. As competitors differentiate their products or change their advertising claims, the seller's advertising enables the consumer to justify his purchasing habit. Typical of such advertising is the campaign based on those other satisfied users who take pride in being repeat purchasers: their habits have strengthened into brand loyalty —they have become "unswitchables."[9]

Competiton for repeat sales helps to explain two quite different phenomena at the manufacturing level. Since World War II, many firms that originally specialized in one type of consumer goods have broadened their output so as to offer a more complete product line. Sometimes this has been the result of acquisition or merger, as in the major appliance industry; sometimes it required the development of a product new to the firm. Certainly it reflects the economies of scale possible in manufacturing and distribution. But it also acknowledges the consumer's propensity to make repeat purchases. Familiarity with one branded product ensures at least some recognition of another product with the same name. Advertising encourages the consumer to make a carryover from one product to another, by emphasizing the quality, dependability, or some specific characteristic of the brand. The consumer's own experience as the best source of information is significant here; if the purchase of one item has not proven satisfactory, and brand recognition has been established, consumers will then be prejudiced against other products in the same line. Even for items such as major appliances, for which repeat purchases of the same product are infrequent, the consumer's own information may outweigh advertising appeals.

Besides building up a product line, some manufacturers seek to establish the identity of the brand, rather than of the seller. The phenomenon of large firms that make and sell competing brands of the same product runs the gamut from automobiles to soap. Even where consumers show clear familiarity with brands, they are much less able to identify the actual makers of the products, unless the firm name has been strongly associated with it.[10] Repeat purchases, therefore, are geared to the brand. The seller who has such a "stable" of brands assumes that a larger share of the total market can be captured by catering to different segments of the market, in which consumers may differ in age or income, or quite simply, in tastes and preferences. Such product differentiation also enables the manufacturer to escape the wrath of a dissatisfied customer, whom an unsatisfactory experience with one brand has made more receptive to the trial of another. In short, such policies assume that the consumer's habit of repeat purchases can be broken.

Empirical data show that "brand loyalty" is nowhere near as strong as most sellers would like (for their own brands, of course). The existence of brand-switching is documented by the shifting shares of the market among nationally distributed brands as well as by the growth of private-label merchandise. Businessmen have looked to advertising research for a solution, and psychology and sociology have been called in to analyze this "habit" of consumers. To some extent, it is clearly a manifestation of the drive for variety that has played such an important part in consumption choice. For example, a marketing survey of consumer preference found that "Bread consumers in general appear to shift their loyalties to another brand about every three to five years . . . from a sense of monotony and a desire for something new and different."[11] Foremost among the remedies, for a manufacturer who has found that buyers are tending to shift away from his brand, has always been the recommendation to maintain and improve the product itself; this recognizes that it is the consumer's own experience with a satisfactory purchase that is of primary importance. But all forms of nonprice competition can be used to encourage the consumer toward switching brands.

Clearly, advertising can help to break, as well as to establish, consumer buying habits. Although some advertising themes are famous for their longevity, typically the seller seeks variety in advertisting campaigns, presumably in order to attract consumers with one or another appeal. It may degenerate into simply advertising competition, with products otherwise undifferentiated, as pointed out in the Federal Trade Commission decision on Clorox:

There does reach a point at which product differentiation ceases to promote welfare and becomes wasteful, or mass advertising loses its informative aspect and merely entrenches market leaders. We think that point has been reached in the household bleach industry. Price competition beneficial to the consumer has given way to brand competition in a form beneficial only to the sellers. Cost advantages that enable still more intensive advertising only impair price competition further; they do not benefit the consumer.[12]

But such advertising has been termed self-defeating:

As manufacturers continue to turn out similar products selling at similar prices and backed with similar advertising and similar promotions, shoppers see little product differentiation and little reason to stick with one brand.[13]

The latter quotation reiterates the usefulness of the consumer's own experience as a source of information. Critics of advertising usually admit that some useful purpose may exist in publishing information about what the product is, what it will do, how it can or should be used, and where it can be purchased. But emotional appeals or farfetched claims are challenged on the ethical grounds that industry is thereby manipulating the tastes and preferences of consumers. The most devastating accusation appears to be that advertising can persuade consumers to buy what they do not "need" and even what they do not "truly want."[14] Such arguments ignore the existence of repeat purchases and consumer buying habits. The habit is established only after the purchase itself has proved acceptable and when, for the consumer to move from "good enough" to maximum satisfaction, a burdensome investigation of alternatives looms, with no real certainty of any enlargement of utility.

The distinction between a one-time purchase and a loyal customer is clearly understood by the advertising industry itself and by sellers who advertise. A typical example was described by the president of Doyle Dane and Bernbach:

"Great advertising can make a bad product fall faster; it gets more people to know it's bad," he says. He notes that DDB's TV commercials for Betty Crocker Rice with Valenciana Sauce won an industry award, and believes they led many people to try the product. But General Mills, Inc., says repeat sales were so disappointing it stopped making the product.[15]

Certain types of merchandise can indeed be "sold" on the basis of advertising—but only once. If the advertising industry could demonstrate its ability to control the consumer, it would have little need to "sell" its own wares, or to engage in advertising research—and both these activities are substantial. Repeat sales must come from satisfied users, and no amount of advertising can overcome the prejudice that has been left by an unhappy experience with the product.

On the contrary, if there is potential gain for the consumer in trying different alternatives, then advertising serves a useful function by spurring the consumer to switch brands, to experiment instead of buying the tried-and-true product, and thus to widen the information on which he bases his subsequent decisions. Many critics emphasize the *monopoly* elements of advertising, yet fail to recognize its role in keeping monopolistic competition *competitive*. They fall into the trap that advertisers themselves were warned about in a famous speech: "Gentlemen, the consumer is no moron, she's your wife."

It can even be argued that, where repeat purchases and habit are the normal buying pattern, the problem of deceptive advertising dwindles in importance. FTC action on misleading claims often appears to be futile; by the time a decision has been reached, the particular advertising appeal has been dropped in favor of another campaign. By that time, however, any consumers who were attracted have had the opportunity to test the product after purchase and have learned much more than the seller can possibly tell them. If repeat sales occur, then the "misleading" claim that prompted the consumer to try the product is irrelevant; if the consumer resumes his former buying habit, he will have gained additional information. This argument is obviously limited: much condemnation of deceptive advertising comes from business itself, which seeks regulation by government as a protection against "unfair" competition. This merely emphasizes the importance of repeat sales, however: the going concern depends on satisfied customers for its continued business success, and therefore objects to the "raid" on its market by false and misleading claims that divert consumers from their established habits. Significantly, among the deceptive advertising claims that businessmen universally condemn are statements associated with "going-out-of-business" sales and "fly-by-night" operators. Neither of these offers the consumer any potential of withholding repeat purchases, nor the established business a potential recouping of its losses by later sales to sadder, but wiser, customers.

In the general atmosphere of nonprice competition, the temporary price reduction or other quasi-price change appears clearly to be an attempt by the seller to induce consumers to change their purchasing habits. Manufacturers who offer "cents-off" and other such "deals" are typically those who produce food or grocery items that the consumer purchases frequently, and which epitomize the kind of intensive brand advertising that was criticized by the Federal Trade Commission. The "deal" exists specifically in order to lure consumers away from competing substitutes, as explained by a General Foods executive: "A cents-off deal is a type of promotion designed to benefit the consumer, to pass along directly to her a limited-time price reduction in order to induce her to try our product."[16] Obviously, however, manufacturers are counting on consumer satisfaction with the product and consequent repeat purchases. A survey that involved 19 brands reported:

Management's attitudes toward deals or temporary price reductions as an element of marketing strategy vary from unqualified acceptance to outright rejection. On balance, however, there appears to be a consensus that price deals can make it attractive for a consumer to try a new or improved product. . . . The broad purpose of price dealing is to sell more of the product—both during and after the promotion period—at a profit.[17]

The cents-off deal may have the reduced price marked on the package; it may consist of coupons that are redeemable for the product at a reduced price by consumers at stores, or of coupons that may be redeemed for money by mailing to the manufacturer. Couponing is less costly to the producer than off-label pricing, since the price reduction is not given to all buyers; it is estimated that only about 10 per cent of all coupons that are issued are redeemed. All such deals, however, rely on the framework of "regular" or "normal" prices to which the consumer has grown accustomed. The manufacturer's price promotion requires cooperation from the retailer; to quote the food company executive already referred to:

We put on our packages: "With (blank) cents off you pay only (blank)," so that she can better understand the offer.

A final specific, the matter of marking the price per ounce on a package. This, we processors feel, is the retailer's area. He determines all the prices and does all the price marking.[18]

Complaints that such price reductions have not been passed along are common, whether this is attributed to a stockboy's oversight or a retailer's deliberate choice:

The trade's behavior in pricing bears no predictable relationships to the allowances tendered by manufacturers, in spite of the fact that consumer incentives and trade offers specify changes in price and in-store cooperations as a *quid pro quo* from retailers. . . . Even the most generous consumer off-label reduction is ineffective without trade acceptance. . . . Retailers usually take what they want from the total price incentive anyway.[19]

Potentially, such cents-off deals offer a twofold benefit to the consumer. The temporary price reduction may or may not result in a temporary shift in his buying pattern; if it does, the consumer has gained increased experience, which may or may not then lead to a permanent change of habit. The price reduction, however, also offers an opportunity for the consumer to gain by building up an inventory, which was probably not the "benefit" the producer had in mind. A survey of in-store brand switching found that "In some product categories shoppers indicated they expected price cuts and made their selections almost exclusively on the basis of which brand offered the most 'cents-off.' "[20] Frequent use of deals also diminishes the strength of *product* differentiation, because they make consumers more and more *price*-conscious. But when any competitive practice is general among sellers of close substitutes, the firm that avoids this practice can thereby secure for itself significant differentiation. Thus Scott Paper Company's decision to drop price dealing a few years ago created an impressive advertising campaign, in which the manufacturer extolled the housewife's good sense in preferring "quality" and "low prices" to coupons, deals, and other promotions.

Premiums are another type of quasi-price reduction that represents a promotional effort to persuade consumers to change their purchase habits. Although such merchandising is more frequently used to introduce a new product than to defend a market share, the aim is nevertheless clearly to establish repeat sales.[21] So-called "direct" premiums are far from new; one of the earliest "free gifts" with a purchase that still survives is probably the small token found in each box of "Cracker Jack." Its direct descendants are the face towels that are enclosed in soap packages, the "free" lessons offered to the purchaser of an electric organ, the scoop attached to the bag of flour or coffee, the box of detergent found in a new washing machine. The type of physical distribution required by the product obviously sets the limits on the use of "direct" premiums; in some cases, they approximate "tied sales," as with the detergent and the washing machine, or the toothbrush taped to a tube of toothpaste.

Like premiums, package variations are merchandising promotions that attempt to attract the consumer away from existing purchase habits. Reusable containers—liquor bottled in decanters, cheese packaged in refrigerator dishes—represent a fairly expensive outlay for packaging per se, and are therefore used only for special promotions. Other forms of packaging appeal shade into product differentiation itself—for example, the disposable tissues or cleansing powder in containers that "no longer need to be hidden—they're attractive enough for your bathroom shelf"—and hence may provide the consumer with a new kind of utility or a higher level of satisfaction, and produce a consequent change in his buying habits.

One description of premium merchandising clearly identifies its role in a market of monopolistic competition:

There is no point in kidding about the differences between competing brands in many industries; often these differences are slight at best, and frequently not material to the quality or performance of a product. To this extent, incentives offer the advertiser an opportunity to inject into his promotion a distinctiveness which he may otherwise achieve only through exaggerating the importance of minor differences or silly slogans.[22]

The theory of monopolistic competition classifies premium merchandising and other promotions as selling costs, like advertising; occasionally, critics have lumped all forms of selling effort together with advertising and called the whole business wasteful. But the analysis of the consumer shopping and buying process makes it clear that there is a consumer reaction to every action by a seller. Nonprice competition in all its forms attempt to cater to consumer tastes and preferences.

If it is the possession of fuller information about available alternatives that helps the consumer to attain a higher level of satisfaction, then the more he experiments in buying products and services the better. Not only does such a buyer immediately become aware of many purchase alternatives, but he also taps an unimpeachable source of information—his own reaction. Yet the consumer's propensity to make repeat purchases and to form buying habits, while it may be based on a natural attempt to economize time and effort, nevertheless militates against his experimenting in this way. Especially when the consumer is moderately satisfied with his purchase habit, the idea of getting more information by whatever means is not very attractive. As a result, promotions or merchandising efforts may provide just the extra inducement needed to break the familiar habit. The consumer's gain from selling costs is buying information, and the greater fulfillment of his individual tastes and preferences.

The argument holds good for consumer goods and services that are purchased fairly frequently. It does not deny that the consumer's own experience may be a faulty guide to potentially harmful products; consumer protection against harmful drugs, adulterated foodstuffs and flammable clothing remains an obligation of any government that is pledged to promote the safety or welfare of its citizens. Finally, the argument has not yet been applied to the many types of consumption expenditure that do not represent frequent repetition. But here, it needs only to be modified.

The Retailer and Consumer Shopping

The consumer, aside from buying a specific product or service, also chooses a type of shopping process in his visiting one or more stores as well as in his making a final selection and purchase. And if one retailer has provided an acceptable *shopping* experience, the burden involved in seeking out information on all the alternative buying methods available may outweigh the possibility of an increase in satisfaction. So the consumer will return to the same store, until successive repeat purchases have culminated in buying habits. The consumer has now become a "steady" customer. Just as the goal for each producer is to establish consumer loyalty to his own brands and to break the consumer's habits of buying other brands, so each retailer seeks to enlarge his clientele of regular patrons by attracting buyers away from other stores or outlets.

Retailing typifies monopolistic competition; the various shopping processes that are offered by competing stores are a type of product differentiation. The broad kinds of retail operations correspond to the general classes of product; the individual stores seek to differentiate their "output" of shopping methods. Thus supermarkets form a general class of shopping process, with First National and Safeway as differentiated sellers, just as prepared soups form a general class of product, with Campbell's, Lipton's, Heinz, and Knorr as differentiated sellers. Retailers use advertising as manufacturers do—in order to establish their differences from competitors, as well as to make consumers aware of their names and identities. But the heart of the shopping process that is offered to consumers by any store is its inventory and display of goods, its particular form of "scrambled merchandising," its assortment of product lines and the breadth or depth of choice in each line. Consequently information on what is being sold, where, how, and at what price constitutes a much larger part of retail, than of manufacturers' advertising, although cooperative advertising arrangements result in some manufacturers' products being mentioned more frequently than others.

Like the professions and other services, as well as some manufacturers, retailers frequently stress their expertise in their effort to turn steady customers into loyal consumers—buyers who will seek advice and the seller's answer to the question "What shall I buy?" Emphasizing the difference in knowledge and skill between consumers and sellers takes quite different forms in large and small retail stores.

In the small specialty shop that has one or more highly knowledgeable salespeople, the expert resembles the professional, for he sells technical advice and counsel as much as the products themselves. His skill may be the result of formal training, but it derives chiefly from experience, not only with what he sells but with consumer tastes and preferences. The activities of such salespeople, along with the personal relations they establish with consumers, color the entire retail operation; the store is differentiated from competing sellers by the individual attention given to each shopper, and by the knowledge and skill available—all of which are often acknowledged in references from other customers. The satisfied customer's repeat purchases and his favorable testimony reflect the utility he has gained from the salesman's advice and help while arriving at a consumption choice. The store encourages consumers to substitute trust for their lack of information, not only by emphasizing the expertise available but also by stressing reliability and dependability. This type of specialty selling occurs in technical fields—such as paint or radios—or in cases where questions of taste are involved—such as clothing or furniture—or in any area where the consumer distrusts his own judgment. Different types of expertise are described by two retailers:

Paint is an unusual product. You cannot examine it like you can many other products. You cannot demonstrate it like you can many other products. You cannot demonstrate it except in a general way . . . you cannot really even see it until it is applied to the surface.

Therefore, reputation of a label holds unusual significance. Most customers buy on faith—they believe the paint they buy will do the job the way they wish it to be done. . . . Essentially the local retailer who backs the product's reputation with his own is the key to the accessibility of the product. His knowledge of application techniques is extremely valuable to the consumer.[23]

Stores of our type are service businesses, in addition to being sellers of merchandise. We are concerned about the appearance of a man who buys any product from us. If it is a suit, it may need quite a bit of tailoring . . . we carry extensive size ranges . . . so that we have the right model to fit the individual . . . a qualified man would know the type of shirt, should this man wear a full cut shirt or a tapered shirt . . . the salesmen are familiar with fashion, color, fit, etc. This assistance, plus the tailoring involved, gives the wearer and others who see this garment on the wearer an entirely different reflection of the product, as compared to a garment sold by inexperienced help or taken off a rack. . . . The consumer does not get as much satisfaction or service out of a garment which is bought in a store that does not give him the proper service.[24]

In the very large stores, the consumer can also build up a feeling of trust for the retailer and its private brands. This type of consumer preference resembles that which is shown for the individual manufacturer more closely than it does that shown for the serviceman, professional, or skilled salesman. Quantitative data on the total production and sale of private branded merchandise do not exist, but scattered reports suggest that such items account for over 10 per cent of Macy's New York sales, more than 90 per cent of Montgomery Ward & Co.'s sales and at least 98 per cent of Sears' volume; by product line, private brands may amount to 40 per cent of the annual tire sales, from 10 to 35 per cent of the packaged food and grocery items sold, and 30 per cent (but that figure is increasing) of frozen fruits, juices, and vegetables. There is general agreement that private brands have grown rapidly within the past decade, and that that growth will continue in the immediate future. As with the erosion of traditional margins and customary prices, private brands represent a renewed use of price competition, but one that depends on a nonprice characteristic—the reputation of the retail seller.

Private brands came into being as soon as retailers grew large enough to exert any considerable buying power: mail-order houses, department stores, and chain stores successively demonstrated that such merchandise was a logical part of large-scale retail operations. In some lines, private brands were an outcome of retailers' attempts to control quality; the buyers for large stores set up specifications for the manufacturers to meet in their output of consumer goods. But in many cases the store sells, under its own label, items that are identical to the output of manufacturers who distribute and advertise national brands. Such a strategy may have been adopted as a defense against discounting, but it relies heavily on the consumer's trust in the retailer, for the private brand is in competition with the national brand. Consequently, although the private brand may represent a lower price to the consumer, it must also be supported by advertising and all the techniques of nonprice competition discussed previously. Significantly, the same survey that reported consumers' general lack of familiarity with manufacturers of national brands found that over 60 per cent of the respondents could identify 3 to 6 chain-store labels, even when they did not shop at these retail outlets.[25] One of the major advantages of private labels cited by retailers is that customers are attracted to the store itself, so that its name can both sell merchandise and gain additional appeal by offering merchandise.

From the point of view of the consumer, the purchase of a private brand obviously represents a substitution of trust in the retailer for trust in the manufacturer. Interestingly, the consumer in this situation recognizes that expertise, or the difference between his knowledge and that of the seller, lies chiefly in the area of *buying;* the retailer seems to him closer to a skilled consumer than to a producer. The notion that large retailers exercise a countervailing market power against that of large producers has long been a familiar one to household buyers, who know quite well that purchases can be made in quantity at lower costs, and suspect that retailing, as a business, entails the sort of amassing of information about available alternatives that the consumer himself cannot, or will not, undertake.

Retailers use private brands, their special expertise, and many other types of nonprice competition in differentiating their output: the trade jargon speaks of a store "image"—which once again demonstrates the principle that it is the consumer's perception of differences that is significant, and not only the seller's attempts to differentiate. Research into shopping habits indicates that a consumer normally deals with several small groups of "acceptable stores," and defines "acceptability" in different ways for different types of stores. Among the criteria for supermarkets may be speed of self-service and accessibility of merchandise; for department stores neither of these may be important. Whatever the store image, or the particular shopping process, that identifies the individual retailer, each seller aims at securing repeat purchases and building up customary buying habits in as wide a market as possible. At the same time, retailers seek to break any habits that consumers have established of dealing with other stores. Again, the basic consideration is to provide a shopping process that actually ensures satisfied customers. The familiar slogan "The customer is always right" implies that there is no arguing with the tastes and preferences of shoppers. Beyond this, however, there are promotional devices that are characteristic of retailers.

Temporary price reductions and merchandising promotions occur just as they do at the manufacturing level, with the same goal of attracting consumers away from competition, and with the same hope that, once they are attracted, consumers will make repeat purchases and establish regular buying habits. Retail "sales" may consist of end-of-season merchandise, discontinued lines, or "dogs"—those examples of the retailer's inability to judge consumer taste and preferences—and in such "clearance" sales the seller is more concerned with using inventory space profitably than with attracting customers per se. In fact such sales may be advertised to "regular" customers prior to public announcement as one means of maintaining consumer loyalty.

Weekly sales, "manager's specials," weekend promotions, department specials—these are traffic-building sales. Along with free gifts or premiums, they offer some reward to buyers who abandon their usual shopping habits and visit the competing store. For consumers, such temporary price reductions, like manufacturer's "deals," present an opportunity to build up inventory. The nonprice effect is on tastes and preferences; if consumers are attracted, they engage in a shopping process that adds to their experience and provides information for later decisions. In short, retailers' promotions, like those of manufacturers, help monopolistic competition remain competitive.

One of the most controversial of such traffic-builders is the use of trading stamps. This retail inducement to repeat purchases is not a new merchandising device, for stamps appeared at least as early as 1892, and the Sperry and Hutchinson Company dates theirs from 1896. At first stamps were used chiefly by small retailers; perhaps it is significant that, although A&P was one of the first S&H customers, it stopped using them once it had attained sizable volume. During the late '40s and early '50s, independent supermarkets introduced trading stamps in an effort to compete with the chains, which eventually also adopted them and thereby triggered a decade's spectacular growth. In 1957 the industry, of which the S&H company remains the acknowledged leader, had attained sufficient stature to form a trade association, the Trading Stamp Institute of America.

310

Though in 1962–63 there began a decline in growth, there has not yet been a significant decline in the number of consumers who save stamps—the figure stands at about some 80 per cent of American families. Stamp saving is undertaken by urban and rural families, consumers at different income levels, men and women. The majority of consumers save more than one kind, although the S&H company claims that 60 per cent of all families are "customers."[26] In 1965 the first decline in interest, if not in activity, on the part of consumers appeared. According to the 1964 Burgoyne index of consumer sentiment, the number of consumers who reported more of an interest in saving stamps than they had on first starting to save declined from 41 to 36 per cent and the number of those less interested was a substantial 42 per cent, a larger fraction than a year previously.

But in all surveys, consumers report the same reasons for saving stamps: to obtain merchandise that they would otherwise do without. Many consumers who believe that they pay for the stamps through higher prices are quite willing to bear the extra cost, for they also believe that they are choosing to buy forced savings. More accurately, they are purchasing forced consumption, as will appear. Aside from finding stamps a useful form of forced savings, or an outlet for thrift, some consumers gain a certain independence out of using them. This is particularly true for the housewife who has a specific dollar allowance from her husband for food or housekeeping, for in effect she obtains purchasing power over a wider range of goods. A second important reason for saving is to take advantage of stamps that are being paid for, anyway. Thus the practice of issuing stamps has become deeply embedded in consumer acceptance. Delegates from three European countries to an international distribution conference agreed that "the consumer's desire for trading stamps makes it difficult to do away with them."[27]

The controversy over trading stamps recognizes that

sellers use them to attract new customers and to hold on to present customers. Since the stamps represent a discount for cash payment, the question is often raised whether they result in higher prices to the consumer. The first seller who introduces stamps covers their cost, perhaps, by the additional sales volume he gains from nonstamp competitors; but when all the supermarkets or all the gas stations in a given area use one stamp plan or another, this is no longer possible. Any increase in total sales of such retailers must represent a shift of consumer expenditures away from other categories of spending, or from saving. No data exist to show that stamps have thus profoundly affected total spending patterns. It does not necessarily follow that their use must result in raised prices, however, for stamps are like advertising or free gifts in their promotional effect. Therefore, the retailer can cover their cost by omitting other types of nonprice competition. The idea that doing away with trading stamps would result in lower prices to the consumer implies that price competition alone would replace them—which is quite unrealistic. Trading stamps are only imperfect inducements to consumer loyalty; buyers choose food stores for their convenience, variety, and all the other facets of the shopping process, rather than for stamps. In short, nonprice competition which deals with tastes and preferences, continues to characterize consumer markets. To investigate whether trading stamps per se affect consumer prices is almost irrelevant.

Viewing the consumer buying process as a counterpart of distribution provides a more trenchant analysis of trading stamps, for they represent a medium of exchange and a source of purchasing power. The consumer "buys" goods distributed by trading-stamp companies. Such firms, their catalogues and redemption centers, compete with other forms of retailing, and offer a distinctive shopping process to the consumer. How, exactly, does this function?

The first step in the shopping process has to do with information and choice. Trading-stamp catalogues and the display of goods in the redemption outlets, or stores, present the alternatives available to consumers. S&H issues more than 32 million copies of its Ideabook annually; it contains 1,742 different items described in 132 pages. The company comments:

Nearly a year ahead of time—at the same time that merchandise items are being chosen—S&H begins planning its Ideabook of gifts. Seventeen photo studios begin taking pictures. Printing begins in January, at six printing plants, and continues for three months.

The catalog is distributed free to all the people who save S&H Green Stamps. It's the largest single printing run of any publication in the U.S.[28]

Like any other catalogue, such verbal and pictured displays provide information for the consumer to absorb at leisure, but with little or no supplementary help from sales personnel. Since catalogues illustrate nationally branded merchandise, however, they utilize the explanatory and selling efforts of manufacturers' advertising and of retailers who stock the same items. Although there is some evidence that consumers may learn of available products from trading-stamp displays and catalogues,[29] the industry devotes little effort to this part of the distribution process. Unlike mail-order houses, the trading-stamp company does not, via private brands, offer additional alternatives to the consumer; unlike many retail stores, it does not supplement the information provided by the maker. Its outlets might be compared to the early discount houses, where little or no customer assistance was provided. And the price information needed for consumer choice is extremely difficult to obtain, if not actually impossible to calculate in any comparative terms, owing to the variations among stamp plans in denominations and "prices" of merchandise.

Stamp companies do very little to add to consumption-choice alternatives. They depend on consumer familiarity with national brands, and they offer an extremely small number and variety of goods. Such a limitation on the alternatives that are available conflicts directly with the functions of a distribution process geared to consumer choice. Families that find it difficult to select any satisfactory item from catalogues are not confined to upper income brackets, and the consumer frequently finds a purchase "acceptable" in part because it represents a use for the hoard of stamps. Since forms of savings are difficult to obtain, the trading-stamp phenomenon consists in actuality of forced consumption.

The consumer's buying process requires him to place an order that describes the final choice. Redemption centers clearly fall short of a "satisficing" shopping process in this respect. Although the S&H Company states that "At last count there were 856 Redemption Centers serving S&H families from coast to coast (another one could have opened while we were counting!)"[30] the only relevant comparison is to 1,700,000 retail stores. While the number of stores selling merchandise comparable to that in redemption centers is of course less, no accurate count is possible. Furthermore, if the consumer's purchasing power were not tied to the stamp medium, all stores would be alternative sources of supply. The redemption center's methods of taking orders and transferring merchandise require the consumer's physical presence and some considerable expenditure of time. Only recently has the self-service device, which had spread so widely through retailing, been adopted by the stamp companies:

Recently, we introduced the concept of super-service in our Redemption Centers—hostesses to help you make selections, conveyor systems to get your gift out faster. . . . S&H has a continuing program called "Patterns For Friendliness" aimed at improving the already high standards of courtesy in our Redemption Centers.[31]

314

Commenting on this development, *Business Week* points out that three such stores existed, as of late 1964; they displayed 900 items, and reduced the consumer's shopping time to a few minutes.[32] The difference between 900 items readily available and 1,742 items in the catalogue may or may not be worth the extra convenience of self-service. The inventory in the redemption centers frequently differs from that shown in the catalogue and "out-of-stock" is a common occurrence. In most cases merchandise is delivered to consumers by mail only if no premium store exists within 25 miles of the consumer's home; this, plus the absence of delivery arrangements from the stores, results in a further limitation of the type of merchandise available.

Paying for the goods, another step in the buying process, obviously consists of the consumer's transferring his stamps to the company; there has been substantial experimentation with the means of payment. Large-denomination stamps provide some convenience to the collector; machines that automatically issue the correct number of stamps have lessened the retailer's burden. The consumer has learned to live with more than one variety of stamps, as retailers have adopted individual plans in an effort to attain more differentiation.[33] But the phenomenon of more than one medium of exchange proved, as did ration stamps during wartime, that the costs of protection may exceed the nuisance level. For the consumer, no means of fractional payment exists and gifts or purchases are sometimes made simply to "use up" odd holdings of books or stamps. It is partly for this reason that many attempts have been made to require that stamps be redeemable in cash.

Finally, there is the question of the consumer's satisfaction after purchase, and here the stamp companies again depend on using only nationally known merchandise:

To select the hundreds of gifts in the S&H Ideabook we look at most of the consumer products made in America—more than 400,000 different items. . . . We look for top quality and good value. . . . The companies we buy from are leaders in their industries, producing quality merchandise with famous brand names.[34]

The consumer's dissatisfaction with the specific product is typically voiced against the manufacturer, particularly since goods are usually transferred in factory-packed cartons. The redemption center's policy on returned merchandise is usually liberal; defective or duplicate merchandise can be exchanged for another item. But the limitation of the medium of exchange prevents any exchange for money.

As a method of distributing merchandise, trading stamps and redemption centers offer the consumer a shopping process that is clearly less satisfactory than that which is provided by established retailers. The chief limitation is on choice: the consumer's available alternatives consist only of certain lines of merchandise, and of a narrow range of products within each line. The redemption centers are slow to adopt innovations in service, or to provide the consumer with the most efficient buying method within the store. The actual progress of a shopper within a redemption center resembles nothing that takes place in any other American retail outlet as much as it does the routine for a consumer in the Soviet Union, who gives his order at one counter, makes payment at another, and receives merchandise at still a third; he is used to standing in line.[35] But setting up such a type of store, or an inventory and selling method like that used in redemption centers, would of course provide an alternative shopping process, and some additional variety, to consumers in this country, *if* they were free to choose other competitive outlets. The proper concern for users of trading stamps—and this includes the stamp companies, retailers, and consumers—is whether this system of distribution provides an efficient shopping method to consumers, and whether abandoning a freely circulating medium

316

of exchange is compensated for by the forced saving and limited consumption that results.

The consumer's choice of an acceptable or "satisficing" product or service leads to repeat purchases and habits or loyalty to a given brand, product, or seller. Because each seller tries to break consumer habits as well as to maintain them, merchandising practices account for the competition in monopolistic competition. Nonprice competition is directed at consumers' tastes and preferences. Two areas important to tastes and preferences remain to be analyzed: the case for protection, in circumstances where consumer experience is not a reliable guide to products involving safety or welfare, and the case of new products, about which consumer experience must be gained for the first time.

chapter *9* Protection of Consumer Choice

*F*rom their own experiences with purchased goods and services, consumers derive the most dependable and exhaustive information about the satisfactions that such expenditures can proffer, in terms of the buyer's own personal tastes and preferences. Unfortunately, tastes and preferences cannot be relied upon to prevent bodily harm to the consumer who may drink a tasty poison or use an electrical appliance whose decorative case hides a lethal charge. In any economy, therefore, some candidates for consumer expenditure are outlawed and others are controlled, in order to assure some measure of public health and safety.

319

"The General Welfare"

Beyond these limits, consumer protection laws are justified by the responsibility of government to promote the general welfare of its citizens. Accordingly, some purchases also may be prohibited or restricted to specific conditions—such as those of certain weapons or drugs; or else they may be required, as in the case of windshield wipers with automobiles, or fences with swimming pools. Government may also affect the alternatives that are available to consumers by regulating sellers: it may make informative labels mandatory for food, drugs, and cosmetics, or require barbers and bakeries to observe sanitary conditions of operation. Such consumer-protection laws restrict business activity and opportunities for profit; they also restrict the consumer's freedom of choice. In that sense, they are clearly akin to social welfare laws, whose curtailment of consumer freedom of choice still raises intense opposition in some quarters.

Some welfare laws make certain types of consumption mandatory, as in the cases of compulsory education and contributory social insurance; others provide certain types of income, such as aid to dependent children and unemployment compensation. Welfare legislation, existing or potential—for example, medical care for the elderly or for all; "free" education through high school or through college; income payments to guardians of dependent children or to expectant mothers— removes one portion of the consumer economic problem from the operations of the market. This is true of both income and consumption programs.

By definition, consumer income is limited; in most cases, this is so because the market limits the returns to the productive factors (labor, capital, a rented house or land) that the

320

individual consumer has available for sale. For recipients of public welfare, however, the limitations imposed by the market are extremely severe: if the consumer is a baby or too infirm to work, the unimpeded workings of the market would reduce him to destitution. Hence, public programs of income payments are designed to remove such stringent limitations and to assure a *minimum* level of income. The definition of "minimum" employed by a society is a value judgment: it involves, among other things, the ethical problem of choosing between providing "subsistence" and "adequate" levels of consumption. Such terms themselves are frequently defined by reference to consumer survey data.*

Public welfare payments may be calculated to enable the consumer to buy specific quantities of goods and services; despite the evidence for a common consumption pattern, however, a national minimum standard for welfare recipients has yet to be agreed upon. Although state welfare arrangements are supported by Federal finance, public assistance for a family of 4 averages $206 per month in New York, while it is only $37 per month in Mississippi. These payments, therefore, provide recipients with money income and some freedom of choice. Social workers, by helping such families and individuals to allocate their income, assist in their process of consumption choice. But some have urged that freedom of choice by welfare recipients should be limited so as to make their consumption more "efficient." This reasoning rests on the fact that public assistance supports those who are unable to gain more than—sometimes, as much as—the minimum consumption level from their own market earnings. (The occasional experiment with food stamps is probably concerned less with controlling consumption choice than with reducing agricultural surpluses.) The concept of the "means test" im-

* Cf. Chaps. 2 and 3.

plies that eligibility for public welfare is the consequence of ineligibility in the market for incomes; it can be argued that the freedom to make consumption choices in the market for goods and services stems from the ability to earn incomes in the market.

Such reasoning also implies that contributory insurance benefits can be paid without any reference to market limitations of income. Recipients of old age and survivors' benefits have themselves provided income for such payments to others; their pensions may therefore represent compensation for these contributions. Although payments of Old Age and Survivors' Insurance are "benefits"—transfer payments that occur without current production on the part of the recipients—it is not logical to calculate the amount of such benefits in terms of minimum consumption levels. No social value judgment —such as a choice between "subsistence" and "adequacy"—need be involved. Nevertheless, the confusion between contributory insurance and public assistance programs still persists. In the U.S., the provisions of social security legislation that disallow benefits to those whose earnings exceed a stated amount limit both consumer income and national output.

This same problem plagues public housing policy. Federal mortgage insurance supports private markets; it merely widens consumers' freedom of choice in their spending of privately earned income. The provision of public housing itself is quite different. Low-rent public housing that is available only to low-income families and individuals resembles public assistance: eligibility for it stems from the inability to earn sufficient income to buy what is regarded as adequate housing in the market. But the sphere of public housing—including the extension of subsidies to middle-income housing in the 1965 law—is concerned not only with the markets in which consumer incomes are earned but also with the market for goods and services. Through government housing programs, an important consumer service is produced in the public sector rather than solely by private industry. Hence the extent of such programs does not depend only on the income criterion, but also on the efficiency of government production.

Other government programs also supply consumption goods and services outside the private-sector market: public education, public parks and recreational facilities, health services, and so on. It can be argued that all Government Purchases of Goods and Services that pay for current production rather than capital structures are forms of consumption.[1] That is, while public school teachers' salaries represent consumer services provided by government, a new school building represents investment for future as well as current consumption. And such programs should be distinguished, as public or collective consumption, from the special efforts associated with war and defense. In most cases, the analysis of government spending is not greatly affected if the courts and the police, legislators' salaries and the expenses of foreign embassies, agricultural research and exchange regulation, are classified as general government expenditures rather than as consumption. A sufficient area of controversy about policy remains: what kinds of goods and services should be provided solely by the private sector? which should come entirely from the public sector? which should be produced in both sectors?

These questions of welfare economics go far beyond any analysis of consumption per se, although a first step toward the answers is frequently assisted by the model of consumer choice presented in Chapter 4. Briefly, there is a case for public-sector activity whenever social costs or social benefits exist apart from costs or returns to private producers. The fact that goods and services are *produced* in the public sector does not mean that questions of distribution and consumption are automatically solved. The consumer's shopping process, which is central to this work, may not seem relevant, yet somehow or other the goods or services must be transferred from producer to consumer. Government can impose consumption, as it does with schooling; it can rely on the price system to ration out consumer supplies, as it does with some services of the Post Office; or it can make services available at zero prices, as it does with public beaches. "Zero prices" does not mean free goods, since alternative uses exist for the resources that make consumer services available, and it is these uses that are the real costs of production. "Zero prices" refers only to payments for consumption: consumer income need not be allocated to goods and services that have zero prices. Each method will result in a different pattern of consumption choice, and therefore much of the analysis that was presented in previous chapters is applicable. But public-sector production also involves other economic problems: the relation of prices to costs; the demands of employment security or economic development, as well as of consumer tastes and preferences; the disposition of public revenues, and so on. All these are questions that either do not occur at all in markets for consumer goods and services, or else are answered automatically there.

For the analysis of consumer choice and market competition, government programs of consumer protection in the market are of more concern than government policies for income and consumption outside the market. And to understand such protection activities, the entire process of consumer choice and purchase provides a useful framework. Consumer protection affects chiefly what alternatives are available and the information that consumers use in reaching a decision, although government credit controls influence the means of payment. Moreover, both legislation and judicial interpretation have changed the avenues that are open to the dissatisfied consumer.

Informing the Consumer

Some government agencies issue educational and informational guides to available goods and services and, more usefully, suggestions for consumers to use in comparing alternatives. These—like formal course offerings in the public schools —are heavily weighted toward the home economics of consumption and deal mostly with food, clothing, and home appliances.

For example, the Government Printing Office in Washington offers "Fish and Shellfish Over the Coals," a booklet of more than 30 recipes, plus practical suggestions from the home economists of the Department of the Interior's Bureau of Commercial Fisheries; "Fitting Dresses," a pamphlet for seamstresses; and "Septic-Tank Care—How the Homeowner May Save Money," which has details on how to care for septic tanks and drain fields. Typical buying guides include "Know the Poultry You Buy," an illustrated wall chart, which shows fresh, frozen, and canned poultry; "Buying Your Home Sewing Machine," which explains the types of machines available, with their advantages and disadvantages; and "An FHA Quick Guide to Buying a Home," which "will help determine whether you can afford to buy a home, where to begin, what to look for, and tells about borrowing money for the mortgage." Such guides illustrate "what to look for in buying" with very specific suggestions: grading and inspection of poultry, service agreements for sewing machines, mortgage terms and conditions. For the most part, however, such government sources tend to provide only background information and cover only a limited area of consumption expenditures.

Most consumer information about relevant alternatives, their availability, and the ruling prices comes from the advertisements, displays, and selling efforts of manufacturers and retailers. Here Federal, state, and local governments operate to require that sellers provide certain types of information and to prohibit them from issuing false or misleading information.

Advertising being such a powerful form of nonprice competition, business has always regarded false and misleading advertising as unfair competition; the Federal Trade Commission Act of 1914 provided that "unfair methods of competition are . . . unlawful." The Commission was empowered to issue a "cease-and-desist" order after finding a specific practice unlawful; but a Supreme Court decision in 1931 curtailed this remedy against misrepresentation when it found no evidence that false advertising had injured competitors. The Wheeler-Lea amendment in 1938 instructed the FTC to place the consumer's interest paramount over that of business; in addition to preventing unfair competition, it was also to prevent "unfair or deceptive acts or practices in commerce." Six sections, governing false advertising of food, drugs, devices, or cosmetics, enabled the Commission to obtain a temporary injunction to stop such practices before initiating the regular procedure of issuing a complaint, holding hearings, and deciding whether or not a cease-and-desist order should follow. The amendment also strengthened enforcement of the act, which now specifically defined "false advertisement" as one that is "misleading in a material respect." The elucidation of those two terms—"misleading" and "material"—have occupied the Commission and the courts for many years.

In proceeding against unfair and deceptive acts or practices, the Commission has dealt with both manufacturers and retailers. Complaints against manufacturers frequently object to their claims for product performance: the mattress that, according to its maker, will correct a sleeper's bad posture; the battery-operated toy that, the manufacturer implies, will respond to voice commands; the drugs and therapeutic devices with unqualified (and untested) promises of cure. A particu-

326

larly knotty area of misleading claims has arisen with television demonstrations of what the product will do, for the medium itself requires some "misrepresentation." Mashed potatoes are ordinarily used as a substitute for ice cream, which will melt; actors normally wear makeup, and their "white" shirts look whiter when they are actually blue. The definition of "misleading" under such circumstances leads to highly philosophical speculations, as the background of a Supreme Court decision in April, 1965, suggests.

In 1959 Colgate-Palmolive Company and its advertising agency, Ted Bates & Company, used television to demonstrate "Rapid Shave's" softening ability by applying it to sandpaper, preparatory to shaving the paper. For technical reasons, a mock-up of sand-colored plastic was used to represent the sandpaper. FTC hearings leading to a cease-and-desist order established that the product did soften actual sandpaper, which could then be shaved, but the Commission's opinion was that, since the genuine article was not shown on the screen, the television demonstration was misleading. A Federal appeals court disagreed, noting that the viewer could see a faithful representation of "a test which has been actually performed," and that "If there is an accurate portrayal of the product's attributes or performances, there is no deceit." This reasoning was then overruled by a majority of the Supreme Court, whose thinking on this matter is particularly relevant to the place of advertising in consumption choice.

Noting that the law prohibits the "intentional misrepresentation of any fact which would constitute a material factor in a purchaser's decision whether to buy," Justice Warren, who wrote the majority opinion, found that the television demonstration involved more than mere information:

The seller has told the public that it could rely on something other than his word concerning both the truth of the claim and the validity of his experiment. We find it an immaterial difference that in one case the viewer is told to rely on the word of a celebrity or authority he respects, in another on the word of a testing agency, and in the present case on his own perception of an undisclosed simulation. . . . If . . . it becomes impossible or impractical to show simulated demonstrations on television in a truthful manner, this indicates that television isn't a medium that lends itself to this type of commercial, not that the commercial must survive at all costs.*

The previous chapter argued that advertising can either provide reassurance to the consumer whose repeated purchases brought a satisfactory level of utility, or that it can provoke the consumer into changing an established pattern of choice and obtaining new information from his experience. The Court's ruling implies that in either case the law protects the consumer from misleading advertising.

Clear-cut cases of false advertising include outright misstatements in the defining or naming of products: the candlemaker's claim that its votive candles consist solely of beeswax; the retail store's advertisement of clothing as supposedly coming from hotel shops in Miami Beach; the "magichrome" that does not contain chrome and cannot be used to restore or refinish chrome. Advertising what the product *is* obviously involves labels and names *on* products: for foods, drugs, cosmetics and therapeutic devices, the Food and Drug Administration has jurisdiction over goods in interstate commerce; for wool, fur, and textile products, it is the Federal Trade Commission that administers specific regulations.

In applying the last three labeling laws, the Commission has consulted members of the industry on technical problems of definition and then issued detailed explanations of correct and incorrect labeling. Textile products must be labeled with the generic name of any fiber that makes up more than 5 per cent of the total weight of the product; with the proliferation

* Compare with Chamberlin's reasoning quoted in Chapter 6, page 235.

of synthetic fibers, such labels may not provide much information to the nontechnical consumer, even though they are accurate in every respect. A product tag that reads "80% arnel triacetate, 20% nylon, exclusive of ornamentation" furnishes an opportunity for the seller to demonstrate his expertise by explaining the mysterious message, rather than providing useful knowledge to the consumer. The rules as they stand have led to the anomaly whereby manufacturers of "fake fur" textiles may not label their fabrics "fake"; deceptive practices are still possible. All textile products must also show the name of the manufacturer or his registered trademark and the country of origin; wool must be identified as "new" or "reprocessed." Regulations that require product identification protect the legitimate business from unfair competition by the deliberate mislabeling of goods; to quote the chairman of the Federal Trade Commission:

A great hue and cry came in 1940 when the Wool Products Labelling Act was passed. Now the very industry that didn't want it now is the greatest supporter of it. Because what did it do? It eliminated that sharpy, that fellow who was in a big hurry. So it made competition fair.[2]

But such business support does not mean that identifying labels necessarily afford much consumer protection; facts about the product's performance would provide more useful information for consumer choice than technical identification.

The laws governing the labeling and advertising of food, drugs, cosmetics, and therapeutic devices deal with both types of information. Products must be identified; they must be named and advertised truthfully; the quantity of the contents in a package must be shown; instructions for use must accompany drugs and devices, and warnings of improper usage must be imprinted on the containers holding certain cosmetics, drugs, and devices.

The question of what is a product raises problems of

329

identity and definition: Federal law recognizes, for drugs, the standards of the United States Pharmacopeia and The National Formulary; the Food and Drug Administration has established standards to identify and define certain food products. For processed foods, such as mayonnaise or jam, the standard dictates those ingredients that must be present in specified amounts, along with other ingredients that are optional for the producer. Many varieties of canned fruits and vegetables must either meet minimum specifications for quality, or else be labeled "Below Standard in Quality," with an explanatory statement. Regulations for some natural foods, like eggs, state that "no reasonable definition and standard of identity" shall be issued; for others, like wheat flour, on the other hand, the regulations specify the type of wheat and describe the technicalities of milling processes in great detail. Standards have also been issued that require packages to contain the maximum quantity of food that can be filled in the container without damage. These standards, like the detailed regulations issued by the Federal Trade Commission, are worked out after consultation with the trade; they often serve to prevent unfair competition as much as to protect the consumer.

The labels of all drugs must contain a list of active ingredients, adequate directions for use and warnings against misuse of the product; cosmetics that contain drugs must comply with the same rulings. In this field the 1962 revision of basic legislation shifted the emphasis in consumer protection from preventing the sale of harmful products to permitting only effective products to be marketed. Preclearance by the Food and Drug Administration for safety of use had previously been required for new drugs and food additives; present regulations require drug firms to submit convincing evidence of the efficacy of their products, as well as of their safety.

The move from ensuring that consumers have adequate

information and are protected against misinformation to setting standards of quality and effectiveness has taken place primarily in the food, drug, and cosmetics fields, where supervising agencies control manufacturing conditions and trial use. The Food and Drug Administration has powers to seize filthy or contaminated food, to inspect factories and processing establishments, and to ban from the market those products whose claims of efficacy and safety are not warranted by approved research. In short, government controls have been extended so as to cover what alternatives are available to consumers as well as what information is available about existing alternatives.

Consumer protection activity by the various states follows the same general pattern established by Federal agencies. As of 1963, 43 states inspected and/or graded meat; 40, poultry; 34, eggs; 31, fruits and vegetables; 44, dairy products; 16, seafood. Similarly, 43 states regulated food processors or distributors, as well as eating and drinking places; 26 controlled food additives, while 36 controlled pesticides and other potentially harmful substances. At the same time, 38 states had regulations that covered drugs and therapeutic devices and 33 regulated cosmetics.[3] The effectiveness of these activities, like those at the Federal level, suffers because the administrative agencies are generally understaffed and overworked. State laws that prohibit false or misleading advertising or deceptive practices are widely varied; they serve to supplement the efforts of the Federal Trade Commission.

At both levels of government, the regulation of advertising includes information about prices, which the consumer considers along with his knowledge about available alternatives when he is to make a choice. In 1958 the FTC issued detailed guidelines against "deceptive practices" in price advertising and labeling, which are reviewed and revised as competitive practice changes. For the most part, these guidelines deal with the sort of advertising that urges the consumer to compare products and prices. As was suggested in an earlier chapter, such a policy of competitive pricing may be adopted to differentiate one type of seller or sale and in a market dominated by nonprice competition, it is not the chief means of attracting consumer purchases. Such statements as "manufacturer's list price $17.98—our price $14.98" or "$5.00 only—usually $7.95—you save a whopping 60 per cent!" must conform to the basic requirement of truthfulness. This implies that sales were actually made at higher prices used for comparison. False and misleading price advertising, like other such claims, can be a powerful method of unfair competition and for that reason has generally been condemned by business. Trade associations or Better Business Bureaus have issued similar guidelines for "ethical" pricing practices.

Another aspect of price information to consumers has been investigated by Senate hearings on packaging and labeling practices, which have chiefly dealt with whether consumers can find, read, and understand, in terms of comparative prices, the details shown on packaged goods. Examples of this type of deceptive packaging include: yellow printing on gold cellophane; minute lettering along the crease of a package; ingredients listed on the reverse of a label, so that they could not be read through the colored liquid in the bottle; informative details molded into a plastic container, with no contrast to make them visible, or price markings superimposed in such a way as to be illegible.

The chief controversy aroused by the legislation that has been proposed in order to remedy such situations turns on whether government agencies should have the power to set standards for containers, their dimensions, and the weights and quantities of their contents. Such regulations could be issued only when they would clearly prevent consumer deception or when, by enabling consumers to compare products and prices, they would prevent unfair competition. The legislation would also strengthen the existing powers of the Federal Trade Commission to prevent deceptive practices and of the Food and Drug Administration to require labels on foodstuffs. Manufacturers' "price deals," which involved "cents-off" labels and advertising, would also be outlawed.[4]

The use of fractional weights and sizes in packages raises the question of what it is, exactly, that the consumer buys. Food processors explained at the Senate hearings that the two dimensions of price and *quantity* considered in economic analysis do not necessarily refer to price and *weight:*

Why do manufacturers provide packages containing fractions of ounces? Because surveys show that consumers prefer to buy some products based on the number of servings rather than by the ounce. . . . After determining how much weight constitutes the desired amount of a serving, the multiple of this weight, times the number of servings, gives the weight to be put in each package, and it may not always be in full ounces. . . .[5]

The mixes, used as a pudding, are designed to produce a certain yield—four servings. We built in this control to aid the housewife, and the repeat purchases over the years testify that the homemakers welcome it.

Now, while the number of average servings is constant, the net weight varies with different flavors because some of the flavor mixes have greater densities than others. Chocolate pudding, for example, comes in 4-ounce boxes, while one needs 3¼ ounces to get four average servings of vanilla.

In both cases, our recipe on the package instructs the consumer to add 2 cups of milk to get the yield she seeks—four servings, equal to a half-cup each. Were we to round off the ounces—bring the vanilla pudding content up, say from 3¼ ounces to 4 ounces, some other things would come out uneven. We would not only have to change the recipe and instruct the consumer to add 2 cups plus so many extra tablespoons of milk, but we would also have to indicate that the contents of the package would make $4\%_{10}$ servings— servings of the kind and size she expects.[6]

The idea of buying volume rather than weight—servings rather than quarts or pounds—has considerable validity, of course, particularly in the food field. The consumer does not insist on a pound of fish if the slice "big enough for two" weighs 15¼ ounces, and planners of picnics recognize that the number of hot dogs may be of more importance than a predetermined weight.* But the concept of a "volumetric" society can be overworked; three years after the quotation above (note 6), the puddings referred to were packaged differently. The vanilla pudding contained 3¾ ounces and the chocolate, 4¼ ounces; the directions remained the same: they called for two cups of milk and promised four servings, each of half a cup. In what sense has this "product" changed? Does the consumer now get a more strongly flavored pudding, or does she get more pudding mix? To what does the term "quantity" apply—to the ingredients in the cardboard box or to the dessert on the table? Presumably only the satisfied or dissatisfied consumer has the answers.

In order to ensure maximum freedom of choice, the consumer should possess sufficient information to be able to calculate price on any of several bases: price per ounce, price per serving, price per package, price per meal. But when two or more factors are arranged for easy computation, the relation cannot be kept stable for very long, in a dynamic economy. While the criticism still remains valid that packaging practices may prevent price comparison, many self-appointed spokesmen for consumers also object to fractional packaging on the grounds that it leads to "hidden" price increases, which occur when the contents of a package are diminished instead of the price being raised. Such a criticism is not well-founded, in terms of consumer choice.

The wide range of nonprice competition discussed in the

* Cf. Chap. 7, pp. 255–56.

previous chapter exists because there are such things as consumer tastes and preferences, because the price dimension is not always uppermost in the making of consumer decisions. The notion commonly held that price increases are honest but quantity decreases deceptive implies that the shopper is quite unaware of product variations in weight, size, and quality, and in countless other dimensions of consumer choice. Given the proclivity for variety, the readiness with which each change making for a wider choice has been accepted, there seems to be no reason to assume a general consumer preference for price as against nonprice competition. Conventional price endings and price points may be a "customary trade practice," but they are also certainly familiar to consumers, who were quite well aware during World War II that the "nickel candy bar" had actually increased in price, even though it continued to cost them five cents. A cursory review of packaged salted nuts in a neighborhood supermarket turned up two brands of different varieties, packed in net weights of 2⅛, 2¾, 3⅜, 4, 4¼, 5¼, 5⅜, 5½, 6, 6⅜, 7, 7½, 8, and 11 ounces, and all of them priced to end in "nines"—at 29¢, 39¢, 49¢ or 59¢ a package. Obviously the consumer recognizes the prevailing uniformity and stability in such prices; once he has become aware of price limits, is the consumer "deceived" when the net weight of a package of salted nuts changes by half an ounce?

Prices go down as well as up, yet the challengers of "misleading" hidden price increases have little criticism to offer of the evils of hidden price decreases. If price is the variable that should always change, why has there been no protest that electric light bulbs have been altered so as to give more hours of use, or that durables such as refrigerators have been changed so as to offer larger capacity and more versatile performance? Narrow-minded interpreters of the "consumer interest" are, in fact, insisting on the inviolability of the product, and advocating that all questions of change be thrown into the price dimension. They ignore the inviolability of the individual consumer's preferences and choice. They overlook the power of consumer repeat purchases, which can make or break a product variation.

It remains true, of course, that consumers should be protected against deliberate deception; still, it is difficult to see why price competition should be the rule and nonprice competition outlawed. A local ordinance to require price tags on all merchandise displayed in New York City shop windows aroused business opposition on the grounds of consumer preference:

Most retailers believe that having the retail price on a major appliance is just one more method of preventing genuine product merchandising . . .

"Prices are good for a supermarket, but there's more to it than price in the appliance business. Your only chance is to be able to talk to the customer . . . find out what she needs . . . tell her about the product."[7]

"Merchandising," previously defined as "getting the right product to the right place at the right time," means, in effect, matching consumer preferences. But business efforts to do this turn on nonprice competition and not exclusively on price competition.

Whenever product variation is an important form of nonprice competition, however, consumer protection involves more than just providing information. The consumer's chief weapon is the threat that repeat purchases will not be made. But this is useful only over a limited range of items—those with a fairly small unit price that are fairly frequently purchased. And the threat of not repeating a purchase is much less often applied to, or as effective with, retailers—if only because the particular transaction may be more important to the consumer than to the retailer. Because his weapons are limited, there is a case for protecting the consumer and for ensuring that all the alternatives available to him meet some minimum standard of quality, whether that is defined in terms of the character or performance of the product, or in terms of the seller's expertise. Just as the responsibility for keeping food labels truthful leads the FDA to attempt to establish standards of definition and quality for foodstuffs, so efforts to clarify consumer information sometimes suggest that standards of quality and "grade-labeling" of products in terms of such standards may be called for.

The relation between consumer information, the "expert" seller, and pressures for standards of quality can be illustrated in the professions and service trades. Wherever consumers seek advice, knowing that they will be unable otherwise to make technically informed choices, the case for assuring a *minimum* level of expertise on the part of sellers rests on consumer ignorance: it is a kind of protection for the consumer against himself. Such minimum standards do not ensure a maximum or even satisfactory level of utility for all buyers, but are merely an attack on that gross *loss of utility* that is represented by actual harm. To sellers, however, the establishment of minimum standards of expertise usually means that there will be fewer suppliers than would otherwise exist, and therefore the possibility of less competition and more monopoly gain. Separating the consumer interest from that of the sellers poses a critical administrative problem, clearly illustrated in the laws that provide for occupational licensing in the service trades and the professions.

Since most services are local, licensing is commonly the prerogative of municipal or state governments; the variety and extent of such regulation suggests that it is often the prospect of new sources for tax revenues that generates licensing provisions. When technical qualifications are required in order to obtain a license, they vary from extreme specificity to vague generalities. The board or agency that evaluates applicants according to the standards must consist, almost by definition, of experts in the particular field rather than of consumers. (The chief exception is to be found in such classifications as nurses, midwives, chiropodists, and naturopaths; here, applicants are examined by physicians rather than by other nurses, midwives, and so on.) And the experts, as sellers, have quite different goals from those held by consumers. Licensing provisions, ostensibly set up in order to prevent consumer disutility, also serve to restrict entry into the field and thereby provide monopoly gains to sellers.

Whenever suppliers themselves rather than consumers call for licensing regulations, that is prima facie case that the intent of the system is to lessen competition. Such a suspicion is, of course, strengthened when the new licensing provisions automatically grant approval to all existing suppliers of the service. Two opposing points of view on this question can be discerned. The National Funeral Directors Association of the United States sponsored a history of the industry, which states:

Licensing boards consisting of mostly, and in some specific cases, all funeral directors have become agencies for the control of the personnel in the field, and thus have exercised some small influence in the restriction of competition for the market.[8]

Such licenses clearly differ from those required by the Oregon law for hearing-aid dealers, which was passed specifically for consumer protection. This contained no "grandfather clause," providing for the automatic licensing of existing dealers, and set up an advisory council to judge qualifications. The council consisted of medical specialists, as well as of members "experienced in the fitting of hearing aids." (These latter also had to demonstrate their competence by way of examination.) The bill aroused intense opposition from the trade; only one dealer supported it from the beginning. As he wrote, a year later:

Anyone placing themselves in the position of a prospective hearing-aid candidate can hardly question the desirability of this law. On the other hand, by tending to place a restriction on the immediate economic gain of the hearing-aid dealer by enforced rules of practice it was bound to and will, no doubt, continue to meet with spirited opposition by dealers and manufacturers alike.[9]

Minimum standards for expertise are most stringent when they include educational requirements for suppliers of consumer services. The definition of a "profession"—as distinct from a trade, craft, or skill—has always referred to formal education; in many trades, education is rapidly replacing on-the-job training or apprenticeship, for the transition to professional status usually means increasing educational requirements. And this establishes another opportunity for control: only approved schools can fulfill educational requirements; where, as in the case of the professions, approval and control of the schools rests with the experts, their power to control the number and character of sellers in that field is complete.

Probably the clearest example is that of health services: the supply of physicians, nurses, and other health personnel has not kept pace with population growth, let alone with the rise in income and with those changes in technology that have also tended to increase consumer demand. Consequently, services must be rationed out by high prices: the mean and median incomes of physicians are the highest for any occupational group; dentists and lawyers come second. While there is no question that the relative shortage of medical services reflects the cost of the investment required,* it is also clear that the supply of such services could be immediately expanded by lowering the minimum standards required. The conflict between protecting the consumer and allowing would-be sellers to compete is clear. The medical profession has emphatically denied that the consumer would benefit from the establish-

* Cf. Chap. 8, pp. 285–87.

ment of less stringent qualifications; the fact that the objectivity of this judgment has not been more widely questioned demonstrates, perhaps more than anything else, the completeness of consumer trust.

Because many products are such as to allow the manufacturer to occupy the same role of "expert-seller" as that played by the supplier of services, the same argument often crops up—that consumers should somehow be assured of minimum levels of quality, that advertising and nonprice competition should not be allowed to encompass product deterioration. Where prices are relatively stable and uniform, and product variation is an important competitive technique, it seems wholly possible for manufacturers to increase their profits by worsening the quality of their output—so long as such changes are not discerned by the generally unknowledgeable consumers.[10] Proposals that government impose minimum quality standards have been stoutly resisted by industry on the grounds that freedom of choice—for both consumer and producer— would be thereby curtailed, that the minimum standard would tend to become the maximum, and that any incentive to improve quality would be removed. It is also said that such controls would be totalitarian, Communistic, or worse.

These arguments pose an interesting contrast with the efforts of trades to become recognized professions, and of professions to raise the standards of training and ability in their ranks. There have been successful attempts, within specific industries, to impose minimum standards. (It is generally agreed that packaging and labeling practices were modified so as to meet the sharpest criticism after Congressional hearings were publicized.) Identifying labels, which may be used only if one meets certain specifications, occur in a number of fields: the word "sterling" on silver is perhaps the earliest such mark, the Underwriters' Laboratory seal for electrical wiring probably the one most commonly seen. Even in industry itself, however, attempts to impose common standards may be rejected by the individual seller who is seeking to differentiate his output.

For example, the National Electrical Manufacturers Association worked out standards for rating the capacity of room air conditioners, and these standards were adopted by all leading manufacturers. But its further program of certification of products according to such standards was turned down by Frigidaire, in a letter distributed to the trade, in the following terms:

We believe that it is the responsibility of the manufacturer to guarantee to the customer that what he says about his product is true and accurate and then stand behind his guarantee. Frigidaire will continue to rate its products in accordance with NEMA standards. . . . We will not have anyone else certify what we put on our certificate.[11]

The implication is clear: although the company does benefit from an industrywide program to increase consumer information, as an individual seller it can be differentiated, and will therefore seek to gain more consumer acceptance and loyalty by refusing to accept minimum standards for product quality.

An emphasis on quality is one of the strongest advertising appeals for brand-name, differentiated sellers. Historical evidence supplies firm grounds for the belief that advertised brands represented an improvement in quality over bulk sales and shoddy, unknown workmanship. The use of product variation is too important a weapon in nonprice competition for the individual firm to be willing to relinquish it in favor of minimum standards; except where there is a clear case for protecting health and safety,* government efforts to require such standards gain little support. But although nonprice

---

* Laws requiring safety devices for automobiles, such as seat belts or padded dashboards, are not yet in force throughout the country, which indicates the difficulty of unequivocally establishing a case for government regulation.

competition can lead to the establishment of product quality well above any mimimum standard, it can also lead to product deterioration in the face of consumer ignorance. That is why consumer repeat purchases are so powerful: whether or not he is technically trained, the consumer can recognize whether or not he is satisfied with a product in use. The same argument, however, can be used to support all government and business efforts to prevent false and misleading information, in order to increase the freedom of consumption choice. Since there are laws forbidding deceptive practices and false advertising, and requiring specific information for certain products and services, resources might better be allocated to more enforcement activities for these laws than to reducing nonprice competition by imposing quality standards and product specifications.

Consumer Credit

Federal and state banking regulations serve to protect the consumer's deposits and hence his purchasing power, but monetary policy has much broader goals than this. Of more immediate concern to the consumer's shopping process are the laws that regulate credit transactions. There are two kinds: those that affect the terms and conditions of consumer credit, and those that provide for information about the conditions that now exist.

Legislation against usury persisted for many years; it had the effect of making pawnbrokers and loan sharks the only source of credit—at exorbitant rates of interest—to low-income consumers. The gradual evolution of model small-loan laws permitted the growth of legitimate business; these laws set interest rates sufficiently high—usually around 3 per cent per month on the unpaid balance of the debt—to cover the costs of extending credit in small amounts. Such state legislation, usually accompanied by licensing and regulatory provisions for consumer finance firms, has widened the choices for consumers. It has enabled small-loan companies and banks to offer a variety of credit services, and thus to compete. During the past two decades, similar regulation of the credit that is extended in purchase transactions has broadened the scope of the laws that apply to money loans.

Purchase credit takes on many different forms, as competing sellers try to differentiate the shopping process. Installment sales contracts for a specific purchase apply chiefly to durable goods; they enable the buyer to make payments over time, presumably enjoying services and satisfaction all the while from such products as automobiles, appliances, plumbing, or carpeting. Charge accounts, or open credit, are offered by the retailer as part of his selling policy; they provide the buyer with the convenience of periodic billing and payment. Specialized firms, such as Carte Blanche, the Diners' Club, and American Express—in addition to more than 100 banks—have extended this charging system to a variety of purchases. "Revolving credit," typically offered by large retailers, enables buyers with a wider range of income to contract a specified amount in charge purchases. Under study is a type of credit card that would be honored by vending machines. There seems to be no reason to expect a decrease in innovations in consumer credit arrangements.

Consumers who use credit can buy either of two quite different services: the conveniences of periodic billing and payment, and the ability to make "fractional payments," commonly known as "buy now, pay later." The latter service was appreciated as early as during the '30s for the BLS commented on the similarity of prices paid by high- and low-income families for major appliances.* To the seller, any extension of

* Cf. Chap. 1, p. 35.

credit involves costs, not only in the transfer of purchasing power from seller to buyer (a shift of capital), but also in the collection process. Such costs must be met:* they are absorbed as a cost of doing business by the retailer who offers "conventional" charge accounts, but there is a variety of service or finance charges to the consumer that are connected with installment sales, bank credit cards, revolving credit, and so on. Protecting consumers against "too high" credit costs by regulating sellers or the fees they charge may have the effect of restricting the alternatives available to consumers; protection that insists on complete information, and prohibits false or misleading claims, can widen the range of consumer choice.

Credit extended for the purchase of merchandise is not subject to laws against usury or to small-loan laws, for the difference between cash and credit payments is a "time-price differential," rather than one of interest. However, just as small-loan laws, which permitted a higher rate of interest than that allowed by most anti-usury laws, enabled new forms of business to offer credit to consumers, so laws that regulate purchase credit may support the efforts of competitive business against the methods used by unscrupulous victimizers of the consumer. Complaints about predatory lending have led to the institution of laws governing installment sales of automobiles in 37 states; these laws specify maximum finance charges. Not as much legislation regulating other installment sales exists; fewer than 20 states have set a maximum finance charge. Because it is not clear whether charges for revolving credit plans are a time-price differential or interest, some states have passed laws that specifically regulate this form of credit. Those laws that include maximum finance or service charges set a rate of 1½ per cent per month on the unpaid balance.

* Cf. Chap. 5, pp. 196–97 and Chap. 6, pp. 237–39.

The chief controversy in the area of consumer-protection legislation centers on information about the cost of credit. Many state laws, and certain proposed Federal legislation called "Truth in Lending,"* require the complete disclosure of all charges, whether these are termed interest, finance fees, service charges, insurance costs, fines for late payments, closing charges, or whatever; the total price to be paid under financing arrangements must also be made clear, as well as the price if there is immediate cash payment in full. Unlike laws that have been enacted at the state level, the proposed Federal legislation would further require the cost of credit to be stated, prior to the transaction, in terms of "the percentage that the finance charge bears to the total amount to be financed expressed as a simple annual rate on the average outstanding unpaid balance of the obligation." In the case of revolving credit, the bills proposed would require a statement of "the simple annual percentage rate or rates at which a finance charge will be imposed," plus, in each monthly accounting to the customer, the finance charge actually imposed, calculated on the basis of a similar simple annual percentage rate. The question then arises: what *is* the cost to the consumer?

Supporters of these various, but similar, bills frequently reason that consumers are unaware of the "real cost" of credit and that the revelation of such costs would deter consumers from using credit. The original argument that a diminution of consumer credit would follow from truth-in-lending legislation, and that such a decrease would promote economic stabiliza-

---

* This familiar title has been applied to a number of bills, introduced in successive sessions of Congress since 1960, by Senator Douglass of Illinois. The Economic Report of the President, January 27, 1966, says in part, "While the growth of consumer credit has contributed to our rising standard of living, confusing practices in disclosing credit rates and the cost of financing have made it difficult for consumers to shop for the best buy in credit. Truth-in-lending legislation would provide consumers the necessary information, by requiring a clear statement of the cost of credit and the annual rate of interest."

tion, has been more or less abandoned; the goal of promoting an informed consumer decision remains. The point at issue is whether consumers need to know what the finance charges are by seeing them stated in percentages, as well as money terms. Arguments that consumers are more concerned with the dollar amount of total charges, or with the dollar amount of monthly payments, or with the number of such payments, conclude that indication of the percentage rate would serve to confuse rather than inform consumers. Many of the "horror stories" about buyers who are forced to pay 2 or 3 times the actual price of the product in finance charges evidence little awareness, on the buyer's part, of any of the *money* amounts involved. Some of the transactions reported by ignorant victims seem to be clear violations of existing state legislation. Consequently, it seems dubious that adding one more requirement—that of stating a *percentage* rate of charge—would improve matters very greatly. Strengthened legislation and enforcement of laws against deceptive practices would increase both consumer information and choice.

But both supporters and opponents of the percentage provisions agree that in many cases consumers would find the charges, once they were expressed as a simple annual rate, "too high." Surveys have shown a remarkable consumer ignorance of the rates that are actually being paid, and a faith that "6 per cent" is some kind of maximum (which some people have traced back to the fact that sixth-grade arithmetic books framed too many explanations and problems of percentage in terms of 6 per cent). There are examples of consumers in upper-income brackets, or with some education beyond high school whose choice-decisions have been influenced by their learning to compare finance charges in terms of per cents rather than dollars.

A severe technical problem arises, however, from requiring an annual rather than a monthly rate with revolving credit accounts. Under the provisions of the New York State law, for example, all consumers sign a contractual agreement that describes the extent of their obligation in great detail; it shows monthly payments for unpaid balances, fixes 1½ per cent per month as the rate at which finance charges will be computed, and provides for the issuance of monthly statements that separate purchases, payments, the unpaid balance, and the service charge. Such full disclosure does not include stating an annual rate, and retailers who offer revolving credit insist that the effort to provide this additional information would be costly and misleading. While the monthly rate multiplied by 12 would give the *maximum* service charge imposed, the actual rate could be much less; in any case, it would vary widely, depending on the consumer's purchases and payments. From the consumer's point of view, to quote a percentage that might be 3 times the actual charge is just as deceptive as to err in the opposite direction; it does not lead to accurate comparisons of alternatives.

The trade practice of billing, and the consumer shopping habit of making payments, on a monthly (or 30-day cycle) basis, is the root of the percentage problem. Annual rates are wholly familiar to consumers who have mortgage payments or saving-deposit accounts. Stating finance charges as a per cent per annum for installment-sales contracts, or for small loans that normally run over a year, would therefore be readily understood. Furthermore, such rates would enable the consumer to compare relevant alternatives: if sufficient savings to pay the cash price are on deposit in a bank that is paying 4 per cent, and the finance charge is stated as 9 per cent (rather than $4.00 per hundred), the consumer's choice is clearly presented. But there is no evidence that consumers decide the *total* allocation of their income on a yearly basis. When asked if they would be willing to incur more debt, most consumers replied in terms of whether they could, or could not, increase the size of their *monthly* payments. Presumably the period for which income is received—weekly, fortnightly, or monthly—influences the length of the period over which it is spent. Consequently, for users of revolving credit (where both purchase and payment are made within a short time period), the monthly rate not only seems more relevant but, in most cases, would allow for an accurate comparison of alternatives. In any event, even if institutional arrangements have developed into firmly established shopping habits and trade practices, there is no certainty that they cannot be altered.

Some form of centralized bookkeeping, involving banks, consumers, and all the sellers to whom they make payments, is a recurrent dream of those who are fascinated by electronic data-processing. The extent to which a universal credit-card system can be employed presumably turns on the cost of making all payments in this way, which would be followed by the disappearance of small change and of other convenience forms of currency. Without contemplating such a marked change as inevitable, it is possible to predict that credit, which already provides for both fractional payment and the convenience of periodic billing and payment, will take new forms, thereby altering cost conditions to sellers and alternatives of choice to consumers.

The Dissatisfied Customer

Positive steps by government to assure consumer satisfaction with purchased goods and services include the development of standards for quality and performance, as previously discussed, and the provision of remedies for the consumer who has not achieved an acceptable level of satisfaction.

Since the laws of warranty have developed out of common law and from specific legislation covering all kinds of sales, they do not represent a primary concern with the family or the individual, who is the "ultimate consumer" of this book. Nevertheless, the existence of warranties has shaped the nature of market competition and therefore of consumer choice.

That a seller has the legal right to transfer goods that have been purchased, and that his goods are of merchantable quality, fulfilling a specific description or being reasonably fit for the ordinary purpose for which they are sold was established as an implied warranty by the courts and translated into statutes early in the century. When producers sell directly to consumers, any breach of this warranty can be used to provide redress to the dissatisfied purchaser. But the growth of large-scale manufacturing and retailing has meant that the producer's responsibilities could be transferred. Court decisions have held the manufacturer liable in certain cases, however, and the courts' interpretations of that "reasonable use" that is implicitly promised with goods of "merchantable quality" has led to the use of disclaimers or express warranties.

Such a warranty is any factual statement or promise made by the seller about the goods that tends to induce the consumer to buy. This applies only to factual statements, not to opinions voiced by the seller, and it holds only if the buyer relies on these statements, not on his own judgment. By specifically restricting his warranty to certain conditions of use or causes of failure, the manufacturer can "guarantee" the consumer replacement, repair, or repayment of the purchase price.

Manufacturers' warranties have become an important form of nonprice competition, particularly for durable goods; they therefore influence the consumer's shopping process. As one authority puts it:

It is common in today's economy for the manufacturer to attach a warranty to his product, advertise it to the consumer, make service facilities available, and otherwise assume control over the selling and distribution process. Such practices represent an intent on the part of the producer to influence consumer purchase and to take responsibility for the results accomplished by the product. While the manufacturer does not, in the legal sense, make the sale to the consumer when distribution is effected through retailers, he is often more instrumental than the retailer in inducing consumers to buy. In view of this fact he often has *economic* privity of contract with the consumer, even though he does not have *legal* privity of contract.[12]

The laws of warranty enable sellers to offer a wider variety of consumption choice, to compete by appealing to consumer tastes and preferences. In some cases firms have offered recompense to the dissatisfied buyer that far exceeds any legal responsibility: the broad warranty extended by Zippo, entitling the consumer to perpetual free repair service, is an obvious example. But in such cases the benefit to the firm stems from the nature of nonprice competition: its product is dramatically differentiated by its guarantee.

Much of the effort at consumer protection discussed throughout this chapter seems to extend the implications of sellers' warranties. The express warranty, which governs facts or promises by sellers, leads logically to the adoption of legislation explicitly prohibiting false or deceptive claims and requiring specific information; the implied warranty of "merchantable quality" develops logically into specific standards for identity, definition, quality, and conditions of manufacture.

The point at which regulations appropriate for consumer protection begins to interfere with consumer freedom of choice remains difficult to determine. It is not without significance that so many consumer-protection activities have had their origin in pressures by business itself to outlaw "unfair" competition. The goal, for sellers, of filling consumer demand means using nonprice competition in an effort to match consumer tastes and preferences; presumably, the more such efforts there are, the greater the likelihood that consumer demands for variety and change will be met. Keeping markets actively competitive, therefore, is undoubtedly the most efficient and powerful technique for protecting consumers. What this means, chiefly, is preserving unlimited freedom of entry for new sellers. A shift in consumer preference can destroy a monopoly more effectively than any antitrust ruling; if firms are free to introduce new and varied alternatives, such a shift becomes possible. It remains, therefore, to analyze the seller's process of innovation, which can, ideally, both protect the consumer and at the same time increase his freedom of choice.

chapter 10 **What Will Consumers Buy?**

*P*roduct variation, or the introduction of new products, epitomizes the two-way relation between consumer preference and nonprice competition by sellers in the market. Both the historical and the empirical data in this work have supplied a major emphasis on variety: the goods and services that consumers buy, the shopping processes through which they buy, have been changing continuously, and constantly offering a wider range of choice. The theoretical analysis of consumer choice rests on consumer tastes and preferences and on the basic craving for variety—the Law of Satiable Wants—which is such an important part of human nature. The analysis of consumer markets discloses monopolistic competition and all the forms of nonprice competition that provide variety. Product differentiation is one of the most powerful forms of competition. But the force of consumer preference is such that mere random variation, any differentiation at all of the product, will not do. Over and over again the success of one product or marketing innovation, or the failure of another, has been traced to consumer acceptance in the one case, consumer rejection in the other. Firms that introduce new products, therefore, have developed ways and means of investigating consumer preference, of gauging what people will buy; such investigations shape both the process of market competition and consumer choice.

Consumer Research and Competition

The development of market research has paralleled the growth of mass production and the proliferation of distribution methods that separate the maker of a commodity from its ultimate purchaser. At the beginning of the century, these techniques of production and distribution were beginning to be typical of the economy. Prior to that time consumers, over half of whom lived on farms, obtained their goods from three possible sources. Many things were home-produced: foods grown on the farm, clothing made by wives and daughters. A second source was the factory that supplied the stock of a general store or a small city shop. Much of what these outlets sold was raw materials for home production: fabrics for making clothes, flour for making bread, lye for making soap. Only a minor part of factory production represented finished consumer goods: men's ready-to-wear clothing, shoes, household utensils, the earliest processed cheeses and canned soups. Typically, these were limited in quantity, quality, and variety, for local or regional manufacturers served small market areas. A third type of supplier, the local producer or craftsman, sold directly to the consumer. The dairyman delivering milk, the farmer (or his wife) with a weekly route for eggs and poultry, the local ice plant or coal yard, the milliner and the seamstress, the cobbler, the cabinetmaker, and the blacksmith—these were small businessmen in direct contact with their customers. In many cases the consumer's order preceded production, and goods were frequently "made to order." The changeover to factory production of almost all final consumer goods brought a growing separation between maker and user.

Market research is the modern version of the craftsman's intimate knowledge of his customers. Originally confined to sales analysis and dependent on reports from distributors or sellers, market research has shifted more and more toward investigating consumers directly.[1] Consumer survey data are arranged to estimate the sales potential of a given product; consumer shopping habits are studied to evaluate the sales potential of a given market. And, as differentiating the product has become central to nonprice competition, firms have sought suggestions from consumers themselves as to how their products should be differentiated. The study of consumer preferences has become central to the introduction of new products, or to variations in existing products. Surveys of the failures of new products reiterate that market research was insufficient (or that the public was fickle); the more accurate the prediction of consumer reaction, it is held, the more successful the innovation.

The extent of market research, and particularly of consumer research or premarket evaluation, in American industry cannot be documented by any data that cover the entire economy. Studies by the American Management Association and the American Marketing Association, by such trade publications as *Printers' Ink* and *Advertising Age*, or by individual investigators, have all been confined to surveys of members, readers, or small groups of firms; no statements can yet be made about "all manufacturers" or even "all consumer goods firms." But all these studies, as well as the current reporting of business activity in trade papers, agree that the investigation of consumer preference is a growing field, both in terms of the number of firms involved in it and the amount of resources they devote to it, as well as of the recognition accorded it by company policy.

One difficulty in measuring market research activity is the number of different functions involved. Manufacturers of consumer goods (or producers of consumer services) who have an established consumer research policy can organize responsibility in many different ways. The firm's own staff may devote its efforts to working out areas for investigation which are carried through by specialized organizations outside the firm. Their reports are then analyzed by the market research staff of the firm. Or the staff may itself be fully versed in all the techniques of consumer research, and draw its own samples of consumers for interviews, mail questionnaires, and product testing. A firm that specializes in market research may provide all these services, from diagnosing the manufacturer's needs for consumer investigations to providing detailed reports and analysis. Or such a firm may concentrate on a particular industry or line of consumer goods, or on a particular research technique, such as motivation research, store audits or mailed surveys, drawing samples or conducting field interviews. Among the other firms that include consumer research among their services to manufacturer-clients are advertising agencies, management consultants, and specialists in packaging or design.

Consumer research is of crucial importance to advertising media, which describe (and differentiate) their "product" in terms of the market they reach. Investigating the number in their "audience," whether these be subscribers, readers, listeners, or viewers, is only a first step: if the audience can be further defined by income, age, occupation, family composition, and other household characteristics, its potential for sellers' advertising appeals can be more specifically delineated. Some newspapers, radio stations, and magazines run extensive surveys of routine purchases; others make special studies of particular product or service lines. The *Life Study of Consumer Expenditures* and the *Look National Appliance Survey* are among the most ambitious of such investigations, for they were both based on a national probability sample, which also provided precise figures on magazine readership. Finally, trade associations and trade publications engage in consumer research.

Not all of these activities, obviously, are concerned with investigating consumer preferences primarily as a guide to the production of more successful new products or product variations. Techniques of premarket evaluation are still being discovered and developed; as in any growing field, there is always a fad for one or another type of research. But the fact that consumer preference research is a vital function in market competition is evidenced in policy statements from more and more companies:

Management cannot afford to spend vast sums tooling up for a product that the consumer will not buy, and even more important, rebuy. On the other hand, management cannot afford to wait for wants and preferences to originate and spread through the market spontaneously or to be created by competition. The marketing research upon which management must increasingly depend must measure and forecast rather than describe.[2]

This statement recognizes the crucial importance of consumer repeat purchases, and the fact that nonprice competition focuses on catering to consumer tastes and preferences. The forces of consumer choice are capable of wreaking havoc on nonprice competition.

For example, in discussing advertising as only one part of

distribution—that is, of the entire shopping process—one consumer goods executive has noted:

> Advertising can only create a new market for products which fill a genuine—though often unexpressed or latent—consumer want. . . . The basic need or desire must be there to begin with.[3]

An expert on styling has said much the same thing:

> Change just for the sake of change is not a positive approach to any problem; rather styling or industrial design should be used as a plus factor in planning a manufactured product. . . . Unless the product actually does something better for the consumer, or unless it costs less, it will not satisfy her in the long run.[4]

Although the skeptic may find such remarks to be only pious rationalizations, they supplement statements of the belief that consumers themselves are the best judges of "wants" and "needs."

> There are two ways to develop a product. One is either from the production or manufacturing end out to the consumer, which some companies do. The other is to begin with the market, and come back and have the production people develop the kind of product the consumer wants.[5]

And, of course, the weightiest evidence that this is not just rationalization or wishful thinking lies in the money and resources devoted to market research by consumer goods firms, and by all the organizations they employ for that purpose. To quote another executive of an innovating consumer goods firm, "Today's consumers have more of a direct say about products than ever before—certainly more than they realize."[6]

The functions of consumer research are therefore to devise ways and means of letting consumers have more of a direct say about products. Precisely how research methods stimulate consumers into furnishing the desired information about their wants and needs can be learned only by exploring widely; in a sense, each project is unique. In general, however, the process that many firms use to "develop the kind of product the consumer wants" comprises several parts.

New Products and Consumer Preferences

Before a new product can be made, or an existing one varied, someone must have the idea of doing so. Since market research as a business activity is conducted and paid for by firms, the investigation of consumer wants and preferences is fairly well defined by the spheres of interest that exist within the firm. There is little point in asking the public the open-end questions, "What do you need, or want? What shall we make?" The consensus appears to be that consumers themselves scarcely ever originate new product ideas, that development of a specific product represents the functioning of creativity in business, and that such creativity may be found among technical research, production engineering, market research, or sales staff, all of whom have been responsible for one idea or another.

Considering the magnitude of choice that confronts the American public, it is easy to understand why this is true. Any household consumer is likely to deal in a far greater variety of products and purchases than any firm, and any consumer's suggestions for new items cover a broader field than that of any business interest. The firm is oriented to production and marketing; the consumer, to his own needs and to an unlimited range of alternatives. The consumer may say, for example, in answer to the open-end question, "What do you want?" "We'd like something to make shoe polishing less of a messy job." For the manufacturer of shoe polish, however, this does not offer clear instructions on how to adapt his paste, liquid, or spray toward even greater convenience. Nor does it produce for the manufacturer of shoes a formula for a plastic shoe that can be so cheaply made, it will be discarded when soiled. One acceptable alternative, for consumers, might conceivably be for drug companies to develop a toughening agent for feet so that shoes are no longer needed for protection, and then for the world of fashion to insist that bare feet are the epitome of style. Thus, consumers' suggestions rarely furnish new product ideas, either because consumers are inarticulate about their own needs, or because they lack the technical competence to specify feasible alternatives.

But consumer "wants and needs," more narrowly defined, have been intensively explored by firms that have been seeking new product ideas. Surveys of household spending patterns, such as those reviewed in Chapter 3, can be analyzed for clues to potential markets, and then augmented by investigations of different design. For example, although food consumption data have been collected since Engel's time, nearly all reports have been in terms of dollars spent, or quantities bought, or nutrients consumed, or different types of foods. Yet the consumer generally eats food in the form of meals: the same amount of bread per week may mean noonday sandwiches for one family; for others, it may mean bread pudding for dinner, French toast for breakfast, scalloped tomatoes for luncheon or cinnamon toast for a midnight snack. A detailed study of eating habits (known as "the menu study") was conducted in 1958 by the Market Research Corporation of America, to record the forms of food used and the types of meals served. Such a special study of consumer behavior—of what consumers do—can be broadly or narrowly defined: it may take in a household activity, such as cleaning chores, or a part of the shopping process, such as having appliances serviced; it may require the consumer to cooperate by recording purchases in a diary, or to be oblivious to the observation of her buying behavior in supermarkets; it may analyze broad social trends, such as the increasing number of married women in the labor force, or the opinions that consumers give about such developments.

A fairly common framework for direct investigation of consumer wants and needs is to set up a discussion topic with a few participants, sometimes under the direction of a psychologist who is versed in small-group dynamics. For example, a food company's market-research staff organizes a panel of teenagers to talk about the ways they like to entertain and their association of "party" with "food"; or a psychologist who is working for an oil company talks with mothers about vacation travels and taking care of young children on the road. The use of depth interviews and motivational research into what people think and feel about such topics, as opposed to what they say about them, has become less controversial now than when it first appeared. But consumer comments in such discussions are apt to be impressionistic or imprecise. For example, after the U.S. Housing and Home Finance Agency convened a "Women's Congress on Housing" in 1956, McCall's magazine sponsored an "Annual Congress on Better Living," attended by 100 women from all over the country, who aired their views on housekeeping and homemaking. This conference reported that 8 out of 10 delegates were favorably inclined toward colored light bulbs, yet at the second conference a year later, while more than one-fourth of the delegates had used colored light bulbs, very few recommended them. Consequently, the final report warned that "the true substance of the Congress is reflected in the thousands of quotations found in the report. . . . Interpretations given should not be projected to the entire population."[7]

All such techniques look for provocative comments with which to stimulate the staff. For a business which traces the origin of a new product to its "surveys of consumer wants and needs," the consumer has provided the catalyst, not the end result.

Once the idea for a new product is at hand, consumers can evaluate it through concept research. Testing consumer reaction before the product itself exists requires that the product be described by words or pictures or by a dummy package. The description is of the *concept* involved in the product rather than of the item itself; it is kept vague precisely so that consumers can fill in specifications. For example, a manufacturer of paper products envisages throwaway doormats of absorbent stock, or a vending-machine company thinks of installing frozen-food dispensers next to a coin-operated electronic oven. The research staff then submits a brief statement to consumers for discussion, asking what they like about the idea; how they would use such a product; what their family's reaction would be; where it should be sold; what items a store should drop from stock in order to carry it; what advantages and disadvantages they can find after thinking about the notion for a time; how they would change it; what else it makes them think about; do they want it? need it? is it good for anything?

The simplest result of such an investigation is a "stop" or a "go" signal. Once consumers have registered wholehearted approval, the company can then ask its technical staff whether the product can, in fact, be made; if the audience interviewed shows little interest in the idea, or violent disapproval of it, the company can shelve the project. Some firms state flatly that concept research to determine consumer approval must precede any directions to their technical or engineering staffs, whose resources are too valuable to waste in developing products that cannot be sold. Some firms even use concept research to set priorities for its developmental work: they list projects under consideration and ask consumers to rank them in order of their importance. More often, such research turns up suggestions for changing the product or using it differently. According to one of the leading experts in this field, "The consumer allowed to define the product herself may well find more value in it than the manufacturer alone could ever see."[8] Most companies agree that this first screening of a new product does not require a representative sample of consumers, for the firm is attempting chiefly to discover all types of reaction. Because the concept is vague, comments from the audience may be irrelevant: they may express dislike for a feature that the firm knows can be changed, or else suggest a modification that the company knows will be technically difficult to achieve. There is no reason to elaborate such reactions by securing them from a "properly designed" sample. If the *concept* survives this very preliminary test, the firm can then move on to more systematic research into consumer preferences that are relevant to the product itself.

On the other hand, concept research is not suitable for dealing with many new products, nor for some variations of existing products. Some investigators are convinced that a consumer must handle the product, use it, or "get involved with it," before any useful reaction can be obtained. In certain cases, the consumer's ability to visualize the new product may be distrusted. For example, once aerosol cans had become available, concept research established rather readily that consumers would favor their use for condiments, polishes, cosmetics, and paints. But if insecticides and window-cleaners had not already familiarized consumers with the use of pressurized sprays, concept research might have been less successful in exploring reactions to the aerosol can itself. In cases in which style will be of major importance to the finished product, companies agree that early consumer approval means little, for, in matters of fashion, the general public still follows rather than leads. Finally, where an existing product is to be changed, the maker can ask consumers directly for their reactions or submit very specific suggestions for their approval.

There are some fairly early examples of consumer research

designed to work out the details of a new product or its variation. In the early '20s, the N. W. Ayer Company, advertising agency for Cannon towels, asked housewives for their opinions about buying and using colored towels, which till then had always been white. The manufacturer gained considerable competitive advantage from introducing differentiated products—particularly, when these were in the colors and specific designs that met consumer preference. In the same decade Cluett, Peabody & Company ordered an extensive consumer survey to gauge the market for collar-attached shirts and to find out what exactly wearers wanted in a shirt. The results —which specified well-anchored buttons, comfort and "fit" in the collar—were used by the firm to design shirts that it introduced in 1928, when it shifted the bulk of its output away from collarless shirts and separate starched collars. What consumers wanted most, the survey showed, was to have both shirts and collars that did not shrink; this knowledge was considerable encouragement for the company to adopt Sanford Cluett's pre-shrinking process, despite the extensive educational campaign that it required for both retailers and consumers.

Market research techniques today seek to discover consumer specifications for a product, by means of questionnaires, interviews, and product sampling. For example, suppose that disposable doormats have passed preliminary screening: using concept research, investigators have found housewives receptive to the idea and have heard suggestions for making use of the product in offices, schools, and other public buildings. A cat fancier saw possibilities of using the mats to line cages and baskets, and one woman pointed out that a material that was strong enough for a doormat might do for umbrellas, which one could use once and then throw away, since they were frequently lost in any case. The firm's market analysts began to collect figures on the sales of fiber, rubber, and plastic matting —the "close substitutes" or competitive alternatives for consumer choice; the sales research staff drew up tentative plans for distribution through variety stores and supermarkets, with different price and discount structures; and technical personnel developed several prototypes, differing in weight and size and in a special process that made the material absorbent on one side and waterproof on the other. At this point, consumer research may enlist company personnel to take home samples for use and to place the doormats at strategic points in offices and factory. Samples may be donated for use in a neighboring school or theater. Visitors to the firm's display center may be asked to view three different mats and then fill out a simple questionnaire about preference. Field workers may seek out housewives who agree to use the product for two weeks and then report the reactions of family members and guests. Sometimes, the firm will invite small groups of consumers to visit the laboratory and handle or taste the new appliance or food item; for other products, it is the reactions of the retail trade that are of paramount importance:

The one thing to be sure of, however, is not that you think the new gadget or the new gimmick is clever or good or cheap or whatever —the important thing to find out ahead of time is whether the fellow you are going to sell it to thinks it is good or smart or new or something, and also whether he thinks he can make money doing with it because he is not interested, fellows, in your making money.[9]

It is significant that consumer research is a fundamental step for many firms that make no consumer goods or sales to retailers. The experience of DuPont in promoting nylon and other synthetic textiles is well known: although the company made only the fiber, its market research program called for developing not only fabrics but garments, and for commissioning designers to create models specifically for the new materials. Such a program is typical of industries that have created new materials—such as aluminum, synthetic fibers, and plastics. All such firms have devoted major energies to developing final consumer goods that use their output as a material, and to securing consumer acceptance of these goods. Typical of their reasoning is the following explanation by an executive of Celanese, Inc.:

We must know the *habits, attitudes, preferences* and *needs* at each level of the flow of our goods starting with the ultimate consumer and working back through the retailer and the various wholesale and process levels until we arrive at our direct customer, in our case the weaver or the knitter, etc.

In our case we spend a very large part of our effort in obtaining a thorough understanding of the *ultimate consumer* in particular. That is the man or woman who buys our product and makes the *final decision* as to whether or not it is worth what he paid for it. We do this through our own direct mail panels, through field surveys of attitudes and preferences and by working closely with retailers and following up the goods that they have sold to customers through their normal channels.[10]

The use of consumer research is therefore not restricted to so-called "consumer goods" firms, and a positive buyer reaction to new products and opinions on their specific characteristics may be essential in order to achieve proper distribution of the innovation.

Depending on the product and the company, this stage of consumer research may or may not involve careful sampling procedures. The process attempts to enlist consumers as judges; their indications of potential losers, however, may be more important than their selections of a winner. If the market for the product is fairly well defined, samplers and testers are chosen from that market: the reactions of bank presidents or their secretaries to a synthetic fabric designed for heavy-duty overalls would be somewhat irrelevant. Some consumer panels are exclusive: a nationally known ice-cream company and an equally famous proprietary drug manufacturer have both asked children for their comments on flavor and taste; a panel of canines supplies useful information to a firm that makes dog food; new mothers are enlisted by their friends to participate in evaluating babies' wear for a clothing manufacturer. In other cases, however, the potential market is still undefined, so that almost any consumer reaction may be relevant. Comments or criticisms direct the technicians and engineers to change the prototypes along given lines, and the firm revises and alters its product in a series of successive approximations to what consumers most prefer. Again, the most useful result may be a simple "stop" or "go" signal; with a prototype in existence, the firm can begin the cost and profit analyses that may also provide such a signal. If consumers agree that a specific modification, whose cost can be predicted, is essential, and if sales research shows that the market for an item priced to cover such costs is limited (or worse, occupied by an entrenched competitor, with a high degree of consumer loyalty), then the company had best shelve the whole project. Consumer preference and cost estimates thus together provide an evaluation of new products before they are placed on the market.

Assuming, however, that product specifications to fit consumer preferences have been evolved and that cost analyses predict no obvious losses, still the size of the market has yet to be determined. The company needs to learn the potential repeat purchases, or—in the case of a major appliance or some other item infrequently purchased—the potential consumer satisfaction that will build the market. In short, although the firm has so far proceeded with a crude "go" signal, it now needs more precise information on just how closely the new product matches consumer preferences.

If the product is a variation, or faces competition from close substitutes, consumer research attempts to learn whether buyers will find it significantly differentiated and whether, once they have tried the product, they will find a level of utility satisfactory enough to warrent repeat purchases. Business executives are keenly aware that it is consumer preference that determines the success of a competitive move to vary the product:

Don't ever test a product that is nearly as good—or just as good . . . if you haven't got a definite advantage then spend your time, effort and money to get a better product or a different product or one with some built-in advantages. . . . Don't bother at all unless you know there is a need for the product. This is one you can't think about. It is so darn obvious and still the mistake is made so many times.[11]

Firms that are introducing a new product or a product variation that will confront powerful competition use blind product testing, to let consumers decide whether or not a "definite advantage" exists. Samples of the new product and of competing items, labeled as A and B or some other anonymous identification, are supplied to households for use under ordinary conditions. Consumers then report their preferences and the details of their experience, including suggestions for product improvement, or for packaging, directions for use, and so on. There are those who find this type of consumer research to be essential:

Don't waste marketing dollars on products which fail to develop a clear and decided product superiority in the customary blind product tests. A new product in a worthwhile field will undoubtedly buck up against one or more strong consumer franchises. Companies owning these established brands will be stimulated to extra effort by the introduction of your new brand. Their combined effort can effectively stunt the new brand's growth unless it is recognized as clearly superior by consumers.[12]

Once again, business credits consumer choice with having sufficient power to defeat competitive effort.

The anonymity of blind product testing is not essential for all new items, especially if no close substitute exists. But household use of the product under normal conditions, whether or not the maker's identity is known, nearly always proves an effective form of consumer research. Visitors to a laboratory who sample several alternative formulas for a food item may agree unanimously on one choice. But most families do not have meals accompanied by a sip of coffee, and then one of tea, followed by milk and a taste of cocoa; it is only rarely that two products are used simultaneously for the same purpose. If the housewife uses product A for one week and then tries product B for another, the differences discerned in side-by-side tests may wash out, or else other reasons for preferring one to the other may show up. Home use can provide useful suggestions for further development. Pretesting of early models of the Princess telephone "considerably reduced the risks involved in introducing this new telephone," for consumers complained that the base of the instrument was too lightweight and hard to grasp, objected to the flat dial, and indicated their preferences for a night light and various colors. Reporting on this experience, a company executive explained that "the modifications we plan to make will be in line with the findings of the studies."[13]

Various homes offer various conditions of use: not only differences in climate, utilities, and the surroundings of household operations, but different degrees of use (and abuse), depending on the consumer's skill and that of the family members, as well as their total way of living. The prospective appliance, which gives outstanding performance when it is carefully adjusted by a technician, may prove thoroughly unsatisfactory to a nearsighted, short-tempered, or hasty housewife. A toilet preparation, food package, or liquid dye, which gives excellent results when measured and prepared in the laboratory, may fail in the face of the lack of calibrated instruments and of ideal storage conditions in the home. On the other hand, use tests may benefit from the inventiveness of consumers: a survey of families who bought cotton-tipped sticks that had been designed for baby care disclosed that these items were also used for children's paints, sportsmen's guns, coffeepots, cosmetics, and glue.

This last example illustrates a major problem in drawing a sample of consumers, either for blind product testing or for reports on use under normal conditions. To gain information from prospective users, the firm wishes to sample potential buyers rather than a cross-section of the total population; yet in many cases the market for the product may not be readily apparent. If one is to rely on the results from any sample, it must be drawn in terms of the universe. For example, to determine the average number of words to a page in this book, one need count the words on only a few pages, selected at random within the book: these pages represent a sample of the universe that includes all the pages within this book. But the universe of buyers of a new product cannot be defined in this way. It would seem obvious to select mothers of young babies in order to test baby oil; yet bachelors have been known to buy gifts for babies, and some enterprising consumer may discover that the oil offers an ideal lubricant for stuck zippers. It follows that the quantitative results from such consumer research can be variously interpreted. For example, home testing of the disposable paper doormat may show overall approval by 70 per cent of all users, but this may mean approval by 85 per cent of families living in the suburbs and only 40 per cent of city families. This may suggest hypotheses for further testing: does the difference represent only location? or does it reflect the presence of children and dogs in suburban families? or the physical difficulties of disposing of trash in the city? Is 70 per cent approval sufficient for the firm to take its product to market? What level of consumer acceptance is "enough" for the firm to proceed with its marketing plans? If the nonusers are violently opposed to the product, while the majority who do approve lack great enthusiasm, how much weight should be given to intensity of feeling? Most firms use quantitative measurement as guidelines; precisely because a new product *is* new and different, each situation is judged independently.

Beyond the details of consumer preference and acceptance gained by the research methods so far outlined, the firm that develops a new product also seeks information on the likelihood of its success in the market. Whether or not the tasters and testers and users like the samples, how many consumers will buy how much at what price? What will be the consumer choice, once the product is introduced into market competition?

Full-scale test marketing can provide some clues to the answer, but such investigations are feasible only with certain types of products, usually with those that have a small unit price and frequent consumer purchase. Food and household supplies, the items stocked by supermarkets and variety stores, predominate in test-marketing activities. New models of automobiles or appliances or furniture, or items such as clothing, for which fashion and style set the pace, cannot be as readily tested in one local market prior to national distribution. Where it can be used, however, test marketing covers a wide range of alternatives for consumer choice.

The simplest question for test marketing is the level of sales: over a three-month period how many items did consumers purchase? if there are close substitutes, how did sales compare to those of competitors? if not, how does the sales level, projected, compare to cost and profitability measures? Most test marketing, however, seeks more information than that; it wants to find out about the volume of repeat sales, the comments from users who are buyers (and therefore differ from previous consumers, whose reported reactions were to free samples), the impact of advertising or promotional campaigns, and so on. By testing in more than one area, the firm can experiment with various product designs, sizes, or prices. To ensure reliable results from such tests, the different consumers who are offered different alternatives must be in distinct groups, preferably not only separate from each other but, even more, unaware of the other possibilities being tested. Such complicated aspects of test marketing have led to the development of highly sophisticated techniques; like all of consumer research, these warrant more lengthy discussion than this brief introduction permits.

The Innovating Consumer

Business programs of consumer research attempt to identify consumer preferences and to adapt new products and product variations to what consumers "want and need," using families and individuals as their source of information. With these methods, producers can estimate the results of consumer choice before submitting their output to market competition. While the implications of this process need not be exaggerated to claim that American industry does, in fact, provide goods and services that are "made to order" for American consumers, the preliminary role of the consumer should nevertheless not be overlooked.

Aside from premarket evaluation, competitive firms recognize the strength of consumer choice by their respect for "word-of-mouth" communication among consumers, which outweighs any effort at advertising or promotion. Data from countless sources and on many different kinds of new products show the same pattern: a growth in sales which, at some point, if the product is successful, begins to accelerate. This "take-off" point may occur early or appear only long after the innovation is first introduced, while subsequent growth may reach moderate or high levels of total sales; but the change in the *rate* of sales growth is largely attributable to consumer acceptance and to the selling efforts of consumers themselves.

A typical example—which can be multiplied many times from trade papers and business comment—is Sakrete, a pre-mixed cement whose sales rose from 40,000 sacks in 1936 to 10 million in 1953. Presumably the growth of do-it-yourself projects around the home, the increase in home ownership, the move to the suburbs, and the rise in real income all contributed to the consumer "want and need" for this product. But the president of the corporation "ascribes the remarkable Sakrete sales curve to . . . word-of-mouth advertising,"[14] for the product became a consumer good only after it had first been sold to industrial users. Satisfied workmen on the job explained the product to "sidewalk superintendents," whose inquiries at local retailers enabled the manufacturer to achieve wider distribution. This was only the beginning of word-of-mouth advertising. "In the following years . . . we've had reports of many similar experiences elsewhere. For instance, when a home owner uses Sakrete to build a driveway, pave a patio, or make some other improvement, his neighbors are impressed with the time and labor saving." The same analysis explained, for the Pepperell Company, its sales of nylon fitted sheets, which were introduced at a premium price:

Until consumers had a chance to try Pepperell Nylon, sheet purchases in some instances were below expectations. However, as more and more of these sheets were used, their popularity grew and sales skyrocketed. Stores, as a result, have been placing rush orders as word-of-mouth advertising spreads.[15]

These examples show how the shopping process fits into market competition: although the most useful and complete source of information to the individual consumer comes from his own experience with using a product or service, running a close second as an influence on consumer choice is the experience of other buyers, which is shared by word of mouth. While the psychologists and sociologists who specialize in communications research have done much theoretical analysis of the ways in which individuals and groups influence the ideas and behavior of other individuals and groups,[16] it is business that has the most data to show the effects of such influence, at least on the introduction of new products. As is true for much of the process of consumer choice, recognition that the phenomenon exists and is important may be helpful even when the nature and cause of the phenomenon are not fully understood. Consequently, firms that introduce new products take word-of-mouth selling into account in their plans. And in a sense, it is business respect for consumer-selling efforts that justifies market research. Quite aside from trying to gauge the size of the market or reduce the risks of innovation, determining the acceptability of new products to consumers is at the heart of consumer research.

An interesting avenue of exploration lies open to those who believe that word-of-mouth advertising can be consciously exploited. If certain consumers are more influential than others, if word-of-mouth approval spreads most readily along one route, then these are the individuals whose preferences business should investigate. Such reasoning has led to the "trickle-down" theory of fashion, or the notion of "America's tastemakers"; such hypotheses, however, have been contradicted by many innovations that have been widely adopted from the beginning, instead of being disseminated by an influential class. If, however, the study of consumer influence is not confined to one particular social or economic class or group, perhaps consumers do differ in their willingness to innovate, and therefore to originate word-of-mouth advertising, based on the fact that their experience provides information to others. This reasoning has led to theories which identify those consumers who are likely to experiment, to try new products, to change their shopping habits.

The difficulty with proponents of such theories is their inability to persuade one another. The "innovating consumer" has been seen as having different characteristics, depending on the observer:

Church people change habits and styles more quickly than nonmembers because they are continually mixing with other people and so pick up new ideas and suggestions readily. . . . Students as a class can be easily induced to try new articles and adopt new styles.[17]

Families that tend to be heavy buyers of convenience products also tend to *try* new products first. There is no indication, however, that these families necessarily remain as heavy buyers of a specific new item.[18]

New products are expected to function within the social order and cumulators, and most often opposed by the savers.[19]

New products are expected to function within the social order and it is the relatively secure and well-adjusted personalities who are most free to accept them.[20]

While all these statements may be relevant in a particular context, they make it somewhat difficult for business to draw a sample of innovating consumers who will test their new products. The innovating consumer may be located between the suburbs and the city, in what has been called "interurbia," for fourteen of these areas "are the pace-setters for the nation . . . where habits formed will continue to influence the nation."[21] Or he may be found subscribing to a magazine: "a classification of people *based on their economic venturesomeness versus their cautiousness* . . . characterized by their willingness to try new products" showed that *Better Homes & Gardens* readers are 43.4 per cent venturesome and 25.9 per cent cautious.[22] Or he may be found elsewhere: "What the *Wall Street Journal* reader learns to use, millions everywhere will yearn to possess."[23]

From this cursory sampling of current theories about influential or innovating consumers it seems safe to conclude that no single group exists that can serve as guinea pigs for business and originators of word-of-mouth advertising. And this is a happy conclusion to have reached. The tenor of this book has been that consumer choice is still the prerogative of families and individuals, and the goal of market competition. The variety of choice that exists, the continual innovation in products and shopping processes, the experiments with forming and breaking consumer habits, the gradual evolution of information and protection, indicate that business does not control consumers and that there is no basis for the belief that consumers are controlled by other consumers.

Conclusion

*I*t is appropriate to conclude with a word on consumer sovereignty, whose absence is frequently deplored by those who view the contemporary scene with alarm, but whose presence is stoutly affirmed by those who look with pride at the American economy. A more dispassionate analyst may ask, "What does consumer sovereignty really mean?"

In its simplest terms, the answer may be that the consumer should dominate the economy, and this makes another question inevitable, "Who is the consumer?" The viewers-with-alarm list various sources of so-called economic power, and mourn the omission of any organized consumer interest from the controversies of big business, big labor, and big government. (The lookers-with-pride maintain, of course, that each of these has the consumer interest at heart.) Yet a recurring theme of this book has been that consumers are people, be they single individuals or family members, that each consumer is the best judge of his well-being, and that the consumer's own experience is the best source of information about how well or how poorly his tastes and preferences are being satisfied. Should there be, *can* there be a "consumer interest"—government department or lobby or power bloc—which will reflect the myriad tastes and preferences and experiences of American consumers?

Or does the phrase "consumer interest" refer not to an organization of (or for) consumers but to a regard for just these goals—well-being, and the satisfaction of tastes and preferences—of the families and individuals who face the problem of consumer choice? Much of the analysis in this book stems from the Law of Satiable Wants, or the human craving for variety, formally stated in the law of diminishing utility. Consumers have two reasons for seeking a variety of products, services, and shopping processes: first, because variety is desired for its own sake as a relief from monotony and an established routine, and second because a change may make people better off if they prefer the new to the old. So if the "interests of consumers" are to rule the economy, variety must be the guidepost for economic activity.

The existence of monopolistic competition means that such a guidepost is now being observed and will continue to serve effectively. Consumers are not threatened with the static equilibrium of a purely competitive model, thanks to continual changes in technology and in consumer tastes and preferences. Nor are they doomed to the frustrations of limited satisfaction and economic waste under pure monopolies—again due to technological change which produces new alternatives for consumers to choose and new challenges to monopoly power. This book has traced innovations in products and services and shopping processes—and has made it clear that innovation will continue, that it is inherent in the nature of competition.

Does the American economy, then, represent the best of all possible worlds for the consumer? Not really, for competing sellers have a certain amount of monopoly power, and the consumer is somewhat hampered in his ability to satisfy his tastes and preferences. Without accepting for an instant the argument that big business can shape consumer choice, it remains true that big business does limit this choice. The chief threat to variety is mass production which provides goods and services at low costs, but also, unfortunately, provides them in standardized models, colors, and flavors. In some lines, for example foods, efficient production need not mean millions of units, and small firms that serve regional or local markets can satisfy the taste for variety. This possibility, however, does not exist in other categories such as automobiles and appliances. The obvious policy conclusion is to open American markets even wider; to let down all barriers to the offerings of foreign sellers.

Finally, the consumer cannot satisfy his tastes and preferences to the extent that he is ignorant. There is a case for government support and requirement of increased information and increased veracity accompanying all products and services and shopping processes. This is probably the only justification for such organizations as Councils on Consumer Information set up by state governments and the President's Consumer Advisory Council at the national level. It is not by chance that the only privately organized consumer activities that have survived —Consumers' Union and Consumers' Research—are information gathering agencies. There is a much stronger case for government enforcement of the regulations which now exist to provide consumers with information—and, therefore, for increased facilities for administrative agencies. The case for minimum standards is not as clear—although the bounds of public safety have surely been reached by the users of drugs and automobiles. But above all, the consumer's own experience is the best source of information to him, and therefore all the devices used by sellers to upset consumer purchasing habits and induce consumers to try new products and shopping processes are to the good. The argument of this book provides no proof that advertising is an economic waste; rather it lends support to the proposition that advertising is a form of communication to the consumer and should be analyzed as such.

This book has explored the direct relationship between consumer tastes and preferences and market competition; and there is room for much more research and analysis. But clearly the efforts of competing sellers to satisfy consumer tastes and preferences are inherent in the economic growth of the American economy, where Adam Smith's classic statement holds true—"consumption is the sole end and purpose of all production."

Notes

Introduction

1. Lionel Robbins, *An Essay on the Nature and Significance of Economic Science* (London: Macmillan & Co., Ltd., 1932), p. 15.

Chapter 1   Consumer Choice: An Historical Sketch

1. Translated from Saint-Beuve, "La Réforme Sociale en France," *Nouveaux Lundis*, No. 9 (Dec. 5, 1864), pp. 163–64.
2. Frederic LePlay, quoted in French in Henry Higgs, "Frederic LePlay," *Quarterly Journal of Economics*, IV (July, 1890), 418–19.
3. Carle C. Zimmerman, "Ernst Engel's Law of Expenditures for Food," *Quarterly Journal of Economics*, XLVII (Nov., 1932), 82.
4. Henry Higgs, "Workmen's Budgets," *Journal of the Royal Statistical Society*, LVI (June, 1893), 255–94.
5. Eighteenth Annual Report of the Commissioner of Labor, 1903, *Cost of Living and Retail Prices of Foods* (Washington, D.C.: GPO, 1904), p. 101.
6. *Report on Condition of Woman and Child Wage-earners in the United States*, 61st Congress, 2nd session, Senate Doc. 645, XVI (Washington, D.C.: GPO, 1911), 64, 191.
7. Ellen H. Richards, *The Cost of Living* (New York: John Wiley & Sons, 1905), p. 81.
8. U.S. Bureau of Labor Statistics, "Conditions of Living Among the Poor," *BLS Bulletin 64* (May, 1906), p. 618.
9. Harvey Wiley, *Foods and Their Adulteration* (Philadelphia: P. Blakiston's Son & Co., 1897), p. 2.
10. USDA, Bureau of Agricultural Economics, *Consumption of Food in the United States 1909–1952* (Washington, D.C.: GPO, 1953), pp. 112, 118–19.
11. "Retail Prices, 1890 to 1911," *BLS Bulletin 105* (1912), Part I, pp. 1–48.

381

12. "Retail Prices 1907 to June, 1915," *BLS Bulletin 184* (Nov., 1915).
13. "Retail Prices 1913 to December, 1919," *BLS Bulletin 270* (1921), pp. 1–26.
14. Massachusetts Commission on the Cost of Living, *The Cost of Living* (Boston: 1910), p. 108.
15. *Report on Condition of Woman and Child Wage-earners . . . ,* *op. cit.,* pp. 145–235.
16. Louise Balard More, *Wage-Earners' Budgets* (New York: Henry Holt & Co., 1907), pp. 236–37.
17. *Ibid.,* p. 165.
18. Frank H. Streighthoff, "Report on the Cost of Living," *Fourth Report of the Factory Investigating Commission 1915* (Albany: J. B. Lyon Co., 1915), p. 1661.
19. Massachusetts Commission on the Cost of Living, *op. cit.,* p. 151, quoting Fred G. Garmon, Leopold Morse Co.
20. NICB, *Wartime Changes in the Cost of Living* (New York: NICB, 1918), p. 36.
21. *Idem, The Cost of Living in the United States* (New York: NICB, 1926), p. 52.
22. *Ibid.,* p. 52.
23. Edith Elmer Wood, *Recent Trends in American Housing* (New York: The Macmillan Co., 1931), p. 40.
24. Richards, *op. cit.,* p. 53.
25. Massachusetts Commission on the Cost of Living, *op. cit.,* p. 254. Cf. Yandell Henderson and Maurice Davie, eds., *Incomes and Living Costs of a University Faculty* (New Haven: Yale University Press, 1928), p. 6: "The most significant aspect of the mode of life of a family is the amount of service that they can afford."
26. Bureau of Applied Economics, *Standards of Living* (Washington, D.C.: Bureau of Applied Economics, Inc., 1919, 1930), Vol. I, pp. 22–23.
27. NICB, *The Cost of Living in the United States 1914–1926* (New York: NICB, 1927), p. 37.
28. "Money Disbursements of Wage Earners and Clerical Workers 1934–36," *BLS Bulletin 638* (1941), pp. 116–67.
29. Massachusetts Commission on the Cost of Living, *op. cit.,* pp. 245–46.
30. Bureau of Applied Economics, *op. cit.,* p. 164, quoting the Western Arbitration of 1927, Exhibit No. 13, a detailed list of the annual expenses of a locomotive fireman.
31. Massachusetts Commission on the Cost of Living, *op. cit.,* p. 249.

32. "Health and Recreational Activities in Industrial Establishments," *BLS Bulletin 458* (1928), pp. 44–48.

33. Massachusetts Commission on the Cost of Living, *op. cit.*, p. 495.

34. Frederick L. Hoffman, "Fifty Years of American Life Insurance Progress," *Journal of the American Statistical Association*, XII (Sept., 1911), 667–760.

35. Frank Hatch Streighthoff, *The Standard of Living Among the Industrial Peoples of America* (Boston: Houghton Mifflin Co., 1911), page 118, compares the amount of insurance purchased by $1.00 in ordinary and industrial policies: At age 21, industrial $32.31, ordinary $65.36; at age 30, industrial $25.77, ordinary $52.41; at age 40, industrial $19.23, ordinary $38.31. He lists Bulletin no. 67 of the Bureau of Labor (not otherwise identified) as his source. Cf. Charles R. Henderson, *Industrial Insurance in the United States* (Chicago: University of Chicago Press, 1909).

36. More, *op. cit.*, p. 42.

37. Charles B. Spahr, *America's Working People* (New York: Longmans, Green, 1900), pp. 13–14.

38. Roswell F. Phelps, *South End Factory Operatives* (Boston: South End House Associates, 1903), p. 32.

39. More, *op. cit.*, p. 47.

40. Louise Marion Bosworth, "The Living Wage of Women Workers," Supplement to the *Annals of the American Academy of Political and Social Science*, XXXVII (May, 1911), 82–83.

41. NICB, *The Cost of Living Among Wage-Earners April 1927* (New York: NICB, 1927), p. 33. Cf. "Tentative Cost and Quantity Budget," *Monthly Labor Review*, IX, 6 (Dec., 1919), 28–29: "No provision is made in this budget for savings, other than the original cost of household furniture and equipment, which would average about $1,000 in value. No definite estimate, of course, can be made as to the amount which a low-salaried Government employee should be expected to save. But an average saving of 12½ per cent of yearly salary during an employee's single and early married life would seem to be the maximum."

42. Raymond S. Goldsmith, *A Study of Saving in the United States* (Princeton: Princeton University Press, 1958), Vol. I, p. 14.

43. See, for example, Dorothy S. Brady, "Family Saving, 1888 to 1950," in *A Study of Saving in the United States*, Goldsmith, ed. (Princeton: Princeton University Press, 1958), Vol. III, Part 2; Milton Friedman, *A Theory of the Consumption Function* (Princeton: Princeton University Press, 1957); Irwin Friend

and Robert Jones, eds., *Proceedings of the Conference on Consumption and Saving* (Philadelphia: University of Pennsylvania Press, 1960); R. C. Jones, "Transitory Income and Expenditure on Consumption Categories," *American Economic Review: Papers and Proceedings*, 50 (May, 1960), 584–92; Margaret Reid, "Consumption, Savings, and Windfall Gains," *American Economic Review*, LII (Sept., 1962), 728–37; Albert Ando and Franco Modigliani, "The 'Life Cycle' Hypothesis of Saving: Aggregate Implications and Tests," *American Economic Review*, LIII (March, 1963), 109–27; Robert W. Clower, "Permanent Income and Transitory Balances," *Oxford Economic Papers*, XV (July, 1963), 177–90.

44. Massachusetts Commission on the Cost of Living, *op. cit.*, p. 499.

Chapter 2   The Consumer's Scarce Means

1. Robert Lampman, "Changes in the Share of Wealth Held by Top Wealth-holders, 1922–1956," *Review of Economics and Statistics*, XLI (Nov., 1959), 379–92. For more recent data, but a different method of analysis based on a sample of one city and its suburbs, see George Katona and John B. Lansing, "The Wealth of the Wealthy," *Review of Economics and Statistics*, XLVI (Feb., 1964), 1–13.

Chapter 3   Patterns of Consumer Choice

1. See especially James N. Morgan, Martin H. David, Wilbur J. Cohen, and Harvey E. Brazer, *Income and Welfare in the United States* (New York: McGraw-Hill Book Co., Inc., 1962) and Richard F. Kosobud and James N. Morgan, eds., *Consumer Behavior of Individual Families Over Two and Three Years* (Ann Arbor: University of Michigan Press, 1964). Work on consumer expectations, although it refers to change over time, plans and the extent to which they are carried out, does not provide the same approach to continuing studies of consumption. See F. Thomas Juster, *Anticipations and Purchases* (Princeton: Princeton University Press, 1964). Several market research firms have maintained a continuous panel of consumers but do not collect complete data on income and spending patterns.

2. USDA Agricultural Marketing Service, Marketing Research Report 340, *Income and Household Size: Their Effects on Food Consumption* (Washington, D.C.: GPO, 1959).

3. Helen H. Lamale and Margaret C. Stotz, "The Interim City Worker's Family Budget," *Monthly Labor Review*, LXXXIII, 8 (August, 1960). See also Robert J. Lampman, *Low Income Population and Economic Growth*, Study Paper No. 12, Joint Economic Committee, 86th Congress, 1st session (Washington, D.C.: GPO, 1959).

4. The interested reader may wish to check the *Recommended Dietary Allowances*, National Research Council; FAO Committee on Calorie Requirements: *Recommendations;* USDA *Survey of Household Food Consumption, 1955;* Victor E. Smith, "Models for Human Diets," *Journal of Farm Economics*, Vol. 16 (May, 1959); and USDA, "Low and Moderate Cost Food Plans," *Agricultural Statistics 1963*, Table 807.

5. USDA, *Agricultural Statistics 1964* (Washington, D.C.: GPO, 1964), p. 580.

6. Cf. S. J. Prais, "The Estimation of Equivalent Adult-Scales from Family Budgets," *Economic Journal*, LXIII (Dec., 1953), 791–810.

7. *BLS Survey of Consumer Expenditures 1960–61* (Washington, D.C.: GPO, various dates).

8. John B. Lansing and James N. Morgan, "Consumer Finances Over the Life Cycle," *Consumer Behavior*, Lincoln Clark, ed. (New York: New York University Press, 1955), Vol. II, p. 36.

9. Paul C. Glick, "The Family Life Cycle," *American Sociological Review*, XII (April, 1947), 164–75.

10. Daniel Suits, "Use of Dummy Variables in Regression Equations," *Journal of the American Statistical Association*, LII (Dec., 1957), 548–51.

11. Morgan, David, Cohen, and Brazer, *op. cit.*, pp. 370–73.

12. A brilliant analysis of both appears in André Danière's *Higher Education in the American Economy* (New York: Random House, Inc., 1964).

13. Cf. Bennett M. Berger, *Working Class Suburb* (Berkeley: University of California Press, 1960), p. 23: "It is a great mistake to equate an income which permits most of the basic amenities of what the middle class calls 'decency' with becoming middle class." Other excellent analyses of the rise in income which is unaccompanied by an adoption of higher-income consumption choices appear in Herbert J. Gans, "Effects of the Move from City to Suburb," *The Urban Condition*, Leonard J. Duhl, ed. (New York: Basic Books, Inc., 1963), and Lee Rainwater, Richard P. Coleman, and Gerald Handel, *Workingman's Wife* (New York: Oceana Publications, Inc., 1959).

Chapter 4 **A Model of Consumer Choice**

1. Adam Smith, *The Wealth of Nations* (New York: Random House, Inc., 1937), Book I, Chap. 4, p. 28.
2. John Stuart Mill, *Principles of Political Economy* (London: Longmans, Green, 1929), Book III, Chap. 1, Sects. 1 and 2, pp. 436–37.
3. W. Stanley Jevons, *The Theory of Political Economy*, 7th ed. (New York: The Macmillan Co., 1931), pp. 36–38.
4. *Ibid.*, p. 51.
5. *Ibid.*, p. 140.
6. George J. Stigler, *Production and Distribution Theories* (New York: The Macmillan Co., 1941), explains that Menger's use of the word "thing" is purposely vague: he meant to refer to useful human activities as well as material goods which can satisfy human wants.
7. *Ibid.*, paraphrasing Menger's *Grundsatze der Volkwirtschafts-lehre.*
8. *Ibid.*, p. 143, quoting Menger; Stigler's italics.
9. John Bates Clark, *The Distribution of Wealth* (New York: The Macmillan Co., 1889), pp. 210–11.
10. Jevons, *op. cit.*, p. 51.
11. Clark, *op. cit.*, p. 215.
12. *Ibid.*, p. 242.
13. Nassau William Senior, *Political Economy* (London: C. Griffin and Co., 1850), p. 11.
14. Clark, *op. cit.*, pp. 379–80.
15. Alfred Marshall, *Principles of Economics*, 8th ed. (New York: The Macmillan Co., 1950), Book III, Chap. 5, Sect. 1, p. 117.
16. *Ibid.*, pp. 118–19.
17. Smith, *op. cit.*, Book I, Chap. 5, p. 30.
18. *Ibid.*, Book V, Chap. 2, p. 821.
19. John Rae, *The Sociological Theory of Capital*, C. W. Mixter, ed. (New York: The Macmillan Co., 1905), pp. 252, 245–47.
20. Thorstein Veblen, *The Theory of the Leisure Class* (New York: Random House, Inc., 1934), pp. 97–98.
21. Marshall, *op. cit.*, Chap. 6, Sect. 6, p. 137.
22. Kenneth E. Boulding, *Economic Analysis* (New York: Harper and Bros., 1948), p. 10.
23. Tibor Scitovsky, *Welfare and Competition* (Homewood, Ill.: Richard D. Irwin, Inc., 1951), p. 29.
24. George J. Stigler, *The Theory of Price* (New York: The Macmillan Co., 1946), p. 90.

25. James T. Duesenberry, *Income, Saving, and the Theory of Consumer Behavior* (Cambridge: Harvard University Press, 1949), p. 22.
26. *Ibid.*, p. 27.

Chapter 5   The Consumer in the Market

1. Flow of goods, 1897–1901, from U.S. Bureau of the Census, *Historical Statistics of the United States* (Washington, D.C.: GPO, 1960), p. 143. In 1965 prices this amounted to $34.7 billion. 1965 data from *Economic Report of the President* (Washington, D.C.: GPO, 1966), consumption spending on goods was $253.8 billion.
2. Harold Barger, *Distribution's Place in the American Economy Since 1869* (Princeton: Princeton University Press, 1955), p. 38.
3. For example, L. D. H. Weld, "Market Distribution," *American Economic Association: Papers and Proceedings, American Economic Review* S, V (March, 1915), p. 133: "The subject of retail distribution is only beginning to be subjected to scientific study"; and Frank W. Taussig, "Price Maintenance," *American Economic Association: Papers and Proceedings, American Economic Review* S, VI (March, 1916), p. 179: "This is a question on which we are much in need of further data. Detailed specific study of retail methods is needed."
4. Massachusetts Commission on the Cost of Living, *The Cost of Living* (Boston: 1910), pp. 317–18, quoting W. C. Brown, President of the New York Central.
5. "Statistics of Retail Trade," *Labor Bulletin of the Commonwealth of Massachusetts,* No. 20 (Nov., 1901), pp. 117–28.
6. Boris Emmett and John E. Jueck, *Catalogues and Counters* (Chicago: University of Chicago Press, 1950), p. 100. Copyright 1950 by The University of Chicago.
7. *Ibid.*, pp. 112–13.
8. Lawrence B. Mann, "The Importance of Retail Trade in the United States," *American Economic Review*, XIII (Dec., 1923), 615.
9. Robert W. Twyman, *History of Marshall Field and Company* (Philadelphia: University of Pennsylvania Press, 1954), pp. 124, 156–57.
10. E. M. Patterson, "Cooperation Among Retail Grocers in Philadelphia," *American Economic Review*, V (June, 1915), 274–80, quoting *Grocer's Review* (1910), p. 246. Similar evidence was given that year as testimony before the Senate Committee on Wages and Prices of Commodities and before the Massachusetts Commission on the Cost of Living, 1909–10.

11. Massachusetts Commission on the Cost of Living, *op. cit.*, quoting Charles H. Jones, Commonwealth Shore and Leather Company, p. 301.

12. *Ibid.*, quoting Alfred P. Lee, The Cloverdale Company, p. 311.

13. "Retail Prices 1913 to December, 1919," *BLS Bulletin 270* (Feb., 1921), p. 8.

14. L. D. H. Weld, "Marketing Functions and Mercantile Organization," *American Economic Review*, VII (June, 1917), 310.

15. R. S. Alexander, Chairman, "1948 Report of the Definitions Committee of the American Marketing Association," *Journal of Marketing*, XIII (Oct., 1948), 211.

16. Massachusetts Commission on the Cost of Living, *op. cit.*, p. 312.

17. *Ibid.*, p. 346.

18. *Ibid.*, quoting Charles H. Jones, p. 301.

19. Helen Rich Norton, *A Textbook on Retail Selling* (Boston: Ginn & Co., 1919), pp. 89, 100.

20. *American Mail Order Fashions 1880–1900* (New York: American Review, 1961), p. 16.

21. *Ibid.*, p. 25.

22. Massachusetts Commission on the Cost of Living, *op. cit.*, quoting Professor J. C. Schwab, author of "an article" in the *Yale Review*, p. 333.

23. *Ibid.*, quoting Bernard J. Rothwell, President of the Bay State Milling Company, pp. 293–94.

24. *Ibid.*, p. 305. Compare the reasoning seven years later: "Retailers and consumers are generally weak so far as accumulation of capital is concerned," L. D. H. Weld, "Marketing Functions . . . ," *op. cit.*, p. 311.

25. Emmett and Jueck, *op. cit.*, quoting Sears' catalogues, p. 86.

26. Weld, "Marketing Functions . . . ," *op. cit.*, pp. 313–14.

27. Massachusetts Commission on the Cost of Living, *op. cit.*, pp. 303–4.

Chapter 6   A Model of Market Competition

1. Edward H. Chamberlin, *The Theory of Monopolistic Competition*, 6th ed. (Cambridge: Harvard University Press, 1950), p. 50.

2. *Idem*, "The Definition of Selling Costs," *Review of Economic Studies*, XXXI, 1 (Jan., 1964), 63: "A retail trader has complete and absolute control over the supply of his 'product' when this is taken to include the advantages, to buyers, of his particular location." Cf. Morris A. Adelman, "The 'Product' and 'Price' in

Distribution," *American Economic Review* /S, XLVII (May, 1957), 266–73, and Margaret Hall, *Distributive Trading* (London: Hutchinson's University Library, 1949).

3. U. S. Bureau of the Census, *U. S. Census of Business: 1958, Retail Trade-Summary Characteristics* (Washington, D.C.: GPO, 1961), Vol. I, App. p. 3.

4. *Discount Merchandiser*, May, 1965.

5. Malcolm P. McNair, William Applebaum and Walter J. Salmon, *Cases in Food Distribution* (Homewood, Ill.: Richard D. Irwin, Inc., 1964), p. 19, quoting an address by McNair.

6. *Grocery Business Annual Report, 1964,* Progressive Grocer, New York, 1965.

7. National Retail Merchants Association, *Stores* (June, 1964), p. 56.

8. *Shopping Center Age* (Jan., 1964), p. 123.

9. *Business Week* (July 29, 1961), pp. 80–81.

10. Chamberlin, *The Theory of Monopolistic Competition, op. cit.,* p. 56.

11. *Ibid.*

12. *Idem,* "The Definition of Selling Costs," *op. cit.,* p. 61.

13. *Ibid.,* p. 60.

14. David Seidler, quoted in *Printer's Ink,* 285, 2 (Oct. 8, 1963), 20.

15. Gerald B. Tallman and Bruce Blomston, "Retail Innovations Challenge Manufacturers," *Harvard Business Review,* 40 (Sept., 1962), 139.

16. An illuminating discussion occurs in M. Yanovsky's *Social Accounting Systems* (Chicago: Aldine Publishing Co., 1965).

Chapter 7   **Price Competition in the Market**

1. Congressman Chet Hollifield, quoted in *Quality and Price Stabilization, 1962*—Hearings before a Subcommittee of the Committee on Interstate and Foreign Commerce, House of Representatives, 87th Congress, 2nd session, H. J. Res. 636, H. J. Res. 637, H. J. Res. 679, H. R. 10335, H. R. 10340, H. R. 10517, H. R. 11227, H. R. 11346, and H. R. 11778 (1962), pp. 68–69. Compare with the following descriptions of competitive pricing at the manufacturing level from Alfred R. Oxenfeldt's *Marketing Practices in the TV Set Business* (New York: Columbia University Press, 1964), p. 55: "Although one finds almost universal criticism of executives in this industry because of their heavy reliance upon price as a competitive weapon, there are a few heretics. One volunteered, 'Maybe television sets *should* be sold mainly on the basis of prices.' He expressed

determination to put his company in a position that would enable it to thrive in a price-competitive environment." And at the retail level from John Gosnell, General Counsel for National Association of Small Business, quoted in *Quality Stabilization, 1963*—Hearings before a Subcommittee of the Committee of Interstate and Foreign Commerce, House of Representatives, 88th Congress, 1st session, H. R. 3669 (1963), p. 184: "Business long ago found out that the pressures of competition—that is, competition between dealers in goods bearing the same trademark—defeat a major purpose of the competitive process with adverse economic effect . . . The competitive system is predicated on reward for quality, efficient service, and productive merchandising effort. Each necessary stage of production and distribution must at least have the opportunity for reward commensurate with efficient performance. This is the backbone of our system, and it should be obvious that senseless intrabrand price cutting defeats the main purpose."

2. Alfred R. Oxenfeldt, "Multi-Stage Approach to Pricing," *Harvard Business Review*, XXXVIII (July–Aug., 1960), 133.
3. Bernard Roshco, *The Rag Race* (New York: Funk and Wagnalls, Co., Inc., 1964), pp. 58–59.
4. Colston E. Warne, quoting a "large food company" in *Packaging Legislation, 1961*—Hearings before the Subcommittee on Antitrust and Monopoly of the Committee on the Judiciary, U.S. Senate, 87th Congress, 1st session, S. Res. 52, Part 1, p. 36.
5. *Ibid.*, p. 40.
6. "The lower a firm's price range the more important price becomes as a competitive factor." Roshco, *op. cit.*, p. 59.
7. Al Perkins, "Some Manufacturers Being Taxed by the Repeal of Excises," *Home Furnishings Daily* (May 28, 1965), p. 15.
8. *Home Furnishings Daily* (July 20, 1965), p. 20.
9. *Home Furnishings Daily* (July 2, 1965), p. 15.
10. Roshco, *op. cit.*, pp. 58–59.
11. "Clairol Puts On a New Face," *Business Week* (June 12, 1965), p. 128.
12. Mary Lou Pack, "Total Lamp Program Keys Furniture Sales," *Home Furnishings Daily* (June 1, 1965), p. 22.
13. Sam Karoll, Director, National Association of Retail Clothiers and Furnishers, quoted in *Quality Stabilization*—Hearings before a Subcommittee of the Committee on Commerce, United States Senate, 88th Congress, 1964, p. 112.
14. Restrictive Trade Practices Commission, *Report of an Inquiry*

into Loss-leader Selling (Ottawa: Edmond Cloutier, Queen's Printer, 1955), p. 84.

15. Paul Rand Dixon, Chairman, Federal Trade Commission, quoted in *Quality Stabilization*, Senate Hearings, 1964, p. 229.

16. "Food producer" cited by Colston Warne, quoted in *Packaging Legislation*, 1961, p. 40.

17. Roshco, *op. cit.*, p. 222.

18. J. Arnold Anderson, Vice President, Safeway Stores, quoted in *Packaging and Labeling Practices*—Hearings before the Subcommittee on Antitrust and Monopoly, Committee on the Judiciary, U.S. Senate, 87th Congress, 1st session (Washington, D.C.: GPO, 1962), p. 236.

19. Malcolm P. McNair, Elizabeth A. Burnham, Anita C. Hersum, *Cases in Retail Management* (New York: McGraw-Hill Book Co., Inc., 1957), p. 241.

20. *Ibid.*, p. 15.

21. See, for example, "Consumer Attitudes and Shopping Habits in Conventional Retail Stores and Discount Houses," a study conducted by Louis Tannenbaum for the Bureau of Advertising of the American Newspaper Publishers Association, 1963: "Women group stores by price and quality of merchandise, rather than by whether or not a particular store is a discount house or department store." Also Gregory P. Stone, "City Shoppers and Urban Identification," *American Journal of Sociology*, LX (July, 1954), 36–45; Pierre Martineau, "The Personality of the Retail Store," *Harvard Business Review*, XXXVI (Jan.–Feb., 1958).

22. Oxenfeldt, "Multi-Stage Approach to Pricing," *op. cit.*, p. 133.

23. Louis D. Brandeis, "Cutthroat Prices," *Harper's Weekly* (Nov. 15, 1913), quoted in *The Fair Trade Question* (New York: NICB, 1955). Compare the following reasoning by Congressman Chet Hollifield, owner of a men's clothing business, quoted in *Quality and Price Stabilization, 1962*, pp. 66–67: "Once having spent this money in advertising, the resulting consumer recognition and acceptance of brand-name merchandise is a real tangible business asset to both manufacturer and retailer. When a woman comes in and says 'I want an Arrow shirt,' and I lay it on the counter and she puts a five-dollar bill on the counter, she is satisfied and I am satisfied, and I do not have to stand there and argue with her for 30 minutes to get her to buy it. She has what is known as consumer acceptance already in her mind, based on merit."

24. Harold Barger, *Distribution's Place in the American Economy Since 1869* (Princeton: Princeton University Press, 1955), Table B-5, pp. 132–40 and Table B-6, pp. 148–49.
25. Joseph V. Heffernan, Association of the Bar of the City of New York, quoted in *Price Discrimination Legislation*—Hearings before the Subcommittee on Antitrust and Monopoly of the Committee on the Judiciary, 88th Congress, 1st session, S. 1815 and S. 1935 (1964), p. 81.
26. Remington Arms Company, Inc., V.G.E.M. of St. Louis, Inc. (Minnesota Supreme Court, 1960), Trade Cases 69, 673, quoted in *Quality and Price Stabilization, 1962*, p. 45.
27. Miles Laboratories Inc. v. Eckert 73 So. 2d 680, 682 (Florida Supreme Court, 1954) quoted in *Quality and Price Stabilization, 1962*, p. 44.
28. Thomas H. Murphy, President, The Home Shop, quoted in *Quality Stabilization, 1963*, p. 199.
29. Lee Loevinger, Assistant Attorney General, Department of Justice, quoted in *Quality Stabilization, 1963*, p. 75.
30. *National Fair Trade Legislation, 1959*—Hearings before a Special Subcommittee on Fair Trade of the Committee on Interstate & Foreign Commerce, U.S. Senate, 86th Congress, 1st session, S. 1083 (1959), p. 168.
31. E. B. Weiss, *Marketing's Coming Readjustment to Low-Margin Retailing* (New York: Doyle, Dane, Bernbach, Inc., 1957), p. 10.
32. Glen E. Weston, Visiting Professor of Law, Northwestern University, quoted in *Quality Stabilization*, Senate Hearings, 1964, p. 341.
33. Charles Frank Fort, President, Food Town Ethical Pharmacies, Inc., quoted in *Quality Stabilization, 1963*, p. 209.
34. "Our Floundering Fair Trade," E. G. Harms, quoted in *National Fair Trade Legislation, 1959*, p. 302.
35. *Quality Stabilization Act*—Report of the Committee on Interstate and Foreign Commerce, House of Representatives, H.R. 3669 (1963), p. 15.
36. Letter from W. H. Sahloff, Vice President, General Electric Co., quoted in *Fair Trade, 1959*—Hearings before the Committee on Interstate & Foreign Commerce, House of Representatives 86th Congress, 1st session, H.R. 768, H.R. 1253, H.R. 2463, H.R. 2729, H.R. 3187, H.R. 5252 and H.R. 5602, p. 741.
37. *Quality Stabilization Act, 1963*, p. 6.
38. Louis Rothschild, Executive Director, National Association of Retail Clothiers and Furnishers, quoted in *Quality Stabilization, 1963*, p. 117.

39. See the extensive hearings on dual distribution held in 1963 by the House of Representatives' Select Committee on Small Business.

40. Cf. Allen F. Jung, "Price Policy and Discounts," *Journal of Business*, XXXIII (Oct., 1960), 342–71.

41. Without attempting to claim completeness in this discussion of manufacturers' efforts to maintain retail prices, Sunbeam's use of consignment selling should be mentioned as should General Electric's cut-off points for cooperative advertising allowances. The former, adopted when fair trading in small appliances was generally abandoned, has been used by other manufacturers as well and should probably be considered a version of direct selling, since the manufacturer retains legal title to the merchandise until it passes to the consumer. G.E.'s system for electric housewares lists minimum prices which the dealer must observe in order to receive compensation for his cooperative advertising with the manufacturer. Although the system has not prevented price cutting below the stated minimums, G.E. has extended it to other lines of merchandise.

42. Stanley Hollander cites a number of cases in *Restraints Upon Retail Competition* (East Lansing: Michigan State University Press, 1965), pp. 53–55.

43. Grant Mauk, First Vice President, International Franchise Association, quoted in *The Impact Upon Small Business of Dual Distribution and Related Vertical Integration*—Hearings before a Subcommittee No. 4, Select Committee on Small Business, House of Representatives, 88th Congress, 1st session, H. Res. 13, Vol. 8, 1964, p. 1729.

44. *Ibid.*

45. Thomas Carvel, Carvel Franchise Systems, quoted in *Dual Distribution*, Vol. 8, p. 1760.

46. David B. Clater, "Some Socio-Economic Footnotes on Franchising," *Boston University Review*, XX (Summer, 1964), p. 27. But see also Lewis and Hancock, *Franchise System of Distribution*, Small Business Administration Management Research Reports (University of Minnesota Press, 1963), particularly their conclusion that success in a franchised field was highly correlated with business ability and willingness to work long hours.

Chapter 8 **Nonprice Competition and Consumer Choice**

1. Herbert A. Simon, "A Behavioral Model of Rational Choice," *Quarterly Journal of Economics*, LXIX (Feb., 1955), reprinted in Herbert A. Simon, *Models of Man* (New York: John Wiley & Sons, 1957), p. 241.

2. *Models of Man*, p. 252. See also *idem*, "Rational Choice and the Structure of the Environment," *Psychology Review*, LXIII (March, 1956), reprinted in *Models of Man*, Chap. 15. Somewhat akin to these ideas is the theory applied to the firm by William Baumol, in his *Business Behavior, Value, and Growth* (New York: The Macmillan Co., 1959). Compare *Probability and Profit*, by William Fellner (Homewood, Ill.: Richard D. Irwin, Inc., 1965).

3. Cf. Gerald Zaltman, *Marketing Contributions from the Social Sciences* (New York: Harcourt, Brace and World, Inc., 1965), p. 24: "Once a permanent adoption decision is made the continued repurchase of a given brand by a consumer does not necessitate his passing through the same stages that led to his initial purchase. Hence, the terms *buying* and *adoption* are used interchangeably here. For purposes of this discussion, they may be redefined as the process *whereby the individual comes to accept an item as the best alternative course of action available at that time. Should 'other things remain equal' and the same need or drive continue or arise again, the same item will be reemployed."*

4. Cf. Doctor X, *Intern* (New York: Harper & Row, 1965), p. 2: "There is an ancient unspoken code of secrecy surrounding the practice of medicine and the men who practice it. According to this code, what the layman does not know is all to the good; the work that doctors do, the way they do it, the kind of men they are and the way they become doctors must be carefully hidden from public knowledge. I am convinced that this attitude is wrong, and unworthy of the great profession that perpetuates it."

5. Walter F. Faxlanger, Secretary, Buffalo and Suburban Gasoline Retailers' Association, quoted in *Summary transcript of representative State Conference on Store Trading Stamps* (Albany: October 2, 1956), p. 34.

6. Tibor Scitovsky, *Welfare and Competition* (Chicago: Richard D. Irwin, Inc., 1951), pp. 402–3. See also the same author, "On the Principles of Consumer Sovereignty," *American Economic Review, Supplement*, LII, 2 (May, 1962), 262–69.

7. For an entertaining and useful account, see Bruce Bliven, Jr., "And Now a Word from Our Sponsor," *New Yorker* (March 23, 1963), pp. 83–130.

8. Faxlanger, *op. cit.*, p. 40.

9. Zaltman, *op. cit.*, pp. 60–64, puts the psychology of it as follows: "Often, after an individual has engaged in a specific activity, he learns of something which, if considered by itself,

might have caused him not to have engaged in that activity. This new information is 'dissonant,' or inconsistent, with the action already taken . . . Customers who are experiencing cognitive dissonance may become dissatisfied customers; consequently, every item must be 'merchandised' after it is sold . . . Advertising must work closely with the sales personnel to accomplish dissonance reduction . . . the customer should be reassured that his decision to buy was a wise one."

10. See, for example, a study by Ralph Head, quoted in *Printer's Ink*, 282, 9 (March 1, 1963), 5.

11. Nathaniel H. Engel, "Bread Buying Habits," *Journal of Marketing*, XXXI, 2 (Oct., 1956), 195.

12. Federal Trade Commission Docket No. 6901, *In the Matter of Procter & Gamble Company, a Corporation*, Opinion of the Commission (November 26, 1963).

13. Nancy Bier, "Who Can Control Brand-Switching?" *Printer's Ink*, 286, 11 (Feb. 7, 1964), 25.

14. Vance Packard is the best-known writer along these lines, but his over-simplifications and lack of documentation come perilously close to exemplifying, in the book-writing business, the type of product differentiation he deplores in business. More respectable sources, whose comments fall within a variety of analytical structures, include Scitovsky, *op. cit.*, p. 435: "The ease with which advertising can sway consumers' preferences has raised doubts as to whether perfect conformity to these preferences is really such an important and desirable goal of economic organization." Cf. Joseph A. Schumpeter, *Business Cycles* (New York: McGraw-Hill Book Co., Inc., 1939), Vol. I, p. 73: "The great majority of changes in commodities consumed has been forced by producers on consumers who, more often than not, have resisted the change and have had to be educated up by elaborate pyrotechnics of advertising." Cf. Carl Kaysen, "The Corporation: How Much Power? What Scope?" in *The Corporation in Modern Society*, Edward S. Mason, ed. (Cambridge: Harvard University Press, 1959), p. 101: "Business influence on taste ranges from the direct efforts through the design of material goods to the indirect and more subtle effects of the style of language and thought purveyed through the mass media . . . one aspect of this broad power . . . is the position that corporation management occupies as taste setter or style leader for the society as a whole."

15. "Ad Alley Upstart," *Wall Street Journal* (August 12, 1965), p. 1.

16. *Packaging and Labeling Practices*—Hearings before the Subcommittee on Antitrust and Monopoly, Committee on the Ju-

diciary, U.S. Senate, 87th Congress, 1st session, Part 2 (Washington, D.C.: GPO, 1962), p. 453, quoting Ellen-Ann Dunham, Vice President, General Foods.

17. Charles L. Hinkle, "The Strategy of Price Deals," *Harvard Business Review*, XLV (July–Aug., 1965), 75.

18. Dunham, *op. cit.*, p. 453.

19. Hinkle, *op. cit.*, pp. 80–81.

20. Bier, *op. cit.*, p. 26, quoting a survey made by Point of Purchase Advertising Institute, New York. Cf. Hinkle, *op. cit.*, p. 77: "Indications are that the industry which relies less on deals of the consumer type has many more loyal customers for various major brands. Conversely, high rates of dealing (as in the regular-coffee industry) induce consumers to be extremely price-conscious . . . Brands which characteristically deal frequently encourage even regular customers to stock up (especially in the very short run) and wait for the next deal before repurchasing."

21. Cf. George Meredith, *Effective Merchandising With Premiums* (New York: McGraw-Hill Book Co., Inc., 1962). Cf. Arnold Corbin, *Premium Use and Supply* (New York: Premium Advertising Association of America), where survey findings show that manufacturers, wholesalers, and publishers list two reasons for using consumer premiums which out-rank all others and are mentioned by half to three-quarters of the respondents. These are first, to get new customers for an existing product and second, to achieve more frequent or regular use. The two reasons cited most frequently by retailers (three-quarters of those replying) were first to bring in new customers and second to hold present customers' goodwill and loyalty.

22. Meredith, *op. cit.*, p. 316.

23. Thomas C. Sullivan, President of the Sullivan Paint Co., Arcadia, Calif., and President of the Paint and Wallpaper Association of America, Inc., quoted in *The Impact Upon Small Business of Dual Distribution and Related Vertical Integration* —Hearings before a Subcommittee No. 4, Select Committee on Small Business, House of Representatives, 88th Congress, 1st session, H. Res. 13, Vol. 1, 1964, p. 114.

24. Sam Karoll, Vice President of Karoll's Inc., Chicago, Ill., and Director of the National Association of Retail Clothiers and Furnishers, quoted in *Quality Stabilization, 1963*—Hearings before a Subcommittee of the Committee of Interstate and Foreign Commerce, House of Representatives, 88th Congress, 1st session, H.R. 3369 (1963), pp. 109–10.

25. *Printer's Ink*, 282, 9 (March 1, 1963), 5.

26. Richard Rosenthal, "Stamp Industry Talking Maturity, Not Growth," *Home Furnishings Daily* (July 8, 1965), p. 8. Cf. Batten, Barten, Durstine, and Osborn Inc., 1956, *Trading Stamps and Premium Credit Plans* which reported that 75 per cent of those saving stamps obtained them in food stores and an equal proportion got them from gasoline stations. The May, 1965, *Monthly Labor Review* article, "Trading Stamps and the CPI" by Ethel D. Hoover and Mary Lou Drake, says, "Rough estimates of the proportions of purchases for which stamps were received were: Food and other commodities commonly sold in foodstores—50 per cent; gasoline and motor oil—30 per cent; toilet goods, drugs, and other commodities commonly sold in drugstores—15 per cent."

27. Lawrence W. Bell, Premium Magazine, New York City, quoted in *Summary Transcript of the New York State Conference on Store Trading Stamps,* October 2, 1956, p. 13.

28. Sperry and Hutchinson Company, "Special Report," *The New York Times,* October 18, 1964, Section 12, Advertisement, p. 14.

29. *Ibid.,* p. 11. Hamilton Cosco, Inc., "A Survey of Trading Stamp Savers," *Consumer Research Report* No. IM-463 (1963), reported 54 per cent affirmative response to the question, "Do you recall having seen any product illustrated in a stamp catalog or displayed in a stamp redemption store that you purchased at a later date from a retail store?" and 16 per cent of the respondents reported that, once they had redeemed stamps with an individual item of a merchandise set, they had purchased the remaining pieces in a retail store.

30. Sperry and Hutchinson Company, *op. cit.,* p. 16.

31. *Ibid.,* p. 16.

32. *Business Week* (Oct. 17, 1964), p. 110.

33. Commonly, any attempt to use stamps "differently"—for example double-stamps—will be widely imitated but nevertheless remains a possible inducement for consumers to break their purchase habits. Meredith, *op. cit.,* p. 15, stresses the self-defeating nature of trading stamps as differentiation: "Trying to define distinctiveness in stamp merchandising in specific terms is like trying to put up a fence. The only natural approach to building a distinctive trading-stamp pattern is in the imagination of the user of the plan. There are, however, four principal areas in which this imagination can be applied to make one stamp plan—or one user's handling of a stamp plan—stand out from the rest: 1. Different premiums; 2. Different service; 3. Different promotion; 4. Different use of the plan."

34. Sperry and Hutchinson, *op. cit.*, pp. 9, 11.
35. Marshall Goldman, *Soviet Marketing* (Glencoe, Ill.: The Free Press, 1963).

Chapter 9 Protection of Consumer Choice

1. Cf. Francis Bator, *The Question of Government Spending* (New York: Harper and Bros., 1960).
2. Paul R. Dixon, Chairman Federal Trade Commission quoted in *Quality Stabilization, 1964*—Hearings before a Subcommittee of the Committee on Commerce, United States Senate, 88th Congress, 1964, p. 239.
3. For these figures and other pertinent information, see *Consumer Protection Activities of State Governments*, Part 1, Seventh Report by the Committee on Government Operations, June 24, 1963, Washington, D.C., and Part 2, Seventeenth Report by the Committee on Government Operations, November 22, 1963, Washington, D.C.
4. See also the recommendations of the National Food Commission, reported in *The New York Times*, March 14, 1966, and published in various reports during 1966.
5. *Packaging and Labeling Practices*—Hearings before the Subcommittee on Antitrust and Monopoly, Committee on the Judiciary, U.S. Senate, 87th Congress, 1st session, Part 2 (Washington, D.C.: GPO, 1962), p. 331, quoting Paul S. Willis, President, Grocery Manufacturers of America.
6. *Ibid.*, p. 452, quoting Ellen-Ann Dunham, Vice President, General Foods.
7. Mary Merris, "New York Retailers Hit Price Tag Ruling," *Home Furnishings Daily* (Aug. 4, 1965), p. 22.
8. Robert W. Habenstein and William M. Laners, *The History of American Funeral Directing* (Milwaukee: Bulfin Printers, 1955), p. 533, quoted in Stanley A. Hollander, *Restraints Upon Retail Competition* (East Lansing: Michigan State University Press, 1965), p. 33.
9. Thomas M. Stipe, quoted in *Prices of Hearing Aids*—Hearings before the Subcommittee on Antitrust and Monopoly of the Committee on the Judiciary, U.S. Senate, 87th Congress, 2nd session, S. Res. 258 (Washington, D.C.: GPO, 1962), p. 238.
10. Cf. E. H. Chamberlin, "The Product as an Economic Variable," in *Towards a More General Theory of Value* (New York: Oxford University Press, 1957), pp. 109, 129–36.
11. Herman F. Lehma, Vice President General Motors Corp., quoted in "If You Ask Me," by Earl Lifshey, *Home Furnishings Daily* (Nov., 1964), p. 22.

12. James G. Hauk, *Technical Service in the American Economy* (Ann Arbor: University of Michigan Press, 1962), p. 47.

Chapter 10   What Will Consumers Buy?

1. Cf. Laura Margaret Hall, John Knapp, and Christopher Winsten, *Distribution in Great Britain and North America* (London: Oxford University Press, 1961), p. 4: "It is no longer as appropriate as it once was to talk of the distributors being, as it were, the eyes and ears of the final consumer, interpreting the consumers' sovereign wishes to the producers and thereby to a dominant extent influencing the character of output. It is still true that manufacturers are dependent on securing the orders of distributors, but, increasingly, it is the distributors and not the manufacturers who play the more passive role in determining the range of merchandise available."

2. Vergil D. Reed, "Changes in Consumer Markets as a Guide to Marketing Management," *Changing Structures and Strategy in Marketing*, Robert V. Mitchum, ed. (Urbana: University of Illinois Press, 1957), p. 50.

3. Howard Morgan, speech presented at NICB Conference, 1960, reported in *Sales Management* (October 7, 1960), p. 132.

4. F. Walter Perl, "Styling—The Industrial Designer and the Product," *Marketing Research in Action* (New York: American Management Association, 1958), pp. 202–03.

5. Clarence F. Manning, "Planning a Product Diversification Program," *New Product Seminar, 1955* (New York: Kastor, Hilton, Chelsey, Clifford & Atherton, Inc., 1955), p. 5.

6. Ronald G. Shafer, "Helpful Consumers," *Wall Street Journal* (June 2, 1965), p. 1, quoting J. B. Catlin, General Manager of consumer products, Kimberly-Clark, Inc.

7. Robert L. French, Final Report, *First Annual Congress on Better Living* (New York: McCall's Magazine, 1958), p. 3.

8. Walter A. Woods, quoted in *Printer's Ink*, 268, 8 (Aug. 21, 1959), 66.

9. Don G. Mitchell, "New Horizons for Business via New Products," *New Product Seminar—1954* (New York: Kastor, Hilton, Chesley, Clifford & Atherton, Inc., 1954), p. 33.

10. J. F. Kurie, "How a Non-Durable Goods Producer Found New Markets," speech at NICB Conference, Sept. 17, 1958. Cf. E. Raymond Corey, *Developments of Markets for New Materials* (Cambridge: Harvard University Press, 1964).

11. A. L. Plant, "Popular Fallacies in Test Marketing New Products," *New Product Seminar—1957* (New York: Kastor, Hilton, Chesley, Clifford & Atherton, Inc., 1957), p. 20.

12. Arthur C. Nielsen, Jr., "Evaluating New Product Movement at the Consumer Level," *New Product Seminar—1957* (New York: Kastor, Hilton, Chesley, Clifford & Atherton, Inc., 1954), p. 13.
13. W. R. Reiss, "The Use of Market Research in Developing New Products," *Successful Marketing at Home and Abroad*, W. David Robbins, ed. (Chicago: American Marketing Association, 1958), pp. 246–47.
14. *Sales Management* (Nov. 20, 1954), pp. 72–76.
15. *Ibid.* (March 15, 1954), p. 73.
16. See, for example, H. G. Barnett, *Innovation* (New York: McGraw-Hill Book Co., Inc., 1953), Herbert I. Abelson, *Persuasion* (New York: Springer Publishing Co., 1959); Richard T. LaPiere, *A Theory of Social Control* (New York: McGraw-Hill Book Co., Inc., 1954); George Gallup, "Absorption Rate of Ideas," *Public Opinion Quarterly*, XIX (Feb., 1955), 234–44; Elihu Katza, "The Two-Step Flow of Communication," *Public Opinion Quarterly*, XXI (Spring, 1957), 61–78; George Fisk, "Consumer Information Channels" (unpublished dissertation in Economics presented to the Graduate School of the University of Pennsylvania in partial fulfillment of the Ph.D., Feb., 1956); George M. Beal and Everett Rogers, "The Scientist as a Reference in the Communication of New Technology," *Public Opinion Quarterly*, XXII, 4 (Winter, 1958), 555–64 and William H. Whyte, Jr., "The Web of Word of Mouth," *Fortune* (Nov., 1964).
17. *Consumer Demand in Lincoln, Nebraska* (1928), pp. 22, 28.
18. *Advertising Age* (October 3, 1960), quoting Curtis C. Rogers, Market Research Corporation of America, p. 85.
19. Pierre Martineau, "Social Class and Spending," *Journal of Marketing*, XXIII (Oct., 1958), 49.
20. Wroe Alderson, "A Functionalist Approach to Consumer Behavior," *Consumer Behavior and Motivation*, Robert H. Cole, ed. (Urbana: University of Illinois Press, 1956), p. 22.
21. "From Today's Big-City Areas," *Printer's Ink*, 259, 4 (April 26, 1954), 41.
22. Thomas Meiller, Speaker at Conference, reported in *Public Opinion Quarterly*, XX (Winter, 1956), 560.
23. "Bob Feemster: A Tie Between Wall Street, Madison Avenue," *Printer's Ink*, 267, 11 (June 12, 1959), 53.

Bibliography

The following pages list sources and references that are basic to this work or to any analysis of consumption and that provide a stimulus for further inquiry. The works have been roughly divided by subject matter: historical material to supplement Chapters 1, 3, 4, and 5; theoretical and empirical data on consumer choices and preferences; and descriptive and analytical approaches to the nature of market competition. At the outset, however, four publications should be mentioned which attempt a more extensive coverage than that given here. For empirical surveys of consumer income and spending before 1935, Faith M. Williams and Carle C. Zimmerman prepared an extensive bibliography, *Studies of Family Living in the United States and Other Countries,* published by the United States Department of Agriculture (Miscellaneous Publication No. 223) in December, 1935. A similarly extensive bibliography, but with a different frame of reference, was prepared for the post-World War II literature by James Morgan and published in *Consumer Behavior,* edited by Lincoln Clark (New York: Harper & Brothers, 1958). The eighth edition of the classic *The Theory of Monopolistic Competition* (Cambridge: Harvard University Press, 1962) contains Professor Chamberlin's latest revision of a bibliography of published material relevant to that work. In the field of new product development, Donald Megathlin and Edward J. Harnett have prepared a collection of titles, *A Bibliography on New Product Planning* (Chicago: American Marketing Association, 1960), for the American Marketing Association.

Historical Insight into Consumer Choice in the American Economy

Addams, Jane. *Twenty Years at Hull House.* New York: The Macmillan Company, 1910.

American Public Health Association. *A Half Century of Public Health.* New York: American Public Health Association, 1921.

———. *Committee on the Hygiene of Housing, Construction and Equipment of the Home.* Chicago: Public Administration Service, 1951.

Anthony, Katharine. *Mothers Who Must Earn.* New York: Survey Associates, 1914.

Bailyn, Bernard. *The New England Merchants in the Seventeenth Century.* Cambridge: Harvard University Press, 1955.

Barger, Harold. *Distribution's Place in the American Economy Since 1869.* Princeton: Princeton University Press, 1955.

Beyer, William C., Davis, Rebekah P., and Thwing, Myra. *Workingmen's Standard of Living in Philadelphia.* New York: The Macmillan Company, 1919.

Boothe, Viva Belle. *Salaries and the Cost of Living in 27 State Universities and Colleges, 1913–1932.* Columbus: Ohio State University Press, 1932.

Bosworth, Louise Marion. "The Living Wage of Women Workers," *Supplement to the Annals of the American Academy of Political and Social Science, May, 1911.* Philadelphia: American Academy of Political and Social Science, 1911.

Bowden, Witt. "Changes in Modes of Living," *Monthly Labor Review,* LXXI, 1 (July, 1950), 23–30.

Brady, Dorothy. "Family Savings in Relation to Changes in Level and Distribution of Income," *Studies in Income and Wealth,* Vol. 15. New York: National Bureau of Economic Research, 1952.

Bremner, Robert H. *From the Depths.* New York: New York University Press, 1956.

Bureau of Applied Economics. *Standards of Living.* Washington: Bureau of Applied Economics, 1920–32.

Butler, Elizabeth Beardsley. *Saleswomen in Mercantile Stores.* New York: Russell Sage Foundation, 1912.

Calkins, Raymond. *Substitutes for the Saloon* (2nd ed., rev.). Boston and New York: Houghton Mifflin Company, 1919.

Chapin, Robert Coit. *The Standard of Living Among Workingmen's Families in New York City.* New York: Charities Publication Committee, 1909.

Clark, John Bates. *The Distribution of Wealth.* New York: The Macmillan Company, 1889.

Clark, Sue Ainslie, and Wyatt, Edith. *Making Both Ends Meet.* New York: The Macmillan Company, 1911.

Clark, Thomas D. *Pills, Petticoats and Plows.* Norman: University of Oklahoma Press, 1963.

Council of Social Agencies. *Chicago Standard Budget for Dependent Families,* Bulletin No. 5. Chicago: Council of Social Agencies, 1919.

————. *Chicago Standard Budget for Dependent Families, 1937.* Chicago: Council of Social Agencies, 1937.

Country Gentleman. *Selective Spending in Rural America.* New York: Curtis Publishing Company, 1940.

Cummings, Richard Osborn. *The American and His Food.* Chicago: University of Chicago Press, 1940.

Dexter, Seymour. *A Treatise on Co-operative Savings and Loan Associations.* New York: D. Appleton and Company, 1889.

Emmet, Boris, and Jeuck, John E. *Catalogues and Counters.* Chicago: University of Chicago Press, 1950.

Gibbs, Winifred Stuart. *The Minimum Cost of Living.* New York: The Macmillan Company, 1917.

Girtin, Thomas. *Nothing But the Best.* New York: McDowell, Obolensky, 1960.

Goldsmith, Raymond S. *A Study of Saving in the United States.* Princeton: Princeton University Press, 1955–56.

————, Brady, Dorothy S., and Mendershausen, Horst. *A Study of Saving in the United States,* Vol. III. Princeton: Princeton University Press, 1956.

Goodrich, Carter. *Earnings and Standard of Living of 1,000 Railway Employees During the Depression.* Washington, D.C.: Government Printing Office, 1934.

————. *Migration and Planes of Living, 1920–34.* Philadelphia: University of Pennsylvania Press, 1935.

Harriss, C. Lowell. *History and Policies of the Home Owners' Loan Corporation.* New York: National Bureau of Economic Research, 1951.

Henderson, Charles R. *Industrial Insurance in the United States.* Chicago: University of Chicago Press, 1909.

Higgs, Henry. "Frederic LePlay," *Quarterly Journal of Economics,* IV (July, 1890), 408–33, 467–77.

————. "Workmen's Budgets," *Journal of the Royal Statistical Society,* LVI (June, 1893), 255–94.

Hoffman, Frederick L. "Fifty Years of American Life Insurance Progress," *Journal of the American Statistical Association,* XII (Sept., 1911), 667–70.

Housing America, by the editors of *Fortune.* New York: Harcourt, Brace and Company, 1932.

Hower, Ralph Merle. *History of Macy's of New York, 1858–1919.* Cambridge: Harvard University Press, 1943.

————. *The History of an Advertising Agency*. Cambridge: Harvard University Press, 1949.

Howey, R. S. *The Rise of the Marginal Utility School*. Lawrence: University of Kansas Press, 1960.

Jevons, W. Stanley. *Theory of Political Economy* (4th ed.). New York: The Macmillan Company, 1931.

Kemmerer, Edwin S. "Six Years of Postal Savings in the United States," *American Economic Review*, VII (May, 1916), 46–90.

Kendrick, John W. *Productivity Trends in the United States*. Princeton: Princeton University Press, 1961.

Lampman, Robert J. *The Share of Top Wealth-Holders in National Wealth 1922–56*. Princeton: Princeton University Press, 1962.

Laver, James. *Taste and Fashion*. London: G. Harrap & Company, 1945.

Leiby, James. *Carroll Wright and Labor Reform*. Cambridge: Harvard University Press, 1960.

Mack, Ruth P. "Trends in American Consumption and the Aspiration to Consume," *American Economic Review: Papers and Proceedings*, XLVI, 2 (1956), 55–69.

MacLean, Arnie Marion. *Wage-Earning Women*. New York: The Macmillan Company, 1910.

Markets by Incomes. New York: Time, Inc., 1932.

Marshall, Alfred. *Principles of Economics* (8th ed.). New York: The Macmillan Company, 1950.

Martin, Edgar W. *The Standard of Living in 1860*. Chicago: University of Chicago Press, 1942.

Massachusetts Commission on the Cost of Living. *The Cost of Living*. Boston: Wright J. Potter Printing Co., 1910.

Mill, John Stuart. *Principles of Political Economy* (7th ed.). London: Longmans, Green, and Company, 1909.

More, Louise Bolard. *Wage-Earners' Budgets*. New York: H. Holt and Company, 1907.

National Bureau of Economic Research. *Recent Economic Changes*. New York: McGraw-Hill Book Company, 1929.

National Industrial Conference Board. *Family Budgets of American Wage-Earners*, Research Report 41. New York: The Century Company, 1921.

————. *The Cost of Living Among Wage-Earners*, Research Reports 22, 24. New York: National Industrial Conference Board, 1922.

————. *The Cost of Living in the United States, 1914–1926*. New York: National Industrial Conference Board, 1927.

————. *The Cost of Living in the United States, 1914–1936.* New York: National Industrial Conference Board, 1936.

————. *Studies in Enterprise and Social Progress.* New York: National Industrial Conference Board, 1939.

————. *Studies in Labor Statistics, Family Expenditure for Clothing.* New York: National Industrial Conference Board, 1955.

————. *Wartime Changes in the Cost of Living.* New York: National Industrial Conference Board, August, 1914.

Nesbitt, Florence. *Standards of Public Aid to Children in Their Own Homes.* U.S. Department of Labor, Children's Bureau Publication No. 118. Washington, D.C.: Government Printing Office, 1923.

New York State Department of Labor, Bureau of Research. *Division of Women in Industry and Minimum Wage. Adequate Maintenance and Protection of Health for Women Workers in New York State.* 1939.

Peixotto, Jessica Blanche. *Getting and Spending at the Professional Standard of Living.* New York: The Macmillan Company, 1927.

————. *How Workers Spend a Living Wage.* Berkeley: University of California Press, 1929.

Phelps, Roswell F. *South End Factory Operatives.* Boston: South-End House Association, 1903.

Potter, David M. *People of Plenty.* Chicago: University of Chicago Press, 1954.

Rae, John. *The Sociological Theory of Capital,* Charles Whitney Mixter (ed.). New York: Macmillan and Company, 1905.

Report of the President's Homes Commission. Washington, D.C.: Government Printing Office, 1908.

Richards, Ellen H. *The Cost of Cleanness.* New York: John Wiley & Sons, 1911.

————. *The Cost of Living, as Modified by Sanitary Science.* New York: John Wiley & Sons, 1900.

Rowntree, B. Seebohm, and Kendall, May. *How the Labourer Lives.* London: Thomas Nelson and Sons, 1913.

Ryan, John. *A Living Wage.* New York: The Macmillan Company, 1920.

Sainte-Beuve, Charles Augustin. "La Réforme Sociale en France," *Nouveaux Lundis,* IX (Dec. 5, 1864), 844–74.

Senior, Nassau Williams. *Political Economy* (6th ed.). London: C. Griffin and Company, 1872.

Shuey, Edwin L. *Factory People and Their Employers.* New York: Lentilhon & Company, 1900.

Sissman, Louise. "Development of the Postal Savings System,"

Journal of the American Statistical Association, XXXI (Dec., 1936), 708–18.

Smith, Adam. *The Wealth of Nations.* New York: Random House, 1937.

Spahr, Charles B. *America's Working People.* New York: Longmans, Green, and Company, 1900.

Stewart, Paul W., Dewhurst, J. Frederic, Field, Louise, and the Committee on Distribution. *Does Distribution Cost Too Much?* New York: Twentieth Century Fund, 1939.

Stigler, George J. *Domestic Servants in the United States 1900–1940.* New York: National Bureau of Economic Research, 1946.

————. *Production and Distribution Theories.* New York: The Macmillan Company, 1941.

Streightoff, Frank Hatch. "Report on the Cost of Living," *Fourth Report of the New York State Factory Investigating Commission.* Albany: J. B. Lyon Co., 1915.

————. *The Standard of Living Among the Industrial People of America.* Boston and New York: Houghton Mifflin Company, 1911.

Twyman, Robert A. *History of Marshall Field & Co., 1852–1906.* Philadelphia: University of Pennsylvania Press, 1954.

U.S. Bureau of Labor Statistics. Bulletin 125, *Retail Prices 1890 to April, 1913.* Washington, D.C.: Government Printing Office, 1913.

————. Bulletin 156, *Retail Prices 1907 to December, 1914.* Washington, D.C.: Government Printing Office, 1915.

————. Bulletin 263, *Housing by Employers in the United States.* Washington, D.C.: Government Printing Office, 1910.

————. Bulletin 357, *Cost of Living in the United States.* Washington, D.C.: Government Printing Office, 1920.

————. Bulletin 541, *Handbook of Labor Statistics, 1931.* Washington, D.C.: Government Printing Office, 1931.

————. Bulletin 822, *Family Spending and Saving in Wartime.* Washington, D.C.: Government Printing Office, 1945.

————, and Federal Emergency Relief Administration. Bulletins 636–641, *Study of Money Disbursements of Wage Earners and Clerical Workers.* Washington, D.C.: Government Printing Office, 1939–40.

————. and Works Progress Administration. Bulletins 642–649, *Study of Consumer Purchases: Urban Series.* Washington, D.C.: Government Printing Office, 1939.

U.S. Commissioner of Labor. *Sixth Annual Report, 1890.* Washington, D.C.: Government Printing Office, 1891.

————. Eighth Special Report, *The Housing of the Working People*. Washington, D.C.: Government Printing Office, 1895.

U.S. Department of Agriculture, Bureau of Agricultural Economics. *Consumption of Food in the United States, 1909–52* (Agricultural Handbook No. 62 and supplements to 1962). Washington, D.C.: Government Printing Office, 1953–63.

U.S. Department of Commerce and Labor. *Women and Child Wage-Earners in the United States.* Washington, D.C.: Government Printing Office, 1910.

————. "Working Conditions and the Relations of Employers and Employees," *Report on Conditions of Employment in the Iron & Steel Industry,* Vol. III. Washington, D.C.: Government Printing Office, 1913.

U.S. Department of Labor, Children's Bureau. *Welfare of Children of Maintenance-of-way Employees,* Publication #211. Washington, D.C.: Government Printing Office, 1932.

Veblen, Thorstein. *The Theory of the Leisure Class.* New York: Random House, 1934.

Westergaard, Harald. "Obituary, Dr. Ernst Engel," *Economic Journal,* VII (March, 1897), 145–48.

Wiley, Harvey. *Foods and Their Adulteration.* Philadelphia: Blakiston Press, 1909.

Williams, Faith, and Zimmerman, Carle C. *Studies of Family Living in the United States and Other Countries,* United States Department of Agriculture, Bureau of Human Nutrition and Home Economics. Miscellaneous Publication 223. Washington, D.C.: Government Printing Office, December, 1935.

Wood, Edith Elmer. *Recent Trends in American Housing.* New York: The Macmillan Company, 1931.

————. *The Housing of the Unskilled Wage Earner.* New York: The Macmillan Company, 1919.

Young, Agnes B. *Recurring Cycles of Fashion 1760–1937.* New York: Harper and Bros., 1937.

Zimmerman, Carle C. "Ernst Engel's Law of Expenditures," *Quarterly Journal of Economics,* XLVII (Nov., 1932), 78–101.

Consumer Choice and Consumption Patterns

Abelson, Herbert I. *Persuasion.* New York: Springer Publishing Company, 1959.

Anderson, Odin W., with Feldman, Jacob J. *Family Medical Costs and Voluntary Health Insurance.* New York: McGraw-Hill Book Company, 1956.

Ando, Albert, and Modigliani, Franco. "The 'Life Cycle' Hypothesis of Saving: Aggregate Implications and Tests," *American Economic Review*, LIII (March, 1963), 55–84.

Bagdikian, Ben H. *In the Midst of Plenty*. Boston: Beacon Press, 1964.

Baker, D. J., and Berry, Charles H. "The Price Elasticity of Demand for Fluid Skim Milk," *Journal of Farm Economics*, XXXV, 1 (Feb., 1953), 124–29.

Bancroft, Gertrude. *The American Labor Force*. New York: John Wiley and Sons, 1958.

Barksdale, Hiram C. *The Use of Survey Research Findings as Legal Evidence*. Pleasantville, N.Y.: Printer's Ink Books, 1957.

Barnett, H. G. *Innovation*. New York: McGraw-Hill Book Company, 1953.

Bator, Francis M. *The Question of Government Spending*. New York: Harper and Bros., 1960.

Becker, G. S. *Human Capital*. New York: National Bureau of Economic Research, 1964.

Bendix, Reinhard, and Lipset, Seymour Martin (eds.). *Class, Status and Power*. Glencoe, Ill.: The Free Press, 1953.

Berger, Bennett M. *Working-Class Suburb*. Berkeley and Los Angeles: University of California Press, 1960.

Beyer, Glenn H. *Housing, A Factual Analysis*. New York: The Macmillan Company, 1958.

———. *Housing and Society*. New York: The Macmillan Company, 1965.

Bogan, Forrest A., and Hamel, Harvey. "Multiple Jobholders in May 1963," *Monthly Labor Review*, 88 (March, 1965), 266–74.

Brown, Bonnar, and Van Alstyne, Carol. *Family Income Patterns 1947–1968*. Menlo Park, Calif.: Stanford Research Institute, 1959.

Brown, J. A. C. "The Consumption of Food in Relation to Household Composition and Income," *Econometrica*, XXII (Oct., 1954), 444–60.

Burns, Eveline. *Social Security and Public Policy*. New York: McGraw-Hill Book Company, 1956.

Chow, Gregory C. *Demand for Automobiles in the United States*. Amsterdam: North-Holland Publishing Company, 1957.

Clark, Lincoln H. (ed.). *Consumer Behavior: Research on Human Reactions*. New York: Harper and Bros., 1958.

———. *Consumer Behavior; the Dynamics of Consumer Reaction*, Vols. 1, 2, 4. New York: New York University Press, 1955–61.

Clarkson, Geoffrey P. E. *The Theory of Consumer Demand*. Englewood Cliffs, N.J.: Prentice-Hall, 1963.

408

Clower, Robert W. "Permanent Income and Transitory Balances," *Oxford Economic Papers*, XV, 3 (July, 1963), 177–90.

Cole, Robert H. (ed.). *Consumer Behavior and Motivation*. Urbana: University of Illinois Press, 1956.

Colean, Miles L. *The Impact of Government on Real Estate Finance in the United States*. New York: National Bureau of Economic Research, 1950.

Consumer Demand in Lincoln, Nebraska. By the Committee on Business Research of the College of Business Administration. Lincoln: University of Nebraska Press, 1928.

Copp, James H., Sill, Maurice L., and Brown, Emory J. "The Function of Information Sources in the Farm Adoption Process," *Rural Sociology*, XXIII, 2 (June, 1958), 146–57.

Corbett, Richmond M. *Pension Trends and the Self-Employed*. New Brunswick, N.J.: Rutgers University Press, 1961.

Danière, André. *Higher Education in the American Economy*. New York: Random House, 1964.

DeGrazia, Sebastian. *Of Time Work and Leisure*. New York: Twentieth Century Fund, 1962.

Dernburg, Thomas F., Rosett, R. N., and Watts, H. W. *Studies in Household Economic Behavior*. New Haven: Yale University Press, 1958.

Dewhurst, J. Frederic, and associates. *America's Needs and Resources*. New York: Twentieth Century Fund, 1947.

Dichter, Ernest. *Handbook of Consumer Motivations*. New York: McGraw-Hill Book Company, 1964.

Douglas, Paul F., Hutchinson, John L., and Sutherland, Willard C. (eds.). "Recreation in the Age of Automation," *The Annals of the American Academy of Political and Social Science*, CCCXIII (Sept., 1957).

Duesenberry, James S. *Income, Saving and the Theory of Consumer Behavior*. Cambridge: Harvard University Press, 1949.

Duncan, Otis D., and Resiss, Albert I., Jr. *Social Characteristics of Urban and Rural Communities, 1950*. New York: John Wiley & Sons, 1956.

Fallers, Lloyd A. "A Note on the 'Trickle' Effect," *Public Opinion Quarterly*, XVIII, 3 (Fall, 1954), 314–21.

Ferber, Robert. *A Study of Aggregate Consumption Functions*. New York: National Bureau of Economic Research, 1953.

———. *Collecting Financial Data by Consumer Panel Techniques*. Urbana: University of Illinois Press, 1959.

Foote, Nelson N. *Housing Choices and Housing Constraints*. New York: McGraw-Hill Book Company, 1960.

409

Friedman, Milton. *A Theory of the Consumption Function.* Princeton: Princeton University Press, 1957.

Friedman, Rose D. *Poverty—Definition and Perspective.* Washington, D.C.: American Enterprise Institute for Public Policy, 1965.

Friend, Irwin, and Jones, Robert (eds.). *Proceedings of the Conference on Consumption and Saving.* Philadelphia: University of Pennsylvania Press, 1960.

Glick, Paul C. "The Family Life Cycle," *American Sociological Review,* XII, 2 (April, 1947), 164–74.

Harberger, Arnold C. *The Demand for Durable Goods.* Chicago: University of Chicago Press, 1960.

Heller, Walter, Boddy, Francis M., and Nelson, Carl L. *Savings in the Modern Economy.* Minneapolis: University of Minnesota Press, 1953.

Hickman, C. Addison, and Kuhn, Manford H. *Individuals, Groups, and Economic Behavior.* New York: Dryden Press, 1956.

Hicks, John R. *A Revision of Demand Theory.* London: Oxford University Press, 1956.

Houthakker, Hendrik S. "Education and Income," *Review of Economics and Statistics,* XLI (Feb., 1959), 24–27.

Hoyt, Elizabeth E. "Want Development in Underdeveloped Areas," *Journal of Political Economy,* LIX (June, 1951), 194–202.

Huntington, Emily H. *Spending of Middle-Income Families.* Berkeley: University of California Press, 1957.

John, M. E. "Classification of Values That Serve as Motivators to Consumer Purchases," *Journal of Farm Economics,* XXXVIII, 4 (Nov., 1956), 956–63.

Jones, Robert C. "Transitory Income and Expenditures on Consumption Categories," *American Economic Review: Papers and Proceedings,* L, 2 (May, 1960), 50, 584–92.

Juster, F. Thomas. *Anticipations and Purchases.* Princeton: Princeton University Press, 1964.

Katona, George. *Psychological Analysis of Economic Behavior.* New York: McGraw-Hill Book Company, 1951.

———, and Lansing, John B. "The Wealth of the Wealthy," *Review of Economics and Statistics,* XLVI (Feb., 1964), 1–13.

———, Lininger, Charles A., Morgan, James N., and Mueller, Eva. *1961 Survey of Consumer Finances.* Ann Arbor: University of Michigan Press, 1962.

———, ———, and Kosobud, Richard F. *1962 Survey of Consumer Finances.* Ann Arbor: University of Michigan Press, 1963.

———, ———, and Mueller, Eva. *1963 Survey of Consumer Finances.* Ann Arbor: University of Michigan Press, 1964.

———, ———, and ———. *1964 Survey of Consumer Finances.* Ann Arbor: University of Michigan Press, 1965.

———, and Mueller, Eva. *Consumer Attitudes and Demand 1950–1952.* Ann Arbor: University of Michigan Press, 1953.

Katz, Elihu. "The Two-Step Flow of Communication: An Up-to-Date Report on an Hypothesis," *Public Opinion Quarterly,* XXI, 1 (Spring, 1957), 61–78.

Kedzie, Daniel P. *Consumer Credit Insurance.* Homewood, Ill.: R. D. Irwin, 1957.

Kemp, Murray C. "The Efficiency of Consumption as an Allocator of Resource," *Canadian Journal of Economics and Political Science,* XXI (May, 1955), 217–27.

Klaman, Saul B. *The Postwar Rise of Mortgage Companies.* New York: National Bureau of Economic Research, 1959.

———. *The Volume of Mortgage Debt in the Postwar Decade.* New York: National Bureau of Economic Research, 1958.

Kohr, Leopold. "Toward a New Measurement of Living Standards," *American Journal of Economics and Sociology,* XV, 1 (Oct., 1955), 93–104.

Kolko, Gabriel. *Wealth and Power in America.* New York: Frederick A. Praeger, 1962.

Kornhauser, Arthur, and Lazarsfeld, Paul F. "The Analysis of Consumer Actions," *The Language of Social Research,* Paul Lazarsfeld and Morris Rosenberg (eds.). Glencoe, Ill.: The Free Press, 1955.

Kosobud, Richard F., and Morgan, James N. (eds.). *Consumer Behavior of Individual Families Over Two and Three Years.* Ann Arbor: University of Michigan Press, 1964.

Kreinin, Mordechai. "Factors Associated With Stock Ownership," *Review of Economics and Statistics,* XLI (Feb., 1959), 12–23.

Kuehn, Alfred Arthur. "An Analysis of the Dynamics of Consumer Behavior and Its Implications for Marketing Management." Ph.D. thesis, Carnegie Institute of Technology, Graduate School of Industrial Administration, 1958.

Kuznets, Simon. "Economic Growth and Income Inequality," *American Economic Review,* XLV, 1 (March, 1955), 1–28.

———. *Shares of Upper Income Groups in Income and Savings.* New York: National Bureau of Economic Research, 1953.

Lamale, Helen Hune. *Methodology of the Survey of Consumer Expenditures in 1950.* Philadelphia: University of Pennsylvania Press, 1959.

———, and Stotz, Margaret C. "The Interim City Worker's Family Budget," *Monthly Labor Review* (August, 1960).

Lampman, Robert James. "Changes in The Share of Wealth Held

by Top Wealth-Holders, 1922–1956," *Review of Economics and Statistics,* XLI (Nov., 1959), 379–92.

Lansing, John B., and Lilienstein, Ernest. *The Travel Market 1955.* Ann Arbor: University of Michigan Press, 1957.

———, Lorimer, Thomas, and Moriguchi, Chikashi. *How People Pay for College.* Ann Arbor: University of Michigan Press, 1960.

LaPiere, Richard T. *A Theory of Social Control.* New York: McGraw-Hill Book Company, 1954.

Leonhard, Dietz L. *Consumer Research with Projective Techniques.* Shenandoah, Iowa: Ajax Corporation, 1955.

Look National Appliance Survey, 1961. New York: Cowles Magazine and Broadcasting, 1961.

Machlup, Fritz. *The Production and Distribution of Knowledge in the United States.* Princeton: Princeton University Press, 1962.

Mack, Ruth P. *Consumption and Business Fluctuations.* New York: National Bureau of Economic Research, 1956.

———. "Economics of Consumption," *A Survey of Contemporary Economics,* Bernard F. Haley (ed.). Homewood, Ill.: R. D. Irwin, 1952.

Marsh, C. Paul, and Coleman, A. Lee. "Farmers' Practices Adoption Rates in Relation to Adoption Rates of Leaders," *Rural Sociology,* XIX, 2 (June, 1954), 180–01.

McCracken, Paul W., Mao, James C. T., and Fricke, Cedric. *Consumer Installment Credit and Public Policy.* Ann Arbor: University of Michigan Press, 1965.

Menzel, Herbert, and Katz, Elihu. "Social Relations and Innovation in the Medical Profession: The Epidemiology of a New Drug," *Public Opinion Quarterly,* XIX (Winter, 1955), 337–52.

Miller, Herman P. *Income of the American People.* New York: John Wiley & Sons, 1955.

———. *Rich Man, Poor Man.* New York: Thomas Y. Crowell Company, 1964.

Mishan, E. J. *Welfare Economics.* New York: Random House, 1964.

Morgan, James N., David, Martin H., Cohen, Wilbur J., and Brazer, Harvey E. *Income and Welfare in the United States.* New York: McGraw-Hill Book Company, 1962.

Morton, J. E. *Urban Mortgage Lending.* Princeton: Princeton University Press, 1956.

National Bureau of Economic Research. *Price Statistics of the Federal Government.* Princeton: Princeton University Press, 1961.

"National Survey of Liquid Assets," *Federal Reserve Bulletin* (June, July, August, 1946).

Neifeld, M. R. *Trends in Consumer Finance.* Easton, Pa.: Mack Publishing Company, 1954.

The New Consumer. Chicago: The Chicago Tribune, 1957.

Norris, Ruby Turner. *The Theory of Consumer's Demand.* New Haven: Yale University Press, 1952.

Orshansky, Mollie. "Counting the Poor," *Social Security Bulletin,* XXVIII, 1 (Jan., 1965), 3–29.

Perlman, Mark (ed.). *Human Resources in the Urban Community.* Baltimore: Johns Hopkins Press, 1963.

Prais, S. J. "The Estimation of Equivalent Adult-Scales from Family Budgets," *Economic Journal,* LXIII (Dec., 1953), 791–810.

―――. "Whose Cost of Living?" *Review of Economic Studies,* XXXVI (2), 70 (Feb., 1959), 126–34.

Quackenbush, G. G., and Shaffer, J. D. *Collecting Food Purchase Data by Consumer Panel.* East Lansing: Michigan State University Press, 1960.

Ratcliff, Richard U., Rathbun, Daniel B., and Honnold, Junia. *Residential Finance, 1950.* New York: John Wiley & Sons, 1957.

Reid, Margaret G. "Consumption, Savings and Windfall Gains," *American Economic Review,* LII (Sept., 1962), 728–37.

Robbins, W. David. *Consumer Installment Loans.* Columbus: Ohio State University Press, 1955.

Rowntree, Benjamin Seebohm, and Laver, G. R. *Poverty and the Welfare State.* London and New York: Longmans, Green and Company, 1951.

Ryan, Bruce. "A Study in Technological Diffusion," *Rural Sociology,* XIII, 3 (Sept., 1948), 273–84.

Sharp, Harry, and Mott, Paul. "Consumer Decisions in the Metropolitan Family," *Journal of Marketing,* XXI, 2 (Oct., 1956), 149–56.

Simon, Herbert A. *Models of Man.* New York: John Wiley & Sons, 1957.

Slichter, Sumner. *Economic Growth in the United States.* Baton Rouge: Louisiana State University Press, 1961.

Smith, Victor E. "Linear Programming Models for the Determination of Palatable Human Diets," *Journal of Farm Economics,* XLI, 2 (May, 1959), 272–83.

Spicer, Edward Holland (ed.). *Human Problems in Technological Change.* New York: Russell Sage Foundation, 1952.

Suits, Daniel. "Use of Dummy Variables in Regression Equations," *Journal of the American Statistical Association,* LII (Dec., 1957), 548–51.

"Survey of Consumer Finance," *Federal Reserve Bulletin,* several issues yearly, 1947 to 1958.

United Nations, Economic and Social Council, Social Committee. *International Definition and Measurement of Standards and*

Levels of Living. New York: United Nations, Mar. 7, 1955, May 4, 1955, Jan. 20, 1956, Feb. 2, 1956.

U.S. Bureau of Labor Statistics. *Average Retail Prices: Collection and Calculation Techniques and Problems,* Bulletin 1182. Washington, D.C.: Government Printing Office, June, 1955.

U.S. Congress, Joint Committee on the Economic Report of the President. Staff of the Subcommittee on Low-Income Families, *Characteristics of the Low-Income Populations and Related Federal Programs.* Washington, D.C.: Government Printing Office, 1955.

U.S. Department of Agriculture. *Agriculture Statistics 1964.* Washington, D.C.: Government Printing Office, 1964.

——— Agricultural Marketing Service, Agricultural Economics Division, *Meat Consumption Trends and Patterns.* Washington, D.C.: Government Printing Office, 1960.

——— Agricultural Marketing Service, Marketing Research Division, *Income and Household Size.* Washington, D.C.: Government Printing Office, 1959.

——— Agricultural Marketing Service, *Levels of Living of U.S. Farm Families.* Washington, D.C.: Government Printing Office, 1957.

——— Agricultural Research Service and the Agricultural Marketing Service, *Household Food Consumption Survey, 1955.* Washington, D.C.: Government Printing Office, 1956–59.

——— Statistics Reporting Service, *Women's Attitudes Toward Cotton and Other Fibers in Clothing.* Washington, D.C.: Government Printing Office, 1961.

U.S. Federal Emergency Relief Administration. "Family Relief Budgets," *Monthly Report* (June 1936), p. 140.

Voluntary Health and Welfare Agencies in the United States, Robert H. Hamlin, study director. New York: Schoolmasters' Press, 1961.

Weisbrod, Burton A. *Economics of Public Health.* Philadelphia: University of Pennsylvania Press, 1961.

———. *External Benefits of Public Education.* Princeton: Princeton University Press, 1964.

Winnick, Louis. *American Housing and Its Use: The Demand for Shelter Space.* New York: John Wiley & Sons, 1957.

Zweig, Ferdynand. *The Worker in the Affluent Society.* New York: The Free Press, 1961.

Market Competition and Consumer Choice

Adelman, Morris. "The Product and Price in Distribution," *American Economic Review: Papers and Proceedings,* XLVII, 2 (May, 1957), 266–74.

Adler, Max. *Modern Market Research*. New York: Philosophical Library, 1957.

The Adoption of New Products. Ann Arbor: Foundation for Research on Human Behavior, 1959.

Alderson, Wroe. *Marketing Behavior and Executive Action*. Homewood, Ill.: R. D. Irwin, 1957.

Andrews, P. W. S. *On Competition in Economic Theory*. London: Macmillan & Co., Ltd., 1964.

Beal, George M., and Rogers, Everett M. *The Adoption of Two Farm Practices in a Central Iowa Community*. Ames: Iowa State University of Science and Technology Press, 1960.

Bell, Carolyn Shaw. "On the Elasticity of Demand at Retail," *American Journal of Economics and Sociology*, XX (Oct., 1960), 63–72.

Benson, Purnell H. "Optimizing Product Acceptability Through Marginal Preference Analysis," *Quality Control and the Consumer Conference*. Rutgers, N.J.: State University Press, 1957.

Board of Governors of the Federal Reserve System. *Consumer Instalment Credit*. Washington, D.C.: Government Printing Office, 1957.

Bogart, Leo. "Inside Marketing Research," *Public Opinion Quarterly*, XXVII, 4 (Winter, 1963), 562–77.

Borden, Neil. *The Economic Effects of Advertising*. Homewood, Ill.: R. D. Irwin, 1942.

Boyd, Harper W., Clewett, Richard M., and Westfall, Ralph. *Cases in Marketing Strategy*. Homewood, Ill.: R. D. Irwin, 1958.

———, ———, and ———. *Contemporary American Marketing*. Homewood, Ill.: R. D. Irwin, 1957.

Brems, Hans. *Product Equilibrium Under Monopolistic Competition*. Cambridge: Harvard University Press, 1951.

Brooks, John Nixon. *The Fate of the Edsel*. New York: Harper & Row, 1963.

Bureau of Advertising, American Newspaper Publishers Association. *Consumer Attitudes and Shopping Habits in Conventional Retail Stores and Discount Stores*. New York: Bureau of Advertising, American Newspaper Publishers Association, 1963.

Cairns, James P. "Suppliers, Retailers, and Shelf Space," *Journal of Marketing*, XXVI, 3 (July, 1962), 34–36.

Canadian Restrictive Trade Practices Commission. *Report on an Inquiry into Loss Leader Selling*. Ottawa: Edmond Cloutier, Queen's Printer, 1955.

Canadian Restrictive Trade Practices Commission. *Report on Advertising Plan for Resale Price Maintenance*. Ottawa: Edmond Cloutier, Queen's Printer, 1955.

Cassady, Ralph. "The New York Department Store Price War of

1951: A Microeconomic Analysis," *Journal of Marketing*, XXII, 1 (July, 1957), 3–11.

Chamberlin, Edward Hastings. *The Theory of Monopolistic Competition* (6th ed.). Cambridge: Harvard University Press, 1950.

———. *Towards a More General Theory of Value*. New York: Oxford University Press, 1957.

Clewett, Richard M. *Marketing Channels for Manufactured Products*. Homewood, Ill.: R. D. Irwin, 1954.

Cole, Robert Hartzell. *Revolving Credit*. Urbana: University of Illinois Press, 1957.

———, and others. *Manufacturer and Distributor Brands*. Urbana: University of Illinois Press, 1955.

Collazzo, Charles J., Jr. *Consumer Attitudes and Frustrations in Shopping*. New York: National Retail Merchants Association, 1963.

Consumer Buying Habits. Wilmington: E. I. DuPont de Nemours & Co., 1935, 1945, 1947, 1949, 1954, 1959.

Corey, E. Raymond. *The Development of Markets for New Materials*. Cambridge: Harvard University Press, 1956.

Cox, Donald F. *Information and Uncertainty*. Unpublished thesis, Harvard University, Graduate School of Business Administration, 1962.

Cox, Reavis. *Distribution in a High-level Economy*. Englewood Cliffs, N.J.: Prentice-Hall, 1965.

———, and Alderson, Wroe (eds.). *Theory in Marketing*. Homewood, Ill.: R. D. Irwin, 1950.

Crisp, Richard D. *Marketing Research Organization and Operation*. New York: American Management Association, 1958.

Davis, Kenneth R. *Furniture Marketing*. Chapel Hill: University of North Carolina Press, 1957.

DeJouvenel, Bertrand. "The Treatment of Capitalism by Continental Intellectuals," *Capitalism and the Historians*, F. A. Hayek (ed.). Chicago: University of Chicago Press, 1954.

Economic Inquiry into Food Marketing, Staff Report to the Federal Trade Commission. Washington, D.C.: Government Printing Office, 1960, 1962.

Enright, Ernest J. *Planning and Administering Test Marketing Campaigns for New Products*. Thesis, Harvard University, Graduate School of Business Administration, 1957.

Entenberg, Robert D. *The Changing Competitive Position of Department Stores in the United States by Merchandise Lines*. Pittsburgh: University of Pittsburgh Press, 1957.

Ethe, Solomon, and Higgins, Elliott F. *New Product Development*

III: Marketing New Products. New York: National Industrial Conference Board, 1954.

The Fair Trade Question. New York: National Industrial Conference Board, 1955.

Ferber, Robert, and Wales, Hugh G. (eds.). *Motivation and Market Behavior.* Homewood, Ill.: R. D. Irwin, 1958.

Fisher, Franklin M., Griliches, Zvi, and Kaysen, Carl. "The Cost of Automobile Model Changes Since 1949," *Journal of Political Economy,* LXX (Oct., 1962), 433–51.

Fisk, George. *Consumer Information Channels.* Unpublished Ph.D. dissertation in economics, University of Pennsylvania, February, 1956.

Foote, Richard J. *Price Elasticities of Demand for Nondurable Goods.* New York: National Bureau of Economic Research, 1955.

Goldman, Marshall I. "Product Differentiation and Advertising," *Journal of Political Economy,* LXVIII (Aug., 1960), 346–57.

Goodman, Charles Schaffner. *The Location of Fashion Industries.* Ann Arbor: University of Michigan Press, 1948.

Hall, Margaret. "Further Reflections on Retail Pricing," *Economica New Series,* XIX (Feb., 1952), 19–26.

————. "Some Aspects of Competition in Retail Trade," *Oxford Economic Papers, New Series,* III (Oct., 1951), 240–45.

————, John Knapp, and Winsten, Christopher. *Distribution in Great Britain and North America.* London: Oxford University Press, 1961.

Haring, A., and Yoder, W. O. (eds.). *Trading Stamp Practice and Pricing Policy.* Bloomington: Indiana University Press, 1958.

Harris, Richard. *The Real Voice.* New York: The Macmillan Company, 1964.

Hauk, James G. *Technical Service in the American Economy.* Ann Arbor: University of Michigan Press, 1962.

Hawkins, Edward R. "Price Policies and Theories," *Journal of Marketing,* XVIII (Jan., 1954), 233–40.

Heflebower, Richard B. "Mass Distribution: A Phase of Bilateral Oligopoly or of Competition?" *American Economic Review: Papers and Proceedings,* XLVII, 2 (May, 1957), 274–86.

Hilton, Peter. *Handbook of New Product Development.* Englewood Cliffs, N.J.: Prentice-Hall, 1961.

Holdren, Bob R. *The Structure of a Retail Market and the Market Behavior of Retail Units.* Englewood Cliffs, N.J.: Prentice-Hall, 1960.

Hollander, Stanley C. *Explorations in Retailing.* East Lansing: Michigan State University Press, 1959.

————. *Restraints Upon Retail Competition*. East Lansing: Michigan State University Press, 1965.

————. *The Rise and Fall of a Buying Club*. East Lansing: Michigan State University Press, 1959.

————. "Theoretical Implications of Empirical Research on Retail Pricing," *American Economic Review: Papers and Proceedings*, XLVII, 2 (May, 1957), 252–66.

Jewkes, John, Sawers, David, and Stillerman, Richard. *The Sources of Invention*. London: Macmillan & Co., Ltd., 1958.

Karger, Delmar W. *The New Product*. New York: The Industrial Press, 1959.

Katona, George. *The Mass Consumption Society*. New York: McGraw-Hill Book Company, 1964.

————. *The Powerful Consumer*. New York: McGraw-Hill Book Company, 1960.

Ketchum, Marshall D., and Kendall, Leon T. (eds.). *Conference on Savings and Residential Financing*. Chicago: United States Savings and Loan League, 1960.

Knauth, Oswald. *Business Practices, Trade Position and Competition*. New York: Columbia University Press, 1956.

Lambert, Gerard Barnes. *All Out of Step*. New York: Doubleday & Company, 1956.

Leibenstein, Harvey. "Bandwagon, Snob, and Veblen Effects in the Theory of Consumers' Demand," *Quarterly Journal of Economics*, LXIV (May, 1950), 183–207.

Lewis, Edwin H., and Hancock, Robert S. *The Franchise System of Distribution*. Minneapolis: University of Minnesota Press, 1963.

Marketing Planning & Strategy Series. Cambridge: Harvard Business Review, 1965.

Marketing Research in Action. New York: National Industrial Conference Board, 1957.

Marting, Elizabeth (ed.). *New Products, New Profits*. New York: American Management Association, 1964.

Marvin, Philip. *Planning New Products*. Cleveland: Penton Publishing Company, 1958.

Mason, Edward S. (ed.). *The Corporation in Modern Society*. Cambridge: Harvard University Press, 1959.

McNair, Malcolm P., and May, Eleanor G. "Pricing for Profit," *Harvard Business Review*, 35, 3 (May–June, 1957), 105–22.

————, Burnham, Elizabeth A., and Hersum, Anita C. *Cases in Retail Management*. New York: McGraw-Hill Book Company, 1957.

————, and Hansen, Harry L. *Readings in Marketing*. New York: McGraw-Hill Book Company, 1956.

———, Applebaum, William, and Salmon, Walter J. *Cases in Food Distribution*. Homewood, Ill.: R. D. Irwin, 1964.

Megathlin, Donald E., and Hartnett, Edward J. *A Bibliography on New Product Planning*. Chicago: American Marketing Association, 1960.

Meredith, George. *Effective Merchandising with Premiums*. New York: McGraw-Hill Book Company, 1962.

National Bureau of Economic Research. *The Rate and Direction of Inventive Activity*. Princeton: Princeton University Press, 1962.

New Products Institute, Inc. *A Digest of the Composite Postwar Experience of 200 Large US Manufacturers in the Introduction of New Consumer Products*. Irvington-on-Hudson: New Products Institute, 1955.

New Products Marketing, by the editors of *Printer's Ink*. New York: Duell, Sloan and Pearce, 1964.

New Products Seminar 1954–1960. Irving-on-Hudson, New Products Institute, 1954–60.

Otteson, Schuyler F. (ed.). *Marketing: Current Problems and Theories*. Bloomington: Indiana University Press, 1952.

———, Pauchar, William G., and Patterson, James M. *Marketing: The Firm's Viewpoint*. New York: The Macmillan Company, 1964.

Oxenfeldt, Alfred R. "Consumer Knowledge: Its Measurement and Extent," *Review of Economics and Statistics*, XXXII, 4 (Nov., 1950), 300–14.

———. *Marketing Practices in the TV Set Industry*. New York: Columbia University Press, 1964.

——— (ed.). *Models of Markets*. New York: Columbia University Press, 1963.

———. "Multi-Stage Approach to Pricing," *Harvard Business Review*, 38, 4 (July–Aug., 1960), 125–34.

Pease, Otis. *The Responsibilities of American Advertising*. New Haven: Yale University Press, 1958.

Pei, Mario Andrew. *The Consumer's Manifesto*. New York: Crown Publishers, 1960.

Phillips, Joseph D. *Little Business in the American Economy*. Urbana: University of Illinois Press, 1958.

Quenon, E. L. "A Method for Pre-evaluating Merchandise Offerings," *Journal of Marketing*, XVI, 2 (Oct., 1951), 158–71.

Reck, Dickson (ed.). *National Standards in a Modern Economy*. New York: Harper & Bros., 1956.

Reeves, Rosser. *Reality in Advertising*. New York: Alfred A. Knopf, 1961.

419

BIBLIOGRAPHY

Rewoldt, Stewart H. *The Economic Effects of Marketing Research.* Ann Arbor: University of Michigan Press, 1953.

Rich, Stuart U. *Shopping Behavior of Department Store Customers.* Cambridge: Harvard University Press, 1963.

———, and Portis, Bernard D. "The 'Imageries' of Department Stores," *Journal of Marketing,* XXVIII, 2 (April, 1964), 10–15.

Robbins, W. David (ed.). *Successful Marketing at Home and Abroad.* Chicago: American Marketing Association, 1958.

Roshco, Bernard. *The Rag Race.* New York: Funk & Wagnalls, 1963.

Sandage, Charles H., and Fryburger, Vernon (eds.). *The Role of Advertising.* Homewood, Ill.: R. D. Irwin, 1960.

Sargent, Hugh W. *Consumer-Product Rating Publications and Buying Behavior.* Urbana: University of Illinois Press, 1959.

Sherrard, Alfred. "Advertising, Product Variation, and the Limits of Economics," *Journal of Political Economy,* LIX (April, 1951), 126–42.

Smith, Henry. "Further Reflections on Retail Pricing," *Economica New Series,* XIX (Feb., 1952), 26–30.

Smith, Wendell R. "Product Differentiation and Market Segmentation as Alternative Marketing Strategies," *Journal of Marketing,* XXI, 1 (July, 1956), 3–8.

Stevens, James Richard. "The Impact of Marketing Research Upon Manufacturers' Consumer Goods." Unpublished Ph.D. dissertation, State University of Iowa.

Tosdal, Harry R. *Selling in Our Economy.* Homewood, Ill.: R. D. Irwin, 1957.

Triffin, Robert. *Monopolistic Competition and General Equilibrium Theory.* Cambridge: Harvard University Press, 1949.

U.S. Department of Agriculture, Economic Research Service, Marketing Economics Division. *Comparative Costs to Consumers of Convenience Foods and Home-Prepared Foods.* Washington, D.C.: Government Printing Office, 1963.

———, Agricultural Marketing Service, Marketing Research Division. *Consumers' Concepts of Fabric.* Washington, D.C.: Government Printing Office, 1959.

U.S. Small Business Administration. *New Product Introduction,* Management Series No. 17. Washington, D.C.: Government Printing Office, 1955.

Voorhis, Jerry. *American Cooperatives.* New York: Harper & Bros., 1961.

Vredenburg, Harvey L. *Trading Stamps.* Bloomington: Indiana University Press, 1956.

420

Warshaw, Martin M. (ed.). *Changing Perspectives in Marketing Management*. Ann Arbor: University of Michigan Press, 1962.
————. *Effective Selling Through Wholesalers*. Ann Arbor: University of Michigan Press, 1961.

Wedding, Nugent (ed.). *Marketing Research and Business Management*. Urbana: University of Illinois Bulletin, Vol. 49, No. 44, Feb., 1952.

Wiles, Peter J. D. *Price, Cost and Output*. Oxford: Blackwell, 1962.

Williams, W. F., and Stout, Thomas F. *Economics of the Livestock Meat Industry*. New York: The Macmillan Company, 1964.

Yamey, Basil S. *The Economics of Resale Price Maintenance*. London: Pitman, 1954.

Zaltman, Gerald. *Marketing: Contributions from the Behavioral Sciences*. New York: Harcourt, Brace & World, 1965.

Index